# ABOLITIONISTS AND WORKING-CLASS PROBLEMS IN THE AGE OF INDUSTRIALIZATION

BETTY FLADELAND

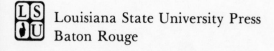
Louisiana State University Press
Baton Rouge

First published 1984 in the United States of America by
LOUISIANA STATE UNIVERSITY PRESS
Baton Rouge

Library of Congress Catalog Card Number 83–82561
ISBN 0–8071–1167–8

Printed in Hong Kong

# Contents

# Acknowledgements

I should like to thank several colleagues in the field of antislavery research who have either directed me to materials, shared their own, or read and criticized these essays: the late Roger Anstey, Richard Blackett, Merton Dillon, Seymour Drescher, George Shepperson, Nicholas Spence, Fiona Spiers, Clare Taylor, James Walvin and John A. Woods.

I should also like to thank the staff members of the British Library (including the Newspaper Library in Colindale and the Library of Political and Economic Science), Dr Williams's Library, the Friends House Library, University College Library and the Public Record Office, all in London; the Rhodes House and Bodleian Libraries in Oxford; Cambridge University Library; Birmingham Reference Library; the John Rylands and University of Manchester Libraries in Manchester; the Central Libraries and Harold Cohen Library in Liverpool; the Mitchell and University of Glasgow Libraries in Glasgow; the University of Edinburgh Library; the University of Hull Library; York Minster Library; the Record Office, Cumbria County; the Boston Public Library Manuscripts Division and Massachusetts Historical Library in Boston; the Historical Library of Pennsylvania; the State Historical Library of Nebraska; Duke University Library; and the Huntington Library. I especially wish to thank Mr Charles Holliday of the Morris Library, Southern Illinois University.

# Introduction

A question of some concern to current historians of the British and American antislavery movements is the degree of working-class involvement in those causes. The issue appears as a recurring theme in several of the essays in a recently published volume edited by Christine Bolt and Seymour Drescher, *Anti-Slavery, Religion, and Reform* (1980), and also in *Slavery and British Society 1776–1846* (1982), edited by James Walvin.[1]

Thomas Clarkson himself raised the point initially when he wrote of the large numbers of people who signed petitions against the slave trade and joined in boycotts of slave-grown sugar.[2] But there the matter rested for more than a hundred years without much attention being paid to it. The earliest works on the American movement, which were published at the turn of the century by A. B. Hart, Alice D. Adams and Mary Locke, did not address the question of mass involvement. The same was true of the standard histories of the British movement by Sir Reginald Coupland, Frank J. Klingberg and William L. Mathieson and of American studies by Gilbert H. Barnes and Dwight L. Dumond, which revived interest in the subject of antislavery among American historians.[3] For the most part, even the succeeding generation of historians of antislavery did not give much thought to the question, but generally accepted as a 'given' that the movements were initiated, led and supported by the middle classes.[4] Aspects which received the most attention were the impact of evangelicalism and the Enlightenment on antislavery attitudes, antislavery as a political issue, and the question of economic determinism.[5]

Yet, some spadework on popular support, including that of the working classes, had begun in the 1950s and 1960s. Bernard Mandel's *Labor: Free and Slave. Workingmen and the Anti-Slavery Movement in the United States* presented the relationship between abolitionists and workers as largely negative. In Britain several people writing theses explored the topic and found decidedly positive connections, especially E. M. Hunt in 'The North of England Agitation for the Abolition of the Slave Trade 1780–1800', and James Walvin in 'English Democratic Societies and Popular Radicalism 1791–1800'. Gloria Clare Taylor pointed out the role of the Scottish churches in disseminating antislavery doctrine to all classes, and more recently Douglas Riach has emphasized the organized attempts of the Dublin abolitionists to reach the working populace.[6]

Building on those foundations, several scholars, both British and American, are currently addressing the problem. Richard Blackett has just completed a study of black American abolitionists' missions to Britain in which he reveals the degree to which they attracted working-class audiences in the thousands. James Walvin has carried forward his initial exploration of the subject to the reform campaign of 1832, and Seymour Drescher has contrasted the degree of mass support for the British movement with the lack of it in France. He argues that as long as the antislavery movement remained elitist, slavery 'pursued its unhampered course', but was abolished when abolitionism became 'a vehicle adopted by underrepresented and dynamic social, regional, and religious groups'.[7] Patricia Hollis, on the other hand, has concluded that the British antislavery movement 'failed to forge a working-class constituency', at least prior to George Thompson's Anti-Slavery League of 1846, and that 'anti-slavery leaders preferred to acquire a more reputable constituency than that of working men'.[8] Alan Kraut, Edward Magdol and John Jentz are among those using quantitative techniques to analyse working-class participation in American antislavery organizations. They have found positive, active involvement to a surprising degree.[9]

The obverse side of the question of working-class interest in the antislavery cause is that of abolitionists' concern with working-class movements. Perhaps it is not surprising how a widespread acceptance of the idea that abolition was largely a conservative, middle-class reform tended to perpetuate the old Dickensian stereotype of emancipationists as a collection of Mrs Jellybys who were oblivious to the fact that exploited white labour at home needed emancipation just as did black slaves in the West Indies or in a far-off section of the United States. Even when historians began to recognize abolitionists as interested in broad-based reform with many interrelated movements, they almost always depicted them, along with reformers in general, as paternalistic, usually evangelical, do-gooders motivated by the need for social control but unhampered by any deep concern for the rights of the working classes.[10] However, Ernest M. Howse in *Saints in Politics* defended the Clapham Sect as men who though they 'unmistakably and inevitably' were men of their own times, yet in many ways were ahead of their times. Frank Thistlethwaite in *The Anglo-American Connection in the Early Nineteenth Century* pointed out that eventually the more 'practical spirits' among the abolitionists 'turned their energies toward linking antislavery to broader political issues' including, in Britain, Chartism and the anti-Corn Law fight.[11]

In his seminal volumes on the intellectual origins and development of antislavery thought, David Brion Davis, while considering the possibility that antislavery 'bred a new sensitivity to social oppression', emphasizes even more the idea of social control and the degree to which the antislavery movement supported the contemporary social order. He sees this not only as an inadvertent result but also as a conscious aim of the antislavery leaders. In citing abolitionists' defences of the existing social and economic structure, particularly their rationalisations of current labour conditions, he tends to resurrect the old stereotype: 'Abolitionists could contemplate a revolutionary change in status precisely because they were not considering the upward mobility of workers, but rather the rise of distant Negroes to the level of humanity.'[12] My impression is that they were, consciously, advocating the upward mobility of the working classes but not solely, and often not primarily, from an economic viewpoint. Civil liberties, political rights and educational opportunity were of equal importance in their vision of the just and good society. Davis was, of course, dealing with the early period of abolition (in which support for the status quo may have been truer than I think it was later), and his evidence is drawn to a large extent from the positions of Wilberforce, James Stephen, Granville Sharp and their colleagues of the revolutionary era. As is apparent in my first essay, I disagree with him on Granville Sharp, and believe that one can find many others of the same period who do not fit so neatly into the category of upholders of the status quo.[13] To illustrate, one has only to name Major John Cartwright, Thomas Hardy, Tom Paine, Capel Lofft, Thomas Walker, Christopher Wyvill and Richard Price – all antislavery and political radicals.

Indeed, Roger Anstey held that even Wilberforce had the potential for 'a more modern syndrome'. Although Wilberforce voted for what Will Cobbett termed the 'gagging and dungeoning' bills, he supported Pitt's abortive reform bill of 1785, subsequent bills to curtail election corruption, and Peel's factory acts of 1802 and 1818. He advocated the expenditure of public as well as private monies to relieve the poor and carry out prison reform.[14] Davis cites the potter Josiah Wedgwood as a representative abolitionist whose concern for black slaves was not matched by a concern for his own labourers, whom he ruled with an iron discipline overlaid with benevolent paternalism. Yet in the riots of 1779 workmen trusted him enough to admit to him, in a large meeting, that they had been destroying machinery, and he acknowledged (at least privately) that their action was the result of their unemployment. In a riot in 1783 which was crushed by military force, one of Wedgwood's workmen was hanged; but Wedgwood deplored the use of soldiers against rioting workers, saying, 'I do not like to have the soldiery familiaris'd to spilling the blood of their countrymen & fellow citizens.' And in another case of recalcitrant workmen he took the 'shortest and easiest' way with the 'rascals' by letting them 'carry themselves off' – that is, run away without being pursued and returned for punishment. To his partner, Thomas Bentley, he admitted that the petty larcenies of the lower classes were 'a mere flea bite' compared to the robberies 'of those above us'. Wedgwood rejoiced over both the American and French revolutions and the spirit of liberty which he saw growing all over Europe.[15] These bits of evidence suggest that Wedgwood as well as Wilberforce had the potential for enough flexibility to accept expanding boundaries of egalitarian thought.

While Davis emphasizes the degree to which Granville Sharp 'helped to frame the boundaries of future controversy' with care to preserve the existing legal system, it seems to me that Sharp was more interested in extending the limits of change in existing legal and social structures than he was in curtailing them. Howard Temperly concludes that, while Davis himself has 'significantly altered the boundaries' of antislavery historiography, yet from his two volumes 'no very clear overall picture emerges'. As for the thesis that the antislavery movement was designed to divert attention from a developing bad situation at home, Temperley writes, 'That this may sometimes have been the case cannot be disproved, although evidence for it is hard to find . . . it is hard to see a movement as formidable as the assault on slavery, with all its implications for radical change, simply, or even largely, as a form of negative response.' Using the Midlands as a test case, Seymour Drescher has found that the antislavery movement helped to stimulate factory and other reforms rather than to divert attention from them.[16]

Abolitionists have traditionally been associated with the laissez-faire doctrines of the Political Economy school of Jeremy Bentham and often therefore lumped with those who opposed business regulation and public expenditures for welfare. Except for R. K. Webb's sympathetic treatment, Harriet Martineau has had to carry more than her share of the odium of inflexible Social Darwinism, with little notice taken of the modifications her theories underwent. Richard Hofstadter left this negative impression of her for thousands of American students who probably knew nothing of Martineau except what they read of her in *Social Darwinism in America*. More recently, Jonathan Glickstein took a hard swipe at her by holding her up as the epitome of abolitionist laissez-fairists who upheld business interests and denied the rights and needs of labourers.[17] David Davis refers to Thomas Babington Macaulay as 'a rising spokesman for laissez-faire and middle-class ideology', contrasting his position with that of Michael Sadler, who led the fight for factory legislation.[18] True, Macaulay generally fits the description, yet one should note that even he voted for the Ten Hours Bill. More importantly, a legitimate question can be raised as to whether Macaulay, or the sons of Wilberforce for that matter, can be taken as representative of abolitionist attitudes. Their devotion to the cause was markedly lukewarm in comparison to that of their fathers. One might as appropriately use Sadler as representative, for he was an abolitionist too.

Patricia Hollis, in 'Anti-Slavery and British Working-Class Radicalism in the Years of Reform', is the most recent upholder of the traditional interpretation of abolitionists as unsympathetic to the rights and demands of labour. In her opinion, even for the period of the 1830s and 1840s, 'Anti-slavery leaders in any case were no radicals, and had little sympathy with a more democratic impulse.'[19] She stresses the degree to which working-class leaders saw antislavery as a rival movement, with the consequence that it evoked antagonism and opposition. Beginning my study of the

period with the same impression, I was instead struck by the surprising amount of co-operation that I found to be emerging in the
1830s.[20] Cobbett, for example, found it politically necessary to
switch from his abolitionist-baiting negrophobia of the 1820s to a
pro-emancipation stance.[21] I learned that labour leaders William
Lovett, John Collins and Richard Oastler were long-time anti-
slavery men, as were George Julian Harney and Ernest Jones after
them. With the completion of emancipation and apprenticeship in
the West Indies in 1838, when abolitionists were free for other
endeavours, Oastler proposed that systematic efforts should be
started to bring them into the movements on behalf of white
labour. Even Bronterre O'Brien and (perhaps with ulterior
motives) Feargus O'Connor co-operated for a time with Joseph
Sturge and his abolitionist followers who formed the backbone of
the Complete Suffrage Movement.[22]

Hollis cites Chartist interruptions of antislavery meetings as the
height of their anti-abolitionism; but, when one remembers that it
was a Chartist tactic to interrupt the public meetings of all organizations which did not give priority to the Charter, one cannot
assume that Chartists were antagonistic to antislavery organizations *per se*. In Glasgow, for example, it was James Moir, a
member of the Glasgow Emancipation Society and a Chartist,
who issued the notice of the policy to interrupt public meetings.[23]

In his essay 'Abolitionism and the Labor Movement in
America', Eric Foner joined those who question the Davis thesis
that antislavery supported the emerging capitalistic order.
Although most American abolitionists, like their British counter-
parts, continued to define slavery as the absence of personal
freedom – that is, ownership by another rather than self-
ownership – Foner points out that their initial disregard of wage
slavery gave way to some concern. He mentions John A. Collins of
New York as being influenced by what he saw of wage slavery
when on an abolitionist mission to Great Britain. Several other
American abolitionists, including both Frederick Douglass and
William Lloyd Garrison himself, were similarly influenced by
their visits in Britain, but initially they were not ready to admit
that the conditions of American labour could be equated with
slavery even though they conceded that working people in
England were wage slaves. Foner believes that antislavery and
American labour-movement principles came together eventually
in the stand of Lincoln and the Republican Party.[24] James B.

Stewart is just finishing a biography of Wendell Phillips that dis-
cusses at length his interest in labour problems. David Eltis has
pointed out how Garrisonian beliefs in personal liberty and the
universal brotherhood of man led to the position that 'Freedom
for the slave should be matched by universal suffrage and the
ballot at home and in the colonies.'[25]

Obviously, one can find plenty of examples both of antagonism
between the working class and abolitionists and of co-operation
between them. Perhaps it is a case of some historians seeing the
proverbial half-empty glass while others see it as half full. Charles
Darwin's remark about research in geology is equally applicable
to history. In 1861 he wrote,

> About thirty years ago there was much talk that geologists
> ought only to observe and not theorize; and I well remember
> someone saying that at this rate a man might as well go into a
> gravel-pit and count the pebbles and describe the colours. How
> odd it is that anyone would not see that all observation must be
> for or against some view if it is to be of any service.[26]

Since the antagonisms between the labour and antislavery
movements have had a longer and fuller press, my purpose is to
give some exposure to the evidences of co-operation between
them. The following essays, a beginning on my way to a longer
study of the association of abolitionists with working-class
movements, provide a few illustrations of cases where abolitionist
leaders grew to see black chattel slavery and white wage slavery as
parts of the same whole. As Richard Oastler put it, the anti-
slavery and labour causes were 'one and the same', or, as
Bronterre O'Brien phrased it, to say that white workers owned
themselves and black slaves did not was to create a 'distinction
without a difference'.[27] Paternalistic the antislavery leaders were,
but they illustrate a capacity for growth and flexibility when confronted with the increasing problem of industrial labour and with
accusations levelled at their short-sightedness. They moved
beyond pity and charity to attempts to gain justice and independent rights for working people and the range of their consideration extended to rural tenant farmers and to artisans as well
as to industrial workers. Hence I have included all of these groups
in my definition of the working classes.

Brian Harrison has pointed out how 'reciprocal rebuke'

resulted in a 'jostling forward' of reforms, an idea I tried to illustrate in showing the relationship between abolitionists and Chartism.[28] In his book *Drink and the Victorians*, Harrison used the phrase 'a broker between the classes' to describe a temperance reformer.[29] I think the concept an apt one to characterize the antislavery reformers discussed in the following essays.

I have not intended these essays to be biographical, and because of my thesis I have usually given less space to my subjects' antislavery activities and have put more emphasis on their work on behalf of poor, white labouring people. Most of all I have tried to present evidence of their emerging recognition of the close relationship between white and black slavery.

# 1 Granville Sharp

Granville Sharp has been immortalized in annals of the anti-slavery movement. As the individual who instituted proceedings in the Somerset case (1772), which contributed so significantly to the death of legal black slavery in England, Sharp was one of the earliest of abolition heroes.[1] What is often not known is the degree to which Sharp was concerned about the plight of the white working classes as well, and that he championed their cause for better social and economic opportunity. His concern for justice extended itself equally to the American Indians, the Caribbean peoples under colonial rule, the Irish, the Scots Highlanders, and both American and French revolutionists fighting for rights and liberties.

It is now accepted doctrine that the reform repulse of the late eighteenth century in Great Britain grew out of merging Enlightenment philosophy, newly awakened evangelical religious vitality, and a practical reaction to increasingly discernible industrial problems.[2] Granville Sharp's thinking embodied all three and he argued from each of those bases in presenting his case for reform. Although a loyal member of the established Anglican Church, he was 'an adoptive member' of the evangelical Clapham Sect of William Wilberforce and Henry Thornton; and he interpreted the Biblical injunction to love one's neighbour as a Christian obligation not only to forgive personal injuries but also 'to oppose every degree of oppression and injustice which affects his brethren and neighbours, when he has a fair opportunity of assisting them'.[3] Sharp was just as adept at arguing from a natural-rights philosophy, but held that to be truly free men must submit to law lest 'natural' liberty become unnatural tyranny. He was equally capable of arguing from the 'higher law doctrine' and both philosophies were mobilized to assert his view that man's law must correspond to God's law. His applications of theory were made to situations in his own world where he could observe injustices to people who were victims of the new commercial–

industrial power, whether at home in Great Britain among factory workers, soldiers and seamen, Scottish peasants being driven from their lands, or in the colonies which Britain was gaining from her imperialist ventures. Although not a lawyer, Sharp was self-taught in legal history and fortified his theoretical arguments by basing them on traditional British rights.

Granville Sharp was born on 10 November 1735 (old style), in Durham. His father was an archdeacon of the Church of England and his grandfather was Archbishop of York, but Granville was despatched at an early age to the business world of London, where he was apprenticed to a linen draper (a Quaker). The apprenticeship was continued under a Presbyterian, and finished under a Roman Catholic, thus giving the young man an acquaintance with other faiths than his own. Later he lived with a person who had no apparent religion, thus further stimulating his lifelong interest in the variety of beliefs. He subsequently learned Greek and Hebrew in order better to equip himself for debating points of scripture. Granville's quick and searching mind destined him for broader spheres of enterprise than being a draper, and before long he moved into Government service as a clerk in the Office of Ordnance in Westminster. There he soon became involved in political issues – so involved, in fact, that he resigned his position in 1777 in protest against Government policy toward the rebelling Americans.[4]

Sharp's concern for those who lacked opportunity probably stemmed from the influence of his father, who set up schools at his own expense to educate poor children, Catholics as well as Protestants. We know that Granville's exertions on behalf of oppressed peoples had begun by 1765, when he succoured a badly mistreated black, Jonathan Strong; and we find in his letter book evidences of continuing and expanding intervention in similar cases. For example, there is a communication of 17 May 1768 to an Alderman Beckford, written on a morning when Sharp had been struck at seeing an advertisement regarding the apprehension of a 'poor Negro boy' who, if found, was to be returned to Beckford. Without hesitation Sharp followed his impulse to make a protest and to use the occasion to lecture the alderman on the evils of slavery.[5]

Sharp was even then indulging his scholarly interests by digging into historical records and old laws to investigate what connections there might be between chattel slavery and ancient villeinage – a search which provided him with a basis for his enduring conviction that oppression manifested itself against the poor and the powerless regardless of race. Moreover, he concluded that ancient villeinage, like slavery, had always been illegal. Both rested on assumptions that were contrary to natural law and divine law; yet powerful interests had sustained the institutions and thereby had given them the sanction of tradition. Common law had eventually triumphed over villeinage, with the result that it was discarded. Now Sharp was worried that eighteenth-century Britain might accept arguments for sustaining slavery which rested on an assumed legality of previous villeinage which Sharp called 'an inadequate foundation'. One can easily picture young Sharp retreating to his room at night after work to pore over musty volumes of old statutes and legal cases. Evidently he acquired a reputation for assiduous research in preference to more frivolous evening activities, for, in a poem addressed to him, one of the directors of the Bank of England, a Mr Payne, prayed, 'Oh may thy labours by the midnight lamp / Pour day's effulgence on thy country's darkness.'[6]

The Somerset decision vindicated Sharp's position on the illegality of slavery in England; but he was aware that proslavery interests in Parliament were concurrently pressing for and might very well succeed in passing a bill specifically recognizing West Indian slavery. His opposition reflects his clear realization that black slavery in America and white slavery in Great Britain had a close bearing on one another. Reasoning from his experience in the Somerset and the Jonathan Strong cases, Sharp concluded (and feared) that legalized slavery in the West Indies would result in England's being overrun with slaves who might be brought there or escape there and who would then threaten the jobs of free labourers. The 'industrious poor' and the working people in general 'would inevitably be involved by degrees in the same horrid slavery and depression; for that *is always the base wherever slavery is tolerated*: of which the gross oppression of *White Servants* (even English, Scotch and Irish) in the British colonies is a lamentable proof'.[7]

Indentured servitude provided ample evidence of the gross oppression of which Sharp spoke. He suspected that the laws governing it were purposely designed to make it possible for masters to extend the length of service for minor offences and to exact exorbitant penalties for trifling breaches of contract, thus degrading white labour 'so that their condition is certainly A Degree of Slavery'.[8] Consequently, when he learned of the intentions of a group of Scottish Highlanders to emigrate to America, he wrote to dissuade them or at least to warn them 'that wherever Slavery or property in Negroes is tolerated, the *Common Working People* are, also, generally involved in the same misery with the foreign Slaves'. New York, Virginia and Maryland were cited as colonies where 'the oppression of the poor is carried to a monstrous pitch'.[9] He wanted to impress on the potential emigrants the fact that not only free Negroes, but also poor white natives of Ireland and Great Britain were often arrested and jailed without redress simply on the suspicion of being runaway servants. He believed that the tyranny of the planters over convicts was as notorious as their treatment of slaves.

Although his warning arrived too late to influence their decision, Sharp was pleased to learn that the Scottish emigrants were bound for Pennsylvania. From the Quaker reputation for justice toward the Indians as well as their stand on slavery, Sharp could deduce that Pennsylvanians would treat white workers also with more consideration. (He did wish, though, that the Quakers would forsake their religious errors!) Sharp then wrote to Anthony Benezet, his antislavery Quaker correspondent in Philadelphia, to alert him to the arrival of the Scots and to express his confidence that the Friends would see to it that these poor strangers did not fall into bad hands and thus find themselves enslaved. Even his use of the word 'enslaved' indicates Sharp's awareness of this condition for whites as well as blacks. Habituated to giving advice, Sharp this time gave as his opinion that each of the colonies ought to take steps to increase its supply of white labour, not to be used simply as servants, but to be allowed a status equivalent to that of British cottagers, or to form nuclei in the settlement of country towns.[10]

Actually, Sharp's solution for slavery was very similar: slaves should be settled on small farms with provision for making systematic payments to their masters. Thus masters would be compensated and the blacks who bought their own freedom would have learned management and acquired a property stake in the community as a basis for citizenship. He drew up plans for a model colony without slavery, in Africa, but one which included the possibility that permission might be given the establishing company to purchase slaves on the condition that the purpose should be to free them. The stipulation was that they be held on a temporary basis only, while working out their own redemption.[11]

His hope was that the American colonies would abolish slavery and extend the British constitution (as he interpreted its justice) so as to protect 'every individual, rich or poor, white, Negroe or Indian without distinction, and ensure to everyone the lawfull product of his Industry, allowing also an equitable reward for Labour'. He was irate when he learned, during the war with France, that British naval officers were guilty of taking free blacks off French ships and selling them as slaves in Jamaica instead of delivering them to Africa or to some island where they could be provided with land and live in freedom.[12]

Independence for the United States did not stop the flow of Sharp's advice. In 1785 he wrote to President James Manning of the College in Providence, Rhode Island, to urge that the new nation should adopt agrarian laws to prevent land monopoly, 'which reduces to slavery' the ordinary labourers. If primogeniture were retained, acreage must be limited. Cottage land and common land should be reserved around every town for the accommodation of the poor, for schools and other public needs. Moreover, regulatory laws must be enacted at once before lands became scarce and high priced, when greed would prevail over reform legislation.[13]

Sharp was extremely sensitive to the violations of natives' rights which accompanied British imperialism. In 1768, when he read of a plot of British soldiers in West Florida to set the Creeks and Choctaws against each other through the device of dressing themselves as Indians and going in to attack and even to scalp, Sharp warned that tactics so despicable would bring such odium on his nation that not even their old Indian allies would continue to trust them.[14] In his later plans for laying out towns on the American frontier, he was careful to include strictures against encroaching on Indian lands; and his proposals for free-labour settlements in West Africa also stipulated that all land should be purchased from the African chiefs.[15]

In 1772, the same year in which he was busy with the Somerset case, Sharp extended his exertions by denouncing the landing of British troops in St Vincent in the Caribbean. He called the efforts to subdue the Caribs the most glaring case of injustice since Ireland was ceded by the Pope to Henry II, and he brought all of the pressure he could on Lord Dartmouth, both by letter and in person, to change the national policy. In Sharp's view a European nation – in this case, France – had no right to cede colonial territories to another nation, and Britain could not claim legal title to any such territory she accepted. He argued that, in addition to destroying colonial peoples, great nations only bled themselves by such actions: witness currently the French in Corsica, the Spanish in Chile, the Portuguese in Brazil, and Holland in Surinam. Above all, Sharp's religious convictions told him that God's judgement would surely be visited on guilty nations; and the loyal Protestant in him worried lest England's record should show up as worse than Catholic Spain's.[16]

Sharp's benevolence was not of the type which came to a focus only on the far side of the Atlantic. Rather, he was constantly responding to distressing situations at home as well. For example, in 1772 a Mr Henry Douglas wrote to him to call his attention to the situation of the salters and colliers in Scotland. Girls at the age of twelve and boys at the age of fourteen who worked in the mines were bound to their proprietors for life, and were even sold with the mines or transferred (i.e. sold) from one colliery to another at the will of the master. If parents took children to the mines to help them work, the children also were bound. Sometimes, like dogs, or some slaves, they were forced to wear collars engraved with the owner's name. Masters had no obligation whatsoever to such workers in sickness or to any who survived to old age.

Sharp answered Douglas immediately with the acknowledgement that, having spoken out so publicly against black slavery, it would be inexcusable if he did less for 'our own distressed Brethren of this Island, that are involved in an *unjust Slavery* almost equally wretched and deplorable'.[17] Again he based his position on historical and legal research which informed him that the Scottish law was meant to apply only to those workers still having a duty to discharge under the old feudal villeinage. Any new application of the law, he emphatically pronounced to be tyrannical. As a matter of fact, in his pamphlet against slavery published three years earlier, Sharp had called attention to the plight of the salters and colliers. Now he promised to give them all the help in his power. Specifically, he suggested to Mr Douglas that the pamphlet of 1769 should be circulated to the members of

Parliament prior to their receipt of a petition from the miners which would ask for legislation to prohibit current practices.[18] He had the satisfaction of seeing such a law passed in 1775.

Crusades to ensure better treatment for seamen, soldiers, convicts and people assigned to workhouses also absorbed Sharp's energies; and he often equated their condition with that of the slaves. No poor man was safe from impressment into military service, which, because it was involuntary servitude, Sharp labelled 'absolute slavery'. Consequently he joined James Oglethorpe's crusade against the press gang. His preference was for a real national militia based on a rotation system in which all men would share the responsibility for the defence of their country. Under the current system those with money could hire substitutes. Not only was such a system unfair to the poor, but Sharp deplored it as an abandonment of the old communal spirit. The result was that the people of the nation were reduced to 'a block of helpless cattle'.[19] A notebook entry reveals his outrage and his religious fears of retribution:

> and if the Gentry continue much longer to permit the *Laws of the Land* to be so openly and notoriously violated with impunity in the oppression of the poor and helpless, they must expect in time to feel the effects of the same lawless Tyranny themselves; because *Violence* & *injustice* will grow strong & more daring by long suffrance & daily execution agt. the *Poor* until they take root by prescription & long usage.... [20]

He encountered such an example of acceptance by long usage when he called on Dr Samuel Johnson to debate with him the issue of impressing seamen. Johnson contended it was part of 'that way of life' – an interesting position for Johnson to take since he was strongly in favour of abolishing slavery, evidently by revolution if necessary. At least he is supposed to have given, at Oxford, a toast to the next insurrection in the West Indies. Several years later, when Johnson was reported to have held forth on the 'garrulosity' of the people about their rights, Sharp exploded against 'the Quondom professed advocate *for Popular Rights & Liberty*' who had 'swallowed' 'perverted notions'.[21]

As he had in the cases of individual slaves, Granville Sharp involved himself as well in specific cases of impressed seamen, most notably that of a Londoner named Millachip, in 1777. In order to present a strong argument (again to Lord Mansfield), Sharp engaged in research to show the number of deaths accompanying pressing. When confronted with the contention that such people as he only persuaded poor people to be unhappier than they actually were, he responded vigorously,

> Happy would it be for this nation, and the eternal souls of such as mislead it, if the feelings of the seamen and other labourious poor had no other stimulation than the recital of their unhappy case by such poor advocates as myself! Are they not surely of the same blood; have they not the same natural knowledge of good and evil, to discern, and the same feelings to be sensible of injuries, as those who cause their sufferings?[22]

Subversion of laws permitted the conviction of poor people for petty offences followed by sentences of long imprisonment and even death. Then the courts, with a show of great mercy, would commute the sentence if the 'criminal' agreed to transportation (exile). Thus, instead of the law being the protector and guardian of the poor, it became an agency for ridding the country of 'undesirables'.[23] In one case involving two pickpockets convicted in the Old Bailey, Sharp volunteered to pay the fees to outfit the men if they would be allowed to enter the King's service instead of being transported. Whether the magistrate happened to be a sympathetic man or was aware of Sharp's reputation as a tenacious opponent is impossible to say, but transportation was suspended until the next session to allow time for the men either to enter the service or to find other employment.[24]

Sharp's opinions on crime and punishment were decidedly modern. He realized that the causes of crime often lay in lack of employment, education and decent living-conditions, and he worked closely with fellow abolitionist Samuel Whitbread, who in 1795 introduced a bill in the House of Commons which would have allowed magistrates to fix a minimum wage and to punish an employer who paid less. Lacking Pitt's support, the bill failed, however. Once a person was convicted and jailed, Sharp argued, the emphasis in his treatment should be on reform, and, no matter how much he might deserve punishment, he should be decently housed and dealt with humanely. Sharp was outraged by the frequent use of the label 'low-born miscreant', insisting that a miscreant was a miscreant no matter what his station or birth. The only distinction was that the 'high-born', with benefit of education, ought to know better and therefore should be dealt with more severely. Sharp found the conditions on the ships used to transport felons to be especially shocking. He called for instruction and employment for them, and apartments for the married; and he wrote to Sir William Dolben to enlist his support for instituting inspection. As a member of Parliament, Dolben was (several years later) the author of a bill to improve conditions on slave ships by limiting the number carried according to the ship's tonnage.[25]

In his concern for female convicts, Sharp antedated the work of Elizabeth Fry, the well-known Quaker abolitionist of the nineteenth century. He advocated a separate penitentiary for women as well as separate facilities for the mentally ill. When he served on the Committee for Bridewell Hospital, he persuaded the administration to experiment, for a time, with his proposals for reforming prostitutes. Emphasizing prevention and rehabilitation as always, Sharp wanted employment with protection provided for 'industrious females' so that, working under regulations, they could not then be discredited for taking factory jobs, which were at that time often both morally and physically degrading. He suggested that if the women in Bridewell were taught to spin wool the profits from their work could go to pay their maintenance and they should be encouraged by being allowed to keep anything above such expenses. Elderly women over sixty could be assigned as matrons in a general asylum where the poor could find work. Children detected in pilfering were not to be whipped and sent back into the streets, as was often the custom, but should be detained and given instruction in some useful work. He also began another crusade that Elizabeth Fry was to continue: improvement in conditions on the ships which transported female felons.[26]

Although Sharp never married he seems to have been sensitive to the subjugation of women in marriage. In explaining to an African chief why polygamy was wrong, he put it, not on a religious basis, but on the basis of women having 'the same passions, and feelings, and love toward the men, that we have toward the women; and we ought, therefore, to regulate our behaviour toward them by our own feelings of what we should like and expect of faithful love and duty from them toward ourselves'.[27]

Poor relief, with the concomitant question of workhouses,

posed as many solution-defying problems in Sharp's day as in
our own; and, when one considers the prevalence even in the
twentieth century of unsympathetic attitudes toward 'the lazy
relief parasites', one can better appreciate what reformers of
Sharp's day had to contend with in public opposition. As abolitionists working against vested interests in the slave trade, men
such as Sharp, William Allen, Samuel Whitbread and Samuel
Romilly, with many others, were quickly learning valuable lessons
in the moulding of public opinion and then capitalizing on it to
influence legislation. They applied the same techniques in
working for the relief of poor whites, but faced decidedly more
obstinate opposition because the spirit of the age was con-
siderably more responsive to crusades for liberty than to those
calling for equality of economic opportunity. Then, as now,
liberal reformers were full of good intentions to elevate the 'lower'
classes by teaching them social discipline and individual responsibility. Freedom meant, therefore, being 'on one's own' and being
responsible for one's own actions regardless of the inequalities in
opportunity. Even in considering slaves, the generally accepted
doctrine was that once they were legally freed they could and
should make their own way. Reportedly, Sharp, frustrated by the
lack of positive response from London's destitute blacks when
given the chance to go to Sierra Leone, distributed leaflets
counselling others not to give them charity which would deter
them even longer. This could be interpreted as a sign of Sharp's
insensitivity to the problems of blacks, or even as revealing a
latent belief in their inferiority; but taken in the context of
Sharp's total philosophy it can be seen as an expression of his
belief that free blacks should be treated as responsible people who
must face the realistic consequences of their own decisions. James
Walvin may be right in attributing it to Sharp's oversanguine
hopes for Sierra Leone.[28] Perhaps it reveals only that Sharp was
human too, and had his fits of impatience when his schemes did
not progress smoothly.

In debates over whether the American slave was worse off than
the British worker, Sharp definitely held that chattel slavery was
the greater evil. He argued that free workers were largely
protected from personal ill usage and could, as a last resort, apply
to the parish for support. He knew, of course, and acted on the
knowledge, that such laws were often honoured more in the
breach than in the fulfilment. According to Gilbert's law of 1782,

parishes could give outside relief and wages could be supplemented, but there was local option on the part of the parish.[29]

Writing to the Bishop of London in 1795, Sharp poured out his sympathy for the poor and his frustration with the system whereby

> an industrious man who labours hard 6 Days in every week shd be subjected to this most humiliating circumstance of applying to his Parish to make up a bare subsistence for his Family, & be thereby deemed a Pauper, & thereby lose his elective Rights as an English Householder not withstanding his utmost diligence in labour but merely because his wages are inadequate to the necessary expenses of a Family!

Sharp concerned himself also when there were strictures on the traditional rights of the rural poor to glean in the fields after harvest. Again he argued that the right was based on the three foundations of English law: reason, the laws of God, and 'the general custom of England'. Biblical example (for instance, the right of Ruth to glean in the fields of Boaz) was of major weight in his thinking.[30]

Not satisfied with doling out charity, Sharp promoted the idea of distributing land to poor cottagers where they could have gardens and potato grounds at least. The financial outlay, he believed, should be accepted as an ordinary expense of the estate. Moreover, while it was proper for the Bishop of London and him to raise money for the instruction of slaves (Sharp even offered a small estate in Essex for that purpose), not all such donations should be used for foreigners; part of the money ought to go for parish schools for the children of poor workers of the soil 'from whence the revenue rises'.[31] Unlike many of his contemporaries in benevolence, Sharp was ahead of his day in recognizing at least a simplified version of the labour theory of value.

Acting on his own advice, Sharp experimented with providing lots for farm labourers, choosing those with the largest families to support. A small rental fee furnished the means for a school for the children.[32] Granville's brother John (certainly with Granville's approval and support) worked out a detailed plan for the use of the old Roman tower in the family home, Bamburgh Castle. It housed schools for both boys and girls, two large granaries for corn for the poor, and a sale room where grains and meal could be retailed to the needy at a set rate even if the market price rose. Other rooms were designated for a library for the neighbourhood, a general dispensary, a surgery for the poor, and an infirmary for sick or wounded sailors who came ashore on the coast (open to all nationalities). Even incurable cases were to be admitted on charity and everything possible done to relieve them.[33]

Benevolence and charity were fashionable in the late eighteenth century and good people of wealth enhanced their own reputations for piety by generous almsgiving for worthy causes. Like so many of his contemporaries of enlightened and/or religious motivation, Sharp was fulfilling an obligation that 'betters' owed to 'inferiors'; but in his case motivation went beyond that sense of *noblesse oblige*. His study of old legal history had thoroughly convinced him that the common people were entitled to rights of which they had been deprived. Consequently, benevolent charity was not enough; there must be a restoration of the old heritage. He was sensitive and realistic enough in his reasoning to conclude that the masses would not remain patient forever. Unless their birthright were restored, they would seize it forcibly while executing vengeance on their oppressors. Sharp's strong belief in God's justice made it possible for him to conceive of such an event as divine retribution, whether carried out by Indians, black slaves or white peasants acting as agents of God's will. Hence one of his missions was to labour for a return of the people's political rights which had been usurped by the upper classes, by Parliament and by big corporations. It is somewhat ironical that Sharp's own privileged position ensured his being allowed to expound such revolutionary doctrine without being branded a revolutionary. His circle of friends included powerful men in the Church and in Parliament, and he even enjoyed a personal relationship with the King. The Sharp family, all musicians, spent many a summer evening floating down the Thames in a boat serenading listeners on the banks, including the royal family at Richmond. On at least one occasion the King and Queen were invited aboard the Sharp yacht.[34]

In arguing for the historic rights of the people, Sharp began with a nostalgic notion of the good old days which was decidedly unrealistic. He conjured up a true community based on the ancient system of frankpledge which provided that all must take a vow of service and loyalty for the common good. Each able-bodied man served in a citizens' militia so that all were trained in defence. Rotation assured that no group or class bore an undue share of the burden. Each individual who freely participated, whether rich or poor, could take pride in the status of a worthy citizen, and suffrage was based on households.[35] Frankpledge became so basic to Sharp's plan for the good society that he recommended it to Benjamin Franklin for the new United States, and to Lafayette to secure the gains of 'the wonderful revolution' in France.[36] He was equally persistent in advising against a standing professional army, as opposed to his citizens' militia, and again he urged that new nations should learn from history: as Cromwell's army had 'enslaved' England, so could a standing army enslave the American people. No doubt he was much relieved by Dr Benjamin Rush's reassuring report that General Washington had retired to the life of a country gentleman and that the revolutionary army had 'quietly melted away into peaceable citizens'.[37]

Taxation without representation was another example to Sharp of how the British Government had departed from its ancient principles. Like the American colonial leaders, he denied that virtual representation sufficed as a substitute for geographic representation, 'for no Parliament or Assembly upon Earth can have any just Right to enact laws for *places*, which it does *not* represent'. Because representation was imperfect at home was no reason to deny it to the areas of the Empire which had none. It was this issue which made Sharp a champion of the American cause and led him to resign his position on the Ordnance Board. He deplored the bad precedent which had been set in Ireland, and defended annual parliaments for Ireland, although in later life Sharp proved to be inconsistent on the Irish issue when he opposed Catholic emancipation.[38]

Arbitrary power was Sharp's 'Public Enemy Number 1', whether expressed in a master–slave relationship, by a standing army repressing civil liberties, by a parliament which had grown away from real representation, or by a judiciary that pronounced judgements contravening the two 'indespensible [*sic*] principles' on which the English consitution must rest: the law of God and the law of nature.[39] Even God, he said, rules under a covenant, and 'no act of injustice can be more flagrant than that of denying to any particular order of Men (whether Soldiers or others) their *natural Right* of appealing to the *eternal Law*, and of acting agreeable to the dictates of their own *Reason* and *Conscience*!'

Sharp was certain that the American colonies need not have been lost had Parliament agreed to reforms, and it was the American situation which provided the stimulus for his co-operation with a growing band of Englishmen who were beginning to agitate for that reform, among them John Wilkes, the Revd Christopher Wyvill, Horne Tooke, Capel Lofft, John Jebb and Major John Cartwright.[40] Like them he deplored the fact that the excesses of the French Revolution were used as an excuse to prevent reform in Britain. He reasoned that the dodges were due to the rejection of moderate reform by those who wanted no reform at all. During that period of radical agitation Granville's brother James was a member of the London Common Council, and supported the radicals. He participated in remonstrances to George III and was on a committee to present one to the King.[41]

Sharp's contributions to the campaign for parliamentary reform (aside from his ever freely-flowing advice given personally) took the form of pamphlets. Many of his proposals are reminiscent of those put forward by the Chartists a generation later and would have sounded even more radical to eighteenth-century ears had it not been for the revolutionary rhetoric bombarding them from America and France. Sharp attacked rotten boroughs as laying the basis for parliamentary corruption, which was 'a harbinger' of 'approaching slavery'. From the law of 8 Henry VI, cap. vii, whereby the right to vote was limited to those holding 'land or tenement to the value of "fourty shillings" by the year', Sharp deduced that, prior to the law, 'All Men, in each county, that were free, howsoever poor, enjoyed a share in the legislature. . . .' In other words, the people had been losing rather than gaining rights and were 'approaching slavery' because of Parliament's arbitrary legislation. Property, not people, had become the basis of representation: 'Thus our pads, our *pigs*, our very *geese*, must all be represented. . . but NOT the people!' Sharp reminded his readers that natural right was an inheritance equivalent with property – the most important 'property' of all to be protected. Some petitioners were calling for triennial parliaments in order to make legislators more responsible to the electors, but for Sharp that was not enough; he called for annual parliaments at least, more often if needed.[42]

Granville Sharp was obviously an obstinate and tenacious – perhaps a meddling – reformer, ready to interfere in any situation where he believed he could help to see justice done or where his advice might lead to an improvement in the human lot. Yet one does not get the impression that he was either a cantankerous zealot or an impractical visionary. Although he exaggerated the happiness of 'the good old days', he was generally realistic about what was possible in the present, modest about his role (he even refused to accept offices in the many organizations he supported), and was reputedly of a winsome personality.[43] His Anglican loyalties did not preclude his working with people of nonconforming faiths, and his debates with Jews, Catholics and Quakers seem to have increased his tolerance rather than to harden his prejudices, except in the case of Catholicism.

Sharp's private pleasures were in music and in friendship. It is refreshing to note in connection with his musical interests that he had a sense of humour. He accepted as his signature:

How much Sharp imbibed of the 'cordial cup' himself is impossible to say, but his list of liquid refreshments for an election dinner on 7 August 1780 included nine gallons of red port, three of Madeira, three of Lisbon and one of Mountain along with twelve bottles each of French claret and Old Hock, one bottle of brandy and one of rum. Evidently it was all drunk, because for another dinner three days later, on 10 August 1780, the list included thirty-four gallons of red port, ten of Mountain, six of Madeira and ten of Lisbon, plus twenty-four bottles each of French claret and Old Hock, and one each of brandy and rum. Obviously he was no teetotaller.[44]

Sharp died on 6 July 1813 and was buried in Fulham, but the vicar would not allow a funeral sermon to be preached in the church because Sharp had supported the British and Foreign Bible Society, which was Nonconformist.[45] He was, of course, immortalized in Westminster Abbey.

It must have been disheartening to Sharp to see the idealism of the Age of Revolution give way to the Age of Reaction, and to witness another period of erosion of the people's rights. Yet he saw one battle won: the abolition of the slave trade. And, since in his mind all forms of slavery were aspects of the same problem of arbitrary power, one can surmise that this man whom James

Stephen said had 'the most inflexible of human wills united to the gentlest of human hearts' died not in despair but in hope that other forms of tyranny too might eventually fall.[46]

# 2 A Quartet of Liverpudlians: William Rathbone, William Roscoe, James Currie and Edward Rushton

The story is told that in the latter part of the eighteenth century the tragedian George Frederick Cooke appeared on the Liverpool stage while intoxicated. When the audience hissed, he 'pulled himself together and said venomously over the footlights that he had not come to be insulted by a pack of men every brick in whose detestable town was cemented by the blood of a negro'.[1] Cooke's bitter accusation accurately reflected the image of Liverpool as a town whose wealth was built on the Guinea trade, and whose ships by mideighteenth century carried a growing percentage of the slaves taken from Africa by the British. Even some of the trading-companies owned by antislavery Quakers found it almost impossible to remain untainted, because bills of credit for slave cargoes became an integral part of general currency exchange.[2]

The surprising thing is that it was possible not only to start but to sustain an antislavery movement in the town. One of the historians who told the George Cooke incident ended his account by reporting that the audience cheered the defiant outburst, and that the cheers reflected the change coming over the attitudes of many Liverpudlians toward the slave trade. Among those residents who deserve credit for the effort to keep antislavery opinion alive were William Rathbone (the fourth of that name[3]), a prominent Quaker lumber merchant; lawyer–banker–writer–botanist and politician William Roscoe; the physician Dr James Currie; and a blind poet, Edward Rushton. Influenced by the humanitarian Enlightenment ideas of the late eighteenth century, as was Granville Sharp, their counterpart in London, all of them abhorred the traffic in human flesh that was the African slave trade and simultaneously expanded their sensitivities to encompass an empathy and sympathy for the powerless poor of their own country and race. Because of their common interests, the four men, and especially the Currie, Rathbone and Roscoe families, became close friends.

Roscoe was the oldest of the group and lived the longest (1753–1831); Currie and Rathbone were three and four years younger but were the most short-lived (1756–1805 and 1757–1809); while Rushton, the youngest (1758–1814), died seventeen years before Roscoe.[4] But all lived through the heady days of the American and French Revolutions when talk of liberty and equality filled the air and people of reason and intellect were posing hard questions about the course of British politics and society. All but Currie lived to rejoice together over the abolition of the British slave trade in 1807, their major victory; none witnessed the passage of the Emancipation Act of 1833, although it was imminent enough for Roscoe to foresee its success before he died in 1831. He was the only one to survive the reactionary period following the Napoleonic wars, and therefore the only one able to savour the beginnings of success in stirring up the British public in favour of their other causes: poor-law and prison reform, special treatment for juvenile delinquents, opposition to capital punishment and press gangs, better treatment for men in the armed services, election and parliamentary reforms, extension of educational opportunity, and greater religious tolerance.

Each of these men's lives was directly affected by the slave trade. The Rathbone family company had got its start trading with the American colonies, and by the nineteenth century had built a trading-empire that stretched to continental Europe, the eastern Mediterranean, India, the Orient, Africa, Australia and both of the American continents.[5] The first William (c. 1669–1739) had a partner who urged him to participate in 'black-birding', a common euphemism for the slave trade, but the second William (c. 1696–1746) who founded the Liverpool firm, remonstrated with his father and won a veto of the proposal. By the last half of the century the Society of Friends was bearing a stronger testimony against the trade, and William the third (c. 1728–1789) extended the Rathbone company's policy against it by refusing to sell timber to firms that built slavers.[6]

The first eight bags and three barrels of American cotton to reach Liverpool from America in 1784 were consigned to the firm of William Rathbone and Son, and as the trade in cotton increased it posed further problems of conscience, settled completely and finally only in 1862 when the firm refused, on grounds of both morality and expediency, to buy any more.[7]

Among the men who worked for the Rathbones was James Cropper, later to become an outstanding abolitionist leader and one of the Anti-Slavery Society's experts on the economics of slavery. The story goes that Cropper, then a country lad from Cumberland, simply walked into the Rathbone office one day, said he had heard of their Quaker trading-firm, and asked for a job. Within three years he was a partner in the company, but eventually left to form one of his own. The families remained close friends and Cropper was of great help to William Rathbone the fifth and his brother Richard when they set up a new firm as commission merchants.[8]

According to Emily Rathbone, who published the *Records of the Rathbone Family*, Roscoe was an opponent of the slave trade from childhood, but she does not explain what the influences on him were.[9] He came of a humble background. His father owned a market garden and kept a tavern, and everyone who has written on Roscoe mentions how as a boy he carried bags of potatoes to market on his head. But he early developed a love of books, in which his mother encouraged him, and he seems to have been very susceptible to their influence.[10] Rising rapidly from his modest beginnings, Roscoe was to become a lawyer, banker, writer of history and poetry, botanist and – long enough to be the public spokesmen for his friends on the slavery issue – a politician. The fates were kind enough to allow him a short tenure in the House of Commons under the 'ministry of all the talents' just when Wilberforce pushed the Abolition Act to its successful conclusion, thus affording Roscoe the honour of speaking and voting in its favour. It is interesting to note that as a banker Roscoe had a partner, Thomas Leyland, who made a fortune in the slave trade, but he also at one time had as an employee the future leader of British abolitionism, George Thompson.[11]

Currie, son of a Scottish clergyman, saw slavery at first hand in Virginia, where he was living when the American Revolution broke out. Although his sympathy was with the colonies, he decided to return to Britain, but his ship was seized and he was detained for a year before he could escape. Upon his return he studied medicine in Edinburgh and then moved to Liverpool to set up his practice.[12] Despite the risk of jeopardizing his career, he was brave enough to oppose the pro-slave-trade sentiments of Liverpool society.

Rushton's father was a barber. After a meagre education at a Liverpool free school, the son was apprenticed to a firm of West India traders before he was eleven years old, and by the age of sixteen was an experienced sailor – so experienced that at that age he confidently took over command of a ship when the captain lost his head in a storm. As a reward for saving the ship he was promoted to second mate, in which position he shipped on several voyages to Guinea. Although living in the midst of the slave trade, instead of becoming inured to its brutalities he reacted against them. Being saved from drowning by a slave whom he had taught to read and who lost his own life in the rescue made a lasting impact on Rushton. Thereafter he intervened more often to protect the slaves on his ships, often getting himself into trouble by befriending them. The end to his career as a seaman resulted from one such incident. Ophthalmia raged below decks and all of the crew except Rushton refused to go into the hold. By going to help the slaves, he contracted the disease, which destroyed one of his eyes and left him blind in the other. It left him, also, a vehement opponent of the slave trade.[13]

Even before the organized antislavery movement began in Britain, Roscoe, Currie and Rushton had begun their individual endeavours to influence the public through their writing, and Rathbone was doing his part as a member of the Society of Friends. When he was only nineteen, Roscoe wrote his poem 'Mount Pleasant', named after the district of Liverpool in which he had been born. The poem begins with a description of the city and the bustling trade of Liverpool merchants which had brought opulence to the inhabitants and made their town's name known in the farthest places of the world. But, Roscoe feared, the 'happier moments' were being lost as people concentrated on piling up wealth even to the point of losing their sense of humanity as they engaged in the business of tearing 'Afric's swarthy sons' from their native soil to labour 'helpless and forlorn' till death relieved them of their torture. The poem ends as a jeremiad against both the city and the nation:

Shame to Mankind! But shame to BRITONS most,
Who all the sweets of liberty can boast;
Yet deaf to every human claim, deny
The bliss to others, which themselves enjoy. . . .

He recalls the better days:

Our drink, the beverage of the chrystal flood,
– Not madly purchased, by a brother's blood –
Ere the wide spreading ills of Trade began,
Or Luxury trampled on the rights of Man

and asks his readers to ponder the verdict of history: 'What now remains of TYRE's imperial pride?'[14] The poem was written in 1771 but not published until 1777. Roscoe's publisher was also the publisher for such advocates of human rights as Joseph Priestley, Horne Tooke and Mary Wollstonecraft.[15]

Ten years after the publication of 'Mount Pleasant', Roscoe followed with the first volume of his second poem against the slave trade, *The Wrongs of Africa*, for which his friend Dr Currie wrote the preface.[16] Part II constituted a second volume in 1788. In his preface Currie noted that the close of the eighteenth century was similar to the fifteenth, in which 'a sudden accretion of light burnt on the human mind', but, like Roscoe, he feared that the spirit of commercialism was degrading the British nation. Although the foundations of liberty had been laid at home, the growing African trade infringed on all principles of liberty and justice, causing untold misery in Africa and the sugar islands. While he appealed primarily to British honour, he also pointed out that from a sheer profit motive the traders ought to realize that, if they continued to rob Africa of its men in their most prolific age, they would soon deplete the supply and run themselves out of business.

Roscoe appealed to the bonds of human brotherhood:

Formed with the same capacity of pain,
The same desire of pleasure and of ease,
Why feels not man for man?

How could anyone, he asked, 'tear with stripes' the 'quivering flesh' of a fellow human being, 'waste his emaciate frame' with grinding toil and deprivation? And how could the people who do such things expect any mercy for themselves? Addressing 'the master of the sable crew', he questioned, 'Can their groans / Add poignance to thy pleasures'; 'Feels not thine harden'd breast a horrid bliss / In the wild shriek of anguish?' And, again challenging his countrymen,

> Blush ye not
> To boast your equal laws, your just restraints,
> Your rights defin'd, your liberties secur'd,
> While with an iron hand ye crush to earth
> The helpless African; and bid him drink
> That cup of sorrow, which yourselves have dash'd
> Indignant, from oppression's fainting grasp? . . .
>
> Forget not, Britain, higher still than thee
> Sits the great Judge of Nations. . . .

Rushton's first and major poem against slavery, *West Indian Eclogues*, came out in 1787 also. His setting was Jamaica and his characters two slaves who recall their homes in Africa to contrast past happiness with present misery. Strong emphasis is given to the sexual lust of the master, who has taken the wife of one of them, and the slave is now tortured by gnawing visions of her succumbing to him, perhaps even willingly as a way to gain comforts and privileges. His decision to kill the master ends in his own death instead. One of Rushton's footnotes makes the plea similar to that in Currie's preface to Roscoe's poem, an appeal to the profit motive. He says the evidence shows that, thanks to kind treatment, on some plantations the blacks have multiplied. Wouldn't it be wise to follow that path, for self-interest's sake, if not from feelings of humanity?[17]

Hardly first-class poetry, both Roscoe's and Rushton's verses were effective propaganda, composed of the ingredients designed to catch the popular notice, especially since they were published just as the first antislavery society was emerging to stir up discussion and agitation. It was in May 1787 that twelve Londoners organized the Society for the Abolition of the Slave Trade, and within a month Roscoe announced that he would donate the proceeds from *The Wrongs of Africa* to the cause. He also whipped out a pamphlet, *A General View of the African Slave Trade, Demonstrating its Injustice and Impolicy; with Hints towards a Bill for its Abolition*, which rejoiced the hearts of the London Society because of the ferment it produced in Liverpool.[18] Supporters of the trade then found a champion in a Jesuit priest, the Revd Raymond Harris, who was voted £100 by the Liverpool Corporation to write *Scriptural Researches on the Licitness of the Slave Trade*, arguing that God sanctioned slavery when, for example, he allowed Joseph to 'buy' the Israelites for Pharaoh during the time of famine. Roscoe then responded with *A Scriptural Refutation of a Pamphlet Lately Published by the Rev. Raymond Harris*, and Currie, too, persuaded a clergyman friend of his to answer Harris by expressing Currie's reaction 'that if such be religion, I would "none on't"'.[19]

Even Currie, though he had no claims at all to poetic ability, put this hand to a poem which he called 'The Negroe's Complaint', the lament of an African stolen from his home and his love; but it was evidently so bad that Roscoe undertook to rewrite it before Currie sent it off to Admiral Sir Graham Moore in London, asking that it be published anonymously. Currie gave himself away, however, when he wrote that he hoped the 'simple ditty' might do some good and confessed that it had already done some 'in diverting a stream of indigation that a certain heart could hardly contain'. Only after Moore obtained its acceptance for publication in the *World* under the title 'The African' did Currie admit its provenance.[20] In a subsequent letter from Moore to Currie on the subject, Moore raised the point that 'Some people who in other respects are not shallow say that the negroes in the West Indies are better off than the labourers in Great Britain. . . .'[21] He denied believing it, yet obviously the idea had provoked him to serious thought, just as it was already leading men such as Granville Sharp to examine the 'slavery' of fellow Britons. The Liverpudlians were to be drawn into the same controversy.

The battle over slavery was already under way in Liverpool when Thomas Clarkson appeared in 1788 to gather statistics for the book which was to become a classic on the subject. In it he names Currie, Rathbone, Roscoe and Rushton along with the Quaker abolitionist Isaac Hadwen as the men he immediately called upon for help.[22] Rathbone and his father, William the third, had already furnished Clarkson with muster rolls of slave ships from the Liverpool Customs House, and now introduced him to people, mostly common sailors, who could provide more information. At first the seamen talked freely but, as Clarkson's aims became apparent, hostility increased and eliciting facts became not only difficult but dangerous. In the tavern where he stayed they took to taunting him by toasting the slave trade in his presence. Luckily Clarkson had with him an ex-slave-trader from Bristol whose size and athletic build warded off physical attack; but one day, when standing on a pier, Clarkson suddenly found himself surrounded by men about to push him into the sea. He was alert enough to sense their purpose, darted forward, knocking one man down, and so escaped.[23]

As the people of Liverpool were awakened to the wrongs of slavery, Currie reported to Sir Graham Moore, 'the struggle between interest & humanity has made great havock in the happiness of many families'. But the small group of abolitionist pioneers were encouraged by Clarkson and by another visitor, Joseph Priestley, who boosted their spirits with his confidence that no effort of even the humblest person is in vain.[24] So they moved ahead with the organization of the Liverpool Anti-Slavery Society, while alarmed members of the town corporation got up a petition to Parliament to uphold the slave trade, the first of many to be sent throughout the 1790s and up to the Abolition Act of 1807. Rushton began to edit the *Liverpool Weekly Herald* as another avenue for attacking the trade.[25] At issue in 1787, 1788 and 1789 was a bill in Parliament introduced by Sir William Dolben to limit, according to the tonnage of a ship, the number of slaves that could be carried on it. Liverpool merchants were naturally up in arms, and looked on its passage as a defeat for them and a victory for the abolitionists. Currie was even radical enough in the beginning to oppose Dolben's motion for fear that it would sidetrack total abolition. Even worse in the eyes of Liverpudlians, he praised the courage of some Africans who retaliated against Liverpool ships because one Liverpool captain had carried off free hostages as slaves.[26]

One of Clarkson's aims in writing his book on the slave trade was to discredit the myth that the African trade provided valuable experience for British sailors, was, in fact, a 'nursery for seamen' who would then serve the nation in its ever-broadening international trade. Clarkson's statistics on the fearful mortality

of sailors as well as captains on the slave voyages were brought to
life by Rushton's poems, especially when people learned that they
were informed by Rushton's own experience. One entitled 'The
Seaman's Nursery' substituted British sailors for Africans as the
victims of the 'trade accursed' that 'blasts each social joy' by
separating the men from their families and sweethearts. They
were doomed to succumb to African fevers, die and be
abandoned in their graves far from home on Africa's shores.[27]
Another, called 'Will Clewline', reprimanded,

> Ye statesmen, who manage this cold-blooded land,
>> And who boast of your seamen's exploits
> Ah, think how your death-dealing bulwarks are manned,
>> And learn to respect human rights.[28]

Roscoe's botanical interests gave him an excellent opportunity
to contact a ship's captain to ask him if he would bring back from
Africa seeds or plants which might be grown in England. Roscoe
pointedly expressed his hopes that Captain Lace himself would
return safely, and then went on to remind him of his responsibility to the 'several hundreds of people' under his control. Roscoe
asked that he exercise 'coolness, vigilance and compassion' so that
the 'poor imprisoned African' might find 'that in all his distress he
is not without a friend', and that Lace would do his duty 'with as
much humanity as is consistent with the nature of this business'.[29]

Already Rushton's thoughts were going beyond the slave trade
to the abolition of slavery itself. When the American Revolution
failed to bring emancipation to the slaves in the new republic, he
composed 'American Independency', praising the colonists for
their determination to be free, but pleading with them,

> And reflect that your rights are the rights of mankind,
>> That to all they were bounteously given,
> And that he who in chains would his fellow men bind,
>> Uplifts his proud arm against heaven.
> How can you, who have felt the oppressor's hard hand
>> Who for freedom all perils would brave,
> How can you enjoy peace, while one foot of your land
>> Is disgraced by the toil of a slave!
> O! Rouse then in spite of a merciless few,

And pronounce this immortal decree,
Whate'er be man's TENETS, his FORTUNE, his HUE,
He is man and shall therefore be free.[30]

When he realized that no action was forthcoming from the shouters for freedom, Rushton's indignation boiled over in a vitriolic address to George Washington. It begins disarmingly enough with praise for the American hero's fight for freedom, and an appeal to set an example for the world, but builds up to a climax of denunciation:

The hypocritical bawd who preaches chastity, yet lives by the violation of it, is not more truly disgusting than one of your slave-holding gentry bellowing in favor of democracy....In the name of justice, what can induce you thus to tarnish your own well-earned celebrity, and to impair the fair features of America with so foul and indelible a blot?...Now, sir, are you sure that your unwillingness which you have shewn to liberate your negroes does not proceed from some lurking pecuniary considerations? If this be the case, and there are those who firmly believe it is, then there is no flesh left in your heart, and present reputation, future fame, and all that is estimable among the virtuous, are, for a few thousand pieces of paltry yellow dirt, irremediably renounced.

On the flyleaf is a note saying the letter was returned to Rushton 'without a syllable in reply'.[31]

Although disappointed with the United States' failure to carry its revolutionary rhetoric on liberty and equality to its logical conclusion of emancipation, liberal thinkers in Britain were profoundly influenced by that rhetoric as they examined their own country's guilt, not only in the slave trade but also in its refusal to allow the free exercise of civil liberties at home. One can easily discern the fusing of these issues in the words and actions of the abolitionists, especially as the French Revolution continued to heighten their sensitivities. The Liverpool Literary and Philosophical Society, founded by the subjects of this essay, proved to be an excellent vehicle for the expression of their liberal ideas. In the first flush of delight in England at the overthrow of tyranny in France, Roscoe's verses enjoyed great popularity. In

1788 he had fused literary and political interests by joining in the commemoration of the Glorious Revolution of 1688, for which he wrote 'Secular Song for the Revolution of 1688'. In it he hailed William of Orange, who represented the cause of freedom over James II, 'the worst heir of a tyrannous line' who 'trampled on reason, religion and laws'. But now

> Round the altar of freedom united we bow,
>   Our libations shall aid her unquenchable flame
> Which here, to submit to our children, we vow,
>   Bright and vivid as when from our fathers it came. . . . [32]

That celebration of liberty in 1788 proved to be the prelude to those which followed to cheer the French revolutionists, and Roscoe's pen remained busy. In 1789 his 'Ode to the French Nation' hailed the people who had inspired all of Europe to 'dash to earth her Tyrants and her chains'.[33] When Liverpool celebrated the fall of the Bastille in 1790, he contributed his famous song to liberty in France that begins 'Unfold Father Time! Thy long records unfold' – records filled with oppression, terror and superstition – and ends with the refrain

> Seize then, the glad moment – and hail the decree
> That bids millions rejoice and a Nation be free![34]

In 1791 both Roscoe and Rushton produced poems to commemorate the Revolution. Rushton's made use of the analogy between the enslavement of Africans and of Europeans, and was a call to revolution by both:

> To be free is a duty man owes the All-wise,
> And he sins who is tamely a slave. . . . [35]

Roscoe's eminently singable 'Song for the Anniversary of the French Revolution' was to be his most popular:

> O'er the vine-covered hills and gay regions of France,
>   See the day-star of Liberty rise. . . .
>
> Let Burke like a bat from its splendour retire

A splendour too strong for his eyes. . . .

O catch the high import, ye winds as ye blow;
  O bear it ye waves as ye roll
From regions that feel the sun's vertical glow,
  To the farthest extremes of the Pole.

*Equal rights, equal laws*, to the nations around
  Peace and friendship, its precepts impart,
And wherever the footsteps of Man shall be found,
  He shall bind the decree on his heart.[36]

Roscoe's allusion to Burke's conservatism was followed up with a sharp satire on the 'Life, Death and Wonderful Achievements of Edmund Burke', who like Don Quixote rushes out to tilt at all he meets, but 'with a backward stroke'. All he accomplished was to hit his best friend, Charles Fox, though he continued to roam about tweaking Whig noses until 'lo! An Amazon stept out / One Wolstonecraft [*sic*] her name. . . .' She cuts him with vigorous strokes before she is joined by Tom Paine, who delivers the *coup de grâce* with a club made of a tree from 'western climates'. Now only Burke's shadow walks as a warning to others. Three years later Roscoe was to publish a third attack on Burke, who, although he had persisted in encouraging the Americans in their fight for freedom, had failed to take the same stand in defence of the French people.[37]

Alfred Shennan in the introduction to Chandler's bicentennial biography of Roscoe avers that the Liverpool Literary and Philosophical Society members' fraternization with French revolutionaries was 'essentially ideological, academic and remote', yet I think the evidence shows that the stirrings of liberty in America and France did more than inspire poetry, that members of the Society took ideas seriously and were ready to suit deeds to words.[38] Currie led off with an attack on the Corporation and Test Acts which resulted in a public meeting at which he presented resolutions against them. The resolutions were unanimously passed and the assembled group of Dissenters then further resolved to back only candidates for Parliament who would bind themselves in advance to oppose the acts. Although Currie was dubious about the wisdom of that resolution, he was willing to bow to the majority and agreed to be one of the group's delegates to a great Dissenting meeting in Warrington to choose delegates to a London gathering. He was concerned about the importance of keeping the people of each congregation involved, not just the delegates, so that the movement would remain democratic. His hope was to use the Virginia Act of Toleration fathered by Thomas Jefferson and James Madison as a precedent for action, believing that to be consistent with respect for the British constitution. Currie argued against the obnoxious acts via an exchange of pamphlets with the Revd Edward Owen, forcing Owen to rescind his diatribe against the Nonconformists.[39]

For years Liverpool had been governed by a self-elected and therefore self-perpetuating town council reflecting the elite slave-owning corporations which enjoyed a monopoly of power in the city. Now in 1791 the inspired reformers led the freemen in petitioning for a change. Reverting to a long-unused custom, an Assembly of Burgesses was convened to pass new bylaws and to elect new councillors, and William Rathbone led in the demand that the Treasurer must submit to an audit. When the demand was defied, the case was taken to court with the result that the reformers won, but a retrial was granted on a technicality. Again they won, but again a retrial ensued. By the time of the third attempt the funds of the reform group had run out, and the excesses of the Reign of Terror in France had turned British public opinion around so dramatically that reform of any kind was giving way to reaction and repression.[40]

Another focus of protest which gained the reformers a popular following in 1791–2 among both merchants and the working classes was the trade monopoly of the East India Company. It was logical that Rathbone, as one of the leading merchants himself, should be named to the committee that called a meeting to voice public opinion; but the East India issue was somewhat lost in the more pressing one of reforming the town's government, and by 1793 the crisis of war with France took precedence.[41] Rathbone and Roscoe were to revive it a decade later.

With the French war looming, the British Government quickly made an issue of loyalty and subversion, and as the nation went, so went Liverpool. When the Pitt ministry put out a proclamation on sedition, the Major of Liverpool, in November 1792, ordered the publication of 10,000 copies of an anti-Jacobin declaration to be posted in the city. Roscoe, with Rathbone's help, prepared a reply in the form of a pamphlet entitled *Equality*, but the local newspaper to which they sent it was afraid to publish it, so the radicals had to have it run off as a handbill.[42] When the Mayor then summoned the citizens to a public meeting of support for the Government, Roscoe and his friends determined to attend to present their own version of what constituted loyalty and British rights, and to call for parliamentary reform. Roscoe drew up the draft which was presented by Joseph Birch, and a stormy debate followed in which Roscoe himself participated. Then, with his proposals seconded by Rathbone, the friends succeeded in carrying the citizenry with them in a victorious vote. The Mayor was forced to announce that the Roscoe address would be printed and circulated. But, since the meeting was on a Saturday, he said it could not be ready for signing until Monday, thus allowing time over the weekend for a mob to tear the address to pieces before it could be signed. 'Loyalists' then found enough people in the crowds to sign a counter address which was sent to the King. The newspapers were afraid to protest against this miscarriage of justice, and, when Rathbone tried to speak at another meeting to ask for Pitt's dismissal, the officials were so afraid of his eloquence that they hired enough people to ensure that he would be shouted down by the mob.[43] The town council reported to King George that it 'observed with concern the prevalence of wild and delusive theories tending to weaken the sentiments of obedience to the laws'.[44] When war with France materialized the following year and Roscoe, Rathbone, Currie and Rushton were among those openly opposing it, they were quickly labelled Jacobins and suspected of plots and conspiracies.

Rushton's poem 'The Fire of English Liberty' bemoaned the expiration of the small spark of freedom inherited from Runnymede and the revolutions of 1640 and 1688.[45] Because of Rathbone's white hair, he was known as 'the hoary traitor', and so suspect that the family doctor asked to pay his calls only after dark for fear of reprisal if his carriage was seen at the Rathbones' door. Rathbone wrote to his London abolitionist friend William Smith that no one who was an abolitionist and a reformer could let his name be used openly in the city. 'If matters continue in their present situation,' he predicted, 'many Reformers will become Revolutionists. . . .'[46] A ballad which appeared locally obviously referred to the Quaker merchant Rathbone and the politician–attorney Roscoe:

> But unluckily then in the Town
> Attorneys were great politicians
> And Quakers were men of renown
> And merchants were metaphysicians. . .
> They'd one family make of all nations
> A State without rulers they'd rule
> And vote me and a negro relations.[47]

Local politics, anti-Government authoritarianism and antislavery were securely blended to create in the public mind the stereotype image of a radical Jacobin.

The connection was reinforced when Roscoe wrote a pamphlet blaming the causes of the insurrection in Santo Domingo on white oppressors. While he deplored the atrocities accompanying the uprising, he declared that no one ought to be surprised by them, because the slaves had learned their lessons in bloodshed from their white masters.[48] Also in 1793 he wrote an antiwar pamphlet in an attempt to convince the merchants that their present economic distress was because the bills of credit on which they operated the African trade had been drawn for two to three years in advance and now the war made it impossible to cash them. Meanwhile territories were changing hands and capital was being destroyed so the future held only ruinous prospects.[49] But in 1793 patriotism and anti-Jacobinism prevented Roscoe from winning allies among the merchants. Their change in attitude would come only as the war with France dragged on.

Roscoe, Rathbone, Rushton and Currie all stood together against the Test and Corporation Acts, Pitt's suspension of habeas corpus, and the French war. While adamantly anti-Pitt on those issues, they were thankful for his co-operation with Wilberforce on the slave trade, and Currie decided to try to capitalize on the Wilberforce–Pitt friendship to approach the Prime Minister on the war question. Currie had been in correspondence with Wilberforce, but also made a trip to London to confer with him, with the result that what had been intended as a private letter to Wilberforce was turned into a public one to Pitt. Somewhat more cautious than his trio of cohorts, Currie believed discretion to be the better part of valour in this case, and signed an assumed name, 'Jaspar Wilson'. Wilberforce, of course, knew the secret, and, while he did not agree with Currie's opinions, he respected his motives and kept his identity in confidence.[50]

Currie's message in the printed letter was twofold: the pragmatic one that the war was ruining the commerce and economy of the nation; and the idealistic one that ideas cannot be conquered by the sword. 'The present generation will probably be swept away before the intellectual earthquake subsides,' he opined, 'but those who succeed them will, I trust, find the air more pure and balmy, and the skies more bright and serene.' That Currie retained faith in the idealistic side of the French Revolution was enough in itself to brand him a Jacobin, but, when one reads the unpublished drafts of his Jaspar Wilson letter, one realizes the full extent of his revolutionary ideas on the rights of the people and on what English society should be. People must have the right of self-government, he argued, and to exercise that right properly they must be instructed. Only through education could poor people learn to 'look before and after' and to act on reason rather than from passion. Pitt needed to realise that poor men who are ignorant will yield to the moment rather than think of future well-being. People who do not govern themselves, people subservient to a domineering authority, will in a few generations 'assume the temper as well as the condition of slaves'.[51]

Currie's thinking was truly compatible with that of Granville Sharp, but somewhat sharper in its expression. He even implied that one of Pitt's war aims was to kill off enough men to keep a balance of population at home. Pitt's repressive acts against civil liberties were already fostering so much bigotry and Toryism in the name of orthodoxy that men of enlightened minds and liberal opinions were being harrassed out of the land to find refuge in America. In fact, Currie himself kept some property in Virginia in case he needed a safe retreat.[52] Although Wilberforce never divulged the identity of 'Jaspar Wilson', he was evidently perturbed about what the effects of Currie's radicalism might be. 'Above all,' he admonished, 'consider what may be the consequence of infusing into the minds of the lower orders anything of a Jacobin principle.'[53]

By 1793 the radical Literary and Philosophical Society felt the constraints of official watchfulness and censure so much that they suspended their meetings, but they were not completely silenced. In 1795 Roscoe and Rathbone drew up a petition against Pitt's bills to suppress seditious meetings and for the preservation of the King and Government, and Roscoe printed a long argument to show the invidious consequences of such measures. Some 4000 Liverpudlians were willing to sign, but the opposition prevailed by gathering even more signatures.[54]

As individuals, the members of the Literary and Philosophical Society continued their efforts to help the poor and the handicapped, and to champion the rights of the common people, heeding Rushton's admonition in verse:

> Go then, ye affluent! go, your hands outstretch,
> And from despair's dark verge, oh! raise the woe-
>     torn wretch.[55]

Even as a boy Roscoe had written verses which reveal an awakening social conscience, as in

> Teach me to sooth the helpless orphan's grief
>     With timely aid the widow's woes assuage
> To misery's many cries to yield relief
>     And be the sure resource of drooping age.[56]

As a member of the Society of Friends, Rathbone, too, had been early sensitized to one's obligation to minister to the poor, and Currie, because of his profession, was more aware than the average citizen of their health problems. He compared society to a great trading-company in which people invest in varying degrees according to wealth and rank. Though all contribute differently, all are concerned with the profit of the whole, and, as in a pyramid, the multitudes of poor at the bottom support those above. Therefore thinking people must realize that attention to the needs of the people at the bottom is not simply charity. It is enlightened self-interest and the basis of a good society.[57]

In the Liverpool of 1790, nearly 7000 of the wretched poor were crowded into cellar dwellings – that is, they lived in the cellars which had once served as warehouses underneath the residences of merchants and tradesmen. After being abandoned the cellars had fallen into decrepitude, unclean and unhealthy, but afforded some shelter for people who had no choice of anything above the level of squalid misery. In 1794, even before the distress of the French war was felt very much, one of every forty of the townspeople was in the workhouse. Confusion and corruption prevailed in the administration of poor rates.[58] Dr Currie took the initiative in reporting the appalling conditions to the town council and was instrumental in getting a commission appointed with himself as a member. Thanks to his leadership, Liverpool earned a reputation as a model for other cities in its Poor Law administration.[59] Currie, like Sharp, was ahead of his time in recognizing that insanity was an illness and that the mentally ill should be placed in separate asylums rather than in workhouses. The establishment of the Liverpool Lunatic Asylum can be credited to his persistence.[60]

Rathbone actively co-operated with his friend not only in improving the administration of the Poor Law, but in trying to get the law itself changed – without success. The fifth William Rathbone recalled how his father knew personally each of the men he employed and went to their aid in times of sickness or special need. Rathbone's wife, Hannah Mary Reynolds, was the daughter of a Quaker philanthropist who made a fortune in ironworks, and she too was dedicated to charitable works. She could not stomach Malthus's ideas on overpopulation, fearing that his solution would lead to even more power for the magistrates and clergy and the consequence would be infanticide for the poor.[61] Currie and Roscoe were interested in savings banks for workers, and, after Robert Owen established such a system in New Lanark, Currie made a trip to Scotland to learn at first hand how successful the plan was. He was impressed, but despaired because he was painfully aware of how meagre a poor man's savings could be and knew the pressure to spend was constant.[62]

In the drafts of his Jaspar Wilson letter, Currie had argued the necessity of educating the poor so that they could intelligently participate in their own government. To that end he enlisted his friend Rathbone to aid him in establishing a school; while Rushton, with the help of Roscoe, gave his energy to founding the Liverpool School for the Blind. As Currie was ahead of his contemporaries in his recognition of mental illness, so Rushton was ahead of his generation in proposing that the school should educate and train blind students for employment – be something more than just a care-taking asylum. His poem on blindness emphasizes how it is a double curse if accompanied by poverty.[63] In another poem, 'Superstition', Rushton plays on the idea that ignorance and superstition, characteristic of either blacks or whites, are equivalent to slavery. Why is earth full of slaves? he asks.

> Britons, yes!
> Seven hundred millions of your fellow men,
> All formed like you the blessing to enjoy,
> Now drag the servile chain. . . .
> How comes it then that minds are thus debased?
> That man, though nature loudly calls 'be free',
> Has closed his eyes against her, and become
> A mean, a grovelling wretch!

The villain is superstition,

> Who wanderest o'er the world, array'd
> In pure religion's mantle; thou whose breath
> Conveys those potent opiates to the brain
> Which brings on reason's sleep. . . .[64]

During Roscoe's short term in Parliament, he was one of Samuel Whitbread's supporters when Whitbread (also an active abolitionist) introduced his bill for the education of the poor.[65]

*Noblesse oblige* was, of course, a fairly common attitude among middle- and upper-class British people during the Age of Enlightenment, but often it went no further than establishing charitable institutions, including schools. What definitely distinguished the quartet of Liverpudlians as radicals was their advocacy of the *rights* of the common people, especially political rights. Rushton was perhaps the most extreme; he was an outright republican.[66] While Currie doubted that extending the franchise would bring about dramatic changes, he believed that Parliament must respond to the demand for wider suffrage. He said he would choose an unstable democracy over a 'close aristocracy' but insisted that extending the franchise must be accompanied by reform in the property laws to do any good. Otherwise landlords could dictate the votes of their tenants. Less radical on this issue than Rushton and Rathbone, he preferred household suffrage, and also approved a literacy test, that being consistent, of course, with his attempts to broaden educational opportunity.[67] Rathbone, on the other hand, favoured universal suffrage (for males). His programme for election reform included the secret ballot, concentrating all elections on the same day for the convenience of the people, and a 'more serious' oath for candidates to hold them to their promises. He also wanted the pubs closed on election days. All these, he pointed out, had been part of election reforms in the United States. Although Rathbone's views on the slave trade were unpopular, his support for the people's political rights saved him in the eyes of the working classes. According to family history, on more than one occasion he rode straight into anti-abolition mobs and persuaded them to disperse.[68]

As the war with France dragged on, and as Liverpool's trade suffered in consequence, the antiwar stance of the radicals gradually grew more acceptable. Merchants' losses of ships on the high seas increased, but of course there was no profit to be made by staying in dock either. Sailors were constantly subject to capture or, if out of work and at home, were the victims of the press gangs. Rathbone's Quaker pacifism marked him as antiwar, and Currie as Jaspar Wilson attacked Pitt for wasting lives uselessly. While editing the *Liverpool Herald*, Rushton attacked the press gang so strongly that the lieutenant in charge of it came to the office to demand an apology. The reply was naturally a refusal to comply, but the loud threats and exchange of curses so alarmed Rushton's partner that they had a falling-out and dissolved their partnership.[69] Roscoe's loathing of the press gang dated back to the days when he was articled to a Liverpool law firm and lodged with a sea captain who lived in such nightly fear of the gang's appearance that he reportedly drank himself to death in the attempt to keep up his courage. Roscoe saw no heroism in the naval and privateering exploits of his countrymen, and detected only brutality in the operations of the press gang as it forced men into the American and French wars.[70]

It is not surprising that Roscoe and Rathbone added to their activities a campaign for improving the conditions of the French prisoners of war, and Currie got himself appointed to a commission to check the prisons. By 1799 there were over 4000 Frenchmen held in Liverpool jails.[71]

Rushton expressed the views of the quartet in his antiwar poems. In one addressed to Robert Southey he grieved over the slaughter, but separated the oppressors who made war from the 'high-minded men' who 'must liberate mankind'.[72] 'The Coromantes', about a group of Africans captured for slavery, blends the themes of the trade in black slaves and that in European 'slaves' who are pressed against their will into fighting for the 'lordlings':

> Oh Britons! behold in these Coromantees
>   The fate of an agonized world,
> Where, in peace, a few lordlings hold millions in chains,
> Where, in war, for these lordlings men open their veins,
>   And again to the dungeons are hurled![73]

His categories of just and unjust wars made it possible, while hating Britain's war with France, to idealize Toussaint L'Ouverture as he rallied the blacks of Santo Domingo in their fight to expel both the British and the French. To Rushton and his friends, Toussaint's was a just war for freedom, not one created by the commercial rivalries and power struggles of the 'lordlings'.[74] While Rushton composed his verses, Currie's dislike of the aristocracy was channelled into writing a biography of Robert Burns, a man of the people.[75]

Meanwhile Roscoe, while encouraging his fellow writers in their more propagandistic pursuits, was earning himself an international reputation as a literary historian. While still a law clerk, he had found a friend in a young schoolmaster who taught him French, and together they learned and read Italian. On evening walks they enjoyed Italian poetry, and would get up early in the morning to meet other friends to read and discuss the classics before their work day began. Falling in love with all things Italian, Roscoe dreamed of making Liverpool into a Venice of the North. Perhaps that accounted, in part, for his hatred of the slave trade, which he saw as sullying the good name of his town. Intrigued by the Italian tradition of art patronage and especially by Lorenzo de' Medici, Roscoe not only wrote a biography of him but also emulated Lorenzo as a banker, poet and patron of the arts. A friend, William Clarke, who went to live in Fiesole for his health, collected and sent documents to Roscoe, and, through the good graces of Lord Holland, the help of the British Embassy was enlisted in transcribing more materials from Italian libraries and archives. A life of Pope Leo X succeeded the one on Lorenzo.[76] Their wide circulation was furthered by translations into most of the languages of western Europe. By sending a copy of *Leo X* to Thomas Jefferson, Roscoe probably helped to publicize them in

America.[77] The American author Washington Irving reported that when he unexpectedly met Roscoe in the Liverpool Athenaeum, 'I drew back with an involuntary feeling of veneration.'[78]

As Roscoe's reputation brought credit to Liverpool, hostility to his political radicalism began to fade. Also fading with the waning of the century was the power of the old families who had dominated Liverpool politics for so many generations. Whigs were challenging Tories, and Unitarians the Established Church. Roscoe, Currie and the Rathbones were all becoming part of the new Unitarian elite (Rathbone having been disowned by the Society of Friends because of his protests against their increasingly rigid sectarianism), and were gradually admitted into the Whig party. Even before they were eligible voters they helped to organize campaigns and select candidates. Ian Sellers writes that by 1806 about five-sixths of the Liverpool electors 'could be described as working men' and Roscoe had won their admiration by his fight against the Corporation.[79] Consequently, perverse views on the slave trade were outweighed by other factors, and despite the fact that he was not yet himself a freeman and therefore had no vote, Roscoe was asked to stand for Parliament in the election of 1806 against two Tory candidates, both military men, Generals Tarleton and Gascoyne. When the Roscoe men put out a placard, 'I have voted for myself. Ben Tarleton', the Tarleton men retaliated with 'I wish I could vote for myself. Will Roscoe.'[80] The election returns indicate the decline of the old Corporation's power, for its candidate, Gascoyne, ran far behind Roscoe in votes. Tarleton also trailed badly.[81]

Roscoe seems to have trimmed his sails a bit to help his election along. In his victory speech at the Golden Lion, he stood firmly for peace with France and for parliamentary reform; but on the slave-trade issue he advocated compensation to those who would suffer losses, putting the blame for the trade on the nation and its government rather than on the Liverpool merchants. Differing from Rushton and Currie, he defended the monarchy and the House of Lords, avowing that the latter was a powerful and, on many occasions, a 'useful barrier' between the Crown and the people. Therefore, it was the Commons that needed reforming by extending the franchise to the 'great towns and extensive bodies of men' not presently represented. Sellers says that Roscoe paid out £12,000, 'most of it' in 'direct bribery' to win the election.[82] In

Liverpool, as throughout Britain, payment for votes was an established tradition. Candidates were also expected to provide banquets for their supporters, with alcoholic beverages supplied in abundance.[83]

Roscoe considered it to be one of the greatest honours of his life that he was privileged to be in Parliament to speak against the slave trade and to join in the vote which pronounced its verdict of death. When his friends gathered to rejoice with him there must have been a note of sadness, too, that one of them, James Currie, had not lived to share their victory. One wonders if it was a consciousness of his old friend's spirit hovering over his shoulder that prompted Roscoe to take the line of argument he did, both in his election victory speech in Liverpool and in his speech in the Commons. Currie had always believed that the trade should be ended gradually and with compensation to the merchants. He was willing to allow each ship already engaged in the trade to continue until it had put in a total of fifteen years, although no new ships should be permitted to enter.[84] Rathbone, too, in acting as mentor while Roscoe prepared his speech for the House, cautioned that some compromise might be wise.[85]

Roscoe incorporated both compensation and gradualism into the speech he delivered on 23 February 1807, but he asked that a grace period of only six to nine months be given the merchants, and compensation only to those who suffered specific losses. He advised delay, he insisted, not because of the traders' interests but because of his concern for the victims of the trade. He feared that, if brought to market, and no market existed, they might be massacred. While he declared that he thought he owed it to his constituents to advocate compensation, he stressed that their real payment would come in the form of an expanded East India trade. Doing away with the monopoly of the East India Company would in itself make up for the loss of the slave trade. Precisely because Roscoe was from Liverpool and yet spoke for abolition, he is credited with having won other votes in the House.[86]

Clearly the abolition of the slave trade took priority in Roscoe's career as an MP, but other liberal to radical programmes were not neglected. Rathbone wrote to him after the slave-trade speech that 'You have now fairly started the East Indian game & we must be prepared to join in the chace [*sic*].'[87] Rathbone was practical politician enough to realize that, if Liverpool trade suffered in the wake of abolition, Roscoe must be prepared to be unpopular among the unemployed workmen; therefore it was important to hold their support by pressing forward to break the East India Company's monopoly.[88] One must keep in mind that, as the head of a great trading-house, Rathbone had a vested interest in the direction Liverpool's trade would take. By this time the Rathbone firm was one of the foremost if not the top company in the trade to America.[89] It is logical to deduce that diverting the ships of the African trade to other world markets would be preferable to the increase in competition that would result if they should turn to America instead. Whether from altruism or self-interest, and it is impossible to measure the percentage of each, while Roscoe worked in Parliament on the East India monopoly Rathbone held public meetings in Liverpool at which he exposed the Company's affairs. At one such gathering at which he proposed that the Government cut off all loans to the East India Company, he carried the crowd with him, with only one dissenting vote. Thereupon Rathbone commended the dissenter for his courage with the observation that minorities are often virtuous.[90] He spoke from long experience in a minority role.

The question of the East India Company's monopoly dovetailed with that of the French war and the British Orders-in-Council to stop neutral nations from supplying goods to the enemy. Again Rathbone's own interests were involved, yet one cannot assume that his motives, any more than Roscoe's, were completely self-serving. They co-operated with the nation's liberal Jacobin spokesmen, who had welcomed Roscoe's election as MP not only for his support on abolition but also in trying to restore peace and gain political reforms. As already noted, the Liverpool spokesmen had established reputations for championing the rights of the common man against the press gang and the 'lordings' who sent them to war.[91] Roscoe championed the people's interests further by supporting Sir Samuel Romilly's bill to require that landed estates be subject to contract debts. That is, if an owner died without paying his debts, the heir should not be absolved from responsibility.[92] As noted, Roscoe also backed Whitbread's bill to establish schools for the poor. Romilly, like Whitbread, was another abolitionist who worked against oppressive laws which ground down the working classes.[93]

On economic issues Roscoe clearly had the people of Liverpool behind him, but, when Parliament was dissolved in 1807 over the question of Catholic emancipation, and Roscoe returned to Liverpool, he quickly learned that not only was antagonism still alive because of his abolitionism, but that he had doubly sinned by standing against the Test and Corporation Acts and in favour of Catholic emancipation. He particularly pointed out the injustice of the Test Acts in keeping Catholics from serving in the armed forces when they were offering to shed their blood in defence of their country. True, sometimes Catholics got in despite the law, but then, even after honourable service for the nation, they had no right to sue either at law or equity and their property could be plundered 'with impunity'.[94]

Hearing rumblings of trouble before Roscoe arrived back in Liverpool, his friends, including Rathbone, and Currie's son Wallace, took the precaution of meeting him on the outskirts of the town, some on foot and others mounted. General Tarleton's crowd, including seamen armed with bludgeons, tried to block the way of the procession escorting Roscoe into the town, and a mêlée ensued. Roscoe's group managed to make their homes without loss of life, but the incident discouraged him from standing for re-election.[95] Apparently he had never really relished the life of a politician with all of its pressures, in any case. When a group of his backers nominated him over his objection, he made no effort to campaign and lost by default. During that one-sided contest the Tories put out a series of mock papal bulls recommending that all 'apprentices, ragamuffins, jailbirds, Presbyterians, rogues, Methodists and whores' should vote for Roscoe, 'the stimulator of His Holiness' person'.[96] In a letter to William Smith, Roscoe noted that both parties in the election were using black men to parade their banners, another indication that Catholicism more than slavery was at issue.[97] In subsequent elections Roscoe rejected proposals from Westminster and Leicester as well as Liverpool that he should have another try.[98]

Although officially out of politics, Roscoe continued his reform activities and especially his fight for peace. During the next two years he wrote several more antiwar pamphlets, including a fierce blast at the Government for its attack on Copenhagen. On one count Roscoe's liberalism was inconsistent, though, for, in his opposition to the British newspapers' attacks on France, he went so far as to advocate Government restraints on freedom of the press.[99] To Wilberforce he entreated, 'with what delight should I see you advocate the cause of suffering Europe, or rather the cause of the civilized world, with the same energy and success as you have done that of the oppressed Africans'.[100] Rathbone, in London to testify before the House of Lords against the Orders-in-Council, also appealed to Wilberforce, and worked closely with Whitbread and Henry Brougham to try to get the Orders repealed. Back in Liverpool the merchants wrote an address to the King to which Roscoe added a plea for peace, and the document carried by a large majority at a meeting in the Exchange.[101]

Rathbone's testimony before the Lords was his last public act, his last attempt 'to plant [his] foot athwart oppression's way', as Roscoe wrote in a sonnet on the death of this, his closest friend.[102] Although Rushton did not die until 1814, evidence in regard to any continuing public activity on his part dwindles away, except for his antiwar verses. However, by the second decade of the nineteenth century the younger generation – William Rathbone the fifth, Wallace Currie and Edward Rushton the younger – were old enough to carry on in their fathers' places in support of Roscoe and reform.[103]

One of the first by-products of the passage of the Abolition Act of 1807 was the organization of the African Institution by a group of abolitionists dedicated to the enforcement of the law and the civilizing of Africa. They believed that the most practical way to stop the trade in slaves was to substitute commerce in other African products. Roscoe was one of its founders, along with such leading abolitionists as Samuel Romilly, Zachary Macaulay, James Stephen, Thomas Clarkson, Wilberforce, Henry Brougham and Granville Sharp, with the Duke of Gloucester as Patron.[104] Roscoe's major assignment was to keep an eye on the ships in Liverpool, to report violations and, upon instructions from Zachary Macaulay, to examine the Customs House records in certain suspicious cases. Sometimes it was necessary to persuade a customs officer to search a vessel, although convictions were difficult to obtain because offending ships evaded the law by carrying three captains, one British, one American and one Spanish, and three sets of papers.[105] Paradoxically, Roscoe's second son was a partner in a mercantile house that had three ships in the African trade which had not yet returned home, but he, too, volunteered to watch for slave ships which tried to continue illegally.[106]

Roscoe's most successful intervention was in the case of the *Monte de Carino*, a Brazilian vessel which arrived in Liverpool with nine blacks, presumably part of the crew, but who had been slaves in Brazil. During the ship's stay, the Captain had these men arrested and held in jail on charges of debt to him; but when ready to sail again procured discharges for them in order to take them back. When the men refused to go, the jailer delayed, thus giving Roscoe time to raise bail for the men and institute proceedings for their release. The blacks were freed.[107]

Prince Sanders, a free New England-born black, was a visitor to Liverpool and Roscoe furnished him with letters of introduction to the Duke of Gloucester and other London friends associated with the African Institution. Sanders was *en route* to Haiti to establish an educational system for the progressive King Henry Christophe, and needed their backing.[108] During the same period one of the Rathbone firm's American captains was the famous Paul Cuffe, a free black engaged in carrying other American blacks to settle in the British colony of Sierra Leone. The Rathbone and Roscoe families entertained these guests in their homes, with no apparent feelings of racial prejudice. Roscoe, incidentally, had a black servant who lived several years in the family and who, like his master, studied French and Italian and wrote verses.[109]

Throughout all of his antiwar pamphlets, Roscoe had sounded like a complete pacifist, but in his zeal to stop the slave-traders he took the position that the British were justified in seizing slave ships of other countries even though such action might result in war.[110] Like Rushton, he had his own standards of what constituted a just war for self-defence or for freedom, in contrast to wars that he believed to be motivated by greedy commercialism and power rivalry. His opposition to Pitt's war had been because he thought it was motivated by exactly such base considerations, and that Pitt had no real comprehension of, or concern about, the significance of the ideas of liberty and equality that underlay the American and French Revolutions. Moreover, in the bombardment of Copenhagen, Pitt had surrendered Britain's dignity and honour; in the expediency of the moment he had acted like Napoleon, not against him. Yet, despite their differences, Roscoe could appreciate Pitt's efforts for abolition and the two men worked together as founders of the African Institution. George Canning and Henry Brougham were also fellow members, but in the election of 1812 they stood as rivals to represent Liverpool. That Roscoe retained enough of a political following for his name to be considered to be useful in Brougham's campaign is evident from one of the songs sung at an election dinner:

> If Roscoe would stand, who's the man of our soul,
> He'd soon, my lads, be at the head of the poll;
> But the cares of the state he declines to resume,
> Though he points out successors in Creevy and Brougham.

It goes on to cheer the Whig candidates as champions of peace, freedom, and reform, and, as for their Tory rivals, 'instead of these broomsticks / We'll send up our Brougham'.[111]

When Canning and Roscoe's old rival Gascoyne were victorious, Canning succeeded Pitt as the target of Roscoe's protests on foreign policy. The attacks were acerbic in both substance and expression, and Roscoe treated Canning's speeches with mocking satire. As both he and Currie had done in an earlier period, he emphasized the effects of war on the working classes: Canning's policy deprived the workers of Liverpool of their jobs, and, while they had been longsuffering and patient, remaining peaceful and orderly in the midst of deprivation and rising tax burdens, Canning had not even bothered to commend them while campaigning in the city. Canning had denied the connection between war and scarcity, provoking Roscoe to scoff, 'Is the next discovery to be "poverty begets peace"?' Would singing the old song 'Let us all be unhappy together' solve their problem? Canning was one of 'those political partizans, who,...always make common cause against the people, and would gladly induce them to believe, that all opposition to their measures is not only useless, but criminal; not only irrational, but insane; not only imprudent, but contradictory to the immutable decrees of Providence'.[112]

Along with their efforts to act as watchdogs over the illegal slave trade and to rescind the Orders-in-Council (successful too late to stop the War of 1812 with the United States), Roscoe and Brougham worked together for parliamentary reform.[113] One cannot say they worked in tandem because, in comparison to Brougham, Roscoe was less of a gradualist, more an immediatist, although he proved to be willing to go along in favour of household rather than complete male suffrage. It is difficult to say whether or not Roscoe was pushed in a more radical direction by his association with such London radicals as Capel Lofft and Major John Cartwright, which seems to have begun when he became an MP. Certainly that association must have reinforced his own inclinations, although he declined Cartwright's invitation to become a member of the Society of Friends of Parliamentary Reform or of the Hampden Club, claiming that 'engagements of a private nature' would prevent. In 1808 Cartwright contacted such 'Noblemen and Country Gentlemen' as were friendly to election reform to ask them to become stewards to propose resolutions on representation, trial by jury, and freedom of press and person at a London banquet. Thomas Clarkson, for one, had agreed to do so. Roscoe answered that he would be honoured to accept, but pleaded distance and work as reasons for declining.[114]

In reading the correspondence, one gets the feeling that Roscoe preferred individual to associated efforts. This raises the question of whether he may have been a bit afraid of public repercussions against such radical groups, particularly as Cartwright seems to be trying to persuade him that they will act judiciously. Yet such a conclusion does not square with Roscoe's fearlessness in Liverpool. Perhaps he did have too many calls on his time and energy and preferred to contribute by using his talent for writing, which he could do at home. It appears that Cartwright accepted without question Roscoe's assurances of wholehearted support for the groups' aims. He continued to write to Roscoe for money, for the use of his name on circulars, and to initiate petitions from Liverpool.[115]

Certainly by 1811 Roscoe was writing to Brougham that it was too late for 'palliative' reform, and Cartwright was commending Roscoe for rejecting the 'miserable water gruel' of the moderate reformers. Roscoe was by then speaking very decidedly of the *rights of* the people rather than of *obligations to* the people, and like Granville Sharp he believed that granting such rights was simply a restoration of what had once been, and was still, rightfully theirs. Thus endangering the constitution was not an issue; rights must be restored regardless of consequences. Roscoe was convinced that it was the power of the Government's ministers that was to be feared, not a larger, more representative House of Commons. Just as he had used the analogy of slavery when he spoke of people being sent to war against their will, he now often used the phrase 'political slavery' in connection with disenfranchisement. In one of his pamphlets he referred to the despotic government of Napoleon, 'which in the true spirit of slavery, considers the rulers *as a superior order of beings to the people at large*'.[116] If Roscoe echoed John Cartwright on there being no middle ground between liberty and slavery, he also echoed his old friend James Currie on political liberty, and his friend Rathbone on procedural reform: that all elections should be held on the same day, and districts should be set up so that no one would have to go far to the polls. To his critics, among them Henry Crabb Robinson, it all added up to 'unthinking, vulgar democracy'.[117]

Roscoe's reputation was such that his help was constantly sought in the growing number of reform causes that characterized the early nineteenth century. Because of his botanical knowledge, and his interest in tenant–landlord relationships, fellow abolitionist William Allen called on him for advice in setting up agricultural colonies for the poor. With Robert Owen he discussed education. And in the last years of his life he encouraged the formation of the Liverpool Association for Superseding the Use of Children in Sweeping Chimneys.[118] But, aside from his major cause of antislavery, most of his energy went into the movement for penal reform, including the crusade against capital punishment. There, too, he was co-operating with antislavery cohorts, Samuel Romilly, Samuel Hoare and Dr Stephen Lushington, for instance.[119]

He got into the subject in 1817 when Lushington appealed to him to write something on capital punishment for the Society for the Diffusion of Knowledge. If his strong faith in the possibility of human improvability had already biased him against the practice, his research on the subject convinced him that it was neither right not expedient. If all other measures for rehabilitation failed, transportation was much to be preferred, for in exile one had a chance to make a new beginning. From capital punishment Roscoe went on to study the prevailing prison system in England and then entered into correspondence with leading theorists of penology and wardens working in the new prison systems emerging in the United States. They included Roberts Vaux and James Mease of Philadelphia, William Tudor and Josiah Quincy in Boston, and G. C. Verplanck of New York, among others.[120]

Roscoe's conclusions, like those of Granville Sharp, were

decidedly modern: the aim of prisons should be reform, not revenge; at present, jails were schools of vice because an inmate lost his status as a human being, he was degraded and ruled by fear; the mixing of sexes, of juveniles and first offenders with hardened criminals was prevalent; severity of treatment produced only longings for revenge and was no deterrent to further crime; crowding and bad conditions within compounded the difficulties of awakening any incentive for rehabilitation. Rescoe disputed the current principle that a prisoner was 'dead in law' – that when convicted he lost all rights. Yes, legal punishments were necessary, but disease, cold, famine, nakedness and polluted air were not legal punishments. While a prison system had to be strict, it should make provision for productive labour and for access to books.

Roscoe was particularly horrified by the trend in the United States toward using solitary confinement as a means of bringing about repentance and reform. Neither should prisoners be watched constantly. When he learned of Lafayette's plan to visit America in 1825, he wrote to entreat him to look into the harsh new penal system which was developing. Lafayette's response was sympathetic because he remembered his own imprisonment without books when all of his thoughts centred on revolution. Perhaps of most importance, for this essay, is the point that Roscoe realized that the prison system reflected the gulf between rich and poor, between the mighty and the lowly. His plea to Lafayette, for instance, was on the grounds of the obligation 'of those who have the good fortune not to be called to account for their great offences, towards those who have been detected in the perpetration of small ones'.[121]

In the period following the Napoleonic wars, Britain persisted in her attempts to get the Concert of Europe, and the United States as well, to unite in putting an end to the slave trade. British abolitionists were hopeful that slavery itself would decline and die or, at least, that slaves would be better treated because of the difficulty in replacing them. Ameliorative measures to that end were introduced; but, as the years went on and the hoped-for results did not follow, antislavery people began to revive their societies to push for an act of emancipation. Gradualism had failed, immediatism became the cry. Roscoe complained that the Abolition Act of 1807 was 'little more than an empty sound'.[122]

Among those initiating action for the new Liverpool Anti-

Slavery Society in 1822 were James Cropper, William Rathbone the fifth, and his brother Richard. Roscoe, then in his sixty-seventh year, was honoured by being invited to take the presidency.[123] One of Roscoe's last published works, perhaps the last, was an article for the Anti-Slavery Society in which he looked back at what had been accomplished and forward to future success. Within his lifetime, he said, he had witnessed a remarkable improvement in the 'moral character and disposition of mankind'. English people had made the important discovery of how to combine the 'mass of society' together to attain a public good: the slave-holder must follow the fate of the slave-trader.[124]

Roscoe died in 1831 before the passage of the Emancipation Act of 1833, but already its success was in sight as excitement rose for the election of a Reform government, which was expected to extend the franchise and implement other reforms as well. News of the Revolution of 1830 in France also gladdened his heart.[125]

In 1953, when Liverpool celebrated the bicentennial of Roscoe's birth, Sir Alfred Shennan wrote that his poetry illustrated his 'century's poetic combination of classical tradition and the awakening interest in human rights and emancipation'.[126] The quotation makes a fitting epitaph not only for Roscoe's poetry but for his life, and for the lives of his friends included in this quartet of Liverpudlians. Like Granville Sharp, they were in the ranks of humanitarians who, even in the eighteenth century, were growing in their awareness of the many dimensions of slavery.

# 3  Joseph Sturge

In the early decades of the nineteenth century, as industrialization proceeded at a rapid pace and as labour developed greater consciousness of exploitation, abolitionists, especially those who were themselves employers, were constant targets of the radical press. T. J. Wooler, editor of the *Black Dwarf*, and William Cobbett in his *Political Register* were especially adept with satirical barbs which portrayed antislavery leaders as pious hypocrites who wrung their hands over the plight of far-off black slaves while at home they eased their consciences by supplying the poor with Bibles instead of bread.[1] Some abolitionists were guilty as charged, but a great many were not. One who did not fit the stereotype was Joseph Sturge of Birmingham.[2]

Sturge's antislavery credentials are impeccable. He came from a Quaker background which had sensitized him to the early testimony of that group against the evil of 'man stealing' and holding one's fellow men in bondage. Although too young to participate in the early battle against the slave trade (he was born in 1793), he was involved in the antislavery movement from the time of its revival in the 1820s, and was appointed Secretary of the Birmingham Anti-Slavery Society when it was organized in 1826. By the time of the passage of the Emancipation Act in 1833 he qualified as one of the more radical abolitionists on two counts: his endorsement of 'immediatism' as opposed to gradual emancipation; and his opposition to compensating slave-owners rather than the slaves themselves.[3] Between 1833 and 1838 Sturge led the fight to discredit the West Indian apprenticeship system as nothing more than disguised slavery. In 1837 he travelled to the British colonies personally to gather evidence to present to Parliament. In the wake of the victory ending apprenticeship he proposed an organization to fight slavery everywhere in the world, and when the British and Foreign Anti-Slavery Society was founded he became one of its driving forces.[4] Although its central committee was in London, Sturge travelled down regularly from

Birmingham (sometimes more than once a week) to participate in its decisions and activities, often acting as spokesman in meetings with Government officials. The fact that he was one of the Society's most generous donors gave weight to his opinions in matters of policy. Sturge was the single most dominant person managing the two world antislavery conventions in London (1840 and 1843), and he travelled to the United States as he previously had to the West Indies in the interests of the cause.[5]

Like Granville Sharp, Sturge worried about the problems facing freedmen as well as about those of slaves. After his visit to the West Indies he tried to form a land-investment company to purchase land which could then be sold or let in small plots to the ex-slaves. Although there was no problem in obtaining financial subscriptions, the Government refused the necessary permission. As late as two years before his death he bought an old sugar estate in Montserrat with the idea of rebuilding it under a reorganized labour system.[6] His interest in the free-produce movement led him to abstain from the use of slave-grown sugar and cotton and to experiment with the manufacturing of free-labour cotton.[7]

Sturge's concern with slavery and black labour has been emphasized by historians of the antislavery movement, and it might appear that he turned to the problems of the white working class only when West Indian emancipation was complete; but it would be a mistake to think in terms of a sharp line chronologically dividing his (any more than Granville Sharp's) activities in the two fields. Sturge's involvement in the problems of the poor whites can be traced back just as far as the beginning of his search for a solution to slavery. Both concerns had a common origin in his Quaker upbringing, which stressed care for the weak and oppressed. In Sturge's case this sensitivity was coupled with a feeling of guilt about the increasing wealth and affluence of the community of Friends – including his own as a 'leading citizen' of Birmingham.[8]

Stewardship was for him a solemn trust, but at the same time he seems to have been a man with an openhearted good will and a generous nature, although these traits were not always apparent to those who differed with him. He could be very stubborn when convinced that he had the right of the matter. After the split of the antislavery movement into anti- and pro-Garrisonians, the latter group found little good to say about Sturge. Disappointed when Sturge did not defend him against the charge of 'infidelism', Garrison characterized his erstwhile friend as lacking in candour – he 'shuffled'. Richard D. Webb, a leading Dublin Garrisonian, was willing to concede Sturge's good intentions and his willingness to stand up boldly for the rights of the poor, but repeatedly called him 'snuffling', 'secretive' and a narrow-minded bigot. Samuel May, an American abolitionist, compared Sturge to the wealthy American antislavery leader Gerrit Smith:

> he cannot forego the distinction, the consideration, which he enjoys, arising from his wealth, & from his position among the Friends. He nurses his dignity, and is forever on the watch to see that it receives no detriment. I have therefore thought him very deficient in candour & fairness. . . . [9]

Sturge himself admitted to a 'peppery disposition' in his youth, but Henry Richard, his personal friend and biographer, says that as an adult Sturge was habitually sunny tempered and serene. The Revd John Angell James described him as a happy man, almost always smiling. This was said in a eulogistic memorial service, but James might as easily have praised him as a serious Christian.[10] Dutiful and determined he certainly was, and he took himself very seriously. He may have been a happy man, but there is little to indicate a sense of humour or an appreciation of wit, let alone a relaxed jocularity even with his intimate friends.

Although the Sturge family had been brought up on the principle of moderation rather than abstinence regarding the use of alcohol, Joseph held himself to strict standards of teetotalism in drink as well as in abstaining from slave-grown produce. In contrast to Granville Sharp or to William Roscoe, he once voted against a music hall for Birmingham because it would sanction frivolous, worldly amusement, an act that left him open to the charge of narrow-mindedness. Yet he seems to have enjoyed sociability as he entertained frequently in his home. In his early life he was devoted to outdoor sports, but gave up hunting because it bothered him to inflict pain on any creature. His vitality led an American friend to remark that it was a blessing Sturge was not a general, because 'with your energy, who can tell what mischief you would do in the world?'[11]

Sturge's enormous store of energy was expended in a schedule of diverse reform activities which matched that of Granville Sharp, and one that would stagger most people. Richard Cobden, who called Sturge the most fidgety man he knew, wrote,

> His energy was so untiring that he never stopped to examine the difficulties of any undertaking which commended itself to his conscientiousness. . . . I have often thought that a few thousand such men would effect a moral revolution in the world. I have not met three men equal to him in these attributes.

Upon reading a particularly despairing letter written by her husband, Mrs John Bright observed that it would discourage 'anybody but Joseph Sturge'.[12]

We have more information about Sturge in his early years than we have about Granville Sharp and can therefore better trace the evolution of his benevolent endeavours and his growing commitment to reform. His public participation in good causes began after he attended a meeting of the Bible Society in Bristol in 1813. He immediately went home and organized one of his own in Thornbury. It was at about the same time that he took his stand as a pacifist by refusing his military draft. As punishment, all his sheep were confiscated. Several years later he was dispossessed of his furniture when he refused to pay the required rates for the Established Church.[13] Joseph joined the temperance movement and, even though it meant a loss for his business as a corn-dealer, refused to deal in barley and malt. He also gave up the customary practice of renting his cellars for wine storage.[14] Such strong public stands at an early age undoubtedly reinforced Sturge's 'psychology of commitment'; they laid a basis for his lifelong support of the peace movement, temperance movement, and the causes of religious dissenters – in fact, for his general anti-Establishment stance on issues of education, antislavery, civil liberties, antimonopoly and political democracy.[15] Although originally Sturge's motivation was an inner religious compulsion associated with his own salvation and his responsibility to God, eventually he evolved a philosophy of justification which co-ordinated all of his activities for 'the good of the people'.

Sturge has gone down in history as a moderate Quaker reformer; but there were occasions in his life when a scratch reveals the latent revolutionary. He refused to pay taxes to support an armed police force in Birmingham; and on one occasion urged a ladies' group in Manchester to use a tax boycott to protest against the Corn Laws, asserting that it might be the only effective way 'of bringing the most aristocratic ministry in the world to terms'. In 1842, when the London labour-leader Francis Place warned Sturge that his planned suffrage conference would be in violation of the law curtailing public political meetings, Sturge's reply was that they must take the risk rather than be bound by such an obnoxious law. He went ahead with the conference. While in the United States he defied the laws of Maryland against distributing abolitionist literature. When the British people were swept by the same wave of revolutionary spirit that animated the French in 1831, Sturge was among those who joined the Political Union formed in the wake of a great demonstration of some 200,000 people of Birmingham; and in 1848 he not only presided at a public meeting of sympathy for the French revolutionists, but was one of four delegates who carried the message of support across the Channel to France.[16] While not a Tom Paine, his Quakerism must have contained some of the same ingredients as those of Paine's own Norfolk Quaker heritage. Both certainly shocked the more conservative community of Friends. Sturge's association with the Chartists was to be his ultimate expression of radicalism. But, several years before that connection was made, he helped to start a paper, the *Reformer*, which was, according to biographer Hobhouse, too radical even for James Cropper, his father-in-law and one of his few sympathetic supporters amongst the Quakers.[17] He had the backing of his brothers, John and Charles, and seems to have been actually spurred on in his radicalism by his sister Sophia, although she was never able to persuade him to take a stand for women's rights.[18]

Elihu Burritt, an American abolitionist, peace advocate and himself an all-round reformer, aptly remarked that Sturge's philanthropy was 'as spherical as the sun itself'.[19] His efforts for peace, begun with the Worcester Peace Society in 1818, eventually took him on missions to France, Germany, Belgium, Denmark, Finland and, in a last-minute attempt to stop the Crimean War, to Russia to interview the Tsar.[20] Richard Cobden had urged Sturge to be aggressive on the peace issue: 'The only way to make your principles triumph is by entering the arena of politics and doing as you did in your anti-slavery efforts. You must make yourself troublesome. . . .' But even Cobden was afraid Sturge had been injudicious in his appeal to the Tsar for peace, because Sturge inserted into the memorial the issue of freeing the serfs.[21]

Closer to home, the man of peace continued to contend for the rights of religious dissenters, and did not confine his focus to Quaker problems alone. In 1850 a wave of anti-Catholicism swept Britain when the Pope announced that he was creating twelve new episcopal sees under the Archbishop of Westminster. Sturge defended the Catholics, as William Roscoe had done before him, and in doing so helped to turn the tide of antagonism in both Birmingham and the nation.[22] He resisted proposals for state education because schoolmasters and clergy serving the state would not only impose the established religion but perpetuate an establishment – that is, 'status quo' – attitude which would obstruct and retard reform and work against the labouring classes in the long run.[23]

His objections to the Sunday operation of railways and to shipping-lines' scheduling of Sunday departures rested on the same twofold basis of religion and concern for the workers: it was offensive to some people as a violation of the Sabbath, and deprived many workers of their day of rest. Sturge was not an adamant Sabbatarian himself, but, when he embarked on a Sunday to sail to America, he felt guilty when he noted the clerks, porters and dock hands who were required to report for duty. As one of the directors of the London and Birmingham Railway, he was in a position of personal responsibility. Thus he proposed to his fellow directors that they not allow the company's carriages and engines to be used on the Sabbath. Although he lost by one vote, he succeeded in getting the issue submitted to a referendum of the stock-holders and was supported by 'upwards of 1500 votes'; but a majority put through an amendment which banned railway service only during the customary hours for religious worship. After a second failure to achieve Sunday closing, Sturge resigned his seat on the board.[24]

Sturge's objection to required Sunday labour probably stemmed from his experiences with Sunday Schools, where he learned something of the resentments of working people. His decision to open a Sunday School of his own originated because of the deplorable lack of educational opportunity for the poor of Birmingham. Children were employed from the age of eight years, sometimes even younger, and by the 1840s only about half the town's children received any schooling at all. Under the impetus of the British and Foreign School Society, an evangelical union connected with the London Bible Society, Sturge opened his first Sunday School in October 1845. Many of the young teachers were apprentice workmen and Sturge supplied them with Sunday breakfast as one inducement to volunteer. The Severn Street Adult School developed out of the arrangement. Eventually a library and a workers' savings bank were appended, and in 1848 a women's Sunday School was added. He was a mover in establishing the Gloucester Working Men's Institute, and was its largest contributor.[25]

Work with the underprivileged young led Sturge to an experiment with a decidedly modern sociological basis. He bought a large house, hired a teacher from London to run it, and persuaded the governor of Birmingham jail to release to his custody sixteen of the worst juvenile offenders. The results were so satisfying that he expanded the experiment, buying an estate at Stoke Prior in Worcestershire which would accommodate sixty boys. It too was a success, so much so that he was approached with an offer to make it a Government institution. Sturge declined, as one of his cardinal objectives was to maintain a 'home' rather than an institutional atmosphere. Years later, when the news of Sturge's death reached the prisoners in Birmingham jail, one of them pronounced a spontaneous eulogy: 'Joseph Sturge is dead! Then Birmingham has lost its *best* friend.' Parks, playgrounds, laundries and the town baths were other results of his perception of the needs of the poor.[26] When he opened his fields on Wheeley's Lane as a playground for poor children, neighbours protested with the usual arguments in such cases: annoyance, noise, deterioration of the neighbourhood, the encouragement it would give to beer shops and to other disreputable vendors. Sturge carried on anyway. His concern for his own workers was reflected in visits to their homes to get to know them as individuals, in providing them with reading-material (and bookcases), and in holding an annual tea party for them. Before departing from London on his peace mission to the Tsar, he sent his brother instructions to furnish their labourers with flour below the market price, since corn was so expensive. A letter from the Sturge employees to Mrs Sturge after his death in 1859 expresses their love for him as an employer and also 'as a dear friend'.[27]

It would be easy to assume that all of this largess was self-righteous, guilt-exorcising, ego-satisfying paternalism, and it would be foolish to deny elements of such motivation in Sturge. After all, he was a child of his age, brought up to take seriously his 'duty' to the poor. But it would be an oversimplification to settle for *noblesse oblige* as the complete explanation of Sturge's help to the needy. Early Quaker teachings shaped his belief in equality and in 'rights' as well as in benevolence. As a boy Joseph was often sent to live with his grandfather for long stretches of time. In that household, family and servants all ate together at one big table. As a business man, Sturge maintained friendly personal and social contact with his employees and their families, which must have reinforced his faith in the basic good sense of the working classes, or else he would not have proceeded as he did to agitate for their rights. Henry Richard, Sturge's biographer, who was also his personal friend and fellow reformer, insists that Sturge's effectiveness in the antislavery movement resulted from his lack of an 'aristocratic fastidiousness', which would have held him aloof from the masses.[28] It was not only logical, but seems inevitable, that concern for the freedom and rights of black people should be inherent in his concern for the exploited and oppressed of all races. But, despite the clarity of such logic to a modern person, the fact remains that many abolitionists saw no such obvious connection and remained either apathetic toward, or even hostile to, white labour movements. Thus many Quakers, relatively conservative themselves, considered Joseph Sturge a radical who was 'untrue' to his own Society when he mixed with the ungodly in politics. David B. Davis has observed that the Quakers, like the evangelicals, had two reform goals: 'to produce a sober, self-disciplined, and industrious working population, and to persuade the upper classes to devote their time and wealth to enobling causes. . . rather than to conspicuous forms of waste and self-indulgence'.[29] Sturge approved those goals, but he went far beyond them.

What, then, were the special influences operating on Joseph Sturge? Unlike Sharp, he was not a member of the Establishment and his rebellion against it seems more natural. We can say that the Quaker tenet of equality took deeper root with him than with many Quakers, but without really knowing why. The one child-hood experience of eating at the same table with his grandfather's servants is meagre indeed. We can conjecture a certain amount of parental influence in the same direction from the fact that his brothers and his sister seemed to share Joseph's bent toward democracy. Neither should the influence of his father-in-law, James Cropper, be underestimated. Sturge's early acts of defiance toward the Establishment deepened the psychological grooves of sympathy for other victims of 'the system'. Between the time of Sharp and the Liverpool radicals and that of Sturge, consciousness of an industrial proletariat was much more clearly defined. Like Karl Marx, Sturge saw the developing alienation of the classes, but unlike Marx retained his faith in the possibility of reconciliation without violence. His mission was to preach that gospel. One could posit that his motive was a selfish one: I save my class, and myself, only by saving my brother. But, to accept that conclusion about Sturge, one must concede that the whole philosophy of brotherhood is essentially one of self-interest. I think Sturge's early experiences in political activity were crucial in fostering an acceptance of a practical working relationship with men who were, up to a point, 'equals', but he never completely lost the sense of special responsibility or stewardship in 'guiding' those who had fewer advantages in education and wealth, even when he was encouraging in them greater independence. Although one can argue that he believed labour must be rescued from its radical elements, yet there is no doubt that his goal was a broader base of political and economic independence for the worker. Let us examine the evidence in his political career.

In the early nineteenth century, Birmingham was a centre of radical and reform politics and of religious nonconformism so that the milieu in which Sturge operated reinforced whatever tendencies in those directions he already possessed. Exactly when he made his political debut is uncertain, but by 1822 while he was still in his twenties, he was elected a town commissioner, a position he held until 1830. In that year he worked for antislavery candidates who would also oppose the Corn Laws, evidently the first time he combined his twin goals of emancipation for the slave and relief for the English poor in a public campaign, although his realization of the connection between the two is evident in earlier correspondence with James Cropper. For several years both men had struggled, as the Rathbones had done, with the problem of their responsibility toward the workers in the context of free trade and antislavery. Should antislavery people advocate a cotton boycott which would close mills and throw men out of work? A boycott of slave produce involved more than giving up cotton clothing, because the sails of Cropper's ships were made of cotton and their ropes of hemp were also produced by American slaves. Ought Sturge's and Cropper's railways (and those of other abolitionist Quakers such as the Peases and Frys) refuse to carry slave-produced cotton and sugar, thereby depriving men of jobs and also contributing to higher prices for those commodities? Had they more obligation to boycott sugar and thus destroy slavery in British colonies than to boycott cotton produced by slaves in the United States?[30] Clear-cut answers were difficult.

One could argue that Sturge's motivation in opposing the Corn Laws was his own business interest as a corn-dealer, and of course his political opponents continued to accuse him of ulterior motives. In 1842 he was charged with holding back grain in order to raise prices, a charge which provoked an editorial in the *Birmingham Journal* defending Sturge and dismissing the accusation as nonsense.[31] As previously noted in the case of his temperance convictions and on the issue of Sunday travel, he trimmed profits rather than sacrifice principle. He was willing to sacrifice free trade to his antislavery principles when the question arose of whether the sugar produced by slave labour in Cuba and Brazil should be taxed or admitted free of duty; but generally both Sturge's profits and principles could be served by the abolition of the Corn Laws. He argued logically that the laws created an agricultural monopoly at home which raised the price of food and contracted commerce, thereby limiting the demand for labour while living costs rose. He never denied commercial interests, but always coupled them with moral grounds: the shame of taxing the food of poor people. While Sturge was in the United States in 1841 the *New York Herald* called him a 'corn monopolist' who was 'heartily engaged in grinding the faces of the poor white slaves of that country, while he impudently and audaciously comes to this country to scatter firebrands and disunion throughout the land'. The *Anti-Corn Law Circular* answered that Sturge was the only large corn-dealer in Great Britain who supported the Anti-Corn Law League *despite* his own corn business.[32]

In 1831 Sturge joined Thomas Attwood's Birmingham Political Union. According to E. P. Thompson, the Union was a model of reform under middle-class control;[33] but, for Sturge, joining it was a radical step which brought on him the severe censure of many in the Society of Friends. Indeed, Joseph and his brother Charles felt obliged to publish a letter to refute the charge that by joining they had violated the rules of the Friend's Society. They argued that there was nothing in the goals of the Political Union that a Christian could condemn; it represented a movement of peaceful co-operation for the recovery of political rights, and would be an influence for good.[34] It was another step of commitment for Sturge in the cause of the rights of labour, because, as the unenfranchised became more and more disillusioned with the Reform Bill of 1832, Sturge too was pushed in the direction of universal suffrage and Chartism.

The Reform Government did pass the Emancipation Act which freed the black slaves in the West Indies, but, as labour spokesmen claimed, at the expense of the British worker, who was taxed for the £20 million in compensation money. On 6 July 1833 the *Poor Man's Guardian*, published by Henry Hetherington and edited by Bronterre O'Brien, announced that the settlement was final: the £20 million was to be 'exacted from the bones of the white slaves of England, Ireland and Scotland'. Worst of all, the money would not go to the slaves, but to their masters.[35] This theme was reiterated for many years in the labour publications. 'What Have We Got for Our Twenty Millions?' Bronterre O'Brien queried later in a piece in the *Northern Star*. His answer was, an apprenticeship system which was worse than slavery. The slaveholders, in his judgement, ought to have been punished for capital crimes rather than compensated, and would have been had the poor been represented in Parliament.[36] Since, as noted, Sturge also was opposed to compensation, and since he was the foremost abolitionist agitating for the end to apprenticeship, he must have been particularly sensitive to such articles. They provided him with support, but at the same time pushed him to extend his attention to comparable conditions of home labour. It would be going too far to say that Sturge and the Chartists consciously bargained for mutual support; but mutual support was, in fact, the outcome.

Richard Oastler was right in perceiving that loosening the shackles of the blacks would inevitably loosen those of the whites as well:

Every tear which watered the floor of the House of Commons, from the eye of Pease, was a sledge hammer acting upon the irons of *his own slaves* in Darlington! Every peal of Brougham's eloquence in the Lords, was a flash of Heaven's lightning *against* his own CODE OF MURDER, *daily* executing in his favourite Bastiles.[37]

Brougham's 'Bastiles' were, of course, the poorhouses to which English paupers were consigned for relief under the new Poor Law of 1834, a law which comprised a large element in the disillusionment of the masses with the Reform Government. Under it, the poor could no longer receive state relief at home ('outside' relief), but were forced into institutions which segregated husbands, wives and children – a system which gave spokesmen for the masses another point of comparison between black and white slavery: the loss of respect for family ties.[38] A letter in the *Birmingham Journal* of 30 March 1839 urged Sturge to do as much for apprentices of his home town as he had done for those of the West Indies. Abolitionists had pointed out that, even when supposedly free, apprentices in the colonies were taken by their masters to be whipped by public magistrates. The correspondent claimed that there had been three cases of whipping white apprentices in Birmingham within the past week. The analogy between black and white slave labour became a patent ingredient of labour rhetoric, even when not directly attacking abolitionist hypocrisy. The *Northern Star* proclaimed that every man who had no vote was, in fact, a slave.[39]

G. D. H. Cole has concluded that it was when Sturge came back from his 1841 visit to the United States that he was prepared to advocate manhood suffrage as basic to other reforms.[40] But the decision must have been in the making for several years prior to that date. One consequence of the Reform Act of 1832 had been to make Birmingham a borough, and in 1835 Sturge was elected an alderman under the new government; so that, during the very years when he was spearheading the movement to abolish West Indian apprenticeship, he was also in a position to be directly touched by the growing labour unrest in the Midlands. As Cole has pointed out, it was from the matrix of economic troubles and political helplessness that the Chartist movement was born as an alliance of factory operatives, artisans, and middle-class radical reformers.[41] A Newcastle meeting in late 1838 provides examples of the rising crescendo of revolutionary rhetoric. Dr John Taylor of Scotland said that he could not predict when they would be driven to the use of physical force, but it would come 'when his country men could no longer stand the yoke of slavery which was now rivetted around their necks'. George Julian Harney rallied the crowd with the old call of 'live free, or die'. In Ashton-under-Lyne William Aitkin said it was time for every Briton to ask himself the question 'To be or not to be. To be slaves or not to be slaves. (Cries of "Not").' An editorial in the *Chartist* of 5 May 1839, headed 'The Coming Revolution', stressed the need to be ready with defensive and other weapons.[42] Their use of the analogy between labour conditions and slavery was quite explicit.

By 1838 and 1839 labour-meetings and demonstrations followed by arrests led to widespread rumours of conspiracy. The Home Office exercised surveillance through its secret agents. Sturge's name appears first in an intelligence report from Birmingham dated 6 November 1839, in which it was alleged that he had been invited to take the lead in 'another agitation' for universal suffrage. The same letter warns of the danger of Russian secret infiltrators rousing the people against the British Government.[43] Fears of trouble in Birmingham in the summer of 1839 led to sending police reinforcements from London and an inevitable confrontation which erupted in violence in the town centre, aptly named the 'Bull Ring'. William Lovett, John Collins and Dr John Taylor were among the Chartist leaders arrested and detained (in chains) while awaiting a hearing.[44] Alderman Sturge was named chairman of a commission of investigation, and made no secret of how much he abhorred the sending-in of outside police, an act he considered to be a dangerous precedent for civil liberty and an outright violation of Birmingham's constitutional rights. When three of the arrested rioters were condemned to death at the Warwick Assizes, Sturge wrote a letter to the Home Secretary pleading for commutation of sentence. It was sent with the unanimous backing of the town council, and won a favourable decision – commutation to transportation (exile).[45]

Sturge's task in the months that followed was to try to balance his principles of non-violence and his conviction that governmental violation of civil rights must be resisted. He was furious when he learned that a bill had been quietly introduced into Parliament which would put the entire control of local police under a special commission appointed by the Home Secretary. Determined not to let such a bill pass unchallenged, he spoke at a large public meeting of protest, denounced the bill as a despotic act, and warned that the Government was treading on 'a smothered volcano'. He could not, he said, find any passage in *his* Bible which ordained that the few and the wealthy should govern the poor and the many. But, while advising the people not to forfeit liberty for security, he cautioned them against falling into the trap of creating a disturbance which the police could use as a justification for interference.[46]

The Home Office kept a watchful eye on Sturge for at least four years following the Birmingham riots of 1839. A letter to the Home Secretary on 11 November 1839 reported, 'Sturge is trying to create a cry against us and there is a meeting to-night on the subject of the rate as to what steps are to be taken. . . .' Sturge refused to pay his taxes rather than contribute to the support of armed policemen. The November reports on him continued. On the 13th:

Sturge and his party are playing a dangerous game, they met last night and the night before privately at the Public Office to consider means to thwart our Police, and are going to have a public meeting on the subject next Monday, when all the bad passions will be roused in aid of their object, and the lawless and wicked be encouraged in their efforts. . . .

On the 19th: that Sturge, Moorsom and others sit daily at the Public Office, 'no doubt for the purpose of concocting measures of annoyance to us'. On the 26th: Sturge 'has made himself lately very conspicuous by encouraging a spirit of opposition to the Police'. And on 24 February 1840: 'Sturge and his party are still inveterate and would be glad, if they could, to find a hole in our coat. . . .' Surveillance continued through Sturge's political conference in the spring of 1842, when the informant noted that he provided bail for a man arrested for distributing placards which did not carry a printer's identification.[47]

One somewhat amusing incident in this running battle with the police occurred in November 1839. Sturge waded into a large mob 'supposing that his presence alone would be sufficient to disperse it'. Instead, he had his coat torn off and his watch stolen. But, when the police recovered the watch (easily identified because his name was engraved on it), Sturge refused to appear in court to press charges against the thief until he was forced to do so by a police summons and was bound over to prosecute the case. It was reported as an 'attempt to pervert the ends of justice for the purpose of carrying out a silly opposition to the police bill'.[48] Perhaps Sturge's pride was wounded by his failure to control the mob.

In 1840 Sturge was chosen to stand for Birmingham in a by-election and the Chartists issued a placard declaring their support for him; but he withdrew from competition either because he did not want to split the radical vote, or because he realised he had less support than the candidate of the Political Union, G. F. Muntz.[49] None the less he issued a platform: he was for separation of Church and state, free trade, more frequent elections of parliaments, extension of the franchise, the secret ballot, abolition of capital punishment and war, and the abolition of slavery throughout the world. Local government and local police should be under the authority of local people. In addition, he favoured Sunday rest for employees, but believed this should be granted by employers, not imposed by law. He reasoned that repeal of the Corn Laws would do more to increase the demand for labour than to reduce the price of bread, and believed one of the good effects of repeal would be to break up monopolies. His stand for shorter parliaments did not go quite so far as the Chartist demand for annual elections; but on the controversial issue of extending the franchise he declared that he had no more fear of granting it to the people than he had of giving liberty to the slaves. Any male twenty-one years of age, of sound mind and never convicted of a crime by a jury should be eligible to vote without the imposition of any property qualification. He hedged on the Poor Law, however, objecting only to its harsh administration.[50]

According to Sturge, his trip to the United States in 1841 had a purely antislavery purpose: to try to reinvigorate Quaker anti-slavery activity and to promote the American and Foreign Anti-Slavery Society in its competition with the American Anti-Slavery Society.[51] Sturge's position in this factional rift was somewhat paradoxical. The Garrisonians advocated a broad spectrum of reform activity, while the Tappanites, with whom Sturge allied himself, opted for concentration on the 'one idea'. Yet no one reformer's activities spread over a broader range than those of Joseph Sturge. In his opinions on democracy and in his attitudes toward labour he was closer to the Garrisonians; yet on the two controversial issues of women's equality and political action he lined up with the more conservative Tappanites. The religious difference may have been the crucial one for him. Even though Garrison thought of himself as being 'almost a Quaker' and even though Sturge was considered a radical Quaker, yet Sturge profoundly distrusted Garrison's religious anarchism.[52]

While motivation for Sturge's trip was ostensibly to promote antislavery, the issue of white labour kept asserting itself. While visiting John Greenleaf Whittier's home in Amesbury, Massachusetts, he visited a woollen-mill. He was pleased with its cleanliness and orderliness and with 'the evident comfort and prosperity of the working people'.[53] He noted that, while the workers were mainly young women, there was no child labour, as no one under the age of sixteen was hired. A visit to the famous Lowell mills was also on his agenda, where again he noted wages, housing, religious and educational opportunies, and concluded that 'the most striking and gratifying feature of Lowell, is the high moral and intellectual condition of its working population'.[54] Applying his observations to the British scene, he was ready to proclaim that 'it is quite evident that the statesmen who would elevate the moral standard of our working population, must begin by removing the physical depression and destitution in which a large proportion of them, without any fault of their own, are compelled to drag out a weary and almost hopeless existence'.[55]

Sturge was not an advocate of Owenite socialism – unlike some of his antislavery colleagues, such as William Allen. He believed that free trade offered the best solution to improve economic conditions and this must be achieved by political action. It would stimulate production and employment and thus raise British workers to the same level as American workers. But, as the years went on, Sturge became more and more discouraged by the intransigence of the British Parliament. Consequently, although he remained a member of the Anti-Corn Law League, he was moving to the Chartist position that the goal would be accomplished only with the extension of the franchise to the working people.[56] The anti-Corn Law question was tied in with antislavery as well, and on this aspect of the problem Sturge was influenced by two Americans, Joshua Leavitt, editor of the New York *Emancipator*, and John Curtis of Ohio. Leavitt had written a memorial to the United States Congress, while Curtis had published a tract on the subject. Both argued that it was to the interest of Great Britain and the United States to trade more in wheat rather than in cotton. The British admission of cotton at a low duty was a subsidy for slavery which made both Britain and the northern states vassals of the South. Trade in wheat would subsidise free labour in the United States and save the starving factory operatives in Britain. Curtis deplored the suicidal policy of the British, who sought luxury goods from the West Indies and India when what they needed to import were essentials for the workers – American wheat, for example.[57] *En route* to see Niagara Falls, Sturge met Curtis, who was on his way to Great Britain on a free-trade mission.[58] Since Curtis was an abolitionist as well as a free-trader, his contacts over there were in Sturge's own circles, and when Sturge returned home he chaired an anti-Corn Law meeting in Birmingham at which Curtis spoke.[59]

When Sturge announced his plan to go to America, his old friend Richard Cobden urged him to take the dispassionate look at his own country which only distance makes possible, 'and I hope you will return with a determination to throw all the weight of your talents and moral influence into the scale of the poor and oppressed millions of your countrymen'.[60] Thomas Clarkson, on the other hand, counselled him not to mix other subjects with antislavery, but to keep the cause pure and 'unspotted', forgetting, it seems, that he had mixed causes himself as an ally of John Cartwright in the parliamentary reform movement of the 1790s.[61] Sturge could not help but relate the causes of black and white labour and reflected, in the light of the Birmingham riots, 'I am sorry to say that amongst some of the middle and higher classes with us there is a feeling almost as bitter toward the working classes as there was towards the slaves by the owners.'[62] Evidently he took Cobden's advice while in America, and his reflections led him to a decisive step.

He knew that, while the Anti-Corn Law League tried assiduously in its propaganda to emphasize the price of food for the poor as its main concern, it never really succeeded in convincing many workers. They tended to distrust its middle-class Whig leadership and feared that such public statements were merely camouflage for the real aim of increasing profits for the merchants. Lower prices for food might simply mean a reduction in wages as well.[63] It was Sturge's despair over this misunderstanding between the classes that led him to the decision that he must organize a movement of conciliation based on supporting the Chartist demand for the suffrage. 'I, therefore, think the time is arrived,' he wrote to Cobden, 'when every friend of humanity, of whatever class, sect or party, should endeavour to obtain and secure for the people a just and permanent control over their own affairs.'[64] To Lewis Tappan, back in the United States, he wrote, 'Our unenfranchised countrymen are *politically* much in the same position as your slaves, and in many of the electors there is nearly as strong a feeling against giving them the franchise as there is with giving it to the slave with you.'[65] Another impact of his American experience was that it confirmed a belief he held in common with James Currie: that universal suffrage was safe if accompanied by universal education.[66] Combined efforts of the classes might get the vote for the worker, repeal the Corn Laws, deal slavery a mortal wound, and elevate the condition of all labourers, black and white. The causes of temperance, universal education and peace would all be carried forward. The Complete Suffrage Movement, therefore, really encompassed the whole range of Sturge's reform interests.

His opportunity to take a first step to organise a coalition for complete suffrage grew out of his alliance with Edward Miall, who had begun to edit the *Nonconformist* in London in April 1841. It had become a mouthpiece for liberal reforms, including repeal of the Corn Laws as a poor man's issue. In October 1841, Miall began publishing a series of hard-hitting letters on the necessity of bringing the middle and working classes into co-operation. Hitherto there had been, he said, 'too much of menace' from the labourers, and 'too much of pride' on the part of the middle class. Like Sturge, he saw the analogy between the situation of British workers and slaves. 'Treat men as slaves', he wrote, and 'they will soon betake themselves to the vices of slavery – would you fit them for freedom, you must make them free'. Society tended to allow a particular libel to be attached to a class, then used that libel as an excuse for withholding rights. Before the West Indian slaves were freed, opponents of emancipation were full of dire predictions of the horrible consequences which would ensue, but what happened? 'Why the world was startled to see a once debased population assume a position and act a part of sobriety, morality, and dignity, unprecedented in the annals of any nation.' The moral effects of giving the suffrage to British workers would be just as great as its political effects. The experiment of emancipation had been made with the West Indian slaves and with Catholic rights in Ireland. 'Why not in this country also?'[67]

Twelve days after the last piece of Miall's series appeared in the *Nonconformist*, Joseph Sturge penned a personal testimony to introduce the articles in pamphlet form:

> It is a distinguishing and beautiful feature of Christianity, that it leads us to recognize every country as *our* country, and every man as *our* brother; and as there is no moral degradation so awful, no physical misery so great, as that inflicted by personal slavery, I have felt it my duty to labour for its universal extinction.
>
> Whilst thus engaged, it has sometimes been pressed upon me, that the sufferings of my fellow-countrymen had a prior claim on my attention; and I freely acknowledge that the Patriot and the Christian fail in the discharge of their duty, if they do not, by all peaceable and legitimate means, strive to remove the enormous evil of class legislation.[68]

Undoubtedly Miall's editorials struck a responsive chord in Sturge, but this was not a case of sudden conversion to universal suffrage. Sturge had been moving steadily toward such a position for several years, especially since the Birmingham riots of 1839, and he had come close to the Chartists in his own platform of 1840. His observations in the United States reinforced his conviction that a democratic spirit contributed to the well-being of the workers. Richard Cobden's continual nagging deserves some credit. He wrote before Sturge's departure for America, urging him to throw the weight of his leadership on the side of the oppressed in Britain. Again, after his friend's return, he argued convincingly that since Sturge's reputation was eminently secure he need not fear losing his standing with the middle class if he took an advanced position. Indeed, Sturge could carry the philanthropic and religious world with him, 'or at least neutralize their opposition', adding that 'without their aid no *moral* victory can be achieved in this age and country'.[69]

Actually, Sturge was already ahead of Cobden in accepting universal suffrage as a right, irrespective of any particular issue. Cobden's aim was a more ulterior and limited one. He wanted the support of the workers to achieve repeal of the Corn Laws, but, if that support were expressed via an outpouring of public opinion, it might be as effective on this issue as it had been on the anti-slavery issue in 1833, even without going so far as to extend the franchise to all. He repeatedly warned groups of workers not to place confidence in those who agitated for suffrage extension but refused to join the anti-Corn Law movement.[70] It was leaders such as Cobden, in fact, who made Sturge's task more difficult, for, when Cobden appealed to the workers to place their faith in the manufacturers, deferring agitation for the suffrage until after the Corn Laws were repealed, it was no wonder they were mistrustful. Middle- and upper-class leaders in the anti-Corn Law movement such as Cobden, Villiers, Bowring and Brougham obviously mistrusted the leadership of militant Chartist radicals, especially Feargus O'Connor. But even non-violent Chartist leaders such as Henry Vincent and William Lovett were, at least initially, mistrustful of the Anti-Corn Law League. In attempting to reconcile 'the classes', much of Sturge's work boiled down to reconciling Chartist and Anti-Corn Law League leadership. And this was complicated by the internal dissents within the Chartist movement itself: physical-force Chartism versus moral-force or Christian Chartism. He had to be a dedicated man indeed, or a man with a large ego, even to try.

An anti-Corn Law meeting in Manchester in November 1841 provided the occasion for publicly launching the movement for complete suffrage, an event heralded by Miall in the *Nonconformist* as 'The Blush of Dawn'.[71] Francis Place, long-time political leader of London artisans and prime mover in the Metropolitan Parliamentary Reform Association, was not so sanguine. He worried that Sturge had deceived himself with 'the notion so sedulously inculcated by the Chartists' that a Parliament elected *by* the people would necessarily legislate *for* the people.[72] But Sturge had by then committed himself to the idea of the *right* of men to vote, just as previously he had accepted the *right* of slaves to freedom, regardless of consequences. This was evident in the 'Declaration' he drew up to be circulated and signed. It embodied the ideas of the American Declaration of Independence: taxation without representation was tyranny; the right to a 'full, free and fair' franchise was based on British constitutional rights as well as on 'Christian equity'. Sturge's Quaker indoctrination was now finding expression in democratic principles as well as in Christian benevolence. Injustices stemming from class legislation could and must be ended, he declared.[73] Response was immediate as people signed petitions, organized meetings, set up committees of correspondence, and drew up a memorial to the Queen. By early 1842 a provisional committee based in Birmingham began preparations for a great conference to be held in April.[74]

Who supported Sturge? The Nonconformist liberal reformers comprised one element – the one most solidly and completely attuned to Sturge's own thinking. In addition to Edward Miall, this group included the Revd J. H. Hinton of London, the Revd J. W. Massie of Manchester, and the Revd Henry Solly of Yeovil. The Revd Patrick Brewster of Paisley was among the ministers of the Established Church as was the Revd Thomas Spencer of Bath, whose more famous nephew, Herbert, made his political debut in the Complete Suffrage Union. Herbert Spencer served in the committee to examine tracts put out by the Union, and two years later accepted the job of assistant editor for Sturge's paper, the *Pilot*.[75] Sturge had made a special effort to recruit religious and philanthropic leaders and his success is reflected in the signatures to his Declaration and Memorial. Anti-Corn Law leaders who joined him included John Bright, George Thompson and Archibald Prentice. Chartists willing to co-operate were Henry Vincent, William Lovett, John Collins, Henry Hetherington and even Bronterre O'Brien. Francis Place's Parliamentary Metropolitan Reform Association included P. A. Taylor and Dr John Bowring, both MPs. Actually the overlapping in these groups makes it difficult to assign most leaders to just one of them. Notable politicians who gave Sturge a somewhat qualified approval were Daniel O'Connell and Lord Brougham.[76] All of the people I have named were known for their antislavery views. Most of them were active abolitionists.

Some of the middle-class reformers embraced the Complete Suffrage Movement out of fear: the labour movement must be saved from extremist leadership and the country from revolution. Some Chartists joined from expediency: an opportunity to gain the franchise through a coalition, if only temporary, with the middle class. Many free traders were likewise motivated by the expedient of bargaining support for the workers in return for help in repealing the Corn Laws. Some would have been quite willing to extend the franchise but stop short of universal suffrage. Others, such as Sturge, though not unmindful of the specific legislative gains to be derived from the alliance, held a broader view of the reconciliation of the classes and stood on a foundation of basic rights.[77] Several members had advanced beyond Sturge in respect to both ends and means.[78]

Two vocal opponents of Sturge's Complete Suffrage Movement were Feargus O'Connor, leader of the physical-force Chartists, who preached that the middle classes could not be trusted; and Edward Baines, abolitionist and liberal editor of the *Leeds Mercury*, who was cynical about the possibility of uniting such a varied lot of reformers and radicals. Also absent was Colonel T. Perronet Thompson of Hull, who had been associated with reform causes as long as Sturge had. He was an abolitionist, an Anti-Corn Law Leaguer, and had helped Lovett draw up the document which became 'The People's Charter'. But, like Baines, he was sceptical about the success of any attempt at union. The problem reminded him of his previous experience in Sierra Leone, where he had been sent by Wilberforce and the early abolitionists to be Governor. There he had learned that to float logs you had to tie some heavy ones to light ones. Sturge was tying Complete Suffrage to the heavy log of Chartism rather than to the lighter log of Corn Law repeal, and Thompson foresaw that it would not float.[79]

The Birmingham conference of April 1842 was a model of harmonious democracy. The Complete Suffrage Union was launched on a platform which protested against class legislation; avowed the inherent right of suffrage; demanded the franchise for every male aged twenty-one who was not deprived of his citizenship in consequence of a jury verdict, and regardless of property qualifications; and advocated the secret ballot, division of the country into election districts, annual parliaments, and remuneration for MPs. All of this was incorporated into a resolution for William Sharman Crawford to introduce into the House of Commons.[80] Sturge enlisted the aid of his old antislavery colleague Lord Brougham to present in the House of Lords the essence of Crawford's motion to the Commons. Although Brougham had reservations about its substance, he agreed to ask that the Lords consider it, and agreed also to present the memorial to the Queen.[81] The enthusiasm resulting from the April meeting led to Sturge's nomination to stand for Nottingham in the summer election as the opponent of the Tory candidate, John Walter, proprietor of *The Times*. The euphoria of unity was so contagious that even Feargus O'Connor decided to co-operate and, somewhat to Sturge's embarrassment, went so far as to join other Chartist leaders (notably Henry Vincent) in campaigning for Sturge. The contest was close, with Sturge taking 1801 votes to Walter's 1885.[82]

It is interesting to note that the *British and Foreign Anti-Slavery Reporter* made no mention of Sturge's candidacy, though, in the annual meeting of the Anti-Slavery Society in May, Sturge begged for support not only against slavery everywhere in the world, 'but against every kind of oppression in this country', some 'closely bordering on slavery'. 'And I have feared', he admonished the meeting, 'there was something of a pro-slavery feeling from which even abolitionists were not always exempt, that censured the working class and their advocates when demanding only their just and equal rights.' The *Reporter* noted that cheers followed – an indication that there was a contingent, at least, of abolitionists with tender consciences on this subject.[83] The most prominent abolitionist leader supporting Sturge was George Thompson, who at a Complete Suffrage meeting in Edinburgh in May 1842 asked the Chartists to forgive the past neglect by the middle class and apologized for his own tardiness in joining their cause. He became a popular lecturer at Chartist meetings.[84]

The Complete Suffrage conference in April had adjourned with the intention of reconvening in the autumn, but developments of the summer militated against such a meeting. Widespread unemployment and hardship led to a repetition of the demonstrations and upheavals of 1838 and 1839. Violent confrontations prevailed over quiet assemblies, and mass arrests were the order of the day. Such outbreaks emphasized the urgency of the situation. Even Feargus O'Connor decided to co-operate, either because he, too, feared more violence or because he sensed that he would lose out to the unionists.[85] But the brave hopes of unity with which the Complete Suffrage Union opened its December conference in Birmingham were short-lived. Despite agreement on goals, passions ran high on choosing a name for the document which would embody them. The Sturgeites disliked 'The Charter' because Chartism carried an image of violence as well as militant radicalism which would frighten off the middle classes. They favoured instead a 'Document of Rights' or 'Bill of Rights'. Chartists were naturally emotionally attached to the name which symbolised their long battle. Why should they yield

to those who had come belatedly into the fray? After two days
Sturge and his followers were voted down and he stubbornly led
his group out of the convention. The *Birmingham Journal* offered
a terse summary of the abortive attempt: it was the old story of
marriage on Monday, quarrels on Tuesday, divorce on
Wednesday. The two partners had agreed on their mutual love
but could not compromise on a name for their child and so had
strangled it.[86]

Disagreement over a label was, of course, the expression of
deeper misunderstandings and distrust, much of it connected
with the rivalry of leadership. Most contemporary accounts as
well as those of historians place major blame on Feargus
O'Connor as the spoiler, and blame him for tactics which forced
Chartist moderates such as Lovett to desert Sturge.[87] But Sturge
comes through as a poor politician. First of all, he was too
generous in his concessions on the method of choosing delegates,
thus allowing O'Connorites a chance to dominate delegations.[88]
Secondly, he failed to consult the Lovett moderates in advance
and they were caught by surprise after his 'People's Bill of Rights'
was already in print. One wonders, too, about Sturge's tact. He
was, after all, stepping in to replace old leaders. Did he really
want to unite, or to take over? How much resentment did this
engender even in moral-force Chartists? Was his manner a
modest one of an equal among equals, or was there still enough of
the old paternalistic manner left to antagonize? Maybe no one
could have achieved unity at that point after the revival of
antagonisms between middle and working classes which were
inherent in the summer's upheavals.

Despite the failure at Birmingham, moderate spokesmen for
the labouring classes seem not to have harboured any long-term
grudges against Sturge. According to Thomas Cooper, Chartist
and poet, Sturge looked 'wretched' when the conference broke
up. Even O'Connor could see that 'that man is not happy. He
does not want to leave us.' Some years later Cooper wrote to R. G.
Gammage, historian of Chartism, that he regretted ever having
been misled into saying one word against Sturge. Mark Hovell,
another historian of the Chartist movement, criticized Sturge for
being somewhat 'pig-headed' and 'hasty-tempered' and 'not very
deep thinking', yet lauded him as one of the few prosperous
business men who 'had not blinded his eyes to the distress and
poverty of thousands of his fellow-citizens'.[89]

Throughout 1843 Sturge continued to tour the country to agitate for Complete Suffrage. Twice thereafter (in 1844 and 1847) he allowed himself to be put forward as a parliamentary candidate, but without success. His newspaper, the *Pilot*, continued to advocate complete suffrage as basic to other reforms, especially the repeal of the Corn Laws.[90] Rejected in politics, he concentrated more and more on the peace movement, education and juvenile reform. In a letter to John Greenleaf Whittier, an American abolitionist and people's poet, he compared his failure to that of the Liberty Party candidates in the United States. He had faced the reality that there was just as much opposition on the part of the British upper classes to allowing the lower class to vote as there was in the United States against political rights for blacks.[91]

Whatever may be said in criticism of Sturge's tactics or capabilities as a politician, the fact remains that his heart was in the right place. He had moved from a consideration of what was 'good for' the people to an acknowledgement that one must stress, as Granville Sharp had, the 'rights of' the people. Like Sharp he amply demonstrated that he was willing to assume as large a burden of leadership on behalf of exploited white workers as he had on behalf of the slaves. He believed in the rights of both; perhaps, also like Sharp, he never completely divested himself of a paternalistic attitude toward either.

# 4 Harriet Martineau

There is a sentence in Harriet Martineau's autobiography which furnishes us with a key to her life: 'So to work I went, with needle and pen.'[1] She is referring to the period after her father died, when the family business failed and she and her sisters were faced with making their own way. Few opportunities were open to women in the England of the 1820s and even fewer to one handicapped by severe deafness. But Harriet did possess pen, needle and an abundant share of the resolute work ethic inherited from her Huguenot ancestors. Throughout her seventy-four years (1802–76) these three resources were constants in the life of this intelligent and strong-willed woman as she made her mark on the society of her time.

In Harriet the Calvinist emphasis on duty merged with her Unitarian necessarianism (learned from J. S. Priestley), which emphasized the need to labour toward good ends even though the results or effects might not be foreseen. That belief merged, in turn, with an optimism that Jeremy Bentham's 'greatest good for the greatest number' could be achieved. A quotation from Milton that she used on the title page of her novel *Deerbrook* illustrates the principle which guided her in her refusal to give up on any task.

>                              with good
> Still overcoming evil, and by small
> Accomplishing great things; by things deemed weak
> Subverting worldly strong and worldly wise.[2]

All of this philosophy left no doubt in Harriet's mind that it was her personal obligation to do what she could to 'improve' individual people whose lives touched hers, as well as to reform society. The offspring of her pen were never conceived with the idea of merely giving pleasure; they always bore a message, even when embodied in fictional form to make the lesson more palatable.

Not only the poor and uneducated were targets for her uplifting; friends of higher rank did not escape. On one occasion when Thomas Carlyle heard that Miss Martineau had been taken ill, he could not repress a reaction of relief that for a time he would be spared her 'didacticalities'.[3] When her pen was not spouting admonitions and instructions, her needles were busily clicking for some one of her numerous causes. Most of her writing was done late at night and into the early morning hours. When she sat down in the daytime, it was almost always with some piece of needlework in hand, usually for the benefit of an antislavery fair in America, or to be auctioned off to support some worthy campaign at home. Probably her last creation before she died was a tapestry for an armchair to be donated for a money-raising effort to fight legislation regulating prostitution.[4]

Although Martineau's writings seem insufferably pedantic to the twentieth-century reader, one must remember that Victorians not only were schooled to the acceptance of homilies and morals in their literature, but also were often critical of works lacking such 'ennobling' sentiments. Her stories illustrating the principles of political economy were written to instruct 'the people', but they won her the respect and friendship of such luminaries as Thomas Carlyle, Elizabeth Barrett Browning, Bulwer-Lytton, Charlotte Brontë, the Wordsworths and a host of other literary and intellectual people – even Sydney Smith, whose devastating satire spared few of his contemporaries. While she lived in London, Miss Martineau was lionized at nightly dinner parties, and, when she moved to Ambleside, pilgrimages were made to visit her in the Lake District. Men in government (Lord Brougham and Lord Durham among them) sought her advice, and numerous reformers (notably Robert Owen) fought to enlist her backing for their causes. The story is told that, when a letter arrived at the London Post Office addressed only 'To the Queen of Philanthropists', the official handling the mail promptly wrote on it, 'Try Miss Martineau.'[5]

It has been suggested that Harriet Martineau was the prototype for Charles Dickens's Mrs Jellyby in *Bleak House*, whose 'telescopic myopia' focused on the poor natives of Borrioboola-Gha to the complete neglect of her own household and children.[6] In Martineau's case, however, interest in her own poor neighbours preceded her commitment to the cause of the far-off black slaves. The two concerns always remained intertwined in her thinking.

Her first writing on slavery, the piece called 'Demerara', was included in her *Illustrations of Political Economy* written to instruct British workers. After being educated in England, its young hero returns to his home in Demerara in the West Indies to protest against slavery and to work for emancipation.[7]

When Miss Martineau went to the United States in 1834, her initial intention, like that of de Toqueville, and in the tradition of Roscoe and Romilly, was to study experiments in penal reform. She went at the suggestion of Lord Henley, who believed that the British might profit by finding out how the Americans had managed to do so well in incorporating 'principles of justice and mercy in their treatment of the least happy classes of society'.[8] It was while she was in America that Martineau became convinced that the abolitionists were not misguided fanatics, and that attention to the 'least happy classes' must include black slaves as well as poor whites. 'Through all eternity', she wrote to an American acquaintance, 'I shall bless God that I have had the privilege of seeing and knowing the apostles of this mighty moral revolution.'[9]

It is difficult to pinpoint exactly when Harriet became a champion of the disadvantaged, but her concern may have been a case of transference or equating her own experience with that of society at large. In her autobiography she reveals that her passion for justice was a result of the fact that, 'Justice was precisely what was least understood in our house, in regard to servants and children.'[10] She maintained that even as a child she had reacted critically to sermons she heard in the family Unitarian church in Norwich, because they seemed always to dwell on the obligations of inferiors to superiors and never the other way around, on responsibility toward the weaker.[11]

Despite assumptions to the contrary, it seems to me that Martineau's concern for the poor never stemmed from sentimentality – an assumption too often made because of Victorian stereotyping. A scholar from childhood, she was a very young adult when she embraced that part of 'scientific' Utilitarianism which called for the reordering of legislation to provide the greatest happiness for the greatest number. Sometimes this demanded of her a stern stand in favour of laissez-faire on the grounds that non-interference with commerce and industry would, in the long run, benefit labour as capital profited, even though such a policy involved great temporary hardship. She thought interference by the Government 'which perplexes the calculations of producers' to be a social crime *against* the workers.[12] Martineau embraced the wage-fund doctrine, which held that the only way to raise wages was either to increase capital or to decrease the labour supply. Capital could best increase itself, and thereby the supply of food and consumer goods, by having free access to world markets – in other words, free trade.[13] For their part, the wealthy classes had an obligation to consume 'productively' by putting their money into enterprises which would build capital and provide jobs; they must forgo self-indulging luxuries and the kind of high living which would end in debts and bankruptcy. Her character Temple in *Briery Creek* personifies the self-indulgent, heartless aristocrat; while Dr Sneyd (modelled on Joseph Priestley) and his son Arthur are the productive consumers with social consciences.

On the other hand, nothing should be done to encourage parasitic dependence on the part of the working classes. Their part was to take the responsibility for not increasing their own numbers too rapidly. Controlled emigration might provide part of the solution, but would not suffice. Education for the masses was absolutely essential so that they could learn Malthus's doctrine of overpopulation. If any part of this was sentimental, it was Martineau's great faith which led her to believe that, once the people knew Malthus's theory, they would act on it and limit their own procreation through delayed marriages and sexual abstinence.[14] It is amusing to read the Martineau correspondence with Francis Place, London workingmen's leader and organizer, in which Place tries, delicately, to give her some practical instruction in sex drives – seemingly without much effect, because she continued to expound her own optimistic theories.[15]

Education became the cornerstone of Martineau's philosophy. Often her stands on the Poor Laws and factory legislation were downright hard-hearted and antagonistic to unemployed and exploited workers alike, and her insistence on patience, courage and the helpfulness of middle-class leadership strike one as but modified versions of pie-in-the-sky. But one must examine the purpose which underlay her idea of education. It was not to teach submissiveness and resignation. Quite the contrary, her aim was to enlighten the working classes on basic economic and political issues so that they could intelligently discuss and then act to help solve their own problems, and so fulfil their role in the good society while retaining their self-respect. The advent of the good society could be anticipated when free trade, industrial development and a more representative government had been given free play. Everything that Harriet Martineau said or wrote on the Poor Laws, factory legislation, Corn Laws and education bears out her adherence to this philosophy.

Harriet saw writing as her own contribution to education, and so she conceived her *Illustrations of Political Economy*, a series of tales (with individual titles of a less imposing nature) that would appeal to and instruct the common people. In fact she wrote them under a 'steady conviction that the work was wanted – was even craved by the popular mind'.[16] Lest readers miss her messages embedded in the stories (though it is hard to see how anyone could), each was concluded with a 'Summary of Principles'. That series was followed by another, called *Poor Laws and Paupers*, sponsored by the Society for the Diffusion of Useful Knowledge, which sold tracts and pamphlets at prices calculated to make them available to the working populaton. But Harriet was fiercely critical of the Society for failing to put out enough material of a political as well as of a literary nature. She charged that Lord Brougham and other liberal leaders 'had not faith enough. . .to entrust them [the people] with political knowledge, but preferred putting out, in the most critical period of the nation's history, treatises on physical science, as a tub to the whale'.[17] The manner in which Martineau's tales were written gives ample evidence of the author's faith that even people in lowly circumstances could help themselves. By contrast, when she wrote on the subject of black slavery, she saw no point in addressing the slaves who could not help themselves. On their behalf she addressed not only the affluent classes but British workers as well, believing them to be capable of aiding others even more downtrodden. Her optimism about self-help explains her later preference for Chartism over poor laws and factory legislation.

As might be expected, the Political Economy and Poor Law tales are replete with uplifting lessons.[18] The 'good' poor learn how to manage on a pittance and preserve their dignity and independence by staying out of workhouses, while the 'bad' poor connive to exploit the charity system and become moral as well as physical paupers. But her vivid portrayal of the daily lives of the poor leaves no doubt about Martineau's awareness of the very real distress in the land. Her attacks on the Establishment are pointed and sharp: on the Government for its unjust system of taxation, on the venal clergy who fail to carry on relief measures for the poor, and even on the do-good Methodist missionaries who visit the workhouses to persuade inmates to resign themselves to God's will. Many years later Martineau's view of do-gooders was expressed in her obituary of Lady Byron. She was 'good' not because she attended charity balls and dispensed soups and blankets and 'maudlin sentiments', Martineau wrote, but because she promoted education.[19]

It is evident that, even while Martineau was inveighing against the Poor Laws and charitable institutions because they created parasitic able-bodied indigents, she never blamed the poor as a class for having brought the situation on themselves. She looked below the surface to find the failure of British benevolence in the British social system and Government policy. What she did chide the workers for was for not exerting themselves more vigorously against a system in which they were the victims. In 'A Tale of the Tyne' she preached the duty of the people to complain until the Government set things straight, and even though times improved they must not rest content but keep on protesting in order to keep on improving.[20] Moreover, Martineau reveals a practical realization of the power of the masses should they resort to rioting. She was careful to insert into her tales warnings of such uprisings if the needs of the workers continued to be neglected, warnings which match those given about slave insurrections (as in 'Demerara') should the planters refuse to emancipate. For example, in 'Cousin Marshall' her workhouse inmates riot to tear down the wall separating the sexes. Sexual segregation was one of the Poor Law provisions designed to make families think twice before committing themselves to public support.[21]

Harriet Martineau has been stereotyped not only as a humourless, Victorian spinster do-gooder, but also as a defender of unmodified laissez-faire.[22] That she was not. Like Bentham himself, she came to realize that positive good might be accomplished through Government action provided the base of representation could be enlarged.[23] To that end she lent support to the Reform Bill of 1832, but for more than that one reason. Riots such as those in Bristol convinced her of the real danger of revoluton if the bill failed, and her list of needed reforms that the Government must see to included not only reconstitution of the

House of Commons, but also cleaning up municipal governments, lightening the burden of the Poor Law, repealing the
Corn Laws and Game Laws, abolishing slavery, granting religious
liberty and providing for public education – quite a list of
Government projects for a laissez-fairist! Of top importance to her
was that 'the industrious must have their deserts of food and
comfort'.[24] It pleased her to learn how interested working people
were in the Reform Bill. She noted that after work they walked
miles to pubs to hear the latest progress reports, and that several
labourers would chip in to buy a newspaper, which would then be
read aloud by the best reader.[25] To Francis Place she wrote that
she was watching his coalition of Radicals and Whigs with intense
interest and expectation.[26]

As soon as the new government was in power, Harriet's help
was called for to revise the Poor Law. Her writing had gained her
a reputation as an expert on the subject and she was already
launched on the writing of her Poor Law tales for the Society for
the Diffusion of Useful Knowledge headed by Lord Brougham.
As Lord Chancellor in the new government, Brougham was in a
position to send her all of the reports of the Commission of
Inquiry into the Poor Laws, out of which she made notes enough
for 'one thousand and one' 'marvellous tales'.[27] But Martineau
was not satisfied with Government reports only. Prior to receiving
its materials, she had written to Francis Place to solicit his help in
collecting information on poorhouses and their management.
Her questions indicate that she was trying to get at the attitudes
of the poor themselves. She wanted to know, for example, how
they regarded emigration and transportation. She suspected they
disliked projects for 'home colonies' just as much as any other
'arbitrary plans for the improvement of their condition'.[28] It was
while she was writing her Poor Law tales that Robert Owen tried
to convert her to socialism. Although he did not succeed, she later
acknowledged that perhaps his ideas could be fruitfully applied
in working out a social state in a new land such as America where
there was a better land–population ratio. When she visited the
United States and noted the conditions of the workers, her
reaction was entered in her journal: 'O, the bliss of seeing not a
single beggar, – not a man, woman, or child otherwise than well
dressed.'[29]

To Lord Brougham Martineau wrote that her aim was to
portray the virtues of the suffering poor and to expose the bad

administration of the Poor Laws.[30] It is therefore ironical that her suggestions for reform turned out to be identical with those that the Government incorporated into the new Poor Law of 1834, which was so hated by the poor that it was made the focus of workers' attacks on the Reform Government. The new Poor Law became a symbol of Whig treachery once the Whigs had attained power with the help of the Radicals. Martineau's support of that new law can be accounted for by her overoptimistic belief that it would correct the abuses of the old law because administration by a central commission would eliminate local corruption and local politics such as parish jobbing. Much of the money raised for relief had been misspent by parish administrators in trying to shift their poor to other parishes. Agricultural parishes would often employ only residents, thus handicapping the development of industry and depriving people of potential jobs so that they had no alternative but the workhouse. Vagrancy laws handicapped workers who wanted to move to find work where it was available. Workhouses were sinks of filth, wretchedness and bad management with no provision to save the children through education. Though parish workers were not actually sold as slaves, their labour was auctioned off to the highest bidder. In short, Martineau concluded, 'the parish servitude imposed the miseries and contumelies of slavery'.[31] Her dissatisfaction with the old Poor Law rested ultimately on her conviction that the poor could help themselves and remain independent if they were not corrupted by a system that encouraged pauperism. Therefore she acceded to a plan that would make workhouses most unattractive, although she never looked on them as institutions created to punish people for being poor. If shunned by most, workhouses would simply fulfil the function of providing for the essential needs of those for whom nothing else could be done – those who were already victims beyond redemption.

Most importantly, Martineau never intended that the Poor Law 'reform' should stand in a vacuum. She said its framers acknowledged that it would never work unless the Corn Laws were repealed. It must be accompanied by tax reform as well. She believed that the trouble with the old system was that it fostered a self-defeating circle of developments: with workhouse relief made too easy, even workers who could support themselves were tempted to become indigent unemployed, thus leaving fewer people in the community to pay the rates and, in the long run, narrowing the tax base. That, in turn, meant cutting off relief for even the truly needy. If property should be increasingly absorbed by poor rates, Britain would become a nation of paupers. She argued for the need to endure temporary pain in order to achieve a long-term cure. Charity must go to enlighten minds rather than to relieve bodily wants,[32] a philosophy with little comfort for the hungry. According to Harriet, she persuaded such eminent humanitarians and fellow abolitionists as Elizabeth Fry and J. J. Gurney of the need for the new Poor Law, and they used their influence to help facilitate its passage. Because Francis Place was a representative of workingmen, she thought he was the ideal person to exercise leadership in the reform.[33]

To the twentieth-century liberal, Martineau's attitude toward strikes and factory regulation may seem even more reactionary than her support of what became a punitive Poor Law, but observed in the context of her own era she appears to have been well ahead of laissez-faire theorists as well as industrialists with vested interests. While the economic starting-point for her opinions was that industrial growth meant progress, she never lost sight of her social goal, which included the welfare of workers along with other groups in society, and she tried earnestly to learn from workers as well as to teach them. She credited Manchester factory operatives with sending her the documents which enabled her to write 'A Manchester Strike', but her research was even more extensive. She obtained from Coventry a great deal of information on matters of employment, including factory wages, and she appealed to Place for sources of information on workers' combinations, how they were run, their expenses and their efficiency. Radical MP Joseph Hume furnished her with parliamentary reports on the subject.[34] The resulting tale was applauded by her Manchester operative friends, who insisted that her fictional hero must be one of their real-life heroes. They told her she wrote as if she had spent her life in a mill. Francis Place wished that he were a rich enough man to place copies of her work in all libraries, clubs and institutions.[35]

'A Manchester Strike' served Harriet's double purpose: to expose bad factory conditions, pitiful wages and the deplorable aspects of child labour, and also to lecture workers on the role which would best further their own prospects. She opposed combination laws and believed it was necessary for workers to organize to balance the wealth and influence of capitalists, but she did not approve of strikes or machinery-breaking, which she held to be self-defeating. She worried also about the potential tyranny of unions.[36] Martineau had no faith in legislation to set terms of employment and wages, but favoured direct negotiation between employer and employee – again the self-help emphasis. Initiative which came from the people would pay off, she firmly believed, in self-esteem as well as in better wages and hours. She opposed both Sadler's and Ashley's factory bills on the grounds that they would deprive labour of that freedom of initiative, but objected to them also because they dealt only with effects, not the causes of the problem. She resented Ashley's neglect of farm workers, about whom, as a landlord, he should be most concerned. Neither Ashley nor Sadler attacked the problem of overpopulation, which to her was the heart of the matter. She even accused Sadler of encouraging the poor to have more children on the grounds that 'God would provide'.[37]

With Lord Durham, himself an employer of coal-miners, Martineau attempted to work out a plan for a workers' union which would obtain the necessary benefits without recourse to strikes. Its core idea was education: provision of schools and libraries for the miners. Lord Durham was to provide £200 per year, but it was not to be an entirely charitable enterprise. Workers would themselves pay fourpence per week. To further interest in the plan, Harriet wrote an article the title of which embodies her ideas: 'The Tendency of Strikes and Sticks to Produce Low Wages, and of Union between Masters and Men to Ensure Good Wages'. Francis Place distributed it to working-class readers. While visiting Lord Durham before writing her *Moral of Many Fables*, Harriet actually went down into a coal pit to observe the miners' situation at first hand, a daring act most Victorian women considered to be quite improper.[38] Although she later wrote another article, 'The Factory Controversy: A Warning against Meddling Legislation', she was impressed enough by the coal-pit experience to come out in favour of Government inspection and compulsory insurance for collieries.[39]

Martineau's early stand against regulatory legislation seems particularly offensive when one reads her argument that people who wanted child-labour laws were thinking 'only of the children's instant welfare', yet when it came to child labour she was always dubious about 'hands-off' principles. In 1833 she had recommended to Lord Brougham that Dr Southwood Smith should be appointed to investigate the 'physical and moral state of the lowest orders' and was much gratified when Smith was appointed to the commission on factory children.[40] She heartily approved of Sir James Graham's addition to the Factory Bill of 1843 which would have provided for compulsory school attendance for factory children, and was most dismayed that her fellow Dissenters lobbied against it because it did not meet their demands for complete separation of Church and state. A real problem of which Martineau was well aware was that many families' subsistence depended on the extra pennies their children earned, and so, if children's hours were limited, even by time taken out for education, their parents must somehow be compensated. Her solution advocated paying men sufficient wages to be able voluntarily to keep their children out of the job market.[41] When she visited the United States she noted that children often earned enough to help their fathers pay off mortgages.[42]

For years Martineau stubbornly clung to her belief that British workers really were free agents. Instead of thinking of the tyranny of the employer over employees, her mind was stuck in the rut of the tyranny of the state over employers. By the 1860s, however, she had grown in her thinking enough to see that workers needed legislative assistance, and she was ready to accept not only regulation of child labour and women's labour but also the Ten Hours Act for adult males. Joseph Hume's suggestion for a system of labour arbitration appealed to her because it left bargaining responsibility with the workers themselves. She had no doubt about the common man's ability to learn quickly how to bargain in his own interest. Here she did apply the same principle to white workers as to black slaves: responsibility and independence could be learned only as they were actually exercised within the context of freedom. 'Immediatism', not gradualism, was the answer.[43]

But she also learned another lesson from American abolitionists, the 'higher law' doctrine. For years she had clung to her theory: 'It is impossible to admit that, under a representative system, it is the proper business of government to regulate the private interests of any class whatever.' But mental growth and experience eventually forced her to concede, 'It is impossible, under the far higher constitution of humanity, to refuse attention to the case of the depressed, ignorant, and suffering of our people.' 'Having permitted a special misery and need to grow up, we must meet it with a special solace and aid.'[44] Just as abolitionists were willing to ignore the American Fugitive Slave Law in favour of obedience to the dictates of a higher law of humanity, so Martineau eventually admitted that humanity must take precedence over adherence to hard-hearted theories of political economy, no matter how logical or 'scientific' they might be.

Schemes that involved workers and employers in co-operative efforts appealed strongly to Miss Martineau because they suited her philosophy of class interdependence for the good of the social order. Possibly they satisfied a need in her to defend her own group. As R. K. Webb has pointed, out, she came from a manu-facturing class 'which was not rich, which ploughed back its profits, and some of whose members welcomed social responsi-bility'.[45] The hero and heroines of her novel *Deerbrook* illustrate this middle-class social responsibility and sensitivity to the hard-ships of the poor.

Going beyond the exposing of bad conditions in factories and mines, Martineau concerned herself as well with the time-honoured abuse of individual apprentices and of men impressed into the Army and Navy. Like Granville Sharp and the reformers of William Roscoe's circle, she saw the situations of both as com-parable to those of slaves. Apprentices were helpless in the face of beatings, starvation and even torture; the shanghaiing of men for the services was similar to the capturing of slaves in Africa. In 'A Tale of the Tyne' her character Cuddie reports that he was flogged 'as if I had been a black slave'.[46] Harriet was strongly supportive of James Silk Buckingham's and Joseph Hume's efforts in Parliament to outlaw flogging in the services. In fact, she signed a petition against its use even in cases where men were convicted of brutal attacks on women and children.[47]

Throughout her life, Martineau worked for the abolition of capital punishment and for prison reform, approaching both, as she did the problem of poverty, by trying to get at underlying causes rather than simply ameliorating current conditions. As we have noted, one of her purposes in visiting the United States was to study the new methods being employed for reform as opposed to simple punishment for offenders. Her first principle was identical to that of Sharp and Roscoe: prisoners should not be degraded. Their dignity as men and women must be encouraged.[48] She appreciated the reforming motives underlying the penitentiary system, even including solitary confinement, because it segregated offenders from corrupting influences, but after a visit to the Philadelphia penitentiary in 1834 she could not conceal her depression. 'But what must be the state of society', she asked, 'where it is humanity to prepare such an elaborate apparatus of human misery?'[49]

Still another problem of the poor — this time the rural poor — which engaged Martineau's attention had to do with the Game Laws. It was associated with her concern about prisons, because British jails were full of peasants convicted of poaching. While the poor were sick and starving, noblemen destroyed food to the value of several million pounds a year, yet 'the life of a hare or a pheasant must still be protected more carefully than the character and liberty of a man'.[50] For centuries British landlords had reserved to themselves the exclusive right to game. Violations were severely punished, and peasants could be forbidden to own guns or dogs. Although the class discrimination of the old laws was somewhat modified in 1831, there were loopholes which enabled landlords to reserve most of the game for their own hunting-pleasure.[51] In the 1840s John Bright led an attack on these laws as part of the free-traders' attack on privileged landlords, and his committee furnished Harriet Martineau with information from which she wrote *Forest and Game Law Tales*. Her aim was to open the eyes of some of the gentry, but she hoped the tales would find their way into the hands of tenant farmers, too, so that they would be encouraged to assert their rights.[52] As in all her causes, Harriet was eager that the people should exert themselves to gain justice, thereby obviating the need for charity.

The Corn Laws, like the Game Laws, served the vested interests of one class, and Martineau's talents were welcomed by anti-Corn Law leaders John Bright, Richard Cobden and Colonel T. Perronet Thompson.[53] Her tales 'Sowers Not Reapers' and 'The Loom and the Lugger' concentrate on free trade, while others, such as 'Cinnamon and Pearls', 'A Tale of the Tyne' and 'Briery Creek', include the theme along with her antimonopoly doctrines. She agreed with American abolitionists that slaveholding was a sin. So was protection: 'It involves more sin, and a greater variety of it, than any system I know of, except slavery', she wrote to Maria W. Chapman.[54] When she visited the American West in 1834 she mused on the connection between the iniquitous Corn Laws and emigration:

The landlords of England do not go and see the great western valley; but, happily, some of the labourers of England do. Far off as the valley is, those labourers will make themselves heard from thence, by those who have driven them there; and will teach the brethren whom they have left behind where the blame of their hunger lies. Every British settler who ploughs a furrow in the prairie helps to plough up the foundations of the British Corn Laws.[55]

Martineau approved of plans to ameliorate the lot of British workers by Government-sponsored and controlled emigration, and harboured hopes that such British emigrants to Texas might help to accomplish the abolitionists' aim of outlawing slavery there.[56] Nothing would please her more than to strike the evils of slavery and the Corn Laws in one magnificent blow. During the American Civil War, while Martineau was busy writing pro-Union articles for the London *Daily News*, she continued to point out that, while the sin of the South was slavery, the sin of the North was protection.[57] By that time, of course, Britain had inaugurated its free-trade policy. In addition to fighting import duties, Miss Martineau employed her popularity as a writer to inveigh against unnecessary excise taxes and against tithes paid to the Church of England.[58]

There can be no doubt about Harriet Martineau's serious concern about rights and justice for poor people, black or white, and it should not be surprising that she had a special sensitivity to discrimination against women. Her research on the problems of the poor convinced her that one of the troubles was that fathers often spent meagre family resources on their own comforts while their wives and children suffered. Yet she was consistent in insisting that women must accept responsibility for themselves and even went so far as to defend the bastardy provision in the Poor Law of 1834, which put the whole burden on the woman. It was a hardship, Martineau admitted, but it recognized that a woman was mistress of herself and did not have to be under male guardianship.[59] Her opposition to laws regulating prostitution (the Contagious Diseases Acts) was partly because she did not want prostitution recognized as legal, but mainly because of the blatant application of the double standard. She described the bills as 'most oppressive, insulting and outrageous in their application to women, while men in the same conditions were wholly exempt from their penalties'.[60] Such laws punished the victims instead of the perpetrators of vice. Any woman could be hauled into court by a policeman merely on his suspicion, and the burden of proof was then on her to establish that she was not a prostitute. Such actions under the law demonstrated that civil liberty for women could be cavalierly disregarded.

Martineau, Florence Nightingale, Josephine Butler and several other women organized a Ladies' National Association to work for repeal of the obnoxious laws. They published a national protest, and in the towns posted placards in the form of letters to people known in the communities. Women were urged to persuade their husbands not to vote for MPs who supported the acts. Working people without the vote were not neglected. Miss Martineau spoke to both men's and women's groups to enlighten them on the subject. The surprising result was that the women won their campaign and the laws were repealed.[61] It was a victory of even larger proportions when one considers the implications of breaking the hush-hush attitudes of Victorian Britain about even discussing such a subject openly.

When Martineau was asked if she intended to write about women's rights in her *Society in America*, her reply was that of course she must, since women constituted half of American society.[62] In the book she compared women's political rights to those of slaves: both groups were without representation in a country that made a fetish of government by the consent of the governed. Obedience to law was demanded of both even though they did not enjoy equal protection of the law. When American males argued with her that women were represented through their husbands and fathers, Martineau was in a good position to remind them that the Americans had fought a revolution because they rejected such 'virtual' representation as inadequate. While deploring the Southern slave society, she paid tribute to the strength, mental vigour and sense of responsibility of the Southern women who presided over it.[63] But she complained about the 'whining discontent' of rich, spoiled women who insulted servants and made life miserable for their husbands. While admiring the courage and competency of the 'advancing woman', she admitted, 'I rather dread the pedants taking possession of the movement, pushing forward their own personal claims, and making the cause ridiculous by their conceit, and offensive by their self-regard' – a statement not without irony, since Martineau herself was so pedantic. She believed that what the woman's movement needed was 'steady sweetness', and obviously thought that she exemplified that approach: 'As for me, I work on in a quiet sort of way in the cause. . . .'[64] After her return to England from the United States, Harriet considered editing a journal dedicated to the cause of women's rights, but the financial hazards seemed too great and she gave up the project. She did write for, and contributed money to, a fund to provide opportunities for women to be educated in the field of medicine.[65]

Martineau made her reputation as a reformer by exposing and protesting society's evils: chattel slavery; the Game Laws; the Corn Laws; oppressive traditions governing apprenticeship, impressment and prostitution; prison abuses; capital punishment; racial, class and sex discrimination of all varieties. She was far more than a muckraker, however, because she devoted equal time to positive solutions in a spirit of complete faith that people could be helped to help themselves. Factory workers could combine to obtain better wages and hours. They could organize agricultural co-operatives, consumer co-operatives, Friendly Societies, and savings banks. Carefully organized emigration would afford new opportunities abroad for some and alleviate unemployment at home. Educational opportunities for all would enable people to get at the crux of their primary problem, over-population. The role of the Government was to sponsor such education, enlarge representation and adopt a free-trade policy. To sum it up in her own words, the result would be 'freedom for bringing food to men, and freedom to go where food is plentiful; and enlightenment for all, that they may provide for themselves under the guidance of the best intelligence'.[66] She sounds very much like a modern feminist in demanding that slaves, black or white, male or female, must have justice, not charity, in order to prove their own worth.

Martineau went to the United States 'with a disposition to admire democratic institutions', and her American experience expanded her thinking on democracy while heightening her dislike of class antagonisms at home. She noted approvingly that American workmen could aspire to any position or office, and their relative power resulted in fewer strikes and a more orderly industrial society. Reflecting then on British workmen, she concluded that 'the highest order' of skilled workers were, as a class, 'the wisest and best men of the community'.[67] With such an attitude combined with her views on self-help and representation, it is not surprising that she did not react to the Chartist movement with the dread and panic so many other middle- and upper-class British people exhibited. To her Chartism was a valid social protest. From her point of view it was not the Feargus O'Connors of the political world who were to be feared, but rather the Whigs with their 'aristocratic self-complacency', who lectured the working classes but knew nothing about their real needs or wants. It was they who would be responsible if Britain experienced a disastrous social revolution.[68] Parliament, she cried, was sitting on a volcano, but in dealing with eruptions 'they threw cold water into the particular crevice, or blocked it up with rubbish, and supposed the fire had been put out'.[69] She saw that the people were disillusioned with the Reform Act of 1834. There were still too many unrepresented, and without a secret ballot intimidation of voters persisted. She acknowledged that the Chartists knew that a choice between Tories and Whigs was no choice at all; therefore there was no alternative but to become radical reformers.[70]

In Martineau's view the National Petition of the Chartists was 'a wonderful document', and she declared that 'No persons in England better deserve a respectful hearing than this million of petitioners.'[71] In another context (regarding sanitary improvements in Norwich) she had written that 'Government *will* stir . . . if urged & supported by the public voice: NOT WITHOUT. Those who wish for this salvation of the people must petition & petition & petition.'[72] That was exactly what the Chartists were doing. While she heartily approved of their goals, their petitions, and their orderly protests, she deplored the demagoguery of some of the leaders and upheld the Government's right to arrest 'torch-bearing' Chartists such as those who led the Newport uprising.[73]

It was during the years of Chartist activity that Harriet refused a pension from the Government, 'as they who provide the means have no voice in the appropriation of it to me personally'. She wanted no part of the proceeds of an unjust tax system: 'I should be haunted by images of thousands and hundreds of thousands of poor tax-payers, − toiling men who cannot, with all their toil, keep their children in health of body, − to say nothing of their minds.'[74]

Of all Martineau's ideas on how to solve the problems of the working poor, none was more important to her than education.

Though her sense of *noblesse oblige* certainly included an element of middle-class paternalism, she seems to have been remarkably free of the spirit of condescension which characterized so many reformers (one thinks of Hannah More by contrast), and remarkably understanding of the needs and aspirations of the people she was teaching. Part of the explanation may lie in her religious unorthodoxy. She felt no need to preach to them about morality, and could be as critical of clergymen who approached reform by trying to deprive people of their beer, tobacco and fun, as she was of those who preached pie-in-the-sky submissiveness to God's will. For her, the British churches were often as blind and hard-hearted about the problems of the poor as American churches were about slavery. While she certainly wanted British churches to be mindful of helping the slave, she was critical of too much concentration on missionary activity at the expense of the needy and downtrodden at home.[75]

When Martineau established herself at Ambleside in the Lake District, she immediately began to give talks to the children in school and then, by popular demand, expanded her effort to include evening classes for working men and their wives. No gentry were admitted, because she wanted to keep the sessions free from constraint. 'I have no ambition to teach,' she said of herself, 'but a strong desire to set members of households consulting together about their course of action toward each other.' Many subjects were practical ones: hygiene and sanitation, intemperance, rents, home-building, communal housing and household economy; but she also included areas which would expand horizons: geography, politics, history and emigration. Under her supervision actual experiments were made in low-rent housing, gardening and cow-keeping on limited acreage.[76]

Harriet's instructional writing remained a constant in her life. She put out numerous little pieces on every aspect of household work, a book, *Health, Husbandry and Handicraft*, and another called *Household Education* which dealt more with attitudes and habits than with specific tasks. There were various articles for Charles Knight's *Penny Magazine* and also for his *Voice of the People. England and her Soldiers* passed on to readers what she had learned about sanitary conditions in the Army from her long acquaintance with Florence Nightingale and the published report of the Royal Commission's investigation.[77] When fellow abolitionists William and Mary Howitt began to contribute to the

*People's Journal*, edited by John Saunders, they persuaded Harriet to contribute also. She produced the series 'Household Education', and a pot-pourri entitled 'Survey from the Mountain', which included random advice on everything from vaccinations and baths to tolerance for new ideas.[78] For many years Harriet sent articles to the *National Anti-Slavery Standard* in the United States, and up until her death she wrote over 1600 leading pieces for the London *Daily News*. These included her arguments for the Northern side during the American Civil War, which she bolstered with aid to distressed workers in England who were hit hard by the cotton blockade. Her purse was opened for donations to the suffering as she busied herself personally with establishing sewing-schools for unemployed factory girls.[79]

Harriet Martineau wrote her own obituary. It was kept in a drawer of the London *Daily News* and published after her death in 1876. Amazingly candid and critical of her own writing, she pronounced that none of it had 'any character of permanence' because it lacked artistry. She felt that she had 'no power of dramatic construction', nor 'poetic inspiration', nor 'critical cultivation'. Yet, 'she saw the human race, as she believed, advancing under the law of progress; she enjoyed her share of the experience, and had no ambition for a larger endowment'.[80] Despite this modest self-estimate, Martineau's influence in her time had been major. One of her most apt eulogies was written by Florence Nightingale: 'She was born to be a destroyer of slavery, in whatever form, in whatever place, all over the world, wherever she saw or thought she saw it.'[81] Another, from Josephine Butler, paid tribute to her as 'faithful to the end to the cause of white slaves of Europe as she had been faithful to the cause of the black slaves of America'.[82]

# 5  T. Perronet Thompson

From the editor's office of the *Chicago Tribune* on 1 May 1866, Horace White wrote to T. Perronet Thompson of Hull, England, 'The question with us now is: Shall the negroes vote? The question with you is not unlike this: Shall the working man vote?'[1] If White knew anything at all about his correspondent, these queries could hardly have been intended to stimulate a new line of thought in the mind of the recipient, for Thompson had already devoted more than half a century to the twin causes of freedom for blacks and greater opportunity for working people. He had enlisted in each of the causes as the soldier that he was and in the same spirit with which he fought his military campaigns in the Middle East and in India: striking hard and repeatedly. On one occasion he advised his son, 'If you hit a man once, always hit him again quickly lest he think the first time was a mistake'[2] – a philosophy the father applied in his own battles with people he considered to be the enemies of reform.

T. P. Thompson came by his reform concerns early – inherited them to some extent through his father's friendship and business connections with the Wilberforces. The father, Thomas Thompson, had a bit of the reformer in him, too, setting an example for his son by his attacks on corporate abuses and on the inadequacies of the poor-relief system. As an MP he stood with the abolitionists in the fight against the slave trade, and subscribed to the African Institution that William Roscoe had helped to found, which aimed at substituting legitimate trade with Africa for the slave trade.[3] It was a natural development, then, that Perronet should become excited at hearing Wilberforce and his father discuss the slave trade and Africa and that Wilberforce should respond to that enthusiasm by recruiting the young man (at age twenty-five) to go to Sierra Leone to act as Governor of the colony that the 'Saints' had established as a home for freed slaves.[4] By the time Thompson went out (1808) the colony had been taken under royal authority, but the 'Saints' still exercised a great deal of influence in the choosing and supervising of personnel.[5]

Whereas Sharp's, Rathbone's and Sturge's philanthropy had a strong basis in their religious convictions, Thompson's, like Rushton's, seems to have stemmed primarily from his experiences and observations. His published writings and his letters have no religious overtones. His Sierra Leone experience followed four years of service in the Royal Navy and a stint in the Army which was cut short in its second year when he was captured by the Spaniards during the British invasion of Buenos Aires in July 1807. The Spaniards freed him after a short imprisonment, and it was during the interim at home that he responded with such enthusiasm to Wilberforce's presentation of the good he could do by helping the young colony of Sierra Leone to develop a sound economic and political base.[6] The combination of his connections with the Army, the Navy, and colonial bureaucracy in Africa convinced him of several things: that slavery could exist under the guise of philanthropy, that it was not confined to black Africans, and that slave labour, whether black or white, would never be so productive as free labour.

A scene Thompson witnessed *en route* to Africa made a deep impression on him: on a British man-o'-war he saw three sailors stripped for torture to extract confessions of crime from them. He simply could not square such abhorrent disregard for humanity with judicial justice or with British traditions of liberty. It made no sense to him that British people should always be crying out for liberty while at the same time they 'have tamely seen their fellow-subjects dragged into slavery [i.e. the Army and Navy] without complaint' – an attitude which must have been unusual for an Army officer of that time. He vowed that, if ever he represented the people in Parliament, one of his aims would be to attack this 'home slave trade'.[7] Several years later he kept his pledge by joining James Silk Buckingham and John Bright in campaigns against flogging in the Army, and he took a strong stand as well against British usage which forced Hindu soldiers to use cartridges greased with animal fat. Handling beef fat violated Hindu law.[8] He, along with Buckingham and Edward Codrington, also backed a bill to establish a Marine Board to regulate shipping and thus provide better protection for seamen. One of his election cards, headed 'Thompson and Liberty', lists the planks of his platform, which included 'No Impressment', 'No

Flogging' and 'Rights of Conscience'. One of his Hull election flags in 1841 combined 'Free Trade and Seamen's Rights' as the essential issues.[9] While his time in the Navy gave him first-hand experience with the treatment of sailors in Government service, his residency in Hull made him familiar with the problems of merchant seamen. Consequently many of his electioneering speeches were addressed to what he termed the 'maritime classes'.

Thompson's efforts against the 'home slave trade' did not indicate an abandonment of interest in the black slave trade. In Sierra Leone his persistence in pressing for an inquiry into what was actually going on in this 'free' colony was enough to get him into trouble with the royal government and with his sponsors in the Wilberforce–Thornton Clapham Sect. Even his own father refused to support him. The contretemps resulted in his being branded a headstrong young man who refused to yield to 'practical' considerations, and finally led to his recall.[10] But he enjoyed a moment of sweet victory a decade later when, in 1820, back in the British Army, which was making conquests in the Persian Gulf area, it was his privilege to write an anti-slave-trade clause into a treaty – a clause that designated the slave trade to be piracy. This time he earned Wilberforce's commendation.[11]

Colonel Thompson's continuing concern about the slave trade in West Africa led him to support Elliott Cresson, an agent for the American Colonization Society, who arrived in England in the 1830s to try to get official recognition for Liberia. The argument was the same as that used by the then defunct African Institution influenced by Granville Sharp's view: that the legal trade in agricultural products could become so profitable that it would drive out the hazardous illegal slave trade. At a time when most emancipationists in both Britain and the United States were denouncing the American Colonization Society as a racist scheme to force free blacks to emigrate, Colonel Thompson stuck to his independent but unpopular view that Liberia, along with Sierra Leone, could be, with official help and recognition, a key base from which to stop slave-trade operations.

Something of an amateur economist himself, it may well have been Perronet Thompson who introduced Cresson to Jeremy Bentham in the hope of enlisting Bentham's influence. Thompson certainly urged his and Bentham's mutual friend, Dr John Bowring, to try to persuade France to recognize Liberia. Bowring was active in commercial negotiations on the continent, and Thompson's idea was that France might recognize Liberia as an independent commercial entity – a status similar to that enjoyed by the old Hansa cities – even if she did not proffer recognition of full national sovereignty.[12]

In considering the question of the racism of the American Colonization Society, and why that did not deter Thompson from supporting Cresson, one must ask whether there was any element of racism in T. P. Thompson himself. His good friend John Bowring left the observation that in Sierra Leone, in cases of conflict between a European and an African, Thompson would automatically decide in favour of the African. On the other hand, a modern historian, Ellen Gibson Wilson, says that Thompson was extremely critical of the blacks who came to the colony from Nova Scotia, because they demanded too much, were insubordinate and rebellious. Thompson's attitude could be explained by his military training; but it is possible that, despite his antipathy for slavery and despite his alignment with the Chartists at a later date, he may have retained some remnants of class and colour prejudice. In his relationship with the Chartists, he was strongly criticized by some of them who objected to his assuming the authority to tell them how to behave.[13]

As a political candidate and off-and-on MP,[14] Thompson repeatedly spoke in favour of stationing British warships at the mouths of African rivers as a deterrent against the slave trade, a stance that put him at odds with pacifist-minded colleagues in Parliament such as Richard Cobden and with many pacifist abolitionists – Joseph Sturge, for instance.[15] The greatest test for his adherence to the anti-slave-trade cause came in the 1840s, when, like Sturge, he had to choose between his antislavery and free-trade principles. The problem lay in whether or not sugar ought to be included in duty-free imports, because an increased demand for sugar would surely stimulate the slave trade to the sugar-producing areas of Brazil and Cuba. Yet a tariff on sugar would raise the price to a prohibitive level for British working people. Thompson was one of the most consistent of free-traders (and is better known historically in that context than as an abolitionist), but his early commitment against the slave trade won out in debates which pitted the Anti-Corn Law League against the British and Foreign Anti-Slavery Society and split the antislavery societies down the middle. He became exceedingly impatient with the British and Foreign Anti-Slavery Society for not 'raising its banner' higher in favour of the sugar duties.[16]

Thompson was forced out of two careers, in the colonial administration and in the Army, for what was deemed headstrong and impulsive action that failed to take account of practical considerations. One might assume, therefore, that as a reformer he would be either of the emotionally fervent variety or of the impractical, head-in-the-clouds brand. Instead he appears to the historian as cool-headed, urbane, witty and decidedly averse to tilting against windmills. Satire, not pious rhetoric, was his forte, and his writings are laced with witticisms. He once remarked that Sydney Smith could do more with a joke than other men could with 'the accumulated wisdom of their lives'. He liked to tell the story of being with Smith at a dinner of the Political Economy Club at the Free-Mason Tavern where there also happened to be a festival dinner for the Welsh School Institution. Suddenly an upper door opened and down the two staircases into the hall came one stream of boys and another of girls. Sydney Smith jumped up excitedly, calling out, 'Where's Mr Malthus? Where's Mr Malthus?' Malthus happened to be there and was brought out 'to view the two streams of population descending'.[17]

Perhaps Thompson's Sierra Leone experience had conditioned him against being too sanctimonious a reformer. When he discovered that actual slavery continued there under the guise of an apprenticeship system, he reacted with aversion to what he considered to be the pious hypocrisy of the 'Saints' and that awakening may have led him to take a more realistic view of what was possible in reform, even from the best-motivated people. At home he counted among his friends some of the leading intellectual and literary personages of his time, whose influence may have tempered his own impulsiveness. Certainly the fact that they represented the political-economy philosophy of the day means that their ideas would have had a braking effect on any belief that the Government could or should 'interfere' to alleviate every social or economic ill. Rather, they generally espoused a philosophy advocating the removal of Government restraints. This explains why, of all reform movements of the day, Thompson associated himself most closely with the one against the Corn Laws. Yet, from time to time he expressed his independence, such as in his stand to retain duties on Brazilian and Cuban sugar, and in his alignment with the Chartists, although they were considered by many Anti-Corn Law Leaguers to be radical and dangerous enemies.

Thompson began to write for the *Westminster Review* when Jeremy Bentham and John Bowring first established it in 1824, and in 1829 he bought the publication to become its editor (although Bentham retained half of the stock and thereby half of the proprietorship).[18] The political aim which underlay Thompson's ambitions for the *Review* was to achieve a reform bill by sustaining a union of Whigs and Radicals in order to 'blow the Tories and Huntites into the air in all directions on both sides of us'.[19] To help in reaching that end he wanted the *Review* to appeal to the interests of the 'mechanical classes', a goal he believed to be attainable because, as he wrote to Bowring, it had once been possible for the *Edinburgh Review* to win the backing of the Glasgow weavers. If a middle-class periodical such as the *Edinburgh* could win over workers, so could the *Westminster*. The electrifying effect of the July Revolution of 1830 in France boosted his optimism even more regarding the possibility of making his *Review* the organ of a people's party.[20] Although the Colonel frequently denounced Will Cobbett as a scoundrel and hoped one day to drive him 'into one of his own tallow barrels', yet he retained a certain admiration for Cobbett's success as a people's publisher, an admiration tinged with envy, perhaps, because the *Westminster Review* never was able to earn the same whole-hearted trust of the working classes.[21]

While Thompson took issue with Cobbett and John Hunt for misleading the people through demagoguery, his attacks were by no means confined to the more radical leaders. He also challenged the theories of J. S. Mill, Robert Owen, and St Simon; Whig political tactics which did not go far enough; and, like Harriet Martineau, he was dubious about the limited factory legislation approach of Michael Sadler and Richard Oastler. His argument with J. S. Mill was because Mill preached the need for a balance of land, labour and capital, which to Thompson implied that, if one of those should be scarce, the others must be curtailed too. Thompson pronounced this theory to be as sensible as the recommendation that, in a diet consisting of bread, beef and potatoes, a dearth of one meant that the others must be cut back as well.[22] Owenism and St Simonism – in fact, most isms – he held to be too visionary about the future. They failed to realise that co-operatives and communities would not always be able to compete favourably in production with individual enterprises.[23]

While admitting that the Factory Act of 1833 had some good features – notably, limiting the hours of work for children and requiring a minimum of education in connection with factory work – he, along with Martineau, doubted that restricting hours would get at the root of the labour problem. It was only 'cursing the pimple and leaving the pox'. He foresaw that either mill-owners would simply dismiss workers under the age of eighteen (and he knew that poor families could ill afford not to let their children work) or the mills would operate only ten hours (if Sadler's bill passed) with a resulting loss in production accompanied by rising costs and a lowering of wages. Machinery would be increasingly introduced to replace men. Moreover, he suspected that the motive behind Sadler's Ten Hours Bill was to deflect support from parliamentary reform, slave emancipation and repeal of the Corn Laws, all of which Thompson saw as more fundamental.[24] However, in 1837, when Thompson was in the House of Commons and Poulett Thompson's Factory Act Alteration Bill came up for a second reading, he voted against changing the section of the 1833 Act which dealt with hours of work for children; and in the 1840s he supported the Ten Hours Bill in response to the wishes of the operatives and even some manufacturers in his constituency. He thought the Government should give direct monetary relief to trades in special distress – for example, the silk-weavers in the early 1830s.[25]

Thompson made the same charge of political motivation in regard to the Poor Law of 1834 as he did about the factory acts; and he was equally dubious about poor-laws affording any kind of real solution, unless accompanied by repeal of the Corn Laws. Indeed, he feared that they only compounded the desperate situation of the workers through pseudo-charity, which contributed to an increasingly 'uneducated, toilworn and ignorant working class'. Even the old individual charity given in a spirit of *noblesse oblige* had preserved some sense of a bond between the classes. He despaired because national education was still an 'abortive philanthropy', the criminal code abhorrent, and the jails were schools of vice. In short, the present social order condoned a horrible waste of the masses.[26]

What was the Colonel's solution? The middle classes, including capitalist manufacturers, must initiate the breaking down of class barriers and class legislation. They must begin by realising that a relationship which consisted only of the exchange of labour and wages was insufficient, was merely heartless and degrading.[27] In an article entitled 'The Suffering Rich', Thompson unleashed a brand of satire that was equal to Cobbett's best: 'The poor are up, are they?' Well, they must pay for having been made paupers of; but, he challenged, can they be expected to pay for being starved to death while being piously admonished to love their enemies?[28] In another article he condemned the commercial policy of England as 'one continuous fraud upon the industrious classes for the benefit of those whose trade and calling it is to live without working'. Yet the poor were expected not only to refrain from appropriating their rich neighbours' property, but to give their lives to defend it. With the exception of Negro slavery, the history of the world revealed to Thompson no example of so glaring an abuse of power stemming from 'giving one selfish class the right of legislation for the rest'. All revolutions, Thompson warned, 'come by there being nobody who had sense to join the people, and give them half of what was the next day taken by violence'. Granted, the workers' attempts to keep their jobs by breaking machines were exercises in futility, but the manufacturers were the ones who ought to realize the necessity of introducing machines gradually to keep a balance between production and demand and so keep labour employed and wages up. The responsibility lay with the mill-owners, not with the workers, for 'The ignorant and the poor, – those who are ignorant because they are poor, and poor because they are ignorant, and whom laws have been passed to make both one and the other, – cannot be expected to reason like doctors in divinity. . . .'[29]

One of Thompson's biggest bugbears was the current tax system, which seemed to be purposely contrived to deprive the poor, bit by bit, of the little they had, and continued, as he said, to squeeze the workers in order to provide the rich with the means to be generous in their charity to the poor! Citing figures, Thompson pointed out that the tax on ordinary tobacco (in 1834) was 1200 per cent, while that on 'Maryland fine yellow' was 240 per cent and that on 'Havannah Segars' smoked by the rich was 105 per cent, all high enough to save the poor from the curse of tobacco. The rate on unrefined sugar was 96 per cent, while that on the refined used by the upper classes was only 34 per cent.

Coarse yellow soap was taxed at 39 per cent, but fine white oil soap at only 20 per cent. On one occasion Thompson referred to the 'smoke-dried operative, whom great men tax in his bread and soap, and then call the unwashed'. Taxes on hotels and inns which served the public were much higher than those on the homes of aristocrats and country gentlemen. Taxes on baptisms and marriages and on numerous household articles always hit the poor the hardest. No teetotaller, Thompson objected also to the malt tax on the poor man's drink. The answer, for Thompson, lay in graduated taxes, with complete exemption for the poor who fell to a level of poverty where any tax at all would be unjust. Beyond that, he wanted provision for workers' wages to keep pace with inflation – the reverse of the current policy of manufacturers, who fought to keep wages low. Thompson believed that, if the Government were to establish a fixed rate between paper currency and gold, depreciation could be checked whenever necessary by withdrawing paper money from circulation. Until the end of his life the old soldier continued to oppose tax plans which did not embody a graduation of rates.[30]

One of the worst taxes in the Colonel's list was the 'tax on knowledge' imposed on newspapers, stamps, advertisements and other instruments that fostered communication and education, and by the mid 1830s he had joined such radicals as Henry Hetherington, John Cleave, Augustus Beaumont and William Lovett in meetings to agitate for freedom of the press. On that issue Lord Brougham became an obvious target. Brougham had won a reputation for being concerned about workers' education through his efforts on behalf of Mechanics' Institutes and in helping to establish the Society for the Diffusion of Useful Knowledge. Yet, when he became Lord Chancellor in the Reform Government of 1830–2, he failed, the *Westminster Review* charged, to use his power to see that taxes on knowledge were repealed. Moreover, Thompson joined Harriet Martineau in asserting that the Society for the Diffusion of Useful Knowledge erred in not providing labouring men with cheap reading-materials which would really help them to understand why their condition was so bad and what could be done about it. Instead they were given scientific treatises or literature which had little relevance to their own lives and problems. This was what he meant by his epithet 'abortive philanthropy' to characterize the current state of national education.[31]

Thompson worked hard to abolish tithes, which he saw as another example of unjust taxation. Although he had been brought up in a Methodist home, he broke away from all narrow intolerance of sect while maintaining a running battle against church hierarchies, both Roman Catholic and Anglican. He argued that the Churches of England, Scotland and Ireland were all better able to pay taxes themselves than were the poor from whom tax pennies were wrung. Thompson claimed that in Manchester in 1830 a tax 'imposed under the pretence of supporting a religious creed' amounted to a prohibition against giving information to the poor about their own political concerns. Always outspoken, on one occasion he accused the Pope of aiming to reduce workers everywhere to the level of those in Naples, Portugal and Spain. Bowring said that Thompson inherited and retained a strong anti-Catholic feeling; William Howitt credited him with opposing both Catholic and Jewish disabilities; while biographer Leonard Johnson holds that the he championed Catholic emancipation in his early career but reverted to anti-Catholicism in old age. At least his stand against tithes was important enough in his election campaigns to win him the support of the Hull Catholics, the Quakers and other Dissenters, and he capitalized on the support of one Jewish family, which enabled him to refer to his 'Jewish constituency'. His concern extended to all Dissenters, and his letters to his Unitarian friend Bowring are filled with references to the subject, often in a humorous vein discussing the legalizing of Unitarian marriages and speculating as to whether or not Bowring's grandchildren could hope to claim legitimacy. In election campaigns he took the practical approach, cautioning Bowring to deemphasize his Unitarianism.[32]

Although the Sabbatarian movement gained some ground in reform circles, Thompson never did back bills restricting Sunday activities and labour.[33] This position is open to several interpretations: one, that on this issue he took the side of the factory-owners; or, that he realized that such a measure would result in decreased earnings, which working people could ill afford – a position consistent with his doubts about the utility of restricting hours for children. While there is no 'hard' evidence, my own impression is that Thompson, who had no strong religious commitment himself, probably found the pressures from the Sabbatarians somewhat distasteful. Even though one of their points was that the workers were entitled to a day of rest, the over-shadowing thrust of their approach was the Biblical injunction to keep the Sabbath holy. Thompson's cynicism about saintliness probably began in Sierra Leone when he realized that slavery persisted even in the colony of Wilberforce, Thornton and Macaulay. It was evident in his attitude toward James Silk Buckingham's pious mien even while they worked together against impressment and flogging, and may have been a subconscious, if not conscious, brake against his full co-operation with so purist a Quaker as Joseph Sturge. The same distaste probably carried over in his attitude toward Sabbatarians.

After dismissing socialism, co-operatives, and factory legislation as failing to get at the heart of economic problems, Thompson settled on repeal of the Corn Laws as the most far-reaching reform possible in order to attain the Benthamite goal of the greatest good.[34] Simply put, the Corn Laws sustained the high prices of food for working people in order that landlords could live in luxury without fear of foreign competition. The fallacy in the thinking that supported the landlords at the expense of the workers was to Thompson the same as that which upheld the interests of the great West Indian planters at the expense of the slaves and the small farmers. As a case in point, in passing the Emancipation Act of 1833 the Government had included £20 million in compensation to the planters. Thompson's inclination was to refuse to pay taxes 'so long as such enormities are committed upon us'. The situation reminded him of an anecdote about soldiers in the Middle East who had forced a shepherd to kill and then feed them a sheep, after which they demanded that he pay them for eating it. Likewise, 'the people of England have been made to pay twenty millions for having their mutton eaten'.[35]

Thompson began writing for the free-trade cause well before such heroes as Bright, Cobden and Villiers emerged as leaders. As usual, his satirical wit was his main weapon. In his *Catechism on the Corn Laws* (1827) he 'answered' the numerous fallacies in popular thinking. The following are a few examples. Fallacy: 'That the operatives are a lazy race and seldom go to work before Wednesday.' Answer: 'The landlords never go to work at all.' Fallacy: 'Plenty is dangerous because we may be deprived of it.' Answer: 'Two legs are dangerous for the same reason.' Fallacies in defence of landlords: 'That they fought the battle against the

Jocobins.' Answer: 'Which other people are paying for.' Or, 'That they sit at quarter sessions.' Answer: 'And strange things they sometimes do there. For instance in Buckinghamshire they sentenced John Doe to five months imprisonment for intending to assault the lord's hen pheasant, and Richard Roe to three, for assaulting the serf's daughter.' He called Britain's refusal to allow untaxed food imports the equivalent of Noah's shutting himself and his family up in the Ark with a determination to eat nothing but what could be grown upon its decks; Shem, Ham and Japhet would have become 'distressed manufacturers' very quickly. To Thompson an island economy faced the same problem as a bee colony: the hive would soon die unless the bees were free to go wherever they wanted to gather honey.[36]

The Colonel's conception of a 'Spaceship Great Britain' was an early-nineteenth-century version of Buckminster Fuller's 'Spaceship Earth' theory of the twentieth. In addition to advocating free trade for Britain, he used every opportunity to send the same message to the rest of western Europe, especially to France and Belgium as they set up new governments in the wake of the 1830 uprisings. Since John Bowring's connections gave him access to revolutionary and reform councils in those nations, Thompson repeatedly counselled him to argue and agitate for free trade and against the slave trade.[37] Free trade had come to have two meanings for Thompson: trade in legitimate products to kill the slave trade by competition, and the removal of national tariffs (except on slave-grown produce) in order to facilitate the exchange of goods, thereby lowering prices on food and fostering manufacturing to keep up employment with better wages. Thus the problems of black slavery and white slave labour were intertwined in his thinking.

By the early 1830s Thompson's platform had focused on three issues; emancipation, free trade and a reform bill to broaden representation; and he was moving steadily into politics to fight for them directly. The strategy he favoured was a political coalition of Whigs (who were the strongest for emancipation) and Radicals (i.e. middle-class political radicals) who should try to win the support of artisans and operatives away from working-class radicals, and keep them from an alliance with the Tories. Thompson thought of himself as a Radical who, since he had many Whig friends, was in a good position to convince them that Radicals were not to be feared. If the Huntites (followers of John and Leigh Hunt, i.e. radical Radicals) should coalesce with the Tories, Thompson's Whig–Radical party must 'crack them both in one nut'.[38]

Having put his faith in working with the Whigs, Thompson was among those who were bitterly disappointed with the performance of the Reform Government. 'Never men so laid themselves out to do what they ought not to do, and leave undone what they ought to do', he moaned.[39] Even the Emancipation Act, widely hailed as so glorious a victory, displeased Thompson as it did Joseph Sturge, not only because of its provision for compensating the planters at the taxpayers' expense, but also because it included a long apprenticeship period rather than immediate emancipation. When Thompson heard that the first bill provided for a twelve-year apprenticeship (later reduced to five years), his angry reaction was, 'I hope the negroes will emancipate themselves in *two*; and the Whigs may be put to the fire and sword in *one*.'[40]

In the general election of 1834 following Peel's dissolution of Parliament, Thompson was nominated to stand for Preston. He lost on his first try, but was successful the following year when he stood for Hull. He was in and out of the Commons from then until 1859.[41] During these years one of the major challenges confronting him was how to balance his sympathy for Chartism and his loyalty to the free-trade movement. In his own mind Chartism and Corn Law repeal should and could go together, a view consistent with his belief in breaking down class barriers and consistent as well with the programme of the early Chartists.[42] But as time went on this stand made him unpopular with both sides. Despite the efforts of several leaders who agreed with Thompson, the Anti-Corn Law League was to remain largely middle-class and hence highly suspect in the eyes of many Chartists.

In 1840, when working with Hull Chartists, Thompson distinguished between 'my Radicals' and the Whig Radicals, in order to defend the former. 'It is manifest the Chartist Radicals are coming round, if anybody will met them half-way', he wrote to Bowring, and 'For my own part, I do not intend to desert my squad. They are in some senses unguidable and wild, but in others they are amenable to reason, and daily coming round. So I mean to march with them . . . or not at all.'[43] In his own election campaign, Thompson chastised the Whigs for overemphasizing Corn Law repeal to the exclusion of other issues when he believed that he was on the verge of bringing over at least the Hull Chartists to acquiesce in repeal as one ingredient of reform.[44]

Yet Thompson's middle-class prejudices show through in his use of the term 'unguidable', and on another occasion when he impatiently called the workers 'utterly impracticable'.[45] During the crisis over slavery in Texas, T. P. Thompson urged the abolitionist orator George Thompson (no relation) to visit Hull to lecture on the subject because 'It is of immense importance to get the men to put themselves forward on anything good, and to amalgamate themselves with the well-thinking and well-doing portions of society' – obviously implying that they were not already in that group.[46] The Colonel believed that the men needed to learn a lesson in practical politics: that co-operation in other causes would earn them reciprocal help, a strategy he thought would result in more success than would the more limited approach of 'bawling' only for their own needs. He was delighted to discover that his Hull Chartists read and were impressed by the American preacher–philosopher William Ellery Channing on the Texas issue and, as usual, Thompson's optimism was confided to his friend Bowring: 'You see the men only want a little pains [taking?] with them, to bring them into union with all worthy things'; and, in another letter: 'It is really a proof of the times to see the Chartists braining their opponents with extracts from Dr Channing.'[47] Obviously, too, Thompson was still thinking of the emancipation of black slaves as an issue with a direct bearing on the emancipation of white workers, and still believed what he had written in a *Westminister Review* article of 1834 that the people would 'no more bear a little Corn Laws, than they will bear a little Slave Trade'.[48]

It is clear from Thompson's correspondence that he had a good working relationship with the Chartists and enjoyed a good measure of their confidence, especially with leaders William Lovett and Henry Vincent, both of whom Thompson hoped to see in Parliament. Speaking at Mechanics' Institutes and before working men's associations, he supported the ballot, triennial parliaments and household suffrage. He helped Lovett draw up the bill which became 'The People's Charter' and spoke at the Palace Yard Meeting in 1838 (one of numerous meetings to elect delegates to a national convention which should launch the Charter).[49] In 1841 both the Leicester Chartists and the Dundee Chartists invited Thompson to stand for Parliament; but he stood for Hull instead.[50] During that campaign he was careful to consult his Chartist following and to see that they were present at meetings with his Whig backers. The Chartists' casuistry delighted him when they privately advised him to speak out for free trade but not to force them into a public confrontation with the Whig repeal coterie. Thompson reported to Bowring that he had learned that one must handle the conscience of a Chartist as delicately 'as you would of a Sepoy'.[51]

Failure of other middle-class leaders to learn this lesson resulted in the collapse of the Complete Suffrage Movement of 1842 led by Joseph Sturge. Fearing that the Chartist label carried connotations of extreme radicalism, the 'Sturgeons' (as Cobden called them) tried to substitute 'Complete Suffrage' for 'Chartism' and 'People's Bill of Rights' for 'The Charter', thus revealing an insensitivity to their would-be allies' point of honour in sustaining loyalty to the Charter.[52] Reporting to Richard Cobden on Joseph Sturge's *rather flat* reception in Leeds, Thompson went on to analyse: 'How should it be otherwise, when the man goes about, inviting all previously formed associations, leagues, and covenants, to put themselves down and merge themselves in him "the great one that was to come". It will be well if he escapes crucifixion; to say nothing of being *rather flat*.'[53] To Bowring he expressed the opinion that 'Joseph Sturge is as utterly without the bump of combination as Feargus O'Connor'; and that 'the aristocrats' were wrong in thinking the people could not produce their own capable leaders.[54] Thompson agreed with Sturge's goal but not with his strategy. He believed that the Chartists must be given time and 'rope' to realize that their insistence on priority for the Charter was not good politics since it would be much more difficult to obtain than repeal of the Corn Laws.

One measure of Thompson's standing as a Chartist leader was in the recognition given him in anti-Chartist attacks. One example appears in a campaign flyer which is headed 'Chartist League Agitators' and which contains six stanzas of doggerel, two focused on 'the Cur-nel'.

> There's Rory Moore, that noisy lad,
>     The Cur-nel's reeght hand chap,
> He's paid by folks ye never saw
>     For spouting ye clap trap.
> He says he wants cheap Corn and Bread –

> Free Trade – cheap Meat and Tea –
> To pull your wages down to naught
>     Is what he wants to de!
> The poor old Cur-nel may gan back,
>     He'll never get in here;
> The folks about him have ne votes;
>     His cheap bread will turn dear!
> The weel paid, windy blithering crew
>     May tell their lees at home,
> For all we ken the dirty tricks
>     Of the mad Chartist gang.[55]

W. J. Linton, famous as an engraver and poet but also as a reformer, believed that Thompson's promotions to the rank of general were delayed because of his Chartist radicalism.[56]

Thompson lost his bid for re-election in 1841 and was not to win again until 1847. Meanwhile, however, he kept up a steady pace of campaigning for his causes and for his own political future.[57] His good relationship with the Chartists continued as he joined them in their meetings in the London Rotunda and even chaired sessions for them despite attacks in the press and the advice of more conservative friends such as Cobden. Thompson claimed that his was the best strategy for bringing the Chartists over to the Anti-Corn Law League position.[58] Back in the House of Commons during the great Chartist meeting on Kennington Common in 1848, Thompson was fiercely critical of the Government's handling of that situation 'in the style so well understood by political tacticians when a fire is not to be allowed the chance of going out for want of stirring'.[59]

Thompson's association with the Chartists represented the height of his radicalism, but he continued to stick his neck out on other unpopular causes as well: the secret ballot, a graduated income tax with complete exemptions at the bottom level, representation for Jews, and not only suffrage for women, which he saw as 'simple justice', but also equal admission of women to all degrees and all professions.[60] On the issue of denied representation, Thompson's views were again the same as Martineau's. He spoke of its similarity to the issue of slavery. Deprived people were always advised to wait patiently for something to be done *for* them rather than encouraged to do the thing for themselves. 'Like the negroes, we are either without representation, or it is burthened with the necessity of baring our backs for cowhiding in case we vote against our lords and masters....'[61] When the House of Commons defeated a bill to prevent cruelty to animals, he jibed that there was no good reason for such action except that animals were not represented.[62]

Thompson's opposition to capital punishment evoked from him the suggestion of a novel tactic: they should persuade the young Queen Victoria to weep as she publicly declared that she did not like men's heads to be cut off. 'What is the use of being governed by babies,' he asked, 'if we are not to turn it to advantage where the thing is capable of it?'[63]

One of the most surprising of this old soldier's stands was his joining Cobden's peace movement against the Crimean War. He urged the voters of the West Riding to support Cobden as their fathers had supported Wilberforce against the slave trade. 'The question is the same in kind', he wrote. 'It is whether the strong shall abuse the weak.'[64] Adherence to this principle was to cause an outright break with his close friend Bowring when, working for the British Government in China, Bowring was involved in implementing a ruthless policy of British imperialism. Thompson had long been a member of both the British India Society and the Aborigines Protection Society. Sympathies developed in those groups carried over in his attitude toward the exploited Chinese.[65]

Although Thompson was not ordinarily susceptible to sentimental, emotional appeals, he seems to have been caught up, along with the rest of the nation, in the excitement of Harriet Beecher Stowe's visit to England in 1853 following her publication of *Uncle Tom's Cabin*. In May of that year he attended the annual meeting of the British and Foreign Anti-Slavery Society in Exeter Hall in London at which he offered a resolution against American slavery.[66] When the Americans Civil War broke out he immediately took his stand with the Union. To him the fight was clearly the struggle over slavery and he had no intention of backing away from a cause he had supported for half a century. Still, he kept his sense of humour, as exemplified by one occasion when he wrote a letter to an American minister in New York, suggesting that he should preach a sermon on a text in the book of Joshua about God's punishment of a wicked nation. The suggestion was accepted, the sermon preached, and then reported in the *Anti-Slavery Standard*, a mouthpiece of Garrisonian abolitionism. Dr Cheever, it reported, had preached 'a thundering sermon' on the text which 'Providence' had commended to him. Thompson's response was, 'It is the first time I ever found myself promoted to a "providence".'[67]

T. Perronet Thompson lived to the ripe age of eighty-six, dying in 1869. Throughout the decade of the 1850s and in the early 1860s he remained active in reform causes, but during the last years of his life he retired to his books, and to his lifelong interest in music and mathematics and the relationship between the two.[68] He had earlier published a mathematical treatise on geometry and a book of instructions to his daughter for playing the 'Enharmonic Guitar'. His Enharmonic Organ was displayed at the Great Exhibition of 1851.[69] In 1867, amid the excitement over the new Franchise Act, Halifax tried to persuade Thompson to stand again for Parliament, but at the age of eighty-four he preferred to stay out of the fray.[70]

Thompson's concern that the strong should not abuse the weak was the guiding principle of his long and active public life, and it was applied equally whether the question was one of the subjugation of a sex, a race, a colony, or an economically deprived class. It was the same basic philosophy which activated Sharp, Sturge, Martineau, Rathbone, Rushton, Roscoe and Currie.

# 6 Patrick Brewster and Henry Solly

It was a common occurrence for American abolitionist ministers to experience sharp conflicts with their congregations or church hierarchies over their radicalism in advocating emancipation of the slaves. In Great Britain, where abolition was a much more respectable cause, there was far less likelihood of such confrontations, but, if an abolitionist clergyman began to equate the situation of the working poor with that of American slaves and boldly preached such a message from his pulpit, then he, too, had to be prepared to stand up to vocal opposition, church discipline, and even the possibility of losing his pastorate. Obviously such ministers touched a chord of guilt that produced a strong defensive reverberation among many British, just as American sermons expounding on the sinfulness of slavery provoked rationalisations of slavery.

Two British clergymen willing to accept the consequences of attacking slavery on both the home front and in the colonies or in the United States were the Revd Patrick Brewster of Paisley in Scotland and the Revd Henry Solly of Yeovil in Somerset. Although Brewster worked within the Established Church and Solly served a Dissenting Unitarian fellowship, their sermons could have been exchanged without either's congregation noticing much difference in the thrust of the message. On the other hand, their personalities and delivery were quite opposite. Brewster thundered denunciations in the style of the Old Testament prophets from whom he liked to draw his texts, while Solly, with a meeker, humbler manner, concentrated on the 'love thy neighbour as thyself' approach of Jesus. They were alike in their willingness to identify publicly with people's causes, even political ones. Both defended the Chartists. They eventually met while delegates to a conference of ministers in Manchester called by the Anti-Corn Law League, and both responded to Joseph Sturge's call for a coalition of Chartists and Anti-Corn Law Leaguers in his Complete Suffrage Union. Solly suffered the more severe penalty for his radicalism in being booted out of his pastorate in Yeovil; while Brewster was forced to stand trial before the Synod of Glasgow and Ayr to receive a sentence of suspension from his pastoral duties. Other disruptions in the Church of Scotland at the time, however, prevented enforcement of the sentence.[1]

Brewster, born in 1788, was already a man of fifty-three when his path crossed that of Solly in 1841. Solly was only twenty-eight at the time and was a new convert to both the antislavery and Chartist causes, in which Brewster had been active for several years. Both came from families of some substance and social standing, able to afford educational opportunities for their sons.

Brewster's father was rector of the grammar school at Jedburgh in Scotland and was ambitious for all of his sons, hoping to see them take orders in the Church of Scotland. Patrick's older brother, who became Sir David Brewster, left the ministry but earned an enviable reputation in education and science. Patrick was ordained in the abbey church of Paisley in 1818, where he remained until his death in 1859. He was twice married: first to the daughter of an Irish colonel, but she died at an early age; and then to the daughter of his predecessor in the abbey church. He fathered twelve children.[2] Solly grew up in London, where his father was in the mercantile business. In his autobiography he recounted that there were plenty of servants in their home – a clue to the family's affluence. Henry began to follow his father in business by taking a job in a counting-house but, in love with the theatre, left work to try his hand at writing drama. When that endeavour proved not to be successful he returned to the mercantile–financial arena but was evidently not attuned to that world. About 1840 he began seriously to examine religious doctrine with the thought of entering the ministry, and after training in a Baptist academy he accepted his first pastorate, not in a Baptist church but at the opposite end of the theological spectrum, in the Unitarian fellowship. Throughout his long life his religion seems to have been more oriented toward a social gospel than dedicated to any specific doctrine or creed.[3]

Brewster became involved in the problems of the labouring poor as early as 1820, when Paisley weavers were in the vanguard of an uprising. Although he had held his pastorate in the abbey church only two years, he was neither fearful nor reluctant to use his pulpit as a forum from which he 'lashed the spoilers of the poor' – some of them members of his own congregation. One of his favourite texts was Ecclesiastes 4:1: 'So I returned, and considered all the oppressions that are done under the sun: and behold the tears of such as were oppressed, and they had no comforter; and on the side of their oppressors there was power; but they had no comforter.' It was the workers, he asserted, who produced the wealth of the country but were robbed of it by the rich. Even the Church was faithless to its trust and actually helped to rob the poor of their inherent rights by preaching that rewards were to be expected in heaven. '"Here and now," he cried, "here and now the people starve; here and now they must be fed; here and now must the oppressor set the captive free."' Looking at Brewster's portrait, which shows a rather rugged face and a high forehead topped with wavy hair, one can easily imagine him, locks in disarray after forceful gestures and shakings of the head, as his jeremiads filled the church with 'an all-compelling swelling eloquence that raised class politics to a white heat, stirred the artisans to frantic enthusiasm, and roused to malignant anger the nobility and snobocracy of the district'.[4]

Brewster's criticisms of the 'Establishment' were first directed at the Scottish Poor Laws, then renewed against the English Poor Law of 1834 and further expanded with the rise of Chartism in the late 1830s. The texts of his published sermons were carefully chosen: for example, verse 2 of Psalm 5 – 'The wicked in his pride doth persecute the poor'; verse 8 – 'He sitteth in the lurking places of the villages...his eyes are privily set against the poor'; and verse 9 – he lieth in wait to catch the poor;...he draweth him into his net'. Others included verse 4 of Psalm 72 – 'He shall judge the poor of the people, he shall save the children of the needy, and shall break in pieces the oppressor'; verse 14 – 'He shall redeem their soul from deceit and violence: and precious shall their blood be in his sight'; and Psalm 82:3 – 'Defend the poor and fatherless; do justice to the afflicted and needy.'[5]

For Brewster it was clear that there was a conspiracy of Church and state against the poor; the priesthood had always lent its power to augment the power of the state. And anyone who exposed the conspiracy by preaching the true gospel to all classes must not only expect to be branded a reckless, seditious disturber of the peace, but must be prepared even to lose his life. So it had been with Jesus when he peeled away the layers of hypocrisy that covered the Pharisees and Sadducees as one peels the skin from an onion. Jesus had not evaded politics, nor had the Old Testament prophets, who exposed and denounced evil rulers. Indeed, the Scottish Reformation was political as well as religious, and had laid the basis for both civil and religious freedom. But present-day Scottish ministers, Brewster charged, had relinquished their independence by preaching that government belonged to the rulers and that the only duties of the people were to exercise obedience and submission. To Brewster, divine right and non-resistance were equally absurd, and both doctrines were props of tyranny.[6] He did not object to kings as such: they could be good; but they could also plunder and enslave. In Britain, more fault lay with the aristocracy, who had wrung power from the monarchy in order to possess it themselves, and had then used it to make the clergy dependent – so dependent that ministers of God served the ruling class (Brewster's label for them was the 'insatiable class') instead of serving God. Consequently both forms of government and systems of religion had been designed to 'enthrall' and deceive the people.[7]

Brewster's sermons were replete with allusions to workers as slaves. Both were held in thraldom, taught only to accept and submit. All were human beings capable of 'unlimited' improvement but were shut up in 'dungeons of darkness'. A destitute labourer was not a slave in quite the same sense as a black West Indian or American chattel, 'But every faculty and energy of body and mind are infinitely more at the command of his employer, and are really more productive of labour, than were ever those of the black bondsmen.' British workers, like black slaves, were subjected to 'Constables, Jails, Bridewells, Stocks, Whips, Collars, and Treadmills' – all instruments or agencies of torture. The suffering of slaves, Brewster cried, whether 'in the WHITE SLAVERY under the imperial and Christian autocrats of European civilization, or in the yet darker regions of Eastern and infidel dominion', was greater in sum total than that following in the wake of all insurrections and convulsions of society when people down through history had burst out against despotism.[8]

Such denunciations of oppression were followed by demands that his listeners do as much for the home variety of slaves as they had done for black chattels in the colonies or were doing for slaves in the United States. Britons had challenged and prevailed over vested interests in the fight for emancipation, he reminded them:

'you are surely, – not less, but more bound, by every obligation of reason and religion...to interfere in behalf of your fellow countrymen at home'. Slavery would never have been abolished if it had been left to the rulers. The people had spoken, and must do so again. Ministers had not hesitated to use their churches to preach deliverance for the slave; why should they not do the same for brethren of their own race? Why should religious men of the present be more timid than the prophets of old? Had Britain's ruling classes 'never themselves touched the spoil, nor rioted in abundance, when the people were pining for want? Have they fed the hungry? Have they clothed the naked? Have they instructed the ignorant?'[9] The answer was obviously no, since Brewster believed that operatives were crushed under the yoke of a master class as surely as if they were Negro slaves. Hunger was as compulsive a force as the lash of a slave-driver's whip. Could there be any torture worse than hearing one's children cry as they starved? What difference was there between a Scottish worker and a black slave? Only that no one cared about the fate of the free worker.[10]

Brewster dissected the Poor Laws with the same vehemence that characterized T. P. Thompson's criticisms. They provided for the poor unemployed, but not for the poor employed who needed to supplement their wages. But, whether employed or not, the poor were entitled to a fixed and legal provision. Brewster agreed with Will Cobbett that such a 'provision' should be considered a *property* right of those in need, not charity for them. The law against begging denied the right to even such relief from people who would be charitable, thus forcing a choice between starving and stealing. If a destitute labourer tried to emigrate or move to another parish where work was available, he was punished for deserting his family. Moreover, the Corn Laws required people to pay exorbitant prices for food. The result of bad laws, and bad administration of bad laws, was to force into idleness and dependence people who were 'vainly supplicating for leave to toil'.[11] Political economists might argue that capitalistic production would provide work and material blessings for all, but Brewster was convinced that the 'art of governing ill' negated the benefits of the industrial Revolution, which might have led to abundance: profits had gone to a few, leaving the poor as destitute as ever. This art of governing ill had included misrule in India and Ireland, unrighteous wars in Afghanistan and China, and the slave trade as well as exploitation of the working classes at home.[12] An example of distorted values was the degree to which military heroes – whom Brewster termed 'beasts of prey' – were honoured for carrying out a ruler's 'unhallowed ambition'. Yet many soldiers were themselves victims of the power structure. They had been driven from their humble cottages, forced to exchange their liberty for soldiering in order to obtain bread.[13] On this issue he was in complete accord with Sharp, Sturge, Thompson and the Liverpool four.

One of Brewster's more extreme heresies was his attitude toward property rights. All, he claimed, had the right to be fed from the produce of the earth, and monopolistic land rights were as false as the false claim to property in slaves. Like Granville Sharp he believed that both of these so-called rights had been gained by usurpation. The Corn Laws were especially bad because they gave landlords the monopoly they needed to keep food scarce and taxes high. Therefore repeal was a matter of justice and mercy – a religious question. Taxes should be on luxuries, not food; on property, not on poverty.[14]

In addition to being destitute the poor were kept ignorant lest they rise up to break their yokes. They were taught according to the Malthusian theory that they must limit their families in order to prevent unemployment when actually, Brewster contended, the causes of unemployment were social and political. Scotland had long been praised for setting a good example in areas of religion and education, but, challenged Brewster, did the people who filled the churches really care about their poor brethren? He answered his own harsh, rhetorical questions: 'Where is your HUMANITY? You have none. . . . Where is your JUSTICE? You have none. . . . Where is your RELIGION? You have none. . . .' So-called Christians who refused to care for the poor and naked were the generation of vipers that Jesus had rebuked.[15] In some of his sermons Brewster came close to advocating rebellion, as when he referred to the French people who rose up against the power structure and by doing so took a step toward freedom. Yet, like Harriet Martineau, he feared violence and so adopted the same tactic she used in England to avoid it in Scotland by warning the rulers of its inevitability should they persist in their short-sightedness, and by cautioning the people that the consequences of violence could be even greater suppression. He emphasized that, even after the revolutions for liberty in France and America, the people had not ended up with the power in their own hands.[16]

It was this stand against violence which led Brewster to espouse the cause of the 'moral force' Chartists in opposition to the 'physical force' Chartism of Feargus O'Connor's group, and which motivated him to join the Edinburgh Chartists in order to keep them in the path of peaceful protest.[17] During the summer and autumn of 1838, the Chartists held a series of public meetings throughout Great Britain to gain publicity and support for their programme. On 5 December a huge torchlit gathering assembled on Calton Hill in Edinburgh and it was a measure of Brewster's leadership that he was able to control the meeting and manoeuvre it into passing resolutions rejecting the use of physical force. The tenor of that meeting reflected his influence in another way – in its use of the white-worker–black-slave analogy, insisting that white slaves must be freed as black slaves had been.[18] The tone was reminiscent of Brewster's sermons, in which he found hope for white slaves in the knowledge that already 'the sable captive has hailed the glad sound of freedom'. It was a portent that every yoke could be broken and 'the oppressed go free'.[19]

Brewster's involvement with the Chartists undoubtedly contributed to the growing tensions within his church, already exacerbated by his attacks on the Poor Laws and on the indifference to the poor shown by rulers of both Church and state. He was becoming altogether too political for the Church authorities, not only by his leadership in the Calton Hill meeting but also by advocating that a convention of Scottish delegates ought to organise a union with like-minded Englishmen to operate on the principles of Thomas Attwood's Birmingham Political Union. The breaking-point was probably when he committed the 'heinous offense' of preaching in a Glasgow Chartist church.[20] The consequence was that he was called to stand trial before his synod. Far from daunted, he used the occasion to turn on his accusers, telling them they were engaged in just such a task as Satan set for idle hands. Despite their opposition, Chartism would prevail, and Chartist demands would one day be incorporated into the British constitution. Evidently he was convincing, for the Synod first dismissed the charge against him. However, the Marquis of Abercorn persisted, arguing that Brewster had violated ecclesiastical order by using his sermons for secular and political ends. Those ends were to rouse the poor to discontent and create a class war by encouraging contempt for rulers and for property rights. Despite the fact that Brewster produced a memorial from his Paisley congregation with the signature of 1600 who supported him, his final sentence (May 1842) was suspension from his pastorate for one year. Even after hearing the verdict Brewster's response breathed defiance:

> I will continue to advocate the rights and claims of the poor, till I see my country emancipated from the iron yoke under which it is crushed. You may attempt to convert the heathen abroad and the heathen at home, but they will not listen to your teaching. You must first strike the fetters from the limbs of your slave – you must restore him to the dignity and freedom of a human creature – you must make a man of him, before you can hope to make him a Christian.[21]

With a reputation as a Chartist leader as well as an abolitionist, it was inevitable that Brewster should be drawn into the debates over Chartism within the Glasgow Emancipation Society (GES), which reached a climax with the arrival of a radical American abolitionist, John A. Collins, in the spring of 1841. Collins was associated with William Lloyd Garrison, who, like Brewster, vehemently denounced both government and churches for protecting slavery. Moreover, Collins believed it to be the duty of every American travelling in Britain to denounce the class system, just as it was the duty of every Briton to take a stand against black slavery when visiting the United States. 'The English can condemn our prejudice against color, our Negro seats and Negro cars,' he wrote, 'while they are exercising the same prejudice against poverty, that we do against color.'[22] Collins suited action to words by openly associating himself with the Chartists.

In Glasgow, Chartists had for several months been active in disrupting meetings of the Emancipation Society, demanding that more attention be paid to 'slaves' in their own factories. The situation was complicated by the fact that during those same months, following the 1840 World Anti-Slavery Convention in London, local antislavery societies throughout Great Britain were being pushed to take sides either with the American Anti-Slavery Society (the Garrisonians), or with the American and Foreign Anti-Slavery Society, a less radical group on issues of Church and state. The American abolitionist Lucretia Mott, who visited

Glasgow after the London conference, admitted that she was 'not very sorry' when Chartists interrupted a GES meeting so that 'they could be heard to plead the cause of their own poor'. She specifically noted in her diary that she was 'much pleased' with Patrick Brewster.[23] Some of the Glasgow antislavery leaders, especially among the ministers, were adversely influenced by reports of Garrison's 'infidelity' and by his open espousal of women's rights. Others favoured the Garrisonian stance in America, but at the same time some of them were reluctant to equate the evils of the British and American social systems and shrank from espousing Chartism or John A. Collins's mission.

Disdainful of such timidity, the Revd Patrick Brewster appeared in Glasgow to champion both Collins and the Chartists. Since the two influential secretaries of the GES, William Smeal and John Murray, favoured the Garrisonian faction, the Chartists saw a chance to capitalize on the complex situation by trading pro-Garrison votes for pro-Chartist support. If the GES would admit a sizable number of Chartists to the Executive Committee, their votes would assure open backing for Garrison's American Anti-Slavery Society. Prodding by Brewster (who alleged that the leaders of the GES were letting the poor of Glasgow die of starvation) accompanied the political manoeuvring for votes. At a meeting on 25 March, Collins won a vote of support, and, at a meeting on 13 April which had been called to give Collins a chance to have his say, Brewster succeeded in getting a resolution passed which censured the GES Committee. However, on the same day, in a meeting of the Executive Committee, the conservatives won a victory by preventing an expression of preference for either of the American factions.[24]

Protests led to the calling of a public meeting in the Bazaar for 27 April. Upon a motion by James Turner of Thrushgrove, a long-time supporter of the working classes, Brewster was called to the chair – an immediate indication that the pro-Garrison and pro-Collins people had the majority. With him presiding, the meeting proceeded to add seventeen men of Chartist sympathy to the Executive Committee, and passed a definitely Chartist resolution:

That, in accordance with the sentiments contained in the Address presented by Mr Collins, & now read, it is the opinion of this meeting, that the People of this Country are entitled to those rights of Suffrage for which they have been contending these last three years, & that we pledge ourselves to use every moral and legal means to obtain our own liberty & the liberty of all mankind.[25]

Although the Bazaar meeting was later voted to have been irregular, its minutes were retained in the records and a subsequent meeting affirmed the appointment of the same seventeen new Committee members. An ensuing issue of the *Chartist Circular* endorsed Garrisonian abolitionism.[26]

Brewster and his allies had won an important victory by having a major British antislavery society endorse Chartist goals. Within a few months he found the opportunity to force consideration of another of his favourite issues, Corn Law repeal. The occasion grew out of George Thompson's championing of Indian Rajah Sattarah against unfair treatment by the East India Company. Brewster agreed with Thompson's condemnation of the monopolistic company, the same company against which Rathbone and Roscoe had fought so long, but questioned why the Rajah should be singled out as a victim when there were thousands of oppressed among the labouring classes of India: 'Why not do justice to the peasant as well as to the prince?' Moreover, there were thousands of destitute at home suffering because of the Corn Laws. Brewster believed they qualified for priority on the agenda of the GES. Thereupon he proposed an amendment to Thompson's resolution to censure the East India Company and to express sympathy for the Rajah. Brewster's amendment voiced sympathy with the rest of the exploited people of India, and

> upon the same principle, and by a stronger claim, . . . with the great body of the British people now suffering under the effects of those most impolitic and iniquitous Statutes – the Corn and Provision Laws of Britain – by which many thousands of industrious labourers and artizans have been thrown out of employment, and reduced to starvation, or driven into exile. . . .

The amendment called for repeal and revision of the twin sources of working-class misery, the Corn Laws and the Poor Laws.[27]

Shortly after his anti-Corn Law speech as the GES meeting, Brewster journeyed to Manchester to attend a national anti-Corn

Law conference. Ministers of all religious denominations had been summoned to consider 'the Subject of the Laws Restricting the Food of the Community'. The leadership was mainly from the Dissenting clergy, but several orthodox ministers such as Brewster were in full sympathy and quite ready to 'preach down' the Corn Laws as they had colonial slavery.[28] In fact, a main theme running throughout the meeting was that the wickedness of the Corn Laws could justly be compared with the evil of slavery. Both were moral issues and therefore the clergy had a responsibility to arouse the zeal of the country against the one as well as against the other. The Revd J. W. Massie of Manchester reminded the visitors to his town of how ministers had 'amalgamated' with the antislavery crusade to the extent that they took it for granted that the cause was compatible with their ministry. The same could now be true in this anti-Corn Law campaign. John Curtis, Sturge's American free-trader and abolitionist friend, spoke in support of transatlantic unity in both causes. Free trade between Britain and the free states of the United States, he promised, could replace trade with the slave states and strike a double blow against both slavery and monopoly.[29]

It was at this Manchester conference that the paths of Patrick Brewster and Henry Solly crossed for the first time and they found themselves in harmony on the issues of slavery, the Corn Laws and moral-force Chartism. Both had been first committed to the antislavery cause and through it had developed sensitivities to the oppression of the British working classes.

Solly's commitment to the abolition of slavery was relatively recent, and he did not take a public stand until the time of the World Anti-Slavery Convention of 1840, when he attended its sessions at the behest of his friend the Revd Francis Bishop, a West of England Unitarian. Several of his earlier friends, however, were strong antislavery thinkers who must have had some influence on his attitudes. Among them were the Revd Charles Wicksteed of Mill Hill Chapel in Leeds, Russell Lant Carpenter of the philanthropic Lant Carpenter family, and John Stuart Mill.[30] Solly met William Lloyd Garrison at the London convention and agreed with his non-resistance as well as his anti-slavery positions. When Garrison returned to Britain in 1846, Solly was among those actively supporting his mission, including the organization of a new Anti-Slavery League. He was also among those Unitarian clergymen who kept a firm position against welcoming proslavery American ministers into British pulpits.[31] Non-resistance convictions were to carry Solly, as the practicality of non-resistance had carried Brewster, into moral-force Chartism. Like Brewster, he believed Feargus O'Connor to be an evil genius among the Chartists and depicted him as such in his Chartist novel, *James Woodford.*[32]

The move from London to his first pastorate in Yeovil marked a momentous turning-point in Solly's life. Sorely missing the intellectual and cultural circles in which he had moved in the city, and stunned and dismayed by the 'anything but sociable & cordial' reception he was given by the only 'gentleman's' family in his new community, Solly turned to people of the artisan class for companionship. He discovered 'a sensible and talkative egg-dealer', a 'clever excellent-hearted superior minded journeyman cabinet-maker', a 'lively good-humoured clever tailor' and a 'nice 82 year old lady who does a great deal to make me happy'. But most important of all was his acquaintanceship and growing friendship with John Bainbridge, leader of the local Chartists and an activist in the Mechanics' Institute. It was Bainbridge who challenged Solly's Christianity by asking him how he could preach Sunday after Sunday and yet never apply Christ's teaching by doing something to help the poor. The upshot of their exchange was that Solly accompanied Bainbridge to a discussion at the Mechanics' Institute and was honest enough to admit that his ministry had fallen short.[33]

Before long, Solly's sermons contained overt comparisons of black slaves and white, 'the miserable victims of oppression, whether of a white skin or a dark, whether pining under tyranny in the old world, or the new'. And he appealed to the emotions of his congregation in a longer comparison:

The miserable father stripped of his children, the wretched husband torn from the wife of his bosom, the helpless woman shrieking under the lash, across the Atlantic waves, – in our own country, the wan and wasted widow, the drooping sickly orphan, the strong man, with his heart breaking at the crimes of his offspring, the wretched felon, with his heartbroken wife, soon to be a widow and the mother of orphans, these and a thousand shapes and forms of misery seem thronging round the doors of your Christian assemblies, while they exclaim in mournful accents, 'Followers of the blessed Jesus! Are you met to try to save us?'[34]

Solly's friendship with Bainbridge was the making of him as a lifelong preacher and practitioner of the social gospel, and from then on he could be counted on to defend Chartism. Although many liberal thinkers approved Chartist principles while deploring Chartist tactics, Solly defended both – even the practice of disrupting public meetings to gain attention for the Charter.

Like Brewster, Solly was not afraid to call public attention to the shortcomings of British royalty, the aristocracy or the Government. At a great public gathering in Yeovil to celebrate the birth of Queen Victoria's first child, Bainbridge moved and Solly seconded a resolution which asked the Queen to give thought to the poor women of her realm to whom the birth of children brought sorrow instead of joy because they could not be adequately fed and clothed. This failure to show proper respect for the Queen marked the beginning of Solly's split with his congregation, and his continuing association with the Chartists led to his eventual expulsion by the church officers. He and Bainbridge were both labelled 'leaders of sedition', and before long Solly received a letter from his church treasurer informing him that his salary could no longer be guaranteed.[35]

One of the acts Solly's congregation deplored was that he allowed himself to be made a delegate of the Yeovil Chartists to the Manchester meeting of ministers called by the Anti-Corn Law League. His mission was twofold: to oppose the Corn Laws, but also to speak for the Charter. By that time Solly had been convinced that the franchise would provide the means for proceeding against all grievances and therefore deserved priority.[36] In this stand he had already gone beyond most of the conference spokesmen, who included the Revd Patrick Brewster, George Thompson, the Revd Thomas Spencer of Bath, the Revd James Massie of Manchester, J. H. Hinton and Richard Cobden.[37]

Solly's conviction that the franchise issue deserved first consideration led to his whole-hearted endorsement of Joseph Sturge's Complete Suffrage Union, and, when Sturge issued the call for his Birmingham conference to be held in April 1842, Solly was delighted to be asked again to represent the Yeovil Chartists and, in addition, the Sturge supporters in Bridport to the south of Yeovil in Dorset. Meanwhile he gave public backing to the Sturge overtures by producing a supportive pamphlet, 'What says Christianity to the Present Distress?' He agreed with Brewster that the cause of the people was a Christian cause and ministers therefore had an obligation to participate and, if possible, to lead their flocks in the fight against the Corn Laws and for the Charter. He agreed with Sturge that the two causes were compatible and should be allied. At the conference Solly's role was to try to reconcile differences of opinion. For example, he was chosen to present a resolution by which the non-Chartist Sturge group acquiesced in calling for annual parliaments rather than insisting on their own preference, triennial parliaments.[38] Solly was among those chosen to serve on the Provisional Council of the Complete Suffrage Union, a product of the Birmingham meeting. Its function was to send out lecturing 'missionaries' to prepare for an autumn meeting which would consummate the union of moral-force Chartists with non-Chartists, including many Anti-Corn Law Leaguers. Dissenting clergymen were prominent among the leaders.[39]

Solly used the time between the April and December meetings to write and lecture for the movement, sometimes addressing Chartists in their Christian Chartist churches, all of which hastened his dismissal from his Yeovil pastorate. But a Tavistock congregation which counted working-class as well as middle-class people among its members was favourably impressed and hired him. In Tavistock he was free to continue his Chartist associations but found the Chartists there to be mainly physical-force O'Connorites, sceptical of middle-class leaders such as Sturge, and fearful that too much conciliation might dilute Chartism. Unable to get their backing, Solly found a Scottish group to support him as a delegate to Sturge's Complete Suffrage conference in December.[40] There is no evidence that Patrick Brewster had a hand in advising the Scots to make Solly their delegate, but it seems possible that he may have brought up Solly's name when one considers how close the two men were in their thinking. During the summer and autumn of 1842, Brewster too was busy lecturing for a union of the working and middle classes, trying to prepare Scottish Chartists for such a step. When Sturge arrived in Edinburgh and was honoured at a Complete Suffrage Union banquet, Brewster was among the local dignitaries acting as hosts. The *Nonconformist* was pleased to report that, when Patrick Brewster asked the blessing 'in his usual strong and emphatic manner', he worked in 'a good hard knock at "the monopolizers of the bread of God's people"'. Brewster also read the address in honour of Sturge.[41]

At the December Complete Suffrage gathering it quickly

became evident that some delegates believed it would be better to base the Union on a document with a new name rather than retaining the highly controversial Charter. The same principles could be enunciated, but with a label less likely to alienate the middle-class public whose support was needed. Both Brewster and Solly worked at attaining harmony, but in the last analysis it became apparent they would take different sides. Brewster stood with Sturge in favour of a new, less intimidating name. Solly, on the other hand, was more sensitive to those with loyalties to the labels 'Charter' and 'Chartist'. Moreover, he was critical of the Sturgeite leaders because they failed to work diplomatically through quiet, advance consultations with such reasonable Chartist leaders as William Lovett. When the final vote came, Solly was among the few abolitionists and among the few clergymen who stood with Lovett and 'The Charter'. Even after the crucial vote, he addressed the rump Sturge faction to try to win them over, but to no avail.[42]

Brewster and Solly personify the positions which point up the failure of a strong working-class and middle-class alliance. Although certainly the more aggressive personality of the two, and although he was undoubtedly a radical in the eyes of the Church and state establishment which he criticized so bitterly, Brewster, like Sturge, retained enough of the traditional *noblesse oblige* attitude to make him think that the working class needed leadership and direction from the middle class. Solly, on the other hand, was able to identify more personally not only with the Chartist rank and file, but with the suffering poor generally. He was able to empathize with their distrust of the upper and middle classes, and could see that in any alliance the concessions must be made from the top down or the people would simply fail to co-operate. For instance, he believed that Henry Vincent, as a consequence of voting with Sturge, lost a good deal of the support of the workers whose champion he had been.[43]

Solly retained faith that the working classes could produce their own leaders. This was well illustrated when he wrote *James Woodford, Carpenter and Chartist*, because he believed that simple people could and should be leading characters in novels, revealing their own thoughts and attitudes through their lives. 'It is time to recognize the fact', Solly wrote, 'that the views of working men with regard to what they want, think, and suffer, must be told by themselves, or by those who have lived among them and thoroughly understand them.' The hero of his novel, a moral-force Chartist, complains that his master's son refers to servants 'as if they were so many niggers'.[44] Using a modern psychological term, we can say that Solly realized the need for role models who came out of the working class itself. He tried to do for British workers what Harriet Beecher Stowe did for blacks when she made lowly slaves the heroes and heroines of *Uncle Tom's Cabin*.

When writing for workers, Solly took advantage of his early love for and experience with theatrical productions. One result was *Gonzaga*, a five-act drama that, while hardly a West End success, was produced by amateur actors of the Artisans' Institute in St Martin's Lane. Based on the historical Florentine conflict between Guelphs and Ghibellines, its hero, Gonzaga, though 'born and bred on dunghill straw', becomes the leader of the people's cause. His soliloquies are pleas for their rights:

> Oh! Men
> Of noble birth, why will you not discern
> That toiling slaves have souls, *and therefore* cry
> For Freedom?...
>
> We do not shrink from *work*, but from the chains
> Which Labour overtasked, ill-paid, reviled,
> And plundered, throws around our souls....
>
> The men whom nature destines for command
> Are born and reared in prisons...
> But silently, in darkness and alone,
> They tear away, with bleeding hands, the walls
> Which Circumstance and Wrong have built around,
> Till Day-light flashes in, – and they are FREE!

But, alas, that man of low birth who utters all the brave speeches for liberty, lets ambition run away with him, and dies a villain.[45] Another 'Dramatic Romance', entitled *The Shepherd's Dream*, was written for the stage but never performed. It was set in the time of the Protestant Reformation, its theme was the struggle against Tudor supremacy, and the plot turned on 'Romish' persecutions. Interwoven in the plot was the Greek legend of Diana and Endymion.[46]

Perhaps more than any other British abolitionist among those I know, Solly tried hardest and succeeded best at learning to know and respect working people on their own terms. He continued his antislavery associations, working with Sturge in politics, and with George Thompson in the Anti-Slavery League,[47] but he really became more and more committed to the belief 'that the slavery of ignorance and intemperance is infinitely worse than any human tyranny, requiring and justifying far greater sacrifices of every kind for its removal'.[48] Unlike so many benevolent reformers or middle-class would-be leaders of the poor, Solly actually went to live among those he wished to help, first by moving into a London slum and later by residing among the Lancashire mill workers. His eight-year-old daughter died of scarlet fever contracted when visiting the poor with her mother.[49] Sharing hardships and sorrows was a far cry from paternalistic do-gooding, and the response of the people among whom he lived and worked was exemplified in the remark of a Lancashire mill hand: 'Thae gentlefolk know nowt about us – cept Solly – he do know summut.'[50]

Solly characterized most charity as just a drop of water to those dying of thirst and, far ahead of most thinkers of his own time, advocated positive Government action to provide employment through public works when necessary. Even that early he was asking why a society capable of making such advances as the British had in science and the arts could not also figure out how to deal with poverty. He believed that society could, if the will to do so was there. The religious community could help by providing as much organization, zeal and money as it did for foreign missions.[51] Of course Solly believed in self-help with education as its base. Upper- and middle-class benevolence could provide Mechanics' Institutes and working men's colleges for adults, but he trusted the judgement of the people themselves to decide what they needed and wanted from such institutions. In Yeovil Solly organized a Mutual Improvement Society, but as his experience grew he realized that most such societies and institutes had a limited appeal, because they ignored the social and recreational element and therefore were doomed to lose the masses to the pubs.

His first suggestion for reaching more people was simply to change labels. Improvement Societies and Mechanics' Institutes sounded too forbidding; 'clubs' had a warm, congenial and inviting connotation. In a club one did not necessarily have to study, although classes and lectures would be available. One could have conversations, conduct business, enjoy dramatic presentations or play games. He sided with Martineau and T. P. Thompson when he wrote, 'That people's lives should be joyless is a great evil.' Play had a 'noble function'. Moreover, food and drink should be obtainable, and smoking allowed. Although Solly was active in the temperance movement, he thought the clubs should emphasize that they were not total-abstinence societies. Above all, clubs should not be managed by their paternalistic benefactors. He stipulated that at least half of the members of each council or executive board ought to be *bona fide* working men. His liberality extended to welcoming women also to the privileges of the clubs. Not all of these ideas were peculiar to Solly. He was generous in acknowledging the work of such forerunners as Lord Brougham and Dr George Birkbeck, and of several women, including Miss Adeline Cooper and Mrs Bayley, who had the good sense to organize the type of club Solly advocated.[52]

While still a Unitarian clergyman, for years Solly gave serious thought to organizing a non-sectarian religious group dedicated to making churches the centres of social religion, where services should not be dominated by the minister but all members could speak and discuss in a democratic fashion. Several of the men whom he consulted approved of the idea, among them George Dawson, a fellow Dissenting preacher, abolitionist and popular lecturer to working men. Others were less sanguine, and, although Solly drew up at least two prospectuses, one for 'The Society of Christian Disciples', and another for a 'Free Christian Union', the plan never came to fruition. Solly did, however, inaugurate Sunday evening lectures for working people who complained that they did not want to go to regular worship, but would like sermons that connected religion to political issues and practical economic problems.[53]

Solly had long been an admirer of Robert Owen and of Fourier and credited them with laying the basis for the co-operative movement which flourished in the last half of the nineteenth century. While working with the poor in London he heard and met George Jacob Holyoake, and endorsed the idea that home colonies could reverse the tide of the population movement into the city slums. He believed that industrial villages in the country would allow the working classes to combine skilled production with cultivation of their own food. Cabinet-making, book-binding and leather work were examples of crafts that would lend themselves to a rural setting. The building of such colonies could be financed from a system of Post Office savings of the workers themselves. Since land and houses were always good securities, payments could be gradual. 'Town rookeries' of moral and physical corruption would be supplanted by healthy living in co-operative social communities which would restore dignity and self-respect to working people.[54] On this issue Solly was overly idealistic. Harriet Martineau was more realistic in facing the fact that most urban workers would dislike being resettled in rural colonies.

When Solly published his autobiography at the age of eighty, he subtitled it 'The Story of an Unfinished Life', a title indicative of his philosophy that even in old age one could execute 'Strokes for Freedom'.[55] In a letter to Solly one of the patrons of his organizations for working people drew a cartoon depicting 'Solly the Slave-driver' cracking a whip over three glum-looking men labelled 'Trustees', as he drives them through a door labelled 'Committee Room'. Ever reasonable and moderate in tone even when presenting radical ideas, Solly could drive people from words to action, and seems to have been extremely effective in convincing people of wealth and title to lend their names, time and purses to his causes.[56]

During the 1860s Solly had a hand in starting and helping to edit a paper called the *Bee-Hive*, the organ of the London Trades Council, which was effective in reminding its readers that the Union cause in the American Civil War was the cause of the workers, personified by President Lincoln as 'the railsplitter'. During the following three decades he tried several editing-ventures: the *Common Good*, which merged with *Capital and Labour*, a monthly *Workingman's Magazine*, and *Our Magazine*. All of them dealt with issues of labour and capital, including socialism, land tenure, unions, the eight-hour day, co-operative movements and parliamentary reform; but financial difficulties ended these endeavours.[57]

Along with such editing projects, Solly continued to lecture and to preach guest sermons, even after his retirement from the ministry. His themes ran the historical gamut from 'The Peasant Wars in Germany' of the sixteenth century to the current women's rights movement (both of which he approved). He discussed literary figures such as Milton, Goethe and Byron, and even ventured into the world of science and pseudo-science with an attack on the reality of ghosts which he based on Sir David Brewster's work. His days were also filled with writing letters to editors protesting injustices, proposing reforms and agitating for community improvements.[58] Apparently his last public effort was to establish a chair of Political Science in the London School of Economics and Political Science, which was started with a subscription fund initiated by Sidney Webb in 1896.[59]

My impression of Solly is that he was a modest man, a man of reason, never the demagogue nor overbearing. There is very little material in the Solly Collection that reveals his personal life, but those few items reflect a happy marriage which lasted long enough to celebrate a golden wedding anniversary, and affectionate relationships with his two daughters (one of whom married the son of his good friend Charles Wicksteed). There is one appealing letter from his young grandson, who had just been learning about industrial villages and how a family with one acre and a breeding sow (because, the boy wrote, pigs will eat anything and pig manure is good for the land) could support themselves. It ends, 'I had such a happy time with you at Tilford g-papa. I must thank you again for it extremely. . . . Your loving grandson, Joe.'[60] One other personal glimpse of Solly and his family relationships comes in a cordial letter from his brother Thomas, anticipating meeting Henry in Paris. Thomas thinks that meeting Henry there 'will be especially piquant, – something like meeting the Archbishop of Canterbury in a billiard room. It is so delightful for poor sinners to discover that even great virtue can still enjoy cakes and ale.'[61]

Solly was present at the great meeting when the abolitionists of Britain packed and overflowed Exeter Hall to celebrate the Emancipation Proclamation, and a few years later he saw the enfranchisement of American ex-slaves. He viewed the extension of the franchise in Britain under the Reform Act of 1867 as a parallel, but also limited, advance, and lived to witness another achievement of the working man with the organisation of the Labour Party in 1900.

I have coupled Patrick Brewster and Henry Solly as two abolitionist clergymen who exemplify my thesis that concern for the black chattel slave and the white wage slave went hand in hand. When Brewster died in 1859 a monument was erected over his grave in Paisley churchyard with an inscription that honours him as 'an elegant and powerful advocate for the political enfranchisement of the people, the abolition of negro slavery, a national system of education, and the repeal of the Corn Laws, the cause of temperance, and the rights of our able-bodied and infirm poor'.[62] Henry Solly lived until 1903. An identical tribute could have been written for him, but I like better one which comes from the pen of a working man in a letter to Solly:

I was delighted when I heard you had come back amongst us. You are at home amongst us. And I know of no one who can do more good amongst working men than yourself, and had I not been so unfortunate at home and had the whole of my leisure [sic] time and my means been continualy [sic] absorbed by years of sickness & consequent expense I would have gladly seconded as best I could the laudable efforts you have been for years making for the social & moral elevation of our class.[63]

# 7 Joseph Barker

In the United States in 1856 emotions were running high in the wake of the 'civil war' in Kansas precipitated by the Kansas-Nebraska Act, which had nullified the old Missouri Compromise. By doing so, it had reopened the territories of the Louisiana Purchase to slavery, thus setting off a rush of settlers from North and South alike, each group intent on controlling the destiny of the region. In November of that year an English immigrant wrote from Omaha City, Nebraska,

> I am not one of those who are anxious about the colored races, and careless about the white ones. But I think we can never secure justice to the whites so long as we deny justice to the colored. Liberty is essential to the development of all races. Liberty is the life of all men. The slave-holders here are the friends of oppression – everywhere. The abolitionists of America are the friends of freedom and progress – everywhere.[1]

The writer of the letter, Joseph Barker, had been active in anti-slavery work in England since the late 1820s, and had aligned himself with Garrisonian abolitionism when he met William Lloyd Garrison and Frederick Douglass while they were on their 1846 missions to Great Britain. Interested in a variety of reforms, Barker was to make antislavery and Chartism two of his major concerns. Thus he is another example of those thinkers who recognized the inseparability of the basic problems of exploited black and white labour. A man given to extremes in dedication, his attitudes toward labour as well as his ideas on governmental authority, social structure and religion were to undergo pendulum-like swings during his career.

Barker was born (1806) into a poor family in Bramley, Yorkshire, whose livelihood came from the weaving-trade. Joseph often recalled the two rooms, one above the other, which housed the family of seven. There were no curtains, no carpets, no rugs, and dust sifted down through the boards from the spinning jennys and looms which were kept upstairs, crowding the beds in which the family slept. Undernourishment and even biting hunger were taken for granted by his parents, who enforced long hours at the looms. When Joseph's legs became crooked they regarded the condition as inevitable; but the boy would go off alone, tie his ankles together and force himself to stand upright for up to an hour – at least so he said – a painful but in the long run an effective treatment.[2]

Life was also sternly religious in the Wesleyan Methodist home. Each day Joseph's father read to the family from the Bible, and took literally the admonition not to spare the rod, except when he substituted a flogging-rope. The impact of this upbringing set up contradictory reactions in the boy. On the one hand he suffered from a fearful guilt about his sinfulness, but on the other hand he very early developed doubts about a God who was so vengeful and a religion which seemed to condone so many cruelties. He was especially tormented about the idea of hell, despite all his mother's efforts to explain and to comfort him. On Sundays he envied the children who could run and play at games instead of attending chapel.[3]

Despite a childhood characterized by deprivation to the point of actual beggary, Joseph was able to pick up the essentials of an education. His older brother and sister taught him to read 'by means of a big thick folio family Bible', and his learning was continued through regular Sunday School attendance. By the age of sixteen he had decided to stop asking troubling questions and publicly to acquiesce in Methodist teachings even though he still harboured private doubts. Accordingly, he joined the church, went to prayer meetings two or three times a week, visited the sick, and even began to function as an 'exhorter' or home missionary. When finally his father's financial situation improved, Joseph was sent to a Methodist school in Leeds, and in 1828 he was ready to begin his probation as a 'New Connexion' minister.[4] Nine years later, in Wortley, near Leeds, he began to publish the *Evangelical Reformer*. His inquiring mind and his restless seeking are evidenced by the fact that in the space of the next ten years he moved from evangelicalism through a brief association with Quakerism to Unitarianism. Later he embraced deism, and then deserted religion for a secular stance.[5]

Family tradition has it that Joseph was a headstrong boy who, according to his mother, 'could be led but not driven'. Even during his early years as a Methodist minister he gave evidence of a tendency to reject authority. For example, 'New Connexion' Church rules forbade marriage while one was on probation circuit, but Barker defied the injunction and married a Miss Frances Salt of Betley, in Staffordshire, even though it meant losing a year's probation credit. Before long he was accused of holding heretical views, yet, able and popular, he managed to gain acceptance to 'full connexion' in 1833. Eight years later he was expelled because he denied that baptism was a divinely appointed rite and refused to administer it. He also began to apply literally the Biblical injunction to take no thought for the morrow, and as a consequence protested against Church funds for retired ministers, Friendly Societies, or any kind of savings or insurance; and he refused any salary, accepting only voluntary donations. Moreover, he began to question John Wesley's writings, believing them to be 'full of confusion and error'. The Church trial which ended in his expulsion lasted seven days before he was voted to be incorrigible; but the measure of his leadership and influence is found in the fact that twenty-nine societies, involving over 4000 members, who became known as Barkerites, then followed him out of the New Connexion.[6]

While seeing in Barker a genuinely inquiring mind, one sees also a man who had little staying-power. Exceedingly enthusiastic, he always made extravagant claims for whatever his current cause or philosophy might be. Then, when he again became dissatisfied, his discouragement led to equally exaggerated attacks on whomever or whatever he blamed. Impetuous in the extreme, his denunciations of opponents were as excessive as his praise for supporters. Richard D. Webb of Dublin, who was associated with Barker in Garrisonian abolitionism, characterized him as unbalanced – whatever hobby horse he rode ran away with him.[7] And George Jacob Holyoake, who also had much in common with Barker in their reform efforts, wrote that 'his rotary imputations were applied by turn to every party to which he ceased to belong', and that 'He left to the adherents of every opinion that he espoused, a legacy of exposition and denunciation....'[8] Holyoake's appraisal of Barker touches on a psychological explanation: that, not being 'well-used' himself, he avenged his lot by never treating anyone else well. It seems possible that his personality may have been warped by the deprivations and sufferings of his childhood. Sitting long hours at a spinning jenny left him with a deformity that was not corrected until his adult years. Conceivably the physical warping was easier to straighten out than the mental. Page after page in his reminiscences is devoted to examining his attitudes toward his parents and disclaiming any lingering bitterness – leaving the reader thinking he doth protest too much. But perhaps it is unfair to label Barker as warped, since any personality quirks he developed must be weighed against his lifelong sympathy with the disadvantaged. 'I can never cease to feel a peculiar interest in the class with which I so long and so grievously suffered', he wrote in 1854.[9]

Someone who knew Barker as a young minister described him as tall and ungainly with long, unkempt hair, inclined to slovenly dress and with rustic manners, but with a countenance and eyes which arrested attention.[10] His reputation as a speaker was based on his simple and sincere forthrightness rather than on oratorical effusions. Obviously there was something charismatic about the man, considering the numbers who followed him out of the New Connexion. As an evangelical he espoused the usual gamut of religious causes, including temperance, charity to the poor and Sunday Schools, always with the underlying theme of help to the working class. On the issue of Sunday Schools, for example, he was considered to be a radical because he advocated using such schools to teach poor, unschooled children to write, and that, the conservatives argued, was Sabbath-breaking.[11]

One of the stands Barker took in the 1830s was in opposition to Owenite Socialism because of its non-religious, therefore 'infidel', character. Writing to the *Gateshead Observer* in 1840, he charged that its aim was to overthrow society and break up the family, 'to have property, women and children thrown into one common stock, and to live and herd together like beasts of the field'. In later years, after he had rallied to defend William Lloyd Garrison and Henry C. Wright from the charge of infidelism, he felt obliged to admit to George Jacob Holyoake in the pages of the *Reasoner* that he had been wrong in his assessment of Owen and socialism.[12] He also took up the defence of the Chartists who were accused of irreligion. Although Barker strongly disagreed with Feargus O'Connor and physical-force Chartism, he defended O'Connor's *Northern Star* by pointing out to its critics that, although the paper carried advertisements for 'infidel' books, it also advertised those with a Christian message. Barker used the second periodical he published for that defence, a paper he pointedly named the *Christian* to show that he held no narrow sectarian bias.[13]

It was during his period of Unitarian persuasion that Barker published the *Christian*. While its first volume, in 1844, carried mostly religious material, one can note a gradual inclusion of more articles on politics and reform issues, especially antislavery and Chartism. By 1845 he was declaring that there was no inconsistency between religion and politics, that Christian people needed to be informed on such issues as universal suffrage; annual parliaments; tax reform; capital punishment; laws, such as primogeniture and entail, which worked against the common people; and the corruptions in the state Church. His first public address on a political–religious subject was in support of the abolition of Church rates. In fact, Barker in the 1840s was already doing what Henry Solly later advocated: giving sermons for workers on subjects of importance to them but without the rituals of worship usual in church services. He declared that all property of the Church of England should be confiscated and the money spent on relief and education for the poor.[14] This shift in Barker's priorities led directly to the establishment of his third periodical, the *People*, in 1848.

No doubt the evolution of Barker's opinions was influenced by some of the friends he made among the Unitarian abolitionists, especially Sir John Bowring. Bowring was closely associated with T. Perronet Thompson in politics, in antislavery endeavours, and in editing the *Westminster Review* with the aim of making it the leading advocate of popular reforms.[15] As a wine merchant and occasionally a diplomat–financier before becoming an MP, Bowring spent a good bit of time in France, where he had associated with anti-Bourbon liberals, including Lafayette, and with the Abbé Gregoire, one of the French antislavery leaders. Because of those radical associations Bowring was arrested in Calais in 1822 and spent several weeks in prison in Boulogne.[16] His business took him frequently to Spain and Portugal as well, and, being fluent in their languages, he published a book on the slave trade in Spanish at the time when Britain was exerting diplomatic pressure as well as holding out financial inducements to those countries to end their participation in the trade.[17]

Bowring used his influence in Unitarian circles to raise money to equip Barker with a steam press, thus enabling him to publish 300 volumes chosen from belles lettres, religion, philosophy, history and science under the title of the 'Barker Library'. People could subscribe at six shillings per book or one shilling a week over four years. On the opening day the Barkers provided a cold dinner for the people assembled in one of the warehouses, and Bowring spoke on the importance of knowledge to all classes, especially to the working people, of whom Barker was one. Then, amid the people's cheers, the first sheet was printed on the new press – a poem written by Bowring himself for the occasion. It ended on a rousing reform note:

> But mightiest of the mighty means
> On which the arm of progress leans,
> Man's noblest mission to advance,
> His woes assuage, his weal enhance,
> His rights enforce, his wrongs redress, –
> MIGHTIEST OF MIGHTY IS THE PRESS.[18]

Barker is credited with being a pioneer in the cause of cheap literature for the masses.[19] Like Harriet Martineau and T. P. Thompson, he had only disdain for reformers who fed the people lofty scientific or philosophical treatises with no regard for political and economic issues relevant to their own problems; yet, speaking from experience, he also insisted that their vision could and should be lifted to broader horizons by introducing them to the great classics of world literature.

Bowring's involvement in politics must have rubbed off on Barker. Elected an MP for Bolton in 1841, Bowring carried on in the House of Commons in favour of the same causes he promoted through the pages of the *Westminster Review*: free trade, popular education, poor laws, suffrage extension and reforms in justice, including the abolition of corporal punishment in the Army – a platform he shared with his friend T. Perronet Thompson.[20] Barker, too, began to acknowledge the role of government in reform, but true to his own personality he carried his views to more radical lengths than either Bowring or Thompson. Like them, he favoured suffrage extension, and like Thompson supported the Chartists, but went beyond him in a more militant, more strident rhetoric of Chartist agitation. Bowring sympathized with republican developments in the

United States and France; Barker denounced the British monarchy and called for republicanism at home. He also lined up with the more radical group on the land question by calling for taxes which would force unused land into production or else force its sale, thus breaking up the immense estates of the rich.[21]

On the question of trades unions Barker was more conservative, although he insisted that he had held the same views as a labourer even before he became an employer in the printing-business. He had no objection to men uniting for better hours and wages as long as they used legal and 'reasonable' means, but he opposed union attempts to limit the numbers of apprentices or the number of men who could join a trade, and he felt it his duty to protect employees who preferred not to join a union. In fact, he had to admit when attacked on the point that he preferred to hire non-union men, though he would never dismiss a worker who joined one. He proudly asserted that he paid higher wages than most employers, even though some applicants had volunteered to work for less.[22]

During Barker's Unitarian phase he came in contact also with William and Mary Howitt (other friends of Bowring and of Harriet Martineau) and they mutually influenced each other. While Barker had fleetingly been drawn to Quakerism, the Howitts were birthright members of the Society of Friends; but, as they had begun to write and moved into sophisticated literary circles, they had gradually and quietly shifted away from Quaker orthodoxy to a broad and tolerant non-sectarian religious position. Barker's disaffection with the Friends was more noisily expressed and he broke with them abruptly as he rebelled against their strictures, making Joseph John Gurney the target of his public attacks on Quaker doctrines. In 1845 Barker was a guest preacher in the Unitarian church which the Howitts had begun to attend, and he arrived with so great a reputation that several noted London Unitarian ministers turned out to hear him. According to Mary Howitt's account, Barker 'preached powerfully in racy [Yorkshire] dialect'. His sermon centred on Jesus the Son of Man, not Jesus the Son of God, Jesus 'the friend and fellow sufferer of the human race, the great Teacher, the lover of each individual man, woman, and child, and Who was, as he expressed it, "a loomp o' luv"'.[23]

Besides Unitarianism, Barker and the Howitts had in common their abolitionist activities, and both of the Howitts had a keen sensitivity toward issues connected with working-class problems, which they addressed in the pages of the *People's Journal* (later *Howitt's Journal*) as Barker did in the *Christian* and the *People*.[24] Each of their papers touted the publications of the other, and, when the first volume of the Barker Library came out, the Howitts' 'Literary Notice' carried fulsome praise for its publisher. They pointed out that, once a common weaver, Barker had acquired knowledge and 'took to spreading it', putting the yarn of knowledge together as skilfully as he had previously manipulated his weft and warp. They liked the fact that he was choosing books for his library without regard for church or sect and that he persisted in teaching simple Christianity minus dogma, despite attempts to discredit him as a heretic.[25] Among others who commended Barker for his 'good work among the humbler classes' was the eminent Unitarian James Martineau, brother of Harriet.[26]

Exactly when Barker became an abolitionist is hard to pinpoint. In the 1820s and early 1830s, when emancipation was such a big public issue, he seems to have been largely absorbed in his own controversial career as a Methodist New Connexion minister, but he later recalled that it was while he was still a circuit preacher in Sheffield that he was first called upon to speak on slavery in a public meeting. There, in a new chapel and before a strange audience, he 'was so confused and fluttered, that I was not even able to read the resolution entrusted to me, without the greatest difficulty, and was altogether unable to speak' – a condition hard to believe of Barker, although he claimed that he experienced the same difficulty in other unfamiliar settings. The Quakers who helped Barker religiously, the Backhouses, Peases and Richardsons, were all prominent abolitionists, and the influence of those contacts was certainly reinforced by Barker's friendship with the Howitts and Bowring. Nowhere in his own voluminous writings does Barker speak of a 'conversion' to an antislavery position, however, thus leaving the impression that he may always have been an abolitionist, perhaps having absorbed that part of John Wesley's teachings while a boy.[27]

At the time of the World Anti-Slavery Convention held in London in the summer of 1840, Barker met some of the American delegates, but not William Lloyd Garrison. It seems natural that Garrison should have been curious about and wanted to meet Joseph Barker, whose vocabulary matched his own in denouncing slavery, and that Barker should have been drawn to that

particular American leader's circle. Barker initiated the acquaintanceship by writing to Garrison in 1842 to tell him that he
sometimes had a chance to read the *Liberator*. He praised his
fellow editor as a lover of truth, free from sectarianism, and he
enclosed a copy of his own pamphlet on non-resistance. Actually,
before they ever met, Garrison had heard Barker's praises sung by
Elizabeth Pease (who had donated £30 for Barker's press) and by
Henry C. Wright, the American Garrisonian who, also at
Elizabeth Pease's urging, met Barker in 1843 and spent three
nights in the Barker home. The two men discovered their like-
mindedness immediately, agreeing on their non-resistance and
peace principles, in their sympathies for exploited workers, and in
their opposition to the Church and state establishment.[28]

In this relationship, too, one sees evidence of Barker's
compulsion always to outdo those with whom he found
compatibility, always to exaggerate his own positions. Since
Wright was as radical as Barker in ideas (adhering to the
Garrisonian concept of 'Christian anarchy'), and even more
eccentric in his personal life, Barker's self-revelations to Wright
are among his most extreme statements, making him sound far
more of an anarchist than he actually was. He declared to Wright
that he could not acknowledge the authority of anyone to rule
him but God, that there were no laws but Christ's laws, and that
governments must be annihilated because it was useless to try to
reform them. Like Harriet Martineau, he vowed that he could
never accept anything (such as a pension) from the Government,
because the money would be taken from the people without their
consent. He did not believe in using the courts to sue anyone, and
thought that not even criminals should be prosecuted. All that, of
course, was completely at odds with what Barker was writing
every day in his own publications and with his on-going efforts to
work through politics, especially in embracing Chartism. Yet
Wright pronounced Barker to be 'the most radical, consistent
and independent-minded reformer I have yet met in England'.[29]

Garrison finally met Barker during his 1846 trip to England
when he travelled to Wortley to see the man who had already
gained notoriety as a radical writer. His enthusiastic verdict was
that Barker was 'a great, active and glorious-minded reformer', in
contrast with whom 'all the popular great men of the day are
pigmies', one of the most remarkable men on that side of the
Atlantic, who would be 'an anti-slavery auxiliary of no small

value'. Garrison was sure that Barker with his new steam press would work a revolution in cheap printing in England. In fact, the two editors discussed the possibility of co-operating on a monthly periodical to be the organ of the newly formed Anti-Slavery League, a plan that was never consummated.[30] Barker was later one of the signatories to an antislavery letter from British Unitarian ministers to Unitarian ministers in Boston, Massachusetts, which Garrison published in the *Liberator* in 1847, and which was followed by Barker's first article in the *Liberator*, entitled 'Free Discussion'. Again Barker played up to Garrisonian Christian anarchism: 'Leave the politics of the world, and meddle only with the politics of truth', he admonished. Yet at home in England he continued to support the Chartist six points for political reform and in the summer of 1847 attended a meeting of electors in Wortley in which he not only urged the election of Joseph Sturge to represent Leeds, but also, a few days later, offered himself as a second candidate.[31]

Frederick Douglass and William Wells Brown were other Garrisonian abolitionists on missions to Great Britain with whom Barker became friendly. Both visited him in Wortley, and Barker published an edition of Douglass's *Narrative*. Unfortunately Barker's enthusiasm for an edition cheap enough to be available to poor workers overran his business acumen and he lost money on the printing – enough of a loss to put a damper on any possibility of doing the same for Brown's autobiography. After Douglass returned to the United States, Barker became an English agent for his paper, the *North Star*.[32]

Of all these American abolitionists Barker was the most intrigued by Henry C. Wright, whose radicalism he found so congenial. At first he was put off by Wright's religious views and objected strenuously to Wright's using the Sabbath to hold meetings not only on temperance and antislavery, but on free trade, universal suffrage and non-resistance as well; but it may have been Wright who convinced Barker that, if such issues were important to Christianity's mission, the Sabbath ought to be used to bring them before the people.[33] Barker's progression from strict evangelicalism to Unitarianism and then to a rejection of churches and of the Bible as revealed truth would probably have occurred without the influence of Garrison and Wright, but association with them accelerated its pace. Indeed, Barker credited Wright with having opened his eyes about the churches. Again he tried to outdo his mentors in denunciation, not only of churches, because as institutions they had strayed from Biblical Christianity, but also in questioning the authority of the Bible itself. In language reminiscent of Garrison's, he denounced Abraham, Isaac and Jacob as 'slaveholders, liars and adulterers'.[34]

Another subject on which Barker agreed with the American Garrisonians was women's rights, although his convictions had been formed before he met them. His associates in Unitarianism, John Bowring and the Howitts, had long been supportive of the women's movement, and the fact that the women of the Garrison group were refused the right to sit as delegates in the 1840 World Anti-Slavery Convention undoubtedly was a factor in their being drawn together.[35]

An area in which British abolitionists, among them Barker, took the lead in influencing American abolitionists was in recognizing that the denial of rights to the labouring classes in Great Britain had an intrinsic connection with chattel slavery in America. 'I see reason enough why we should seek the destruction of slavery,' Barker wrote, 'but none why we should enslave ourselves to the most cruel and heartless monopolists that ever plundered and oppressed a nation.... If I cannot put down slavery abroad, without practising robbery at home, I will let it stand.'[36] The visits of Garrison, Douglass, and Wright to Great Britain in the mid 1840s came in the wake of the failure of Joseph Sturge's Complete Suffrage Movement and when Chartist rebellion was building up to its 1848 climax. Because of the agitation of the issue in abolitionist circles, these three Americans (and several others as well) announced publicly their support for Chartist principles, a stand which raised them even higher in Barker's estimation.[37] At a meeting in Holborn, Garrison declared that he did not want it said of him that he had come to England only to capitalize on the popularity of the antislavery cause and had done nothing to cheer on the working men 'in their labour to effect redemption for themselves'. He gloried in the fact that he was a working man, having learned his trade as an apprentice printer, and had worked hours as long as those of plantation slaves.[38]

Garrisonian abolitionists in America had taken the stand that political activity violated antislavery principles because any political activity, even voting, supported a system which rested on the US Constitution's recognition of slavery as legal. In Great

Britain, however, where emancipation was already accomplished, there was no such barrier to political activity; so Americans travelling there were not being philosophically inconsistent when they supported Chartism. Trouble would follow, however, when Barker emigrated to the United States and carried his support for political abolitionism with him. Over there, his deviation from Garrison's leadership led him into acrimonious debates with the Ohio abolitionists among whom he settled.[39]

The beginnings of Barker's connections with both antislavery and Chartism seem to have been based on his religious beliefs and activities. The *Christian* for 1847 reports his preaching on the churches' responsibility toward slavery, and his insistence that English clergymen who visited the United States had a duty to speak out against the evil. At the same time he was lecturing the churches on their obligation to assist the poor through education, cheap libraries and political reforms.[40] By 1848 he was preaching in the Christian Chartist churches which had been organized by Arthur O'Neil, and also speaking to working men's groups on religious topics.[41] As in the cases of Patrick Brewster and Henry Solly, Barker's religious orientation dictated his choosing 'moral force' over 'physical force' Chartism. Like Solly he went further than most abolitionists by defending the Chartists' refusal to unite with Joseph Sturge in the Complete Suffrage Union if it meant giving up the 'whole Charter', including the name. He insisted that it was not the Chartists who separated themselves from the middle classes, but the middle classes who abandoned the Chartists.[42] None the less, he campaigned for Sturge in 1848 when Sturge stood for Leeds, and still supported the idea of a coalition of all reformers.

To that end Barker co-operated in a meeting to organize 'The People's League'. Colonel T. P. Thompson was in the Chair and among those attending were William Howitt; Joseph Sturge and Sturge's friend Edward Miall, whose *Nonconformist* was the official organ of the Sturge movement; Sturge's son-in-law, Charles Gilpin; Sharman Crawford, MP; and the Chartist leaders Henry Vincent and William Lovett. Yet in this middle-class assemblage Barker admitted that he liked the lower classes better than the middle classes; they were more honest. True, there were many who were ignorant and depraved, but they would improve with education, guidance and justice. Just as slave-holders made brutes of men and then declared them to be unfit for freedom, so the British upper and middle classes acted toward the British working classes and toward the Irish. Later Barker was to abandon the coalition approach in favour of a genuine working-class movement not dependent on middle-class liberals.[43]

In the late spring of 1848 Barker extended his Chartist role by beginning publication of the *People*, whose subtitle, 'Their Rights and Liberties, their Duties and their Interests', indicated the thrust of his intentions. But, in taking up the cause of political Chartism, Barker, as usual, outdistanced the platform of those he now championed. He advocated not only universal suffrage, equal electoral districts, the ballot and annual parliaments, but also the abolition of the monarchy, the aristocracy and the Church of England.[44] For 'God Save the Queen' Barker proposed to substitute a 'people's anthem' whose refrain should be 'God Save the Poor'.[45]

Given the fears of the times over revolutions in Ireland and on the continent, and Chartist upheavals in the wake of hard times in England and Wales, it is not surprising that the authorities worried as the circulation of the *People* climbed to 20,000 and as the masses poured out to hear Barker lecture. He was a principal speaker at one meeting in Leeds where the attendance was estimated at between 10,000 and 15,000, and the crowd at one of his lectures in the West Riding was estimated at 20,000. He had also, by then, expanded his publications to include *The Reformer's Almanac, and Companion to the Almanacs*, dedicated 'To the Suffering Masses, as an Expression of Sympathy with Them in Their Sorrows, as an Expression of Indignation against Their Tyrant Plunderers and Tormentors, and as a Pledge of His Desire to Aid in Annihilating Oppression and Wrong the Wide World Over, This Volume Is Inscribed by the Author.'[46]

At the Liverpool summer assizes in 1848 a bench warrant was issued for the arrest of Barker as a Chartist agitator. Still he continued his lecturing as well as his 'incendiary' writings and refused an invitation from a man in Oldenbury who offered to hide him in his house, 'a very retired place', until the storm subsided.[47] Within a few weeks Barker was arrested in Manchester, detained overnight, and then released on bail. Public support for him was evidenced by the fact that on the same day as his arrest he was elected an MP for Bolton by an 'immense' majority, and while he was awaiting trial he was elected to Leeds town council. A Quaker friend, James Bryce, offered to be bound for Barker, but bail had been quickly raised and a 'penny tribute' fund provided financial assistance. One of the specific charges was that Barker had conspired to burn Manchester, but the witness (reportedly a Manchester Chartist but possibly an *agent provocateur*) was unable to identify Barker in Court and proved to have perjured himself. Barker steadfastly refused to give bonds or plead guilty, so the prosecution was abandoned with the issuance of a *nolle prosequi*. Barker was lucky that he was not prosecuted on a separate charge of violating publication laws, because one of the men tried at the same time was sentenced to two years in jail simply for circulating Barker's pamphlets.

Of course Barker capitalized on the event by publishing a special account of his imprisonment, complete with details of his cell fifteen feet below ground with only a small window at the top through which a bit of light entered. One of his jailers was a 'tyrant' who withheld his water rations, but the other turned out to be a sympathetic reader of the *People*. Barker charged that the authorities had kidnapped him to prevent his election to Parliament. Actually, there was a contest over the technicalities of the election and Barker never took his seat. Although a hero to many, others considered him far too radical. As a result of the notoriety, he suffered public insults, people 'took liberties with his property', he was denied insurance, his children were refused admission to schools, and mothers refused to let their daughters play with his – all of which, of course, simply strengthened his hatred of the Government.[48]

Meanwhile American abolitionist friends had been urging Barker to come to the United States 'to sow the seeds of truth in the vast prairies of the West', as Frederick Douglass put it.[49] No doubt he was flattered by such entreaties and paid more attention to them as his disillusionment with the prospects of liberty in England grew. At first he had not favoured emigration as a solution to the problem of British workers. He thought the doctrine of surplus population to be a fallacy, and considered the attempt to get poor people to limit their families to be a wicked plot of the 'priests and aristocrats' who supported their own indolent families at the expense of the working class. It would do his heart good, he said, to see the British aristocracy and royalty shipped off to the American West. He suspected that one reason why the Government boosted emigration to Australia was that it feared the growing strength of a democratic United States.[50]

As Barker became more enthusiastic about going to America himself, he began to see emigration as the bright hope for British workers, and he began to publish letters from America (all favourable) in every issue of the *People*, the *Reformer's Almanac* and the *Reformer's Companion to the Almanacs*. Several were from his brother, who was already living in Ohio, and he extracted pieces from James Silk Buckingham's account of his travels in the New World. Barker's advice was both practical and ideological. People who emigrated, he advised, should 'wash yourselves thoroughly from head to foot before you start', to avoid illness on the voyage. They should also 'Leave a curse behind' on Great Britain,

> on all its oppressions and cruelties; on its villainous Church Establishments; on its tyrannical Government; on its hypocritical Priesthood; on its plundering aristocracy; its extravagant Court; on its prison-like Poor-houses; on its wicked Laws; on its unjust system of taxation; on its middle-class selfishness; on its Parliamentary corruptions. . . .[51]

Moreover, they were to support the abolitionists and treat coloured people with respect.

Once more Barker's zeal led him to inspire utopian visions, this time in the minds of potential emigrants. Irish abolitionists James Haughton and R. D. Webb were critical not only of Barker's raising false expectations, but believed that in his zeal to push emigration he was underplaying the evils of American slavery.[52] Barker, like many Chartists, including Arthur O'Neil, William Lovett and F. R. Lees, believed that American slavery was used by some people in Britain purposely to vilify American democracy, and consequently to check the development of democracy and working men's rights in their own country.[53] It is possible that in this case Barker did give Chartism priority over antislavery.

Another paradox that appeared in his current enthusiasm for emigration was the ease with which Barker overlooked the rights of the American Indians. In fact, he was accused of not opposing intrusions on their territories on the grounds that only with European immigrants would the lands be cultivated and developed for the common man – white man. In England Barker advocated a tax on land to break up big holdings; for America he called for a tax on land alone as a cure for monopoly, thus antedating Henry George's 'Single Tax' idea by several years.[54] Even when he acknowledged injustices to Indians and slaves and to free blacks in the North, Barker still believed the American Government was an advance over the aristocratic rule in Britain. True, the power of the Southern slave-holding oligarchy, sustained by the three-fifths clause in the Constitution, was similar to the power of the British aristocracy, but he had great faith that American democratic trends would obliterate that power along with the abolition of slavery.[55]

Carried away with his own advice, Barker decided to make an exploratory trip to the United States in 1849. He sailed from Liverpool on 23 June and arrived in New York on 15 August 1849, purposely choosing to cross on a common emigrant vessel in order to see at first hand what conditions were like. He was delighted to find several fellow passengers reading copies of his own publications. After dreaming about America for thirty-six years, as he reflected, his first sight of land was a moving experience: 'And now I see it' – the land of hope 'for the perishing millions' of Europe, a 'refuge for the wronged and tortured sons of toil'. During his visit of approximately two months he had time to visit his three brothers in Ohio, went on through Indiana, Illinois and into Wisconsin as far as Milwaukee, and also dipped into the upper South, where his first sight of a slave excited in him 'a strange, indescribable feeling'. In New York he called on Horace Greeley, who must have further encouraged Barker's inclination to return to settle.[56]

Pleased with his impressions and 'dreadfully out of love with' the British Government, the enthusiastic visitor was ready to pull up stakes in England and take his family to America, only to find his spirits take a downward slide when he got word of the Compromise of 1850 with its new Fugitive Slave Act, which made it much easier for slave-holders to reclaim runaways.[57] Bursting with indignation, he wrote to tell Garrison that, if the nation accepted such an act, he could not possibly live there. American slavery was to him 'the most revolting piece of inhumanity with which the earth was cursed', and one of the greatest props of European tyranny. The infamous law would make America 'a proverb for inconsistency and inhumanity' throughout the world.

He now realized, he went on, that there were people worse off than 'the plundered and starving Irish', for the Irish could run away to seek a living elsewhere. Irish landlords, bad as they were, did not pursue their workers with whips, bowie knives and bloodhounds. But, Barker continued, if he were to emigrate and the Fugitive Slave Act was not abolished, he would then prefer to return to 'monarchical and aristocratical' England. His new revelation told him that, although the United States might excel in some social and political institutions, yet the people of England were 'more enlightened, more virtuous – a more respectable and worthy set of people'.[58]

Despite such intransigence, Barker's restless spirit won out, and 1851 found him on his way to the United States. Ray Boston has noted the large number of Chartists who escaped to America because of pressure from either central or local authorities in Britain, but classified Barker as one of 'those "tired old men", anxious for a rest from agitation'.[59] Possibly Barker was weary of Chartist upheavals, but certainly not of agitation *per se*. Controversy was an engrained part of his life and a habit impossible to shed at the age of forty-five (or even, as it turned out, at the age of seventy-five). Indeed, when he first decided to go to the United States he requested that both Garrison and Douglass should publicise his arrival in the *Liberator* and the *North Star* – hardly an expression of a wish to withdraw from the public arena.[60]

The Barker family chose to settle in Knox County, Ohio, not too far from Joseph's brothers. The decision clearly reflected his wish to be a Western pioneer while at the same time living in proximity to one of the most active Garrisonian abolitionist communities in the country. The *Anti-Slavery Bugle*, published in Salem, welcomed him with fulsome praise: 'His enlarged liberality – his habit of radical investigation and his ardent love for freedom will always make him welcome to our columns.'[61] Barker's first letter to the *Bugle* reiterated his egalitarianism by reaffirming his hatred of slavery 'of every kind'; but perhaps of more importance in his new American setting was that the letter contained a portent of future contention with his new associates. From his previous contacts with American abolitionists he was well aware of the issues that divided them: political action, women's rights, whether the Constitution was a pro- or antislavery document, and, more recently, the advisability of advocating the dissolution of a Union which recognized slavery as legal. It was within the Garrisonian ranks that the disunion movement was emerging.

Barker announced that he intended to work with abolitionists of all shades of opinion as long as they all agreed on the injustice of the new Fugitive Slave Law, a seemingly conciliatory declaration that on its surface should have offended no one.[62] But actually the abolitionist rivalry ran so strong that the last thing the Garrisonians wanted was for someone to co-operate with the opposition, especially with those who had organized the Liberty and Free Soil parties. At the same time, Barker's interpretation of the Bible, in addition to the Constitution, as a proslavery document was too radical for most of the Tappanites or 'New Organization' evangelical and political abolitionists, and even for some Garrisonians. Thus eventually he was to find himself at odds with both camps.

From the time he arrived on American shores, Barker was swept up in the excitement of the pot-pourri of heady isms being debated by American reformers – not only abolitionism, but also spiritualism, vegetarianism, pacifism, feminism (including 'free love'), Mormonism, Free Soilism, and labour versus capitalism. He said he arrived in the country thinking that only one reform was needed, emancipation, but discovered that all laws and all institutions were seemingly in need of remodelling.[63] Barker's zeal and his forensic and writing abilities were quickly pre-empted by the most radical Garrisonians, and within months of his arrival he was named a vice-president of the American Anti-Slavery Society.[64] Although he was busy building a home, planting fields and generally settling into the life of an Ohio farmer from 1852 to 1854, he found time to travel to New York, Pennsylvania and New England for antislavery and anti-Bible, or 'Free Discussion', conventions, gave series of lectures in both Philadelphia and Boston, attended antislavery and women's rights conventions nearer home in Ohio, and organized both reform and recreational groups in his own community. The three topics to which he gave priority were abolition, women's rights and secularism, with the last of these becoming more and more dominant, although in Barker's mind the three were inseparable.

The first round of fighting was with those who objected to his insistence that the Bible sanctioned slavery because the slave-holding patriarchs of the Old Testament were blessed of God – the very argument that Southern slave-holders had used for years to restrain American churches from taking an antislavery position. Barker thought it was obvious that the Mosaic law recognized slavery, and pointed out that even the American Pilgrims accepted such an interpretation. Thus, to his way of thinking, they too were at least theoretical if not actual slave-holders.[65] So to impugn the reputation of the Pilgrim fathers was hardly the best way for a British immigrant to endear himself to patriotic Americans.

In November 1852, Barker called a 'Free Discussion' convention in Salem, Ohio, to 'investigate' the authority and influence of Jewish and Christian scriptures and to consider the possibility that the old scriptures had fulfilled their mission and that the time had come for a new dispensation which would replace them. Barker and H. C. Wright were the principal speakers against the Bible, with an Ohio minister, the Revd Jonas Hartzell, carrying the main burden of the opposition.[66] This meeting opened a continuing controversy between Hartzell and Barker, culminating in a nine-evening debate the following summer. The debates were reported by the *Anti-Slavery Bugle* with the explanatory note that its editors were not like some aboli-tionists who refused to go to meetings with infidels. They would 'go to meeting' with all, regardless of whether their abolitionism rested on a Biblical base or on the opposite, as did Joseph Barker's and William Lloyd Garrison's. A relevant point to note for this essay is how Barker, although starting with Bible arguments, worked around to his Chartist and free-trade ideas. His oppor-tunity came when Hartzell asked him what good the abolitionists had done. Barker's answer was that reform could not be left to the churches. British antislavery leaders had quickly learned that lesson and had resorted to holding public meetings and issuing propaganda to arouse the masses against the clergy as well as landlords. For Barker, 'priests and aristocrats' were equal to slave-holders in tyranny, and he claimed antislavery leaders as champions of the people. By awakening the nation to an anti-slavery crusade they had opened the way for 'the men who after-wards wrenched from the heartless landlords the food monopoly, and opened the ports for the free importation of grain and fruit, thus saving the toiling millions from want and starvation'.[67] Anti-slavery, he argued, had a broader definition than the eman-cipation of American slaves; it meant universal freedoms, including freedom of speech.

In the Garrisonian anti-Bible convention in Hartford, Connecticut, in the summer of 1853, Barker learned the practical lesson that Americans were just as adept at disturbing public meetings as Englishmen were. This one was interrupted by theological students defending the Bible so resolutely that Barker found himself left alone on the platform. His colleagues, he remarked laconically, understood the American 'Judge Lynch' better than he did.[68] The following December, while giving a series of lectures sponsored by the Sunday Institute of Philadelphia, his denials of the divine authority of the Bible so enraged the crowd that he needed a police escort to reach the safety of the home of James and Lucretia Mott. Barker himself says that one would have thought he would have learned a lesson, but he 'was daring to madness', and within a month engaged in an eight-night debate with a Revd Dr Berg in the Philadelphia Concert Hall. There Barker held forth on the erroneous concept of God presented in the Bible. He charged that it makes God out to be a person, a horrible person: unjust, capricious, vengeful, and with all the other 'vile' faults of a human being.[69]

From Philadelphia Barker proceeded to Boston for another lecture series, in February 1854. By that time it was evident that he was more carried away with attacking the Bible than he was concerned with fighting slavery, and even some Garrisonians were beginning to regret the acclaim he had been accorded. The Revd Samuel J. May, a Unitarian clergyman from Leicester, Massachusetts, wrote to Richard D. Webb in Dulbin to express his disappointment that 'so candid and so fair a man' as Barker was pushing his anti-Bible diatribes to such an extreme. May's estimate of him had fallen 'many degrees'. It was then that Webb responded with the comment about all hobby horses running away with Barker.[70] Along with his lectures, Barker carried on debates via letters published in the *Liberator*, among them several exchanges with a woman, Elizabeth Wilson of Cadix, Ohio. His focus in these letters was on all of the 'revolting and indecent' passages in the Bible.[71] Garrison admitted that several of his readers cancelled their subscriptions, but one suspects that the lively exchange may have added others. By that time Barker had moved far beyond his earlier stand of defending abolitionists from the charge of being infidels; now he was glorying in the label as a positive asset, claiming that infidels were the only ones promoting the antislavery cause. Indeed, at the Women's Rights

Convention in Cleveland in the autumn of 1853 he argued that the abolition movement 'could only succeed by subverting the Bible'.[72]

While Barker's anti-Bible stance probably provoked the most controversy, certainly his support of radical feminism was alienating too, especially when he related the two by pointing out that the Bible made man master and lord and woman subject and slave. 'Shall injustice and cruelty like this be charged to God?' he challenged. He also inveighed against the laws which denied women equal educational opportunity and equal property rights and taxed them without representation.[73]

The sanguine impressions of America with which Barker arrived in the United States were quickly put to the test in the society of frontier Ohio. 'Just think of Knox County!' he reminisced later.

> The small silent towns the long distances... the curious, silent, reserved, half-hermit-like uncomfortable people... in the unfinished yet decaying and ill-looking and ill-kept houses. No comfort, or but little, and that not at all of the genial, English kind. Even children silent, solitary, cheerless, joyless.[74]

He was dismayed as well by the prevalent overuse of alcohol, and by his neighbours' prejudice against blacks. He soon found himself defending blacks from the usual charges of laziness and other stereotypical characteristics, and rebutting opinions that they should all be shipped back to Africa. In one argument with a man who wanted to rid the United States of 'black blood', Barker asked him how he could possibly separate black blood from white, since so many white men had chosen to mix with blacks, making slavery itself 'the great amalgamator'. He told his neighbours that in opposing freedom and the franchise for blacks they were as bad as the 'princes and priests' of England who opposed rights for the common white people.[75]

Barker, of course, set out with determination to educate the community through lectures and writing. Besides slavery, he addressed his audiences on spiritualism, temperance, women's rights, the treatment of criminals and the rights of labour. Temperance had been one of his early causes (after he gave up drinking to please his mother). In England he was a co-editor of the *Star of Temperance* and he had presided over an early, perhaps the first, conference of the British Association for the Promotion of Temperance. Throughout his life he remained adamantly against the use of alcohol, and even more emotionally set against tobacco because he never lost his own desire for a good pipe. He constantly preached to working people that the first step in raising themselves from poverty was to give up both vices. It is probable that Henry C. Wright was responsible for awakening an interest in spiritualism in Barker, for when Wright visited the Barkers they held a seance during which a medium evoked the spirits of Joseph's father and older brother.[76]

Several visitors from the East journeyed to Ohio to be entertained in the Barker home, among them Garrison, Theodore Parker (in whose church Barker preached in Boston) and Wright. Barker's friendship with the unorthodox Wright seems to have been the most congenial of all his abolitionist associations in America. Wright had made himself an authority on family relationships, especially the rearing of children, and, after staying with the Barkers in their log house on their 160-acre farm for several weeks in the winter of 1852, he painted a happy picture of a warm family circle characterized by affection, intelligence and tolerance. 'The enslaved, the oppressed, the outcast, the despised, of all colors and conditions have in them outspoken and efficient friends', he reported.[77] Besides Joseph and Frances Barker and their two sons and a daughter, the family circle included the children's tutor, Theodore Suliot, also an abolitionist, whom Wright had met previously in England, where Suliot was associated with a Mechanics' Institute. He had served also in Quaker schools in both Ireland and England, where he taught the children of the Gurneys, Frys and other prominent Quaker abolitionist families.[78] Suliot was a fellow student of Richard Webb in a Quaker school near Dublin, and Webb described him as 'imaginative, reflective, irritable, capricious, and very attractive from his intellectual gifts and graces' – words that might easily have been used to characterize Barker as well. Webb agreed with Wright about the cheerful atmosphere in the Barker home, but his acute insight attributed the close-knit family relationship to the isolation which resulted from Barker's radical and heretical doctrines.[79]

Advertisements in the *Anti-Slavery Bugle* invited other children to join Suliot's classes for the young Barkers, and Suliot helped in the attempt to stimulate educational and cultural activities through the presentation of musical entertainments as well as community meetings on reform. The *Bugle* declared the music to be the best since the famous Hutchinson family of anti-slavery singers had toured Ohio. As a matter of fact, the Hutchinsons were among the abolitionists who visited the Barkers, a visit Joseph recalled in his old age as having been a most pleasant one. During the day they all joined in the work to be done in the fields and evenings were made jolly with singing, dancing and games. Barker played the piano and all of his life continued to find solace in music. As a boy, he said, one thing that could make him forget the gnawing hunger pains in his stomach was to listen to singers who came out from Leeds to perform in Bramley. Frederick Douglass recalled an evening of singing in the Barker home in Wortley which corresponds with the genial atmosphere described by Wright. When Garrison visited Ohio, he and his host discussed forming an association of liberal people who would combine mutual improvement with recreation; after Garrison's departure Barker carried through with the idea. The group met regularly to 'talk, read, laugh or play', hear and discuss a lecture, and then round off the evening with singing and dancing.[80]

Richard Webb was probably wrong in attributing Barker's happy home life to the fact that his opinions caused the family to be ostracized by the people of rural Ohio, for the happy home life had existed in England as well; but Webb was right in recognising that the Barker family's isolation from the community stemmed from Joseph's radicalism. If he had been the type of radical who was willing to live and let live, things might have been different, but he always felt impelled to convert others to his persuasions. No doubt his abolitionism was unpopular, but his attacks on the usual Christian interpretations of the Bible were downright obnoxious to the average Ohio settler. In any case, it was not long before Barker experienced frontier retaliation. During one of his lectures on religion in Knox County, a group of young men began to pull down the log schoolhouse in which he was speaking. Supplied with rotten eggs, they pitched the missiles at what they thought was their destined target, but in the dark mistook another man for Barker and pelted him instead. Frustrated with their lack of success, they came at night and pulled down the fences around Barker's farm.[81]

Disgusted with the whole affair, Barker sold the farm and

moved to Salem, from which, at first, he issued glowing reports. He found his new neighbours to be more friendly, more intelligent and refined, and the location was much nearer the railway, thus more convenient for lecture trips.[82] Everything was wonderful – so much so that one suspects Barker of welcoming an excuse for moving a bit closer to civilisation. But of course he carried his own contentious personality along to Salem, where he continued to provoke many of his fellow abolitionists by his insistence on the correctness of political activity, and even more of them, as well as the non-abolitionists, by his continuing attacks on the Bible and his disregard for the Sabbath.

Given Barker's continued adherence to the need for political action against slavery, one might ask why he did not choose to affiliate with the New Organization people of the American and Foreign Anti-Slavery Society in preference to the Garrisonians of the old American Anti-Slavery Society. The answer is that, while the politicians may have accepted him, his attacks on the Bible must have driven evangelicals such as Lewis Tappan to a Biblical gnashing of teeth; and by the 1850s Lewis Tappan was single-handedly running the American and Foreign. The fact that Barker was not ostracized from the American Anti-Slavery Society is a tribute to Garrison's tolerance, for at their meetings Barker plagued his colleagues with the issue of political action. For example, at the Anniversary meeting of the Western Anti-Slavery Society in Salem in 1853, he insisted on emphasizing the similarities with, rather than the differences from, the other faction. He announced that were he a US citizen he would have voted for Liberty and Free Soil Party candidates, and provoked the convention to put him down by passing an anti-Free Soil Party resolution.[83] Before long Barker was himself attacking the Free Soil Party, not for what it did but because it did not go far enough when it took a halfway position of opposing only the extension of slavery into the Western territories, but not slavery *per se*. Agitation, he argued, must not stop short of the goal of total abolition, even though such pressuring might lead to the secession of one or the other section of the country.[84]

Another question that should be asked is why Barker never affiliated himself with the labour movement in the United States, then in only the embryo stage and in need of help. The answer lies in his background. In England he had opted for Chartism in preference to unionization as the route for labour to go. Once workers had gained the vote and political leverage, all else would follow – or so his optimism allowed him to believe. In America, white working men had the vote, so from Barker's point of view their destiny was already in their own hands if they chose to exercise their power. Living on the Ohio frontier he was much closer to the concern over land monopoly versus the continuing availability of land for the immigrant. Despite his disappointment that the Free Soil Party fell short on the slavery issue, there was no question about his endorsement of its 'free land to the settlers' platform. In his speeches Barker condemned American capitalists who thought of their workers only as cash assets rather than as people, but he found so much less land monopoly than in England, and a far more equitable system of taxation. Neither were men in the United States dragooned into the army and navy by roving press gangs. Thus on the whole he did not see American labour as being exploited.[85]

In the spring of 1854 Barker returned to England on business and the first thing that struck him as his ship docked was the sight of poorly clad workers, beggars and ragged street boys, such a picture as he had not seen anywhere in the United States.[86] It seemed to reawaken his conscience and one finds that in his speeches and writings while in England he constantly returned to the theme of wage slavery as being akin to chattel slavery. When he heard attacks on American slavery he countered with the charge that thousands of English and Irish workers were starving to death, while other thousands were imprisoned or transported. The British Government did not keep men in bondage because of their colour, but 'They pledge their whole power to keep men in bondage on account of their poverty and humble birth.' '. . . my conviction is', he wrote, 'that where one poor slave has been whipped, or starved, to death in America, fifty have been starved to death in England. . . . Instead of spending any time and strength in disputing about the comparative merits of the two forms of injustice and villainy, we ought to be warring with them both.' Therefore, Barker vowed, he would never let his concern for the oppressed African keep him from pleading the cause of the oppressed and plundered Englishman, or *vice versa*.[87] Barker was firmly convinced that 'Every blow they [abolitionists] strike at the monster slavery is a blow at the old-world despotism.'[88] He went too far in his further conclusion that the death of American slavery would also mean the death of European despotism, unless one holds that neither is yet dead.

As was to be expected, Barker carried his old contentiousness with him back to Britain, where he immediately indulged in an anti-Unitarian crusade because Unitarians had become voters and office-holders and thus were now part of the Government establishment. At an antislavery meeting in Manchester where Unitarians and pro-Bible abolitionists were numerous in the gathering, Barker got his come-uppance. After the American Garrisonian Parker Pillsbury had delivered an address, Barker jumped to his feet demanding the right to speak before he left to catch a train, although another American, the Revd Samuel R. Ward, was next on the agenda. Cries of 'Ward', 'Ward' drowned out Barker, and when he persisted the audience resorted to thumping the floor with sticks and unbrellas to win their point. Pillsbury reported that Barker was 'certainly gagged' and 'unquestionably for his principles'. Barker himself blamed it on the 'priestly president' of the meeting and his 'priestly' supporters.[89] In Britain as in the United States, Barker's predilection for giving an anti-Christian twist to everything was rapidly straining his acceptance by moderate Christian abolitionists. After his departure for America again, Eliza Wigham, of one of the prominent Scottish abolitionist families, wrote to Samuel J. May, Jr, that she was not sorry Barker had left them.[90]

Abolitionist apprehension over the passage of the Kansas–Nebraska Act was mounting by the time Barker returned to Ohio in the spring of 1855. Passed because of the politics of railway competition, it had reopened the territories to slavery by designating that the settlers themselves could vote on whether the institution should be allowed or prohibited. Competition between the North and South to send emigrants to these territories was about to explode in the violence which has gone down in history as 'the civil war in Kansas'. In a surge of Northern reaction against the Act, the Republican Party was born, and it posed an urgent challenge for Garrisonian abolitionists who had hitherto objected to political means to accomplish their goal; but it gave Joseph Barker an extraordinary opportunity to push his contention that they must become politically active. With his usual lack of tact he rushed into confrontation, this time with the equally tactless, equally extreme Stephen Foster, whom Barker accused of saying that every political abolitionist was 'destitute of honor, of conscientiousness, – is a ruffian, a knave, a villain, a slaveholder, a kidnapper, a thief and a murderer'. I have not located that quotation in Foster's words, but the language is not uncharacteristic; neither would it have been beyond Barker to have exaggerated the language. When the *Anti-Slavery Bugle* defended Foster against Barker's 'offensive personal accusations', Barker turned his guns not only on the publication but on the whole Western Anti-Slavery Society.[91]

It is difficult to say to what extent the falling-out with the Ohio Garrisonians influenced Barker's decision to pull up stakes again and move on farther west. His on-going disputes with neighbours and the ire of the community over his denunciations of their Christianity were certainly ingredients. Barker said that the feeling against him was so strong that anyone in Salem felt free to treat him with impunity. An abolitionist bookseller refused to pay him the $50 he owed, neighbours tore down his fences, his children were ostracized because they did not attend the public school, and even the family maid declined to leave when fired because she claimed that Barker had promised her three years of service. Constant law suits ensued.[92]

Yet, despite his troubles with both the antislavery community and the wider community, one suspects that the lure of the West may have been the biggest reason for moving on. Barker's restless spirit condemned him to be always on the move. Oddly enough, there is nothing in his memoirs or in his 3000-page diary to indicate that he wanted to go to Nebraska to join the antislavery settlers in keeping the territory free of slavery. On the trip out aboard river steamers he was more horrified by what he saw of the conditions under which the boat hands worked than he was by what he learned of slavery from his conversations with Southerners. First, he had considered moving only as far as Chicago, then to Iowa, over which his enthusiasm blossomed after a lecture trip there in 1855; but finally he pushed on to Nebraska, a territory inhabited at that time by only 5000 whites among Indians, along with buffalo, deer, wolves and rattle-snakes. According to family history, he carried with him warrants to purchase some 6000 to 8000 acres near Omaha.[93]

During the Nebraska period from 1856 to 1860 Barker's connections with his old antislavery colleagues were gradually weakening and his lecture trip back to Philadelphia in 1857 was more concerned with religion than with slavery. When he did write to Garrison and Wright it was to chide them for refusing to vote and for their lack of understanding of political means to gain abolitionist ends.[94] At first the large farming and stock-raising operations in Nebraska prospered, but the Panic of 1857 hit Barker hard and was, at least partly, the impetus for his return to England in 1860. His oldest son was left to tend to the Nebraska property. But Barker was already beginning to feel the first twinges of remorse about the anti-Christian position into which he had fenced himself and (at least so he said in retrospect) he wanted to put more distance between himself and his heretical associates in America.[95]

The reconversion was not immediate, however, because in June 1860 Barker allowed himself to be named as one of the editors of the *National Reformer*, a secularist publication, and his language sounded as vehement as ever: 'Religion is insanity. Religion is torment. Religion is vice. Religion is ruin.'[96] He also continued his secularist lectures and entered into public debate with another old reformer, Thomas Cooper, who had gone back to religion.[97]

Yet Barker's doubts about his own thinking were growing. According to his testimony, the breaking-point came when he was sent a secularist book to review which openly undermined marriage and advocated extra-marital sexual indulgence. Shocked at such licence, he resigned his position as editor to begin a paper of his own, *Barker's Review of Politics, Literature, Religion, and Morals, and Journal of Education, Science and Co-operation*. Meanwhile he began to reread the Bible, with the result that he was 'overpowered' by Jesus.[98] By 1863 he was ready to announce publicly that he had been reconverted to Christianity, having worked his way back through Unitarianism to New Connexion Methodism.[99] Once again he became a Christian minister, a publisher of Christian materials, and an indefatigable hounder of infidels.

It is not surprising to find that the return of the prodigal to religion was marked by a concurrent rejection of the American abolition movement — or at least of the course it had taken. If his old friends were among those responsible for seducing him away from God, they were also in error in the means they advocated for achieving emancipation. One can trace a steady progression from his criticisms of the abolitionists to a defence of the secession of the Southern states to an almost unbelievable defence of slavery —

unbelievable in actuality if one remembers how Barker was so often carried away in argument to say extreme things in the heat of the moment. His inconsistencies and exaggerations make the task of unravelling his real beliefs even more difficult.

First of all, unlike Harriet Martineau, Henry Solly, T. Perronet Thompson and most other British abolitionists, but like most British people in general, Barker did not immediately see secession and war in America as stemming primarily from the slavery issue, particularly so long as President Lincoln and the Republican Party refused to acknowledge that emancipation was a war aim. In the first issue of *Barker's Review*, he proclaimed the basic quarrel between the sections to be overprotection for Northern industry versus free trade for Southern cotton in exchange for British manufactures. Protection reflected selfish monopolistic interests detrimental to the working classes; free trade between the South and Britain would obviously be advantageous for British labour, so Britain should maintain a neutral stance.[100] Within a few months, however, Barker was coupling protection and slavery as joint causes of the war, and then dropped the protection issue completely to concentrate on slavery, although he could never forgive the Republicans for their tariffs any more than he could forgive President Lincoln for being so hesitant in moving against slavery. By the time the Emancipation Proclamation was finally announced, he was so disenchanted with Lincoln that he joined in the hue and cry raised by *The Times* that Lincoln's aim was to stir up a slave insurrection and that the Proclamation's consequence would be a strengthening of the South's determination to fight.[101]

For years leading Garrisonians had been insisting that slavery would die faster if the Union were dissolved, because it was the federal Constitution which legalized, and therefore the Federal Government's power which sustained, the 'peculiar institution'. For even longer, abolitionists, both 'Old School' and 'New Organization' (except for a minority of militants), had insisted that they did not favour force to accomplish emancipation and had denied the accusation of the opposition that their aim was to instigate a servile war. Now Barker saw the antislavery people backing Lincoln and the war; thus they were departing from both principles while he remained constant in upholding them. His main thesis, reiterated over and over again, was that slavery was wrong but that it was also wrong to resort to war to eradicate it.

As he had so many times before in making criticisms, Barker again forgot all moderation, and in becoming anti-abolitionist resorted to making out not only a pro-Confederate but also a pro-slavery case. Yet one must also understand his defence of slavery in the context of his consistent belief that white workers in England and Ireland were just as badly off, even worse off in their physical and material wants than most slaves in America. When criticising John Brown's raid on Harper's Ferry, he pointed out that there were millions of suffering people in the world, but that did not justify 'Quixotic expeditions' to relieve them.[102] He credited Brown with a good character and unselfish motives but believed that the war had begun with his raid. While Barker did not object to insurrections under some circumstances, and certainly did not agree that one must always turn the other cheek, the fact still remained that Brown was completely unrealistic as to the success of his plan; therefore his lack of foresight had precipitated an unjustifiable bloodbath. The question was not whether slavery was evil – of course it was; but did Brown take the best possible course to get rid of it? No, he was fanatical to the point of insanity.

But then Barker went on to say that slavery was 'natural and inevitable' during certain stages of human development. It did not follow that it should be permanent, because civilization is always the foe of slavery and eventual abolition was inevitable. Besides, the system of slavery was 'self-improving'; Negroes were more intelligent, moral, happier and more useful, and vastly more numerous than their ancestors were or than they would have been if never taken from Africa – a startling position indeed for an abolitionist. Barker deplored the fact that his old political activist hero, Joshua Giddings, not only approved of Brown's raid but seemed to be encouraging similar efforts in the future; but his most severe censure was for Wendell Phillips, whose speech on Brown's martyrdom had been 'the effusion of a madman, or something worse'.[103]

Even before John Brown's suicidal attempt, Barker admitted, the abolitionists had been guilty of goading the South into rebellion. The fact that slavery was evil did not justify dealing with slave-holders in a spirit of hatred any more than it sanctioned stirring up a spirit of insurrection among slaves. The 'vicious meddling' by 'Northern fanatics' had helped to make 'inhuman monsters' of white Southerners. Yet masters fit on a spectrum that encompassed all degrees of cruelty and indulgence. No doubt some slaves were happier than many of the wretched poor of Europe; and, so far during the Civil War, the slaves who escaped to the North were worse off than they had been in bondage. Constitutionally speaking, the North had deprived the South of her legal rights in the Western territories. It followed that secession was a legal recourse. Barker labelled the Civil War the 'American Revolution', thus endowing it with more dignity, a fight for rights worthy of respect. Moreover, a sudden collapse of the slave power could bring disaster on all; it must be brought down gently and safely. He cited the anti-black draft riots in New York as a demonstration of the greater danger of precipitious change.[104] Barker was now arguing that there was a basis for believing the Confederacy itself might end slavery, because it had ended the slave trade and because a majority of its population did not hold slaves.[105]

Running as a connecting thread through all that Barker said or wrote was his concern for British workers caught in the 'cotton famine' that resulted from the Union blockade of the Confederate States. At first he inconsistently advocated that Britain should both remain neutral and break the blockade, but by the end of 1862 he adopted the more realistic position that France and Britain ought to recognise the Confederacy and then mediate a peace. Meanwhile English factories should inaugurate shorter shifts to allow more workers part-time jobs, and the Government had an obligation to seek alternative supplies of cotton elsewhere (India, China, Egypt), as well as to help workers who wished to emigrate.[106] He clung to his belief that the operatives of Lancashire were asking for freedom for the slaves – and more: they were asking that it be given in 'the best and safest way'. When Frederick Douglass, in addressing the people of Lancashire, charged them with a share in the guilt for American slavery because they bought slave-produced cotton, Barker struck back defensively. How could factory workers determine which cotton was slave-grown? He then took the offensive. Did the 'war party' of the North abstain from the use of Southern cotton? Of what was Douglass's own shirt made? Who raised the sugar he ate? Was not Douglass's land taken from the Indians? As an accomplice of John Brown, and a supporter of the war, Douglass was guilty of destroying the lives of blacks and whites both.[107]

Unfortunately for Barker's image as an abolitionist, several of his statements exposed an underlying racism in him. At one point he called unqualified emancipation unqualified injustice and immediate emancipation 'the extreme of folly' because blacks were not equal. However, he added that it did not follow that they should therefore be enslaved or degraded. On another occasion, while assailing the fanaticism of abolitionists (mentioning Garrison, Wendell Phillips and Wright by name) he wrote, 'They talk, and reason, and act as if negroes and white people were exactly alike – as if the word MAN always stood for the same being', and as if right were always an absolute. But slavery was a dangerous institution and there was need for modified freedom even for inferior races. In one of his speeches on 'The American Question', he capitalized on prejudice when he asked his audience if they favoured as a solution to slavery the suggestion that every white man should take a black wife.[108] It should be noted that, in spite of this racial bias, Barker treated with respect the individual black people that he knew or met. On one occasion when he was preaching he was asked to read an announcement that Jack Birch, 'a nigger player', would lead a service. He changed the wording to Mr John Birch and omitted the pejorative epithet, declaring that, 'I was not going to say *Jack* Birch and *Nigger* player.' On another occasion, when a black man who had heard Barker lecture took off his hat to him in the street, Barker told him to put it on again. His diary contains several such incidents. One of the last abolitionists with whom Barker retained friendly relations was the veteran black member of the American Anti-Slavery Society, Robert Purvis of Philadelphia.[109]

Of course Barker did not escape – no doubt sought – public confrontations. His own lectures were disrupted and he retaliated in kind. At one meeting of the Burnley Union and Emancipation Society the usual resolution in support of Lincoln was moved for adoption. Thereupon Barker and a local resident proposed a counter-amendment which, to the consternation of the meeting's organizers, was adopted. On another occasion, when Barker attempted to lecture in Manchester, the opposition made so much noise – for three hours – that he was finally forced to give up. Barker challenged such antislavery pro-Union spokesmen as George Thompson and Henry Vincent to debate with him, but found no takers. Thompson's attitude of disdain for Barker is evident in a letter written to his daughter Amelia in 1861:

Joseph Barker was lecturing on the 'American Crisis' at the same time with myself last evening. He in the Old Lecture Hall – I in a beautiful New Church – His audience I have heard was very small – mine was a very fine one. I should have liked to have heard him. He would have liked to have heard me. Two papers this morning report me. Of his discourse there is no report. Joseph is at a discount in Newcastle.[110]

Failing to find willing debaters, by 1863 his tactic was to follow speakers for the Union and Emancipation Society and deliver rebuttals in separate meetings of his own. Much of what he said was a repetition of what he had already written in his *Review*, always maintaining that he had no wish to rebut what they said about slavery, for all were agreed on its evil; the question was *how* it should be abolished. His opposition favoured 'fire and sword'; he favoured peaceful and bloodless measures. By that time Barker had chosen to stand with the 'peace party', commonly known in America as the Copperheads. Many of them were Confederate sympathizers, some were proslavery, but many were neither, rather, were simply willing to settle for 'peace at any price'.[111] Barker fell into the last category in his belief that some remedies were worse than the disease, and that this was one such case. In Manchester the Revd Dr James Massie, speaking for the Union and Emancipation Society, had said that they were gathered in the name of Jesus. Barker countered by contending that, yes, Jesus had died for the Negro, but he did not kill others in so doing. One could sympathize with the Negro without condoning an iniquitous war which had gone on for two years; it was time to bring it to an end. Britain and France together should demand an end. Evidently he did not think his position through enough to realize that the consequences of such a demand might be to enlarge the scale of the war.[112]

Barker fit also into the mould of the Copperheads who defended the Confederacy on constitutional grounds. He held that, since the states had seceded peacefully and had sent commissioners to negotiate with the Federal Government, they had followed proper procedures. Their rejection of the Constitution was no worse than the Garrisonian abolitionists' rejection of it. Actually, he contended, the Confederate States were not anti-Constitution; they only demanded respect for it and for its recognition of the legality of slavery – a recognition the

Garrisonians had acknowledged in their own anti-Constitution stand. Now he was willing to defend the constitutionality of even the Fugitive Slave Law of 1850, the law that had almost kept him from emigrating to America.[113] Barker ended his last lecture on 'The American Question' with a burst of euphoria: Britain could recognise the Confederacy without danger of the United States declaring war. Recognition would lead to desertions from the Union Army and hasten the end of fighting. The Mississippi River would be opened, trade with Britain revived, British labourers could go back to work. In the end the North would be grateful to be separated from the South and thus relieved of the guilt and responsibility of slavery. Southerners would improve the conditions of slaves as they, in gratefulness, 'imbibed' British ideas. Abolition was inevitable.[114] All would live happily ever after.

In the end, of course, Barker was on the losing side. Thomas E. Barker (no relation to Joseph), who was on the Executive Committee of the Manchester Union and Emancipation Society, reported to Garrison that Joseph was among the most conspicuous advocates of the Confederacy, along with John A. Roebuck and James Spence, but (with a touch of malice), 'Joseph soon after found that the cause of the South did not pay well enough to command his services and advocacy, and he has therefore gone back to one of his old religious circles, and is no more heard of in the arena of politics or secular questions.'[115] A pro-Union newspaper, the London *Morning Star*, characterized Barker as 'a sort of controversial free lance, constantly changing his flag and his uniform', who was at present not even on speaking terms with his former self. 'Consistency can reasonably be looked for only in a fossil', was its editor's terse philosophical summary. A broadside, put out in 1863, quoted the Barker of 1856 on what he thought of slave-holders and slavery then, in contrast to his current opinions. The question at the bottom of the sheet asked, 'Working men of Lancashire, will you be foolish enough to be led by Joseph Barker?' A correspondent for the *Manchester Examiner* concluded that 'The Joseph Barker of 1856 does not now exist', and the *Star*'s editor opined that this seemed a convenient statute of limitations: 'Every liberal atom which fled from the body of Joseph Barker was replaced by one of pro-slavery tendencies.' He wanted to know what diet had effected such a transformation.[116] No doubt William Lloyd Garrison took some satisfaction as he reprinted the piece in the *Liberator*. Within a year Thomas Barker reported a second time to Garrison that 'Rev. Mr Verity and Rev. Joseph Barker have gone stark out of existence. With all their power of tongue and face, and conscience, they have been frowned down, and have quitted the public platform ignominiously so far as the American question is concerned.'[117]

It is hard to say whether Barker's perorations on slavery revealed a change of opinion on the inherent inferiority of the black race, or whether they exposed a belief he had long held without expressing it. The same question arises in regard to his attitude toward women. Reading his speeches at women's rights conventions in the United States, one assumes that he was a full-blown champion of sexual equality. Yet, in writing in his *Review* about blacks being 'different', he equated their problem with that of women, who are also 'different', always adding that neither group should on that account be denied their rights. While he deplored laws that discriminated against women in property rights, in the labour market and in divorce cases, he allowed that females were certainly not equal in physical properties nor 'in intellectual capacity' nor in 'fitness to command' nor 'for the more arduous labours of peace'.[118] One can only imagine the reactions of his old friends Lucy Stone, Ernestine Rose and Lucretia Mott, if his message reached them.

One is on surer ground in saying that Barker's attitudes toward labour were changing. While he was steadfastly concerned about unemployment and poverty, he forsook his Chartist position that, if given the vote, labour could wield the power necessary to effect its own salvation. In 1861 his writing began to reflect disillusionment about the working class's ability to make proper or wise decisions for itself. Indeed, he doubted that 'respectable' working men were themselves eager for an extension of the suffrage. People needed the leadership and guidance of those 'above' them. In America, he said, he had observed situations where universal suffrage and 'popular sovereignty' were bad – for instance, in Kansas, where a proslavery government had been the result. He doubted that a government based on universal suffrage would provide any more respect for minority rights, for the rights of labour, or for protection of capital; it would be no better at securing peace or in advancing cultural and scientific development. Pushing to his logical extreme, he concluded that if some got the vote all must have it, including women, criminals and even the insane.[119]

By 1862 Barker was totting up all the reforms which had been achieved in Britain without universal suffrage: repeal of the Test and Corporation Acts, modification of marriage laws, rights for Catholics and other religious dissenters, the abolition of slavery and the slave trade, parliamentary reform, free trade, postage reform, better management of the colonies, and a better land law for Ireland. When a new monthly periodical, the *Working Man*, appeared in 1862, he wished it well while declaring that it was too revolutionary. Yet, since he could remember how he had been carried away by the Chartist excitement of 1848, he knew he should not judge others too harshly. None the less he did. When the Reform Bill of 1867 came up, Barker was among its opponents. Throughout his diary for these years he expressed his disapproval of striking workers and admitted that he now believed the Government was justified in acting against them with severity, as government had back in 1816 against the Luddites. His diary also contains many comments on how well-off workers had become by mid century, yet they were never satisfied. All of their complaints were contrasted with the greater sufferings he had endured during his years of poverty, but in this he was, of course, no different from most people in their sixties. As he became more conservative both religiously and politically, he emphasized more and more that it was the 'vices' of the lower classes that kept them down; they were responsible for their own predicament.[120] Christianity, he was sure, would eventually check democracy and both improve and strengthen a conservative government which 'will outlive the streams of equality, communism, women's rights'. By the late 1860s he was praying for the defeat of liberal candidates at each election, and concurrently discovering more and more virtues in both the Anglican and Roman Catholic churches.[121]

When the American Civil War ended, Reconstruction politics and the fate of the freedmen absorbed Barker's interests, and, the more he read, the more bile he stirred up in himself against Lincoln, Radical Republicans, and especially his old abolitionist cohorts. He denounced Lincoln as having 'inflicted more misery on the Negroes than slavery would have inflicted in a thousand years'. 'When shot, he received, as I think the due reward for his deeds.' The only reason to regret the assassination was that it would provoke the North to a more vengeful policy. As for the abolitionists, 'I cannot but look on Garrison, Wendell Phillips, Miss Beecher Stowe, and the antislavery revolutionists generally as the maddest of Fanatics, if not the greatest of criminals.' Like Lincoln, they too had caused more misery than slavery ever had or would have had it lasted another hundred years. One prospect that satisfied his need for revenge was that 'The ruin is likely to reach its authors.' The North, and especially New England, could expect to be dragged down along with the South. Another comfort was his thankfulness for his own change of course: 'I am glad I got cured of Garrisonian abolitionism and democratic republicanism.' He saw Radical Republicans and abolitionists as power-hungry madmen: 'They are of Robespierre's spirit: the spirit of conscientious, unsparing murderous philanthropy; on[e] of the most horrible forms of fanaticism.'[122]

Unable to 'stay put' long, either geographically or philosophically, by the end of the decade of the 1860s Barker was becoming restless again. His wife's illness prevented moves other than within England for several years, but, after her death in 1871, he set off with his daughter and two sisters-in-law to rejoin his sons in Nebraska. Between his arrival there in 1872 and his death in 1875, he divided his time between lecturing in the East on religion and resting on the farm. No longer in the limelight of any popular, or unpopular, cause, and advancing in age, he mellowed somewhat in his attitudes toward controversial public issues, substituting the theme of ungrateful children as the focus of his bitterness.[123] After visiting the scenes of the Civil War, including Harper's Ferry, Barker confessed that he had been much moved, and that he really had not been able to understand the Northern point of view until his return to the United States. By then he had already backtracked enough in his assessment of the abolitionists to concede that 'Poor Lloyd Garrison and H. C. Wright and many others of their companions in unbelief had noble minds at one period. They were goaded into error. And some of them retained their virtue, I believe to the last.'[124] After reading Frederick Douglass's autobiography in 1874 his reaction was, 'I am glad and thankful slavery is abolished. It was a horrible system. It was put down by a horrible process; but its destruction by almost any means was a lesser evil than its continuance.'[125] He had come full circle.

I have found no evidence that Barker was ever reconciled with Garrison and Wright or that they ever met again, but while visiting in Philadelphia in 1874 Barker attended, at the invitation of Robert Purvis, some meetings of a radical club to which several of the old abolitionists belonged. His diary tantalizingly mentions an engagement to see Lucretia Mott, but there is no follow-up as to whether or not a meeting occurred.[126] One wonders if he ever changed his mind on the equality of the races. His last diary entry on the subject was after someone had tried to elicit agreement from him on the inferiority of blacks; but he refused to comply because of 'conflicting views'. His reply was that it was not an issue worth arguing about because all people were God's children.[127]

If Ralph Waldo Emerson was right in saying that consistency was the hobgoblin of little minds, certainly no one can accuse Joseph Barker of small-mindedness. He was widely read in the classics: belles lettres, theology, economics, politics and science. He loved music, was fond of gardening, planting flowers and trees, walking out in the woods and fields. Never provincial, but interested in world affairs on a broad spectrum, his mind was ever sharp as it moved from subject to subject, and one can easily understand why he was known as a formidable debater. Aside from the fact that he repeated himself so often, his writings compare favourably with other propaganda written in the mid-nineteenth century, and his diary is fascinating not only for the attitudes expressed there on public issues, but also because of his self-revelations. A psycho-historian would find him an ideal subject. Barker was self-analytical. He asked himself why old men turn conservative. He acknowledged his pettiness, selfishness and abrasiveness, and knew that his propensity for controversy indicated a desire to suffer: 'against wind and tide I did my work', he wrote. He admitted that he was too prone to look on one side only and to carry a point to extremes. While blaming others for leading him astray, he realized that he became 'as wild or wilder' than they. But then he nicely absolved himself of the responsibility by deciding that, in bemoaning his lack of wisdom and castigating himself for the past, he might be blaming God, who surely must have led him in those mysterious paths. Besides, he could tot up many merits for never having entered 'a Brothel, a gambling hell or low public house or dancing saloon', not to mention never having fornicated or seduced anyone. He said he was never a tyrant and, above all, had 'always studied the interests of the masses'. 'How much of the red Indian there is in me!' he exulted; 'I can feel his passion, his revenge, – his love of adventure, – of a wild hunter's and a warrior's way of life.'[128]

Despite all of his life's conflicts, from the poverty of his childhood to the bitterness of his family relationships in old age, Barker still swung from his pessimistic reflections to an optimism about the world. Four years before his death he wrote, 'What glorious events I have witnessed including the abolition of West Indian, American and Russian slavery, the multiplication of books, schools, libraries, and other helps to knowledge.' And in the last entry in his diary, written when death was imminent, he summed up, 'What joys, what sorrows I have tasted! And more than tasted. I have drunk deep of both. But God is good, and I can trust Him and I still am tolerably happy.'[129]

Joseph Barker was egomaniacally desirous that his biography should be written. 'What a story the story of my life would be!' is but one of dozens of diary entries on the subject.[130] Yet he is known to only a handful of historians, more perhaps to those working in Chartist than in antislavery history. Maybe he turned more people away from his causes than he brought in as supporters; even his co-workers became uncomfortable with him. But like other social and political gadflies he helped to sensitize the people of two nations, despite themselves, to the twin evils of chattel slavery and wage slavery.

# Epilogue

The reform careers of the subjects of these essays spanned over a hundred years, from the time of the American and French Revolutions to the turn of the twentieth century. Sharp, Roscoe, Rathbone, Currie and Rushton were products of both the Enlightenment and the Age of Revolution, their convictions a mixture of reason and the excitement of the new radical ideas of liberty and equality, of faith in gradual progress spurred by a practical realization that their age constituted one of those tides in the affairs of men which must be taken at its full. What they saw in their own world could scarcely be reconciled with their vision of the future unless men such as they accepted the obligation of leadership in changing public attitudes and national laws. Slave-trading, with all of its violations of natural law, reached its height in the era when commercial growth and industrialization were changing the British nation demographically, forcing the working population into slum areas of cities where their poverty and degradation were highly visible.

Charity at home would have been a normal response even had there been no issue of African slavery and the slave trade. But, because chattel slavery was the most obvious violation of human rights and did provoke such a strenuous response, it was inevitable that discussions of it should sooner or later be carried over to the home situation, transforming the trust in charitable benevolence to sustain life for the poor into the belief that rights must be granted to the people in order to sustain national well-being. The very vocabulary of slavery when applied to conditions of the lower classes heightened sensitivity and guilt in the minds of the middle and upper classes, while it stirred restlessness, anger and demands for those rights from the oppressed, white as well as black.

In the eighteenth century, when commercial power was still stronger than industrial power, and when so many wars were being fought because of national commercial rivalries, it was logical that comparisons of white and black slavery would be centred on such issues as impressment, flogging in the Army and Navy, corn-laws, monopolies and poor-laws; while the revolutions in France and America turned attention to civil liberties and representative government. By the nineteenth century, as industrial power grew, old economic issues between landlord and tenant, employer and employee, and disputes regarding the role the Government ought to play in these relationships took on a sharper edge. Thus the generation that included Sturge, Martineau, Thompson and Barker had to face the fact that the working classes themselves were mobilizing both economically and politically. Therefore for concerned reformers to find their own niches as co-operators, leaders or followers was decidedly more difficult. Martineau, Thompson, Barker and Solly lived to see the extension of the franchise in 1867 go beyond that of 1832, and to see the co-operative movement, unionization and the use of direct economic weapons give real leverage to labour's demands. Only Solly lived to witness the organization of the Labour Party.

It has sometimes been assumed that only after emancipation in the British Empire was accomplished could abolitionists give their full support to reforms at home. My study has convinced me that antislavery and home reform went hand in hand from the beginnings of both, and were more often mutually supportive than they were antagonistic. Of course there were rivalries between reform movements, but those contentions often gave each movement more publicity than it otherwise would have enjoyed. Despite temporarily delaying one another, I believe the various reforms edged one another forward in the long run. Brewster, Solly and Barker as clergymen, and even lay Christians such as Rathbone and Sturge, represent the force of religion in pricking consciences and prodding reformers in all causes that had a bearing on relief – and then rights – for the oppressed. Both the evangelical impetus toward perfectionism and Unitarian rationalism contributed significantly to the growing optimism about progress that characterized the Age of Romanticism. In Barker, for instance, one sees them combined and easily carried over into his secularist search for the good society.

Of course, each generation stood on the shoulders of its predecessors. Consider Henry Solly. Like Granville Sharp he believed that the old Saxon system of frankpledge could be used to provide security for home colonies. Like Sturge he envisioned ideal villages with schools, libraries, sports fields, wash houses and public baths. Like Harriet Martineau he pictured the poor exercising their rights to vote and bargain, and to flourish on British soil as much as did pheasants, partridges and foxes, or, for that matter, the landed gentry. Like Brewster he believed that the clergy had a special responsibility to hold the economic troubles of the people before their more affluent parishioners. Like all of them he knew that 'criminal' and 'pauper' were relative terms and insisted that the disadvantaged must not be made objects of degradation in institutions. Also like the rest of them, Solly was optimistic that the capitalist system was capable of being beneficent in providing more jobs, better wages and increasing comforts. He went a step farther than they did by heartily endorsing the trades unions as a means by which working people themselves could regulate raw and greedy capitalism.[1] But, while the nineteenth century saw the African slave trade and chattel slavery legally abolished in the Western world, while the Poor Laws were changed and the Corn Laws repealed, while the brutalities of the press gang were mitigated, and while the franchise and educational opportunities were expanded, yet poverty persisted, crime flourished, and the powerful continued to exploit the weak, making it necessary for Henry Solly to face the same fundamental problems as had confronted Granville Sharp. That the later reformers were aware of their continuity with the past and took up their tasks with hope rather than with cynicism is a tribute to the on-going antislavery spirit of a 'saving remnant' in the human race.

When one studies a group of individuals with such diverse personalities one is bound to react to them individually, as I have done. Sharp, Currie and Brewster came from families of some gentility; Solly, Martineau, Thompson, Rathbone and Sturge were of the bourgeoisie; Rushton and Roscoe were of the working class, and only Barker of the poorest of the poor. One is tempted to conclude that therefore it is obvious why Barker, who had the most to be bitter about, was the most contentious. Rushton, too, had 'just cause' in the tragedy of his blindness to react as ferociously as he did. But there is no equivalent reason to explain why Brewster was sometimes abrasive beyond the point of ordinary civility. While Barker was the most explosive and controversial, the most demogogic, especially in the expression of his antireligious views, he was really no more radical than some of the others in his political and economic opinions. Rushton's espousal of republicanism and Solly's support of a good measure of socialism marked them as just as radical intellectually, each in the context of his own time. From one point of consideration, Harriet Martineau was the most revolutionary simply by virtue of what she did as a woman in Victorian England. Yet I doubt that she ever thought of herself in that light. She simply accepted the task before her, as the rest did: some things needed doing, and they did them.

It is a bit difficult to like pious Joseph Sturge, the most single-minded of the lot as a reformer; easier to be drawn to Rathbone and Sharp, who wore their piety more lightly. Yet I could never doubt either Sturge's utmost sincerity or the trust of the poor in Birmingham that he really was their friend. T. P. Thompson easily wins the best-sense-of-humour award. He strikes one, also, as the least emotional, most objective, with Martineau, Solly, Rathbone and Currie close behind in their realism.

Were these people 'typical' abolitionists? Decidedly they do not fit the old stereotype of 'telescopic' philanthropists who focused their benevolence only on black slaves 3000 miles across the Atlantic Ocean. Neither were they the victims of a decline in class status. Some of them were in the mould of paternalists motivated by *noblesse oblige*, but the interesting point is the degree to which they broke out of that mould. I think one can perceive a gradual weakening of that approach as one moves from abolitionists of the late eighteenth century such as Rathbone and Roscoe to Sturge, Martineau and Thompson in the middle of the nineteenth century, and on, in another stage, to Barker and Solly (discounting Barker's swing to conservatism in old age). However, as I have tried to show in these essays, even the early abolitionists were beginning to think of 'the people' not only as objects of charity, but as citizens with rights – both political and economic rights. They repeatedly voiced objections to 'class legislation', thus indicating an ideology which rejected the view of labour as simply one factor in an economic equation. Economic gains were essential, but were far from being an exclusive goal. Civil liberty and intellectual awareness, to be achieved through education, were integral parts of their vision for the evolution of a future society that would be both just and conducive to the 'pursuit of happiness'. They were not out to overthrow capitalism, but they insisted that it be capitalism 'with heart', capitalism as a servant of human values. That philosophy underlay Sharp's actions as much as it did Henry Solly's. Most of these reformers had trouble divesting themselves of the paternalistic attitude that the lower classes needed the guidance of the middle or upper classes. Again it was Solly and Barker who moved the furthest away from that pattern; Solly lived to see the realization of his hope that the working classes would produce their own leaders.

I am not trying to create a new stereotype of an abolitionist as someone who always balanced concern for the slave with concern for the white working man. We need many more studies on that question – one, for instance, on abolitionist mill-owners and their employees, their attitudes toward one another and the conditions under which they operated. Neither am I arguing that abolitionists were always radicals or even liberals in their approach to social and political reform. In the 1950s and 1960s I was one of several historians who addressed the question, 'Who Were the Abolitionists?' in an attempt to see if a profile of a typical American abolitionist was possible.[2] After some thirty years of studying them in both America and Great Britain, I am still faced with the impossibility of categorizing them by wealth, class, religion, politics, or psychological motivation. But, when more studies of individual British abolitionists have been done, and as research proceeds on mass involvement, I suspect that we shall conclude that the antislavery movement was both for the people and by the people to an extent we hitherto failed to realize.

# Notes

The following are generally identified by surname only: Joseph *Barker*, Sir (Dr) John *Bowring*, the Revd Patrick *Brewster*, Lord Henry *Brougham*, Richard *Cobden*, Dr James *Currie*, William Lloyd *Garrison*, the Marquis de *Lafayette*, Harriet *Martineau*, Francis *Place*, William *Rathbone* the fourth, William *Roscoe*, Dr Benjamin *Rush*, Edward *Rushton* the elder, Granville *Sharp*, the Revd Henry *Solly*, Colonel (etc.) T. Perronet *Thompson*, William *Wilberforce*, Henry C. *Wright*.

The notes for each chapter are self-contained, with full publication or location details on first reference to each source. With manuscript collections, authorship is to be attributed to the subject of the collection unless otherwise stated.

*Abbreviations used in the notes*

| BL | British Library |
|---|---|
| BPL | Boston Public Library, Boston, Mass. |
| *DNB* | *Dictionary of National Biography* |
| GES | Glasgow Emancipation Society |
| HO | Home Office |
| PRO | Public Record Office |

## NOTES TO THE INTRODUCTION

1. *Anti-Slavery, Religion and Reform: Essays in Memory of Roger Anstey*, ed. Christine Bolt and Seymour Drescher (Folkestone: William Dawson, 1980); *Slavery and British Society 1776–1846*, ed. James Walvin (London: Macmillan, 1982).

2. Thomas Clarkson, *The History of the Rise, Progress, and Accomplishment of the Abolition of the African Slave Trade, by the British Parliament*, 2 vols (London, 1808).

3. Albert Bushnell Hart, *Slavery and Abolition 1831–1841* (New York and London: Harper, 1907); Mary S. Locke, *Anti-Slavery in America from the Introduction of African Slaves to the Prohibition of the Slave Trade (1619–1808)* (1901; repr. Gloucester, Mass.: Peter Smith, 1965); Alice Dana Adams, *The Neglected Period of Anti-Slavery in America (1808–1831)* (1908; repr. Gloucester, Mass.: Peter Smith, 1964); Sir Reginald Coupland, *The British Anti-Slavery Movement* (London: Oxford Univ. Press, 1933); Frank J. Klingberg, *The Anti-Slavery Movement in England: A Study in English Humanitarianism* (New Haven, Conn.: Yale Univ. Press, 1926); William L. Mathieson, *British Slavery and its Abolition, 1823–1838*

176

(London and New York: Longmans Green, 1926); Gilbert H. Barnes, *The Anti-Slavery Impulse, 1830–1844* (1933; repr. New York: Harcourt Brace & World, 1964); Dwight L. Dumond, *Antislavery Origins of the Civil War in the United States* (Ann Arbor: Univ. of Michigan Press, 1939).

4. Louis Filler, *The Crusade against Slavery 1830–1860* (New York: Harper & Row, 1960); Dwight L. Dumond, *Antislavery: The Crusade for Freedom in America* (Ann Arbor: Univ. of Michigan Press, 1961); Christine Bolt, *The Anti-Slavery Movement and Reconstruction* (London: Oxford Univ. Press, 1969); Howard Temperley, *British Antislavery 1833–1870* (Columbia: Univ. of South Carolina Press, 1972); Betty Fladeland, *Men and Brothers: Anglo-American Antislavery Co-operation* (Urbana: Univ. of Illinois Press, 1972); Merton Dillon, *The Abolitionists: The Growth of a Dissenting Minority* (DeKalb: Northern Illinois Univ. Press, 1974). One could carry this list on to younger writers as well.

5. Eric William's *Capitalism and Slavery* (Chapel Hill: Univ. of North Carolina Press, 1944) stimulated an on-going debate over the economic factor in the antislavery movement. Two of the strongest rebuttals are Roger Anstey, 'Capitalism and Slavery: A Critique', *Economic History Review*, 2nd ser., vol. 21 (1968) pp. 307–20; and Seymour Drescher, *Econocide, British Slavery in the Era of Abolition* (Pittsburgh: Univ. of Pittsburgh Press, 1977).

6. Bernard Mandel, *Labor: Free and Slave. Workingmen and the Anti-Slavery Movement in the United States* (New York: Associated Authors, 1955); E. M. Hunt, 'The North of England Agitation for the Abolition of the Slave Trade 1780–1800' (unpublished MA thesis, University of Manchester [1959]); James Walvin, 'English Democratic Societies and Popular Radicalism 1791–1800' (unpublished PhD thesis, University of York, 1969); Gloria Clare Taylor, 'Some American Reformers and Their Influence on Reform Movements in Great Britain from 1830–1860' (unpublished PhD thesis, University of Edinburgh, 1960); Douglas Riach, 'Ireland and the Campaign against American Slavery, 1830–1860' (unpublished PhD thesis, University of Edinburgh, 1975).

7. Richard Blackett, *Building an Antislavery Wall* (Baton Rouge: Louisiana State Univ. Press, 1983). James Walvin, 'The Rise of British Popular Sentiment for Abolition 1787–1832', and Seymour Drescher, 'Two Variants of Antislavery: Religious Organization and Social Mobilization in Britain and France, 1780–1870', both in *Anti-Slavery, Religion, and Reform*, ed. Bolt and Drescher, pp. 149–62 and 43–63; Seymour Drescher, 'Capitalism and the Decline of Slavery: The British Case in Comparative Perspective', in *Comparative Perspectives on Slavery in New World Plantation Societies*, ed. Vera Rubin and Arthur Tuden, Annals of the New York Academy of Sciences, vol. 292 (1977) pp. 132–42. Quotations from pp. 138 and 139. Several other essays in the Bolt–Drescher volume which contribute to the theme are those by Serge Daget, Pieter C. Emmer, G. M. Ditchfield, and esp. Brian Harrison, 'A Genealogy of Reform' (pp. 101–18), and Eric Foner, 'Abolitionism and the Labor Movement in Antebellum America' (pp. 254–69). See also Royden Harrison, 'British Labour and American Slavery', *Science and Society*, vol. xxx (Dec 1961) pp. 291–319. In *Slavery and British Society*, ed. Walvin, see esp. Seymour Drescher, 'Public

Opinion and the Destruction of British Colonial Slavery' (pp. 22–48), and James Walvin, 'The Propaganda of Antislavery' (pp. 49–68).

8. Patricia Hollis, 'Anti-Slavery and British Working-Class Radicalism in the Years of Reform', in *Anti-Slavery, Religion, and Reform*, ed. Bolt and Drescher, pp. 294–315. Quotations from p. 295.

9. Alan M. Kraut, 'The Forgotten Reformers. A Profile of Third Party Abolitionists in Antebellum New York', in *Antislavery Reconsidered: New Perspectives on the Abolitionists*, ed. Lewis Perry and Michael Fellman (Baton Rouge: Louisiana State Univ. Press, 1979) pp. 119–45; Edward Magdol, 'A Remonstrance against the Nebraska Bill: Ogdensburg, NY Antislavery Petitioners', and John B. Jentz, 'The Abolitionist Constituency in Jacksonian New York City', papers delivered at 1978 session of the Organization of American Historians; John B. Jentz, 'Artisans, Evangelicals and the City: a Social History of the Labor and Abolitionist Movements in Jacksonian New York' (unpublished PhD dissertation, City University of New York, 1977).

10. For example, Clifford S. Griffin, *Their Brothers Keepers: Moral Stewardship in the United States, 1800–1865* (New Brunswick, NJ: Rutgers Univ. Press, 1960); and Charles I. Foster, *An Errand of Mercy: The Evangelical United Front 1790–1837* (Chapel Hill: Univ. of North Carolina Press, 1960). This portrayal is evident more recently in David B. Davis, *The Problem of Slavery in the Age of Revolution* (Ithaca, NY: Cornell Univ. Press, 1975).

11. Ernest M. Howse, *Saints in Politics* (Toronto: Univ. of Toronto Press, 1952) p. 116; Frank Thistlethwaite, *The Anglo-American Connection in the Early Nineteenth Century* (Toronto: Univ. of Toronto Press, 1959) p. 119.

12. Davis, *The Problem of Slavery*, chs 8 and 9. Quotations from p. 467.

13. I was amused when an article of mine was criticised by an anonymous reviewer for including too many abolitionists who were not in David Davis's index.

14. Roger Anstey, *The Atlantic Slave Trade and British Abolition 1760–1810* (London: Cambridge Univ. Press, 1975) pp. 179–81. For Cobbett see *Cobbett's Political Register*, 29 May 1830.

15. Josiah Wedgwood to Thomas Bentley, 16 and 18 Sep, 3 and 16 Oct, 17 Nov 1779, and Wedgwood to Dr Darwin, July 1789, Wedgwood Correspondence, John Rylands Library, Manchester; Paul Mantoux, *The Industrial Revolution in the Eighteenth Century* (London: Jonathan Cape, 1928) pp. 411–12.

16. Davis, *The Problem Slavery*, pp. 377, 390; Howard Temperley, 'Anti-Slavery as a Form of Cultural Imperialism', in *Anti-Slavery, Religion, and Reform*, ed. Bolt and Drescher, pp. 339, 342; Drescher, 'Cart Whip and Billy Roller: Antislavery and Reform Symbolism in Industrializing Britain', *Journal of Social History*, vol. 15, no. 1 (Sep 1981) pp. 3–24. See also essay on Sharp in this volume.

17. R. K. Webb, *Harriet Martineau, A Radical Victorian* (London: William Heinemann, 1960); Richard Hofstadter, *Social Darwinism in American Thought* (Boston, Mass.: Beacon, 1955) pp. 52–3; Jonathan A. Glickstein, '"Poverty is Not Slavery." American Abolitionists and the Competitive Labor Market', in *Antislavery Reconsidered*, ed. Perry and Fellman, p. 217.

See essay on Martineau in this volume.

18. Davis, *The Problem of Slavery*, p. 357 n.; G. D. H. Cole, *Chartist Portraits* (New York: Macmillan, 1965) p. 104.

19. Hollis, in *Anti-Slavery, Religion and Reform*, ed. Bolt and Drescher, P. 295.

20. Betty Fladeland, '"Our Cause Being One and the Same": Abolitionists and Chartism', in *Slavery and British Society*, ed. Walvin, pp. 69–99.

21. *Cobbett's Political Register* for 1821 carried a series of letters to James Cropper in defence of West Indian slavery. See also the issues of 6 and 13 Dec 1823, 29 May and 26 June 1830, for examples of his racism. For his switch, see the *Register* throughout 1831; also, Archibald Prentice, *Historical Sketches and Personal Recollections of Manchester* (London, 1851) p. 353.

22. Fladeland, in *Slavery and British Society*, ed. Walvin.

23. For rebuttal, see ibid., and Hollis, in *Anti-Slavery, Religion and Reform*, ed. Bolt and Drescher.

24. Foner, ibid. For American abolitionists who were influenced by their encounters with British wage slavery and with Chartism, see Fladeland, in *Slavery and British Society*, ed. Walvin.

25. David Eltis, 'Abolitionist Perspectives of Society', ibid., pp. 195–213.

26. Quoted in Moses I. Finley, *Ancient Slavery and Modern Ideology* (New York: Viking, 1980) p. 65. My thanks to Seymour Drescher for the quotation.

27. *Northern Star*, 5 May 1838; *Poor Man's Guardian*, 17 Nov 1832.

28. Fladeland, in *Slavery and British Society*, ed. Walvin.

29. Brian Harrison, 'A Genealogy of Reform', in *Anti-Slavery, Religion, and Reform*, ed. Bolt and Drescher, p. 122; and *Drink and the Victorians: The Temperance Question in England 1815–1872* (Pittsburgh: Univ. of Pittsburgh Press, 1971) p. 25.

## NOTES TO CHAPTER ONE: GRANVILLE SHARP

1. It is now understood that the Somerset case did not result in freedom for all blacks in England. Numerous cases were brought between 1772 and 1833 and their decisions indicate ambiguity and confusion. It was not until the Emancipation Act of 1833 that the issues were finally settled. See James Walvin, *Black and White: The Negro in English Society 1555–1945* (London: Penguin, 1973) chs 7–8.

2. See, for example, Roger Anstey, *The Atlantic Slave Trade and British Abolition 1760–1810* (London: Macmillan, 1975); David B. Davis, *The Problem of Slavery in the Age of Revolution, 1770–1823* (Ithaca, NY: Cornell Univ. Press, 1975); and Betty Fladeland, *Men and Brothers: Anglo-American Antislavery Co-operation* (Urbana: Univ. of Illinois Press, 1972).

3. Anstey, *Atlantic Slave Trade*, p. 243. Sharp was much concerned about the re-establishment of the Anglican Church in the United States after the Revolution, and sent numerous letters of advice to his American correspondents. See Rush to Sharp, 27 Apr and 15 May 1784, Sharp to Rush, 10 Oct

1785, and Rush to Sharp, 23 Apr 1786, in 'The Correspondence of Benjamin Rush and Granville Sharp, 1773–1809', ed. John A. Woods, *Journal of American Studies*, vol. I, no. 1 (Apr 1967) pp. 1–38. The quotation on loving one's neighbour is from *Memoirs of Granville Sharp*, ed. Prince Hoare, 2nd edn, 2 vols (London: Henry Colburn, 1828) vol. II, p. 382.

4. 'Extracts from a Small Memoranda Book', entries for 26 July 1775 and 10 Apr 1777, transcripts of G. Sharp Papers at Hardwicke Court in possession of John A. Woods. I am greatly indebted to him for allowing me to use these papers. For factual data on Sharp's life see also *Memoirs*, vol. I, pp. 41–6, 184–8; and Albert F. Pollard, 'Granville Sharp', *DNB*, vol. XVII (London: Oxford University Press, 1917) pp. 1337–42.

5. *Memoirs of Sharp*, vol. I, pp. 22–3; Sharp to Alderman Beckford, 17 May 1768, Granville Sharp Letter Book, York Minster Library, York.

6. Sharp, 'Some Remarks on the Case of John Hylas and his Wife Mary', p. 14, and Sharp to Joseph Banks, 20 Feb 1772, Sharp Letter Book; *Memoirs of Sharp*, vol. I, p. 212. See Davis, *The Problem of Slavery*, ch. 9, for an extended treatment of Sharp's theorizing on the subject of villeinage. For more background see Christopher Hill, 'The Norman Yoke', in *Democracy and the Labour Movement*, ed. John Saville (London: Lawrence and Wishart, 1954) pp. 11–66.

7. Sharp to Mr Lloyd (Gray's Inn) for the Archbishop of York (Dr Drummond), 30 July 1772, Sharp Letter Book.

8. Sharp to James Sharp (brother), 12 Sep 1769, ibid.

9. Sharp to the Revd Findlay, 21 July and 14 Aug 1772, ibid.

10. Sharp to A. Benezet, 23 Sep 1772, ibid.

11. Sharp to Rush, 18 July 1775, ff. 80, 88, 89, Benjamin Rush Papers, Library Company of Philadelphia, Historical Society of Pennsylvania, Philadelphia. See also [Sharp], *A General Plan for Laying Out Towns and Townships, on the New-Acquired Lands in the East Indies, America, or Elsewhere; In order to promote Cultivation, and raise the Value of all the Adjoining Land, at the Price of giving gratis the Town-Lots, and, in some Cases (as in new Colonies), also the small Out-Lots, to the first Settlers and their Heirs, so long as they possess no other Land; and on other equitable Conditions* [n.p., 1794]. Inherent in Sharp's plan was a revival of the old English frankpledge under which each settler agreed to take his turn at militia duty and other community obligations.

12. The quotation is from Sharp to James Sharp, 12 Sep 1769, Sharp Letter Book; Sharp to Wilberforce, 4 June 1795, Wilberforce Papers, Duke University, Durham, NC.

13. Sharp to James Manning, 21 Feb 1785, and to Benjamin Franklin, 17 June 1785, J. A. Woods Transcripts.

14. Sharp Letter Book, entry for 4 Aug 1768.

15. Sharp to Rufus King, 30 Jan 1797, J. A. Woods Transcripts; [Sharp], *A Short Sketch of Temporary Regulations (until Better Shall be Proposed) for the Intended Settlement on the Grain Coast of Africa, Near Sierra Leone*, 2nd ed (London: H. Bladwin, 1786). He included in this plan a rule for an eight-hour work day.

16. Sharp to Dr Fothergill, 27 Oct 1772, Sharp Letter Book; Sharp to A.

Benezet, 21 Aug 1772 and 7 July 1773, ibid; Sharp to Lord Dartmouth, 10 Oct, 27 Nov and 31 Dec 1772, and 16 Jan 1773, ibid. As late as 1796 Sharp was evidently still trying to interest other reformers in this question. See Sharp to Wilberforce, 7 Feb 1796, Anti-Slavery Papers, Cornell Univ. Library, Ithaca, NY. Sharp's seriousness in upholding 'true' Protestantism is evident in his sense of national rivalry with Catholic Spain, but also in his arguments over the Jewish religion and his denunciation of the dangerous opinions of Joseph Priestley. He did not want the Scottish emigrants to Pennsylvania to come under Priestley's influence. He seems not to have worried so much about the possible influence of the Quakers, although he did deplore what he considered the Friends' doctrinal errors. See also Sharp to the Revd Findlay, 16 Mar 1773, Sharp Letter Book.

17. Henry Douglas to Sharp, 15 Dec 1772, and Sharp to Henry Douglas, 21 Dec 1772, Sharp Letter Book. See also Paul Mantoux, *The Industrial Revolution in the Eighteenth Century* (London: Jonathan Cape, 1928) p. 74, on the conditions of these workers.

18. Sharp to Henry Douglas, 21 Dec 1772, Sharp Letter Book.

19. Sharp to Wilberforce, 25 Mar 1794, 4 and 27 Aug 1796, and 'Notes on Impressment', J. A. Woods Transcripts; Sharp, *Tracts Concerning the Ancient and Only True Legal Means of National Defence, by a Free Militia*, 3rd ed (London: Dilly, 1782); *DNB*, vol. xvii, pp. 1337–42.

20. 'Notes on Impressment', J. A. Woods Transcripts.

21. Sharp Diary, entries for 20 May 1779 and 26 May 1783, ibid.; Fladeland, *Men and Brothers*, p. 25.

22. *Memoirs of Sharp*, vol. i, pp. 238–55. The quotation is from p. 253.

23. Sharp to Henry Douglas, 21 Dec 1772, Sharp Letter Book.

24. Sharp Diary, entry for 11 Sep 1793, J. A. Woods Transcripts.

25. Sharp to William Dolben, 1777, J. A. Woods Transcripts; Sharp Diary, entries for 1793, ibid.; 'Remarks on the Answer of a Learned Writer to Mr King's Signs of the Times', ibid.; Fladeland, *Men and Brothers*, p. 51; Mantoux, *Industrial Revolution*, pp. 469–70; Roger Fulford, *Samuel Whitbread 1764–1815. A Study in Opposition* (London: Macmillan, 1967) p. 51. Whitbread is another good example of an abolitionist who was involved in measures to relieve the white working classes.

26. Sharp Diary, entries throughout 1794, J. A. Woods Transcripts; Sharp to Josiah Dornford, 9 Jan 1807, ibid.; *Memoirs of Sharp*, vol. ii, pp. 194–5, 226; *Memoir of the Life of Elizabeth Fry with Extracts from her Journal and Letters. Edited by Two of her Daughters*, 2 vols (London, 1847) vol. i, pp. 320–2.

27. *Memoirs of Sharp*, vol. i, pp. 226–7.

28. Davis, *The Problem of Slavery*, p. 382; Walvin, *Black and White*, p. 147. Walvin calls Sharp 'gullible' for believing the rosy reports from Sierra Leone.

29. Sharp to the Bishop of London, 14 Jan 1795, J. A. Woods Transcripts; Mantoux, *Industrial Revolution*, p. 446.

30. Sharp to the Bishop of London, 14 Jan 1795, and to Capel Lofft, 24 Dec 1785, J. A. Woods Transcripts.

31. Sharp to the Bishop of London, 14 Jan 1795, J. A. Woods Transcripts. The estate was Fairsted, which was willed to Sharp by the widow of General

James Oglethorpe. Sharp's proposed disposal of his estate revenues did not work out because of legal entanglements. *Memoirs of Sharp*, vol. II, pp. 187–99.

32. Sharp to Josiah Dornford, 9 Jan 1807, Sharp Letter Book.

33. John Sharp, 'An Account of the Uses to which the Old Roman Tower in Bamburgh Castle is at the Present Appropriated', J. A. Woods Transcripts. John Sharp was also an abolitionist. *Memoirs of Sharp*, vol. I, pp. 26–7.

34. The yacht belonged to Granville's brother James. Sharp Diary, entry for 29 Aug 1777, J. A. Woods Transcripts; John A. Woods, 'James Sharp: Common Councillor of London in the Time of Wilkes', in *Statesmen, Scholars and Merchants. Essays in Eighteenth Century History Presented to Dame Lucy Sutherland*, ed. J. S. Bromley and P. G. M. Dickenson (Oxford: Clarendon Press, 1973) ch. 14; *Memoirs of Sharp*, vol. I, pp. 214–15.

35. Sharp, *Tracts Concerning the Ancient and Only True Legal Means of Defence*; see also Sharp to Wilberforce, 25 Mar 1794 and 27 Oct 1796, J. A. Woods Transcripts.

36. Sharp to Benjamin Franklin, 17 June 1785; Sharp to Lafayette, 2 Aug 1789; and Sharp to Rufus King, 30 Jan 1797, J. A. Woods Transcripts.

37. Sharp to Rush, 21 Feb 1774, Rush Papers; Sharp to Rush, 4 Aug 1783, and Rush to Sharp, 28 Nov and 27 Apr 1784, in *Journal of American Studies*, vol. I, no. 1.

38. Sharp to Rush, 21 Feb 1774, Rush Papers; Sharp to Lord Carysfort [?], 5 Dec 1781, J. A. Woods Transcripts; *DNB*, vol. XVII, pp. 1337–42; Sharp, *A Declaration of the People's Natural Right to a Share in the Legislature; which is the Fundamental Principle of the British Constitution of State*, 2nd edn (London: B. White, 1775). The quotation is from Sharp to Joseph Banks, 20 Feb 1772, Sharp Letter Book. Sharp's diary entry for 17 Dec 1781 reveals that he told the Bishop of Chester that he thought all of Britain's troubles in America were caused by the slave trade (J. A. Woods Transcripts).

39. Sharp, *A Declaration of the People's Natural Right*; Sharp to Earl Stanhope, 27 Apr 1812, J. A. Woods Transcripts; Sharp to Rush, 27 July 1774, in *Journal of American Studies*, vol. I, no. 1. Sometimes Sharp's fears combined with his religious intensity led to rather eccentric conclusions, such as the belief that Napoleon represented the 'Little Horn' of Daniel's prophecy. See *DNB*, XVII, pp. 1337–42. Sharp was also sensitive to people's misuse of their power over animals: if people would mistreat dumb beasts although it might be contrary to their own pecuniary interests, it followed that they would mistreat slaves as well. Sharp to the Revd Findlay, 14 Aug 1772, Sharp Letter Book. On 19 June 1793 he noted in his diary the cab number of a coachman whom he had seen beating his horse, presumably to report him (J. A. Woods Transcripts).

40. Numerous diary entries and letters throughout the period of the American Revolution, J. A. Woods Transcripts; Sharp to John Wilkes, 12 Jan 1780, Wilkes MSS, Add. MS 30872, f. 168, BL.

41. Sharp to Wilberforce, 25 Mar 1794, J. A. Woods Transcripts; Woods, in *Statesmen, Scholars and Merchants*, ed. Bromley and Dickenson.

42. Sharp: *The Legal Means of Political Reformation, Proposed in Two Small*

*Tracts, viz. The First on 'Equitable Representation', and the legal means of obtaining it (1777); The Second on 'Annual Parliaments, the ancient and most salutary "Rights of the People"' (1774). To which are added A Letter to a Member of the Surry [sic] Committee, in Defense of the Right of the People to elect Representatives for every Session of Parliament, viz. Not only 'every Year once', but also 'more often if Need be' (1780); A Circular Letter to the several petitioning Counties, Cities, and Towns, to warn them against the late Proposition for triennial Elections (1780); Appendix to the Legal Means of Political Reformation and the Claims of the People of England,* 8th ed (London: H. L. Galabin, 1797); and *An Appendix to the Second Edition of Mr Lofft's 'Observations on a late Publication, entitled "A Dialogue on the Actual State of Parliaments"': and on some other Tracts equally inimical to the Constitution of 'Free Parliaments': Being a Farther Examination of the Argument, lately published by Mr Hatsell, (in his Precedents of Proceedings, &c.) against the antient Law and Constitution of this 'Kingdom, that the King ought to hold Parliaments elected annually'* [London, 1783].

43. The word 'winsome' is used by Ernest M. Howse in *Saints in Politics: The Clapham Sect and the Growth of Freedom* (Toronto: Univ. of Toronto Press, 1952) p. 21.

44. *Memoirs of Sharp*, vol. I, p. 219; wine lists for election dinners, J. A. Woods Transcripts.

45. Sharp's death is recorded with other family deaths on the cover of Memo Book 2, J. A. Woods Transcripts.

46. Stephens is quoted by Pollard in the *DNB* article on Sharp (vol. XVII, pp. 1337–42).

## NOTES TO CHAPTER TWO: A QUARTET OF LIVERPUDLIANS

1. Ramsay Muir, *A History of Liverpool* (London: Williams & Norgate, 1907) p. 204; Gomer Williams, *History of the Liverpool Privateers and Letters of Marque with an Account of the Liverpool Slave Trade* (London: William Heinemann, 1877; repr. New York: Economic Classics, Augustus M. Kelley, 1966) p. 594; Jean Trapp, 'The Liverpool Movement for the Abolition of the English Slave Trade', *Journal of Negro History*, vol. XIII (July 1928) pp. 265–85.

2. Roger Anstey, *The Atlantic Slave Trade and British Abolition 1760–1810* (London: Macmillan, 1975) pp. 4–8, 10 (n. 26). We now know that, contrary to contemporary perceptions, profits from the slave trade were not excessive on the average, and not high enough to form the basis of the British Industrial Revolution. See ibid., pp. 46–51. Also, Emily A. Rathbone, *Records of the Rathbone Family* (Edinburgh: R. & R. Clark, 1913) ch. 2, on the importance of the slave trade to Liverpool.

3. There were six William Rathbones in succession, but unless otherwise specified my references in this essay are to the fourth.

4. There is far more material available on Roscoe than on the others, so his name dominates these pages. There is less on Rathbone, much less on

Currie, and least of all on Rushton. I think the lack of evidence accurately reflects the descending order of their roles. Of course, Roscoe lived much longer than the others.

5. Emily Rathbone, *Records of the Rathbone Family*; Sheila Marriner, *Rathbones of Liverpool 1845–1873* (Liverpool: Liverpool Univ. Press, 1961).

6. Emily Rathbone, *Records of the Rathbone Family*, ch. 1; Eleanor F. Rathbone, *William Rathbone. A Memoir* (London: Macmillan, 1905) p. 8. This is a biography of the fifth William Rathbone (1787–1868) but also includes a good bit of material on the fourth William.

7. Emily Rathbone, *Records of the Rathbone Family*, ch. 2; Marriner, *Rathbones of Liverpool*, p. 13. Evidently the Rathbone firm in the time of the sixth William, at least, traded in American cotton. Eleanor, in *William Rathbone*, p. 136, says that on his visits to the United States he heard and saw the best side of slavery and was influenced by Southern charm.

8. Emily Rathbone, *Records of the Rathbone Family*, pp. 88–89, 166.

9. Ibid., p. 69.

10. Henry Roscoe, *The Life of William Roscoe*, 2 vols (London: T. Cadell, 1833), is a major source of information on Roscoe, as is a more modern biography, George Chandler's *William Roscoe of Liverpool* (London: B. T. Batsford, 1953).

11. Chandler, *Roscoe*, p. xv. For the information on George Thompson I am indebted to Nicholas Spence, a descendant of Thompson, who is currently working on a biography of him.

12. Emily Rathbone, *Records of the Rathbone Family*, pp. 137–9. Currie's son William Wallace Currie edited *Memoir of the Life, Writings and Correspondence of James Currie, MD FRS of Liverpool*, 2 vols (London: Longmans, Rees, Orme, Brown and Green, 1831). See also MS of the Journal kept by Dr James Currie during a voyage from Nixonton, NC, to the Island of St Martin's, 1776, James Currie Papers, Central Libraries, Liverpool.

13. Emily Rathbone, *Records of the Rathbone Family*, pp. 142–6; Mary G. Thomas, *Edward Rushton*, no. 1 of *NIB Biographies* (London: National Institute for the Blind, 1951) pp. 5–7. After thirty years of blindness Rushton's eyesight was partially restored by surgery. For several years he lived in destitution on four shillings a week given him by his father after his stepmother turned him out of their house. See ibid., pp. 144–6.

14. Chandler, *Roscoe*, pp. 340–2. Pt II of this book, pp. 171–470, contains poems by Roscoe.

15. Ibid., p. xxvii. The introduction to Chandler's book was written by Sir Alfred Shennan, who notes that Roscoe has been called Liverpool's greatest citizen. The book was published for the bicentennial of Roscoe's birth.

16. Henry Roscoe, *Life of William Roscoe*, vol. I, p. 78; [Roscoe], *The Wrongs of Africa, A Poem* (London: R. Faulder, 1787); Chandler, *Roscoe*, pp. 343–78.

17. [Rushton], *West Indian Eclogues* (London: W. Lowndes [1787]). This poem was dedicated to the Right Revd Porteus Beilby, Bishop of Chester,

in gratitude for his efforts on behalf of West Indian slaves.

18. Henry Roscoe, *Life of William Roscoe*, vol. I, p. 78; Williams, *History of the Liverpool Privateers*, pt II, ch. 4: 'The Abolition Movement'. The names of Roscoe and two Rathbones appear on the list of Liverpool men (eight in all) who contributed to the Society for the Abolition of the Slave Trade in Jan 1788.

19. Muir, *History of Liverpool*, p. 203; Williams, *History of the Liverpool Privateers*, pp. 572–75, with quotation from Currie on p. 574; Roscoe, *Life of Lorenzo de' Medici Called the Magnificent with a Memoir of the Author*, ed. William Hazlitt (London: George Routledge, 1883) p. xxix.

20. Currie to Admiral Sir Graham Moore, 16 Mar 1788, and Moore to Currie, 23 Mar 1788, Currie Papers. The poem is found in Chandler, *Roscoe*, pp. 272–3. George Chandler, the biographer of Roscoe, believed that Currie did not share Roscoe's 'moral fearlessness' but was more sensitive to popular opinion in support of the slave trade.

21. Moore to Currie, 1 Apr 1788, Currie Papers.

22. Thomas Clarkson, *The History of the Rise, Progress and Accomplishment of the Abolition of the Slave Trade, By the British Parliament* [abridged by Evan Lewis] (Wilmington, Del.: R. Porter, 1816) p. 119.

23. Ibid., pp. 119–25; Williams, *History of the Liverpool Privateers*, pp. 575–9; Eleanor Rathbone, *William Rathbone*, p. 8.

24. Currie to Graham Moore, 23 Mar 1788, Currie Papers.

25. Williams, *History of the Liverpool Privateers*, pp. 609–13; Ian Sellers, *William Roscoe, the Roscoe Circle and Radical Politics in Liverpool, 1787–1807*, repr. from *Transactions of the Historic Society of Lancashire and Cheshire*, vol. 120 (1968) pp. 45–62. There do not seem to be any extant copies of the *Liverpool Herald*.

26. Currie to Miss Cropper, 23 May 1788, in W. W. Currie, *Memoir of James Currie*, vol. II, pp. 278–80; Currie to Miss Cropper, 24 June 1788, Currie Papers; Anstey, *Atlantic Slave Trade*, pp. 269–70, 419–420.

27. Rushton, *Poems* (London: T. Ostell, 1806) p. 107.

28. Thomas, *Rushton*, p. 11.

29. Roscoe to Captain William Lace, 12 July 1792, in Williams, *History of the Liverpool Privateers*, pp. 614–15.

30. *Poems and Other Writings by the Late Edward Rushton. To Which Is Added, A Sketch of the Life of the Author*, ed. William Shepperd (London: Effingham Wilson, 1824) pp. 38–40.

31. [Rushton], *Expostulatory Letter to George Washington, of Mount Vernon, in Virginia, on his Continuing to Be a Proprietor of Slaves* (n.p., 1797).

32. Henry Roscoe, *Life of William Roscoe*, vol. I, p. 104; Chandler, *Roscoe*, p. 287.

33. Chandler, *Roscoe*, pp. 379–81; [Roscoe], *Ode to the People of France; Imitated from a Canzone of Petrarch: with the Italian Original* (Liverpool, 1789).

34. Chandler, *Roscoe*, pp. 264–5; Henry Roscoe, *Life of William Roscoe*, vol. I, p. 106.

35. Rushton, 'Song in Commemoration of the French Revolution, 1791', *Poems*, pp. 102–4.

36. Chandler, *Roscoe*, pp. 70, 384–5.
37. Ibid., pp. 83, 386–90; Henry Roscoe, *Life of William Roscoe*, vol. I, p. 115.
38. Chandler, *Roscoe*, p. xxv.
39. Currie to Dr Thomas Percival, 27 Jan and 7 Feb 1790, and to the Revd Edward Owen, 24 Feb 1790, Currie Papers; W. W. Currie, *Memoir of James Currie*, vol. I, p. 140; Sellers, *William Roscoe, the Roscoe Circle and Radical Politics*. Warrington was a centre of Nonconformism because of its Dissenting Academy. Priestley had been one of its teachers, and Jean-Paul Marat was a tutor there in the early 1770s. William Shepherd, a friend and fellow member of the Liverpool Literary and Philosophical Society, had been a student there.
40. Muir, *History of Liverpool*, pp. 225–7; Sellers, *William Roscoe, the Roscoe Circle and Radical Politics*.
41. Ibid.; Emily Rathbone, *Records of the Rathbone Family*, ch. 2; obituary of Rathbone, *Monthly Repository*, vol. IV (1809) pp. 232–8.
42. Emily Rathbone, *Records of the Rathbone Family*, pp. 104–5; Sellers, *William Roscoe, the Roscoe Circle and Radical Politics*.
43. Emily Rathbone, *Records of the Rathbone Family*, pp. 106–7; *Monthly Repository*, vol. IV (1809) pp. 232–8; Sellers, *William Roscoe, the Roscoe Circle and Radical Politics*; Henry Roscoe, *Life of William Roscoe*, vol. I, pp. 121–4; Dr Thomas Stuart Traill, *Memoir of William Roscoe* (Liverpool: George Smith, Watts, 1853) p. 22. Traill, Roscoe's physician and friend, prepared the *Memoir* for Liverpool's centennial celebration of Roscoe's birthday.
44. Muir, *History of Liverpool*, p. 227.
45. Rushton, *Poems and Other Writings*, p. 17.
46. Rathbone to William Smith, 3 Feb 1793, Smith Papers, Duke University, Durham, NC; Eleanor Rathbone, *William Rathbone*, pp. 14–15, 27.
47. Quoted in Chandler, *Roscoe*, p. 52.
48. Henry Roscoe, *Life of William Roscoe*, vol. I, pp. 89–97. I have been unable to locate a copy of this pamphlet of Roscoe's.
49. [Roscoe], *Thoughts on the Causes of the Present Failures* (London: J. Johnson, 1793).
50. Jaspar Wilson [Currie], *A Letter, Commercial and Political, Addressed to the Right Hon. William Pitt, in which the Real Interests of Britain in the Present Crisis Are Considered, and Some Observations Are Offered on the General State of Europe* (Dublin: P. Byrne, 1793); Wilberforce to Currie, 21 Jan 1794, Currie Papers. An undated fragment in the Currie Papers explains the origin of the letter.
51. There are several Jaspar Wilson drafts in the Currie Papers.
52. Sellers, *William Roscoe, the Roscoe Circle and Radical Politics*.
53. Wilberforce to Currie, 21 Jan 1794, Currie Papers. Evidently Wilberforce had less compunction about subjecting the West Indies to upheaval. He wrote in a letter to Currie, 13 Apr 1793, that, even if he thought that immediate abolition of the slave trade would cause an insurrection, he would 'not for an instant remit my most strenuous endeavour'.
54. Emily Rathbone, *Records of the Rathbone Family*, p. 109; Chandler, *Roscoe*, pp. 87–8.

55. Rushton, 'The Swallow', *Poems and Other Writings*, p. 21.
56. Quoted in Chandler, *Roscoe*, p. 12.
57. Currie to Mr Gore, 25 Aug 1789, Rathbone Papers, Harold Cohen Library, Liverpool.
58. Muir, *History of Liverpool*, pp. 272–6.
59. Ibid.; Chandler, *Roscoe*, p. xxii; W. W. Currie, *Memoir of James Currie*, vol. II, pp. 373–8.
60. Ibid., vol. I, p. 140; Currie to Mr Gore, 25 Aug and 15 Oct 1789, Rathbone Papers.
61. Emily Rathbone, *Records of the Rathbone Family*, pp. 149, 366–9; William Rathbone, Jr, *Social Duties Considered with Reference to the Organization of Effort in Works of Benevolence and Public Utility* (London: Macmillan, 1867); Eleanor Rathbone, *William Rathbone*, p. 30.
62. Currie to the Earl of Galloway, 25 Dec 1802, in W. W. Currie, *Memoir of James Currie*, vol. II, pp. 373–8; also p. 153.
63. Fragment, Currie to Rathbone, Rathbone Papers; Thomas, *Rushton*, pp. 3–5, 12–14. A commemorative plaque of 1888 names Roscoe as well as Rushton among those deserving credit for the School for the Blind.
64. Rushton, *Poems and Other Writings*, pp. 137–40.
65. Chandler, *Roscoe*, p. 115; Henry Roscoe, *Life of William Roscoe*, vol. I, p. 386. Whitbread was another abolitionist much concerned about the rights of the working classes. As early as 1795 he introduced a bill in the House of Commons to allow magistrates to fix a minimum wage and to jail employers who paid less. He also worked for election reform, more representation of the people in Parliament, and for Poor Law reform. See Roger Fulford, *Samuel Whitbread, 1764–1815. A Study in Opposition* (London: Macmillan, 1967); and Samuel Whitbread, *Substance of a Speech on the Poor Laws: Delivered in the House of Commons, on Thursday, February 19, 1807* (London: J. Ridgway, 1807).
66. Rushton, *Poems and Other Writings*, p. xxvii.
67. Intended Letter to D____ H____ in Edinburgh, 29 Aug 1792, and Currie to Sir William Maxwell, 16 Mar 1793, in W. W. Currie, *Memoir of James Currie*, vol. II, pp. 300–15.
68. Eleanor Rathbone, *William Rathbone*, pp. 14–19, 28.
69. Rushton, *Poems and Other Writings*, p. xvi; Thomas, *Rushton*, pp. 10–11.
70. Chandler, *Roscoe*, p. 59.
71. Muir, *History of Liverpool*, p. 231; Sellers, *William Roscoe, the Roscoe Circle and Radical Politics*.
72. Rushton, *Poems and Other Writings*, pp. 33–7.
73. Ibid., pp. 72–6.
74. 'Toussaint to his Troops', ibid., pp. 94–7.
75. W. W. Currie, *Memoir of James Currie*, vol. I, p. 240.
76. J. R. Hale, *England and the Italian Renaissance: The Growth of Interest in its History and Art* (London: Faber & Faber, 1954) pp. 85–92; Hazlitt, 'Memoir of William Roscoe', in his edn of Roscoe's *Life of Lorenzo de' Medici*, pp. xx–xxxiv; Alfred Shennan's introduction to Chandler's *Roscoe*. Materials from the library Roscoe built up are among the holdings

of the Picton Reference Library in Liverpool, and his magnificent collection of early Italian masters is in the Walker Art Gallery. When Roscoe went bankrupt in 1820, his friends bought up as much as they could of his collections and presented them to the Royal Institution which Roscoe had founded.

77. Henry Roscoe, *Life of William Roscoe*, vol. I, p. 321. Roscoe also wrote some delightful poetry for children, the best known being 'The Butterfly's Ball', which at the request of George III and the Queen was set to music for the young princesses. See Chandler, *Roscoe*, pp. 113–14, 410–11.

78. Washington Irving, 'Roscoe', *The Sketch Book of Geoffrey Crayon, Gent.* (London: J. M. Dent; and New York: E. P. Dutton, 1906) pp. 11–17. Roscoe was also known in America as a naturalist, because he had founded the Liverpool Botanical Garden, which was copied in Philadelphia. See Chandler, *Roscoe*, p. xvii; Henry Roscoe, *Life of William Roscoe*, vol. I, pp. 253, 265.

79. Sellers, *William Roscoe, the Roscoe Circle and Radical Politics*; Williams, *History of the Liverpool Privateers*, p. 620. On Rathbone's disownment by the Society of Friends, see Eleanor Rathbone, *William Rathbone*, pp. 28–9; and Rathbone, *A Memoir of the Proceedings of the Society Called Quakers, Belonging to the Monthly Meeting of Hardshaw in Lancashire, in the Case of the Author of a Publication, Entitled A Narrative of Events Which Have Lately Taken Place in Ireland, &c.* (London: J. Johnson, 1805). James Cropper, who accepted a place on the committee that voted to disown Rathbone, did so with the hope of moderating its judgement, but to no avail.

80. Richard Brooke, *Liverpool as it Was During the Last Quarter of the Eighteenth Century 1775–1800* (Liverpool: J. Mawdsley and Son, 1853) pp. 310–15.

81. Henry Roscoe, *Life of William Roscoe*, pp. 355–7.

82. Ibid., pp. 358–9; Williams, *History of the Liverpool Privateers*, p. 595; Sellers, *William Roscoe, the Roscoe Circle and Radical Politics*.

83. Muir, *History of Liverpool*, pp. 274–5, says that by the early nineteenth century the estimated value of each vote was £20.

84. Currie died in 1805. His views on ending the slave trade are found in an undated fragment in 'Drafts Relating to the Jaspar Wilson Letter', Currie Papers; Currie to Wilberforce, 31 Dec 1787, in W. W. Currie, *Memoir of James Currie*, vol. I, pp. 112–26.

85. Mr Houlbrooke to Roscoe, 12 July 1807, Roscoe Papers, Central Libraries, Liverpool. Houlbrooke was tutor to the Rathbone children and seems to have written the letter for Rathbone, although he – Houlbrooke – opposed any such compromise. See also Roscoe to Rathbone, 14 Feb 1807, Rathbone Papers.

86. *Cobbett's Parliamentary Debates*, 1st ser. (London: Hansard, 1806–20) vol. 8, pp. 961–2; Henry Roscoe, *Life of William Roscoe*, vol. I, pp. 366–78.

87. Rathbone to Roscoe, 28 Feb 1807, Roscoe Papers.

88. Rathbone to Roscoe, 22 April 1807, Roscoe Papers.

89. Sellers, in *William Roscoe, the Roscoe Circle and Radical Politics*, says that the Rathbones and Croppers were so prominent in the American

trade that 'they were already acting as a kind of unofficial consular service for the American government in England'.

90. Obituary of Rathbone, *Monthly Repository*, vol. iv, pp. 232–8.

91. See, for example, Capel Lofft to Roscoe, 6 and 17 Nov 1806, 9 Jan 1807, and several more letters throughout 1808 and 1809, Roscoe Papers; Mrs Rathbone, for her husband, to Roscoe, 27 Feb 1808, and one which follows, undated, ibid. The Rathbone letters, especially, convey the sense of excitement in the behind-the-scenes manoeurving of these liberals and/or radicals.

92. Henry Roscoe, *Life of William Roscoe*, vol. i, pp. 378–82.

93. See *Memoirs of the Life of Sir Samuel Romilly, Written by Himself; with a Selection from his Correspondence, Edited by his Sons*, 2nd edn, 3 vols (London: John Murray, 1840).

94. Chandler, *Roscoe*, pp. 115–16; Henry Roscoe, *Life of William Roscoe*, vol. i, pp. 382–5.

95. Ibid., pp. 391–4; Emily Rathbone, *Records of the Rathbone Family*, pp. 289–92, has an extract from the diary of Elizabeth Greg Rathbone (wife of William the fifth) for 2 May 1807, containing a vivid description of the physical confrontation with the Tarletonites.

96. Henry Roscoe, *Life of William Roscoe*, vol. i, p. 403; Sellers, *William Roscoe, the Roscoe Circle and Radical Politics*, includes the quotation.

97. Roscoe to William Smith, 11 May 1807, William Smith Papers, Duke University, Durham, NC.

98. Henry Roscoe, *Life of William Roscoe*, vol. ii, pp. 29–34.

99. Roscoe: *Considerations on the Causes, Objects and Consequences of the Present War, and on the Expediency, or the Danger of Peace with France* (London: T. Cadell & W. Davies, 1808); and *Remarks on the Proposals Made to Great Britain for Opening Negotiations for Peace, in the Year 1807*, 2nd edn (London: J. M'Creery, 1808). The foregoing are included in a volume entitled *Occasional Tracts Relative to the War Between Great Britain and France, Written and Published at Different Periods, from the Year 1793, Including Brief Observations on the Address of His Majesty, Proposed by Earl Grey, in the House of Lords, June 13, 1810* (London: T. Cadell & W. Davies, 1810). See also Henry Roscoe, *Life of William Roscoe*, vol. i, pp. 434–7.

100. Roscoe to William Wilberforce, 30 Jan 1808, quoted ibid., p. 428.

101. Rathbone to Roscoe, 30 Mar 1807, 24 Apr 1808, and one undated, probably 1808, Roscoe Papers; Henry Roscoe, *Life of William Roscoe*, vol. i, pp. 434–7, 448–9.

102. Eleanor Rathbone, *William Rathbone*, pp. 33–4; 'Sonnet on the Death of W. Rathbone', in Chandler, *Roscoe*, p. 280.

103. Rushton's son is described as 'an ardent social reformer' in Thomas, *Rushton*, p. 15, and Emily Rathbone mentions that he helped the fifth William Rathbone in 1831 in a campaign against election abuses (*Records of the Rathbone Family*, pp. 190–4). Wallace Currie became the first mayor of the Reformed Corporation of Liverpool. See ibid., p. 139. Both the fifth (1787–1868) and sixth (1819–1902) William Rathbones are worthy of individual essays to exemplify my thesis. Richard (1788–1860) and Philip (1828–95) were also reformers, as was Eleanor in a later

generation (1872–1946). I contemplated centring this essay on the Rathbone family, but soon realized it would require a whole book to do them justice.

104. Roscoe to Rathbone, 19 Apr 1807, Rathbone Papers. For a complete treatment of the passage of the Abolition Act, see Anstey, *Atlantic Slave Trade*, chs 15 and 16. For a discussion of the purposes of the African Institution see George Harrison, *Some Remarks on a Communication from William Roscoe to the Duke of Gloucester, Dated March 20, 1809 as Stated in the Appendix of the Third Report of the African Institution; Respectfully Submitted to the Duke* (London: George Ellerton, 1810); and *Reply to 'Some Remarks' (by George Harrison) on a 'Communication from William Roscoe to the Duke of Gloucester. . . .* (dated 7 Mar 1811 and signed 'W.R.').

105. Roscoe correspondence with Zachary Macaulay, Thomas Clarkson and the Duke of Gloucester, 1807–12, Roscoe Papers.

106. Roscoe to Lord Macaulay, undated draft, Roscoe Papers.

107. Henry Roscoe, *Life of William Roscoe*, vol. I, pp. 477–9; Resolution of the African Institution thanking Roscoe, Roscoe Papers.

108. Henry Roscoe, *Life of William Roscoe*, vol. II, pp. 65–8. For more on Prince Sanders and King Henry and their connection with the English abolitionists see Betty Fladeland, *Men and Brothers: Anglo-American Anti-slavery Co-operation* (Urbana: Univ. of Illinois Press, 1972) pp. 98–103.

109. Emily Rathbone, *Records of the Rathbone Family*, p. 231.

110. Roscoe to the Duke of Gloucester, one undated and 17 Mar and 13 Aug 1810, Roscoe Papers; the Duke of Gloucester to Roscoe, 26 Apr 1810, ibid.

111. A printed copy of the song, sung at an election dinner in St George's Place on 29 Sep 1812, is in the Roscoe Papers.

112. Roscoe, *Review of the Speeches of the Right Hon. George Canning, on the Late Election for Liverpool, As Far as They Relate to the Questions of Peace and Reform* (Liverpool: Egerton Smith, 1812).

113. See the correspondence between Roscoe and Henry Brougham, 1810–12, Roscoe Papers. Included is the draft of a letter from Roscoe rejoicing over the revocation of the Orders-in-Council. There are also several letters dealing with Brougham's help and advice in getting Roscoe admitted to Lincoln's Inn.

114. Major John Cartwright to Roscoe, 6 and 12 Feb 1809, 1 Sep 1811, 24 Feb and 15 May 1812, Roscoe Papers.

115. Printed circular of meeting of Friends of Reform, 30 Mar 1811, with note from Cartwright to Roscoe, Roscoe Papers; Cartwright to Roscoe, 7 Aug 1812, ibid.; and printed circular for reform dated 3 Nov 1812, ibid.

116. Roscoe, *A Letter to Henry Brougham, Esq. MP on the Subject of Reform in the Representation of the People in Parliament* (Liverpool: James Smith, 1811); Cartwright to Roscoe, 6 Aug 1811, Roscoe Papers; John Merritt, *A Letter to Wm Roscoe, Esq. Occasioned by his Letter to Henry Brougham, Esq. MP on the Subject of Parliamentary Reform* (Liverpool: Wright and Cruikshank [1811]); and Roscoe, *An Answer to A Letter from Mr John Merritt, on the Subject of Parliamentary Reform* (Liverpool: M. Galway, 1812). The quotation is from the last.

117. Quoted in Chandler, *Roscoe*, pp. xxv–xxvi.

118. William Allen to Roscoe, 16 June 1824, Roscoe Papers; Henry Roscoe, *Life of William Roscoe*, vol. II, pp. 62–5, 73–4; Chandler, *Roscoe*, p. xvi.
119. Henry Roscoe, *Life of William Roscoe*, vol. II, ch. 16.
120. Roscoe: *Observations on Penal Jurisprudence, and the Reformation of Criminals. With an Appendix Containing the Latest Reports of the State Prisons or Penitentiaries of Philadelphia, New York, and Massachusetts; and Other Documents* (London: T. Cadell & W. Davies, 1819); and *A Brief Statement of the Causes Which Have Led to the Abandonment of the Celebrated System of Penitentiary Discipline, in Some of the United States of America. In a Letter to the Hon. Stephen Allen, of New York* (Liverpool: Harris, 1827). Roscoe to Thomas Jefferson, 28 Feb 1819, T. F. Buxton to Roscoe, 16 June 1819, Roscoe to James Mease, 4 Mar and 1 May 1821 and 17 July 1822, Mease to Roscoe, 21 Apr 1821, and Samuel Hoare to Roscoe, 18 Jan 1823, Roscoe Papers.
121. Roscoe to Lafayette, 30 Mar 1825 and 29 Aug 1830, Roscoe Papers.
122. For elaboration see David B. Davis, 'The Emergence of Immediatism in British and American Antislavery Thought', *Mississippi Valley Historical Review*, vol. XLIX (Sep 1962) pp. 209–30; Fladeland, *Men and Brothers*, chs 4–8, and 'Abolitionist Pressures on the Concert of Europe, 1814–1822', *Journal of Modern History*, vol. XXXVIII (Dec 1962) pp. 355–73. The quotation is in Roscoe to James Cropper, 15 Jan 1823, Roscoe Papers.
123. See Cropper–Roscoe correspondence, 1822–6, and Adam Hodgson to Roscoe, undated, Roscoe Papers. It is unclear whether or not Roscoe accepted the presidency or even membership. In a letter to Cropper of 15 Jan 1823 he says he cannot take on any more without neglecting his other 'undertakings'. But Cropper, in one of 27 Jan 1823, expresses pleasure that Roscoe will come to the meeting.
124. [Roscoe], no title, but begins, 'The Present age...', and is so listed in the British Library catalogue. It is bound with other antislavery pamphlets and a notation on the first page says 'Liverpool Anti-Slavery Society', so it probably came from the Society's library.
125. For Roscoe's last illness and death see Traill, *Memoir*, pp. 41–2. On his reaction to the Revolution of 1830 see Roscoe to Lafayette, 29 Aug 1830, Roscoe Papers.
126. Chandler, *Roscoe*, p. xxxvi.


NOTES TO CHAPTER THREE: JOSEPH STURGE


1. *Black Dwarf* (London), 18 Mar 1818, 26 July 1820, 8 Aug 1821 and 7 Aug 1822. Wooler was no gentler with West Indian planters. See, for example, the issue of 3 Mar 1824, in which he argues that, if slaves are no more than brutes, planters must be punished for bestiality. Also, if slaves are brutes, they cannot be tried for insurrection. See Cobbett's *Political Register*, 23 Mar 1805 and 29 May 1830. Cobbett changed to a pro-emancipation stance when pushed by popular opinion in his constituency in the early 1830s. Even then his writings reveal a good deal of racial bias.
2. Sturge has had somewhat more recognition than most of his colleagues as a

man concerned about white workers as well as black slaves. There is plenty of evidence in the biography by Stephen Henry Hobhouse, *Joseph Sturge, His Life and Work* (London: J. M. Dent, 1919), but that work seems to have been largely unused by later historians. G. D. H. Cole included an essay on him in *Chartist Portraits* (New York: Macmillan, 1965), and Sturge is given passing credit in both Christine Bolt, *The Anti-Slavery Movement and Reconstruction: A Study in Anglo-American Co-operation 1833–77* (London: Oxford Univ. Press, 1969) pp. 15–16, and Howard Temperley, *British Antislavery 1833–1870* (Columbia: Univ. of South Carolina Press, 1972) p. 72; but no one has hitherto analysed the development of Sturge's dual concern.

3. After the abolition of the slave trade in 1807 the energies of the British anti-slavery movement subsided to some extent and were largely taken up with ameliorative measures. It was not until the early 1820s that the new impetus for total emancipation was revitalized and organised. For Sturge's participation see Henry Richard, *Memoirs of Joseph Sturge* (London: S. W. Partridge, 1864) pp. 79–86; Hobhouse, *Sturge*, ch. 4; Birmingham Anti-Slavery Society Minute Book, Birmingham Reference Library.

4. I am not trying to claim a 'first' for Sturge on this proposal. In a forthcoming biography of Charles Stuart, A. J. Barker points out that he made the suggestion too. Such a move occurred to several of the leaders at about the same time. In a letter to Maria Weston Chapman, 1 May 1846, Catherine [Mrs Thomas] Clarkson credits Sturge with shortening the apprenticeship period. See *British and American Abolitionists: An Episode in Transatlantic Understanding*, ed. Clare Taylor (Edinburgh: Univ. of Edinburgh Press, 1974) pp. 261–2; Temperley, *British Antislavery*, ch. 4; Betty Fladeland, *Men and Brothers: Anglo-American Antislavery Co-operation* (Urbana: Univ. of Illinois Press, 1972) pp. 244–50; Sturge and Thomas Harvey, *The West Indies in 1837; Being the Journal of a Visit to Antigua, Montserrat, Dominica, St Lucia, Barbadoes, and Jamaica; Undertaken for the Purpose of Ascertaining the Actual Condition of the Negro Population in Those Islands*, 2nd edn (London: Hamilton, Adams, 1838). Sturge was examined at length by the parliamentary investigating committee. See Minute Book of the Anti-Slavery Society, 7 June 1837, Rhodes House Anti-Slavery Collection, Oxford.

5. For Sturge's continuing role in the Anti-Slavery Society, see Minute Books and the Sturge Letters, Rhodes House Collection. His travels in the United States were published as *A Visit to the United States in 1841* (London: Hamilton, Adams, 1842; repr. New York: Economic Classics, Augustus M. Kelley, 1969).

6. At one point Lewis Tappan had suggested to Sturge that they buy an estate in Jamaica together; but it was at the time of the Crimean War and Sturge was too busy with his peace activities. Richard, *Memoirs of Sturge*, pp. 196–9, 488, 533; William R. Hughes, *Sophia Sturge, A Memoir* (London: George Allen & Unwin, 1940) pp. 16, 111, 176–7; Hobhouse, *Sturge*, pp. 47–8. The Birmingham Reference Library has a *Prospectus, The Montserrat Company Limited* dated 1875. The names of four Sturges appear in the list of directors.

7. Hobhouse, *Sturge*, p. 111; Richard, *Memoirs of Sturge*, pp. 384–96. There

is a letter in the Rhodes House Anti-Slavery Collection written by Sturge to John Scoble, 11 Feb 1850, after one of his visits to the London office in which he asks if a silk handkerchief was found after he left. While a silk handkerchief may be a sign of Sturge's wealth, it is also an indication of his personal boycott of cotton goods.

8. On Sturge's guilt about wealth see Hobhouse, *Joseph Sturge*, pp. 22–5.

9. Garrison to Helen Garrison, 10 Sep 1846, and R. D. Webb to Maria W. Chapman, 16 Nov 1845, Garrison Papers; R. D. Webb to Maria W. Chapman, 16 July 1846, Weston Papers; and Samuel May to J. B. Estlin, 4 Dec 1846, May Papers. All these collections in the BPL.

10. Richard, *Memoirs of Sturge*, pp. 18–20, 429; John Angell James, *Christian Philanthropy: As Exemplified in the Life and Character of the Late Joseph Sturge, May 22, 1859* (London: Hamilton, Adams, [1859]).

11. Hobhouse says that the Sturge family letters were full of love and affection, but indicated a 'marked reticence in speaking of God or religion' (*Joseph Sturge*, pp. 8–9). He notes that none of the family felt called to the ministry, a somewhat unusual record for a large Quaker family of those days. The quotation on Sturge's vitality is ibid., p. 188.

12. Extract from Cobden's diary, 5 June 1859, and John Bright to Sturge, 19 Oct 1857, Sturge Papers, Add. MS 43845, ff. 54, 65, BL; Cobden to Mrs [Hannah] Sturge, 1 July 1859, ibid., Add. MS 43722, f. 322; Hobhouse, *Sturge*, p. 189.

13. Richard, *Memoirs*, pp. 21–4; Hobhouse, *Sturge*, pp. 13–14. Many wealthy Birmingham Quakers paid their rates in order to avoid trouble with the Government, but about 1824 the stricter Friends, including Sturge, voted to disown such temporisers.

14. Richard, *Memoirs of Sturge*, p. 52; Hobhouse, *Sturge*, p. 27.

15. Silvan S. Tomkins, 'The Psychology of Commitment: The Constructive Role of Violence and Suffering for the Individual and for His Society', in *The Antislavery Vanguard: New Essays on the Abolitionists*, ed. Martin Duberman (Princeton, NJ, 1965) ch. 12.

16. *Nonconformist* (London), 16 Feb 1842; Sturge to Place, 28 Mar 1842, Place Papers, Add. MS 27810, f. 128, BL; Rhodes House Anti-Slavery Collection; Hobhouse, *Sturge*, pp. 52–8, 85.

17. Ibid., p. 54. There is a bit of human interest in the story, which Hobhouse credits, that the radical Will Cobbett hated Quakers and had a personal grudge against Cropper because Cropper had refused him passage on his ships to bring home Tom Paine's bones from America (ibid., p. 22). Cobbett denies this, and bases his attack on Cropper on Quaker hypocrisy toward the poor (*Political Register*, 15 Sep 1821). Cropper was the father of Sturge's first wife, Eliza, who died in childbirth about a year after their marriage.

18. Hobhouse, *Sturge*, pp. 35–6, 53, 83. John and Sophia Sturge were both active in the antislavery movement, and John joined the Birmingham Political Union along with his brother in 1838. He was the author of two pamphlets: *Report on Free Labour, Presented to the General Anti-Slavery Convention, by John Sturge, Esq. of Birmingham* (London: Johnston & Barrett [1840]); and *A Short Review of the Slave Trade and Slavery, with Considerations on the Benefit Which Would Arise from Cultivating*

*Tropical Production by Free-Labour* (Birmingham, 1827).

19. Quoted in Augustus Diamond, *Joseph Sturge, A Christian Merchant*, published for the Friends' Tract Association in the series *Friends Ancient and Modern*, no. 12 (London: Headley Bros, 1909).

20. C. Fell Smith, 'Joseph Sturge', *DNB*, vol. LV, pp. 130–1; Cobden to Sturge, Cobden Papers, Add. MS 43656, f. 60, BL; Cobden to Michel Chevalier, 8 Mar 1848, ibid., Add. MS 43647.

21. The quotation is in Cobden to Sturge, [?] 11 Sep [1848], ibid., Add. MS 43656, f. 28; Cobden to Sturge, 3 Nov 1856, Sturge Papers, Add. MS 43722, f. 167; Richard, *Memoirs of Sturge*, p. 45.

22. Hobhouse, *Sturge*, pp. 87–8.

23. *Nonconformist*, 4 Aug 1841, 4 June 1843; Arthur Miall, *Life of Edward Miall* (London: Macmillan, 1884) p. 90.

24. *Birmingham Journal*, 24 Feb 1838; *Nonconformist*, 29 Sep 1841; Richard, *Memoirs of Sturge*, pp. 252–3.

25. Hobhouse, *Sturge*, pp. 166–70; Richard, *Memoirs of Sturge*, p. 548. Sturge also supported schools for the West Indian freedmen. See ibid., pp. 200–1.

26. Ibid., chs 27 and 28. The quotation of the prisoner appears on p. 536. Sturge's reform house for boys eventually became the Saltley Reformatory. His humane attitude toward animals was expressed in the construction of stone drinking-fountains for the dogs and horses of Birmingham. See Hobhouse, *Sturge*, pp. 176, 182.

27. Richard, *Memoirs of Sturge*, pp. 55–6, 540–1; To Sturge from Various Inhabitants of Edgbaston, 3 Apr 1855, Sturge Papers, Add. MS 43845, f. 48.

28. Richard, *Memoirs of Sturge*, pp. 7–8, 79.

29. David B. Davis, *The Problem of Slavery in the Age of Revolution* (Ithaca, NY: Cornell Univ. Press, 1975) p. 246.

30. Cropper–Sturge Correspondence, 1825–30, in Cropper Letters, Birmingham Reference Library. See esp. Cropper to Sturge, 4 July 1827.

31. *Birmingham Journal*, 6 Aug 1842.

32. *Scotsman* (Edinburgh), 4 Aug 1841; *Birmingham Journal*, 2 Feb 1839, 1 Feb 1840; *British and Foreign Anti-Slavery Reporter*, 3 Apr 1844. G. D. H. Cole defends Sturge from the charge of being merely an agent of the Anti-Corn Law League. See *Chartist Portraits*, pp. 181–2. For a defence of James Cropper's stand on principle see David B. Davis's two articles 'James Cropper and the British Anti-Slavery Movement, 1821–1823', *Journal of Negro History*, vol. XLV (Jan 1960) pp. 241–58, and 'James Cropper and the British Anti-Slavery Movement, 1823–1833', ibid., vol. XLVI (Jan 1961) pp. 154–73.

33. E. P. Thompson, *The Making of the English Working Class* (New York: Vintage, 1963) p. 815.

34. Richard, *Memoirs of Sturge*, pp. 68–9. The letter of Joseph and Charles Sturge was dated 16 May 1832. Attwood was pledged to an antislavery vote in Parliament. See Birmingham Anti-Slavery Society Minute Book, clipping dated 4 Aug 1832.

35. *Poor Man's Guardian* (Manchester), 6 July 1833.

36. *Northern Star* (Leeds), 14 Apr 1838. For reiterations of this position see also the *Northern Liberator* 24 Aug 1839; *Operative* (London), 19 May 1839;

*Northern Star*, 3 and 10 Mar 1838.

37. *Northern Star*, 5 May 1838. In the *London Dispatch and People's Political and Social Reformer*, 23 Apr 1837, there is an especially nasty cartoon of Brougham smacking his lips over a bowlful of sprawling, squirming little people. One is impaled on his fork.

38. See, for example, a letter to the Editor, *Nonconformist*, 26 May 1841.

39. *Birmingham Journal*, 30 Mar 1839; *Northern Star*, 29 Dec 1838, clipping in HO 40/37, PRO. For an elaboration of this subject see Betty Fladeland, '"Our Cause Being One and the Same": Abolitionists and Chartism', in *Slavery and British Society 1776–1846*, ed. James Walvin (London: Macmillan, 1982) pp. 69–99.

40. Cole, *Chartist Portraits*, p. 181.

41. G. D. H. Cole, *A Short History of the Working Class Movement 1789–1927*, 2 vols (New York: Macmillan, 1930) vol. I, p. 141.

42. The Newcastle meeting is reported in a clipping from the *Northern Star*, 29 Dec 1838, in HO 40/37, an indication that the Government was keeping tabs on the radical papers. The Ashton-under-Lyne meeting is also reported ibid. Aitkin's use of Shakespeare must have appealed to the 'Shakespearean Chartists' led by the poet Thomas Cooper, who had organised literature classes for working men. See *The Life of Thomas Cooper. Written by Himself* (London: Hodder and Stoughton, 1879); *Chartist* (London), 5 May 1839.

43. William Cardo to Home Office, 6 Nov 1839, HO 40/37. These files are filled with reports of agents (including *agents provocateurs*), and of mayors and military officers, on Chartist meetings, lists of names, suspected caches of arms, arrests, and depositions of informers. An anonymous letter in HO 40/59 stresses the danger from French agents.

44. *Birmingham Journal*, 6 and 13 July 1839; *Northern Star*, 13 July 1839; *London Dispatch*, 21 July 1839. The *Dispatch* blamed the London police for provoking the violence.

45. *Birmingham Journal*, 17 Aug and 14 Sep 1839; Richard, *Memoirs of Sturge*, pp. 258–61.

46. Richard, *Memoirs of Sturge*, pp. 262–7.

47. Letterbook, 1839–42, labelled 'Police. Birmingham', in HO 65/10. Captain C. R. Moorsom was an active abolitionist and also sympathetic to the plight of the working people. See also, *Birmingham Journal*, 30 Nov 1839. On 19 Nov 1839 the head of the police force reported that he had four troops of Dragoons and two companies of the Rifle Brigade in readiness in Birmingham.

48. HO 65/10, entries for 26 Nov 1839 and 29 Nov 1840; *Birmingham Journal*, 30 Nov 1839.

49. Hobhouse, *Sturge*, pp. 65–6; HO 65/10, entry for 17 Jan 1840; Cole, *Chartist Portraits*, pp. 170–1.

50. *Birmingham Journal*, 1 Feb 1840; Hobhouse, *Sturge*, p. 66. Sturge did not include women when he spoke of suffrage extension, and he opposed seating women delegates in the World Anti-Slavery Convention in London in 1840. See Fladeland, *Men and Brothers*, p. 267.

51. Ibid., p. 281.

52. Garrison to Elizabeth Pease, 1 Mar and 1 June 1841, in *British and*

*American Abolitionists*, ed. Taylor, pp. 141–2, 152–3.

53. Sturge, *Visit to the United States*, pp. 102–3.
54. Ibid., p. 141.
55. Ibid., p. 147.
56. Ibid., pp. 148–58.
57. Ibid., pp. 148, 155–8; *Anti-Bread Tax Circular* (Manchester) 21 Oct 1841.
58. Sturge, *Visit to the United States*, p. 110. Curtis's lectures in Great Britain are reported in the *Anti-Bread Tax Circular*, 1841–2.
59. *Nonconformist*, 24 Nov 1841. The meeting was interrupted by Chartists led by a man named White. The angry crowd rushed to seize White, who had to be escorted out by Sturge to save him from physical harm. The connection between the antislavery movement and the anti-Corn Law movement will be one part of my study of antislavery–labour connections. Besides Sturge, other prominent abolitionists who were active in the anti-Corn Law movement included MPs Dr John Bowring and C. P. Villiers; George Thompson, who had been run out of the United States because of his anti-slavery agitation; the Revd J. W. Massie of Manchester; the Revd J. H. Hinton of the Broad Street Committee of the British and Foreign Anti-Slavery Society; the Revd Thomas Spencer of Bath; and the Revd Patrick Brewster of Paisley, Scotland. Cobden and John Bright were both antislavery in sympathy but not active in the organized movement.
60. Cobden to Sturge, 3 Mar 1841, quoted in Richard, *Memoirs of Sturge*, p. 226.
61. Thomas Clarkson to Sturge, 5 Mar 1841, in Richard, *Memoirs of Sturge*, p. 227.
62. Ibid., p. 267.
63. For expressions of such worries see the *Chartist*, 2 Feb 1839; *Operative*, 13 Jan 1839; *Charter* (London), 24 Feb 1839; and *Nonconformist*, 14 Apr 1841.
64. Sturge to Cobden [1841], in Richard, *Memoirs of Sturge*, p. 292.
65. Sturge to Lewis Tappan, ibid., p. 296.
66. Sturge to the Electors of Nottingham, 1 May 1842, in *Nonconformist*, 25 May 1842.
67. Ibid., 13 Oct–1 Dec 1841.
68. Introduction by Sturge to Edward Miall, *Reconciliation between the Middle and Labouring Classes* (Birmingham: B. Hudson, 1842).
69. Cobden to Sturge, 21 Nov 1841, in Richard, *Memoirs of Sturge*, p. 299. It is interesting to note the strong moral tone Cobden uses with Sturge; while in the House of Commons his tactic was to argue from expediency as that seemed the only way to convince his fellow MPs.
70. *Nonconformist*, 22 Dec. 1841.
71. Ibid., 24 Nov. 1841.
72. Place to Henry Ashworth, 5 Apr 1842, Place Papers, Add. MS 27810, f. 185.
73. See Richard, *Memoirs of Sturge*, p. 301, for the 'Declaration'. The *Scotsman*, 20 July 1842, has an article discussing Sturge's philosophy of the 'natural right' of the suffrage. He had advocated emancipation on the ground that every person has a right to liberty; now he is advocating the

political emancipation of his own countrymen on the grounds that every person has a natural right to an equal voice in making the laws he is called upon to obey. The *Northern Star*, 19 Mar 1842, facetiously objected to Sturge's 'Declaration' because it advocated the franchise for all who were not burdens on the state. This, the editorial opined, would exclude all of the clergy, all of the upper class, and most of the middle class.

74. One can follow all of these developments in the *Nonconformist* from Nov 1841 to Apr 1842. It was officially designated the organ of the Complete Suffrage Union. See also Fladeland, in *Slavery and British Society*, ed. Walvin; the *Birmingham Journal* for 1841 and 1842; Richard, *Memoirs of Sturge*, pp. 301–3; Hobhouse, *Sturge*, pp. 72–5; Place Papers, Add. MS 27810, esp. f. 124, and Place to Sturge, 23 Mar 1842, which contains Place's warning about the law forbidding communication between political societies under penalty of seven years' transportation.

75. Herbert Spencer, *An Autobiography*, 2 vols (London: Williams & Norgate, 1904) vol. I, pp. 218–19, 247–57; Hobhouse, *Sturge*, pp. 78–9; *Nonconformist*, 22 Feb 1843. The *Pilot* (Birmingham) was published from 1844 to 1846 after the failure of the Complete Suffrage Union.

76. Brougham and O'Connell both had somewhat stormy relationships with Chartists, Anti-Corn Law Leaguers and the Complete Suffrage Movement. See letters to and from O'Connell in the Lovett Collection, Birmingham Reference Library; *Chartist*, 2 Feb 1839, and *Anti-Bread Tax Circular*, 14 Feb 1843, for typical articles.

77. All of these positions and their arguments were aired in the *Nonconformist* for 1842. See also Robert George Gammage, *History of the Chartist Movement, 1837–1854*, 2nd edn (London, 1894; repr. New York: Economic Classics, Augustus M. Kelley, 1959) pp. 198–203. For interesting analyses of Place's role see W. E. S. Thomas, 'Francis Place and Working Class History', the *Historical Journal*, vol. V, no. 1 (1962) pp. 61–70; and D. J. Rowe, 'The Failure of London Chartism', ibid., vol. XI, no. 3 (1968) pp. 472–87, and 'Francis Place and the Historian', ibid., vol. XVI, no. 1 (1973) pp. 45–63.

78. One such advanced thinker was the Revd Henry Solly from Yeovil, who was forced out of his pastorate because he was too radical for his Non-conforming Unitarian congregation. See essay on Solly following in this volume.

79. On O'Connor see *Birmingham Journal*, 5 Mar 1842, and William Lovett, *The Life and Struggles of William Lovett, in his Pursuit of Bread, Knowledge, and Freedom; with Some Short Account of the Different Associations he Belonged to, and of the Opinions he Entertained* (London: Trübner, 1856) pp. 274–5. On Baines see *Nonconformist*, 9 Mar, 28 Sep and 8 Oct 1842. On Thompson see L. G. Johnson, *General T. Perronet Thompson, 1783–1869. His Military, Literary, and Political Campaigns* (London: George Allen & Unwin, 1957) pp. 26–8, 243. See essay on Thompson following in this volume.

80. Printed circular, 'National Complete Suffrage Union', which contains a report of the conference, Place Papers, Add. MS 27810, f. 201. The day-by-day proceedings of the conference are in the *Birmingham Journal*, 9 Apr

1842; *Nonconformist*, 6 and 13 Apr 1842; and Lovett Collection, Birmingham Reference Library. This collection includes the memorial to Queen Victoria as well.

81. *Nonconformist*, 27 Apr and 25 May 1842; Sturge to William Lovett, 27 Apr 1842, in Lovett Collection; Richard, *Memoirs of Sturge*, p. 300.

82. Ibid., pp. 305–15; Hobhouse, *Sturge*, pp. 76–7; *Nonconformist*, 18 and 25 May, 8 June, 10 Aug 1842. Sturge took his defeat with good humour, declaring he had never really been eager to go to Parliament and would just as soon go to Newgate for an equal time if that would serve the country, adding that he expected he would find an equal number of honest men in both places (*Nonconformist*, 31 Aug 1842). His disclaimer was honest. When Walter was disqualified because of currupt practices, Sturge declined to stand again.

83. *Nonconformist*, 18 May 1842.

84. *Scotsman*, 7 May 1842. George Thompson's lectures at both Chartist and Anti-Corn Law League meetings are thoroughly covered in the *Nonconformist* throughout the summer and autumn, 1842.

85. O'Connor's most recent biographers credit him with sincerity in his switch. They say that after the failure of the Chartist National Petition he realised his mistake and saw the need of co-operation between the classes. Donald Reed and Eric Glasgow, *Feargus O'Connor, Irishman and Chartist* (London: Edward Arnold, 1961) pp. 101–3. His contemporaries were less charitable. Miall said O'Connor would have nothing to do with the December conference until the method of choosing delegates was changed, which gave him a chance to pack the meeting (*Nonconformist*, 23 Nov 1842).

86. *Birmingham Journal*, 31 Dec 1842. Bronterre O'Brien named the Revd Thomas Spencer, the Revd Dr J. Ritchie of Edinburgh, the Revd Patrick Brewster of Paisley and Lawrence Heyworth of Liverpool as the Sturgeites who were most opposed to using the name of the Charter (*British Statesman*, 31 Dec 1842).

87. For accounts of the December convention see the *Nonconformist*, 28 and 31 Dec 1842; Cooper, *Life*, pp. 220–7; Lovett, *Life and Struggles*, pp. 274–85; Gammage, *History of the Chartist Movement*, pp. 241–4; Mark Hovell, *The Chartist Movement* (Manchester, 1918; repr. New York: Economic Classics, Augustus M. Kelley, 1969) pp. 264–5; Preston Slosson, *The Decline of the Chartist Movement* (New York: Columbia Univ. Press, 1916) pp. 72–7; and Cole, *Short History of the Working Class Movement*, vol. I, pp. 162–3. For leadership ego and clashes see also Cobden to William Lovett, 25 Apr 1842, Lovett Letters, Add. MS 47663F, BL; and the *Northern Star*, 16 Apr and 3 Dec 1842. Bronterre O'Brien was one of O'Connor's fiercest critics. See his *British Statesmen*, 5 Nov 1842 and following issues.

88. If Sturge was naïve on this count, so, it must be noted, was such an old-time politician as Place. His London delegation was one of those 'taken over' by the O'Connorites.

89. Copper, *Life*, pp. 226–7; letter from Cooper dated 26 Feb 1855, in Gammage, *History of the Chartist Movement*, Appendix, pp. 404–8; Hovell, *The Chartist Movement*, p. 242.

90. *Pilot,* 14 Dec 1844.
91. Sturge to John Greenleaf Whittier, 19 Aug 1844, Whittier Papers, Clark Collection, Central Michigan University, Mount Pleasant, Mich. Sturge died in 1859.

## NOTES TO CHAPTER FOUR: HARRIET MARTINEAU

1. *Harriet Martineau's Autobiography and Memorials of Harriet Martineau,* ed. Maria Weston Chapman, 2 vols (Boston, Mass.: James R. Osgood, 1877) vol. I, p. 110, hereinafter referred to separately as *Autobiography* (vols I–II) or *Memorials* (vol. II).
2. Martineau, *Deerbrook* (London: Smith, Elder, 1858); R. K. Webb in *Harriet Martineau, A Radical Victorian* (London: William Heinemann, 1960) pp. 80–90, gives a lucid explanation of her necessarianism. He does not think Martineau was a true Benthamite. While the Benthamites were legal and administrative reformers, she was 'doctrinaire, utopian, and woolly'. To me, 'doctrinaire' and 'woolly' seem contradictory. Despite her beginning with doctrinaire principles, she grew to be fairly flexible in practice, but not, I think, because she was 'woolly'.
3. Theodora Bosanquet, *Harriet Martineau, An Essay in Comprehension* (London: Frederick Etchells & Hugh Macdonald, 1927) p. 133. The Carlyles were good friends of Harriet's none the less, and, in a letter to Emerson, Carlyle described her as 'a genuine little poetess, buck-rimmed, swathed like a mummy into Socinian and Political Economy formulas; and yet verily alive in spite of that' (ibid., p. 1).
4. John Cranston Nevill, *Harriet Martineau* (London: Frederick Muller, 1943) p. 121.
5. *Memorials,* p. 193.
6. Vera Wheatley, *The Life and Works of Harriet Martineau* (Fairtown, NJ: Essential Books, 1957) p. 337. The Martineau–Dickens relationship was at first amiable and Martineau supplied Dickens with material for *Household Words*. She praised many of his works and loved Pickwick, especially, as an unsurpassably humorous character. But later she criticized his characters and situations as exaggerated and unrealistically sentimental. In 1873 she wrote to Maria Weston Chapman that 'At all times, in all his writings, Dickens opposed and criticized all existing legal plans for the relief of the poor' (*Memorials,* p. 521). While he was in the United States, Dickens praised Martineau's travel book as the best that had been written on America, but, when Anne Weston expressed her gratitude for Martineau's writing on slavery, Dickens 'assented... with something of a stare' (Anne W. Weston to Deborah Weston, 4 Feb 1842, Weston Papers, BPL).
7. Martineau, 'Demerara', *Illustrations of Political Economy,* vol. II (London: C. Fox, 1834).
8. Martineau, *Autobiography,* vol. I, p. 203. Henley was referring to poor white workers, not slaves.
9. Martineau to William Ware, 25 Jan [?], English Manuscripts 244 (11), BPL.
10. Martineau, *Autobiography,* vol. I, p. 14.
11. Ibid., p. 16.

12. Martineau, 'Briery Creek', no. xxii in *Illustrations of Political Economy*, (London: C. Fox, 1833) p. 155.

13. Richard Hofstadter, in *Social Darwinism in American Thought*, rev. edn (Boston, Mass.: Beacon, 1955) p. 52, says that William Graham Sumner learned the wage-fund doctrine by reading Martineau. Hofstadter points out Martineau's objections to government charity but leaves a distorted impression of her as a hard-hearted Social Darwinist by failing to explain her position fully: that, if government allowed more representation, tax reform and free trade, such charity would be unnecessary.

14. After the repeal of the Corn Laws, however, she believed the population crisis was over. Martineau thought Malthus to be one of the most amiable and virtuous men she knew, who did more 'for social ease and virtue' than any man of his time (*Autobiography*, vol. i, pp. 158–60).

15. See particularly Place to Martineau, Place Papers, Add. MS 35149, f. 189, BL.

16. *Autobiography*, vol. i, p. 122.

17. Martineau: 'Lord Brougham', *Biographical Sketches* (London: Macmillan, 1869) p. 160; and *Poor Laws and Paupers*, 2 vols (London: C. Fox, 1833).

18. The tales in which she deals with the problems of overpopulation, poor laws, and charity include 'Weal and Woe in Garveloch', 'The Hamlets', 'The Town', 'Cousin Marshall', 'The Parish' and 'The Land's End'.

19. Martineau, 'Lady Noel Byron', *Biographical Sketches*, pp. 316–25. Martineau drew on their friendship to place two American fugitive slaves, William and Ellen Craft, in Lady Byron's school at Ockham. R. D. Webb to M. W. Chapman, [?] Apr 1851, Weston Papers.

20. Martineau, 'A Tale of the Tyne', no. xxi in *Illustrations of Political Economy* (London: C. Fox, 1833) p. 61.

21. Yet in a later work Martineau defended the segregation of workhouse children as necessary to their moral safety and re-education. See Martineau, *A History of the Thirty Years' Peace*, 4 vols (London: George Bell, 1877) vol. ii, p. 504.

22. In addition to the Hofstadter citation above (n. 13), see Max E. Fletcher, 'Harriet Martineau and Ayn Rand: Economics in the Guise of Fiction', *American Journal of Economics and Sociology*, vol. 33, no. 4 (Oct 1974) pp. 367–79. Percy Colson, who in a most unsympathetic study calls her 'joke-proof', must have read only her pedantic tales, but neither her travel accounts nor her letters – *Victorian Portraits* (Freeport, NY: Books for Libraries, 1932). My reading of Martineau is that she had a lively and active sense of humour. How could anyone who lacked one have remained a friend of Sydney Smith? More recently, Jonathan A. Glickstein has written of her, 'One would be hard pressed to find among leading American abolitionists a real equivalent to the antislavery Englishwoman Harriet Martineau, with her use of vulgarized laissez faire tenets to defend the interests of manufacturing proprietors and deny the right of laboring men to compulsory relief.' Then he goes on to contrast 'The ethic of Christian love and responsibility for the poor and downtrodden that animated American abolitionists. . . .' (Glickstein, '"Poverty Is Not Slavery"; American Abolitionists and the Competitive Labor Market', in *Antislavery Reconsidered: New Perspectives on the Abolitionists*, ed. Lewis Perry and Michael Fellman (Baton

Rouge: Louisiana State Univ. Press, 1979) p. 217). A major exception to the above stereotyping is R. K. Webb's biography.

23. J. Bartlett Brebner in 'Laissez Faire and State Intervention in Nineteenth Century Britain', *Journal of Economic History*, Supplement VIII (1948) pp. 59–73, argues that in practice the laissez-faire of nineteenth-century Britain was as much a 'Hands-on' as a 'Hands-off' policy. He points out that, when it dawned on Bentham that all governments were out to get the 'greatest happiness' for those by whom, rather than for whom, governments were run, he immediately set about to get 'the greatest number' into the government.

24. Martineau, *Thirty Years' Peace*, vol. II, pp. 311, 443–52.

25. Ibid., p. 436.

26. Martineau to Place, 12 May 1832, Place Papers.

27. Martineau to Brougham, [n.d.], no. 14,000, Brougham Papers, University College, London.

28. Martineau to Place, 1 June 1832, Place Papers.

29. The quotation is found in *Memorials*, p. 245, and Martineau, *Autobiography*, vol. I, pp. 174–6. Martineau thought that Owen was an 'amiable enthusiast' who lacked reasoning power, but she characterised his life as 'virtuous and benign' ('Robert Owen', *Biographical Sketches*, pp. 307–15).

30. Martineau to the Committee of Useful Knowledge, Mar 1833 [a copy], Brougham Papers.

31. These themes run throughout her tales in *Poor Laws and Paupers*. See also her *Autobiography*, vol. I, pp. 168–70, and *Thirty Years' Peace*, vol. I, pp. 108–16, and vol. II, pp. 492, 501–4. The quotation about slavery is from vol. I, p. 112.

32. Martineau, 'Cousin Marshall', no. VIII, in *Illustrations of Political Economy* (London: C. Fox, 1832) pp. 49–52, 130–1. The same themes can be followed in 'The Land's End', 'The Parish', 'The Hamlets' and 'The Town'. See also *Thirty Years' Peace*, vol. II, pp. 487–8, 507.

33. Martineau, *Autobiography*, vol. I, pp. 173–4. In a letter to Place of 28 Mar [1834], Place Papers, Martineau implies that she will nominate him for appointment as a Poor Law Commissioner when she next sees Brougham. In Place's answer of 31 Mar he pooh-poohs the idea that either Brougham or James Mill would think of putting into office 'the Radical Tailor'. It must be remembered, however, that, while Place seemed radical to middle-class Whigs, he was a leader of skilled artisans and not a spokesman for the workers at the bottom of the heap.

34. Martineau, *Autobiography*, vol. I, p. 163; Martineau to Place, 29 Mar [1832], Place Papers.

35. *Memorials*, p. 221; Place to Martineau, 4 Mar 1834, Place Papers.

36. Martineau, 'A Manchester Strike', *Illustrations of Political Economy*, vol. III (London: C. Fox, 1834) and 'Thirty Years' Peace', vol. III, p. 94; Wheatley, *Martineau*, pp. 103–5.

37. Martineau, *Thirty Years' Peace*, vol. II, pp. 513–15, and vol. IV, pp. 206–7, 212–16; Webb, *Martineau*, pp. 108–12, 214–16; Wheatley, *Martineau*, pp. 104–5, 221.

38. Lord Durham to Martineau, 18 Jan 1834, in *Memorials*, pp. 221–2.

Martineau confided to an American friend, William Ware, that, although she did not have entire confidence in Lord Durham, she trusted him more than any other statesman of the time – Martineau to Ware, 25 Jan [?], English Manuscripts 244 (11), BPL. See also Martineau, 'The Moral of Many Fables', *Illustrations of Political Economy*, vol. IX (London: C. Fox, 1834), and *Autobiography*, vol. I, p. 193; Webb, *Martineau*, pp. 130–2.

39. *Memorials*, pp. 456–8. The article was rejected by the *Westminster Review* because it contained attacks on Charles Dickens and a factory-inspector as well as on the Factory Acts themselves. But the *Westminster Review* was to be one of her major publishers, and, when it hit upon hard times in later years, Martineau took over its mortgage, she says, because it had been her 'organ of communication' with the world (*Memorials*, p. 455).

40. Martineau, *Thirty Years' Peace*, vol. II, p. 513; Martineau to Brougham, Apr 1833, no. 14,002, and also no. 14,003, which carries no date but is obviously also 1833, Brougham Papers.

41. Martineau, *Thirty Years' Peace*, vol. II, pp. 513–15, and vol. IV, pp. 210–12; *Memorials*, pp. 214–15; Martineau to Charles Buller, 15 June 1843, Washburn Collection, Massachusetts Historical Society, Boston, Mass.

42. Martineau, *Society in America*, 3 vols (London: Saunders & Otley, 1837) vol. II, pp. 247–8.

43. Her faith in people's learning to bargain in their own interest is one theme in 'Cinnamon and Pearls', no. XX in *Illustrations of Political Economy* (London: C. Fox, 1833) esp. p. 51. See also Webb, *Martineau*, pp. 215–16, 346–9.

44. Martineau, *Thirty Years' Peace*, vol. IV, p. 204.

45. Webb, *Martineau*, p. 172.

46. Martineau: 'A Tale of the Tyne, no. XXI in *Illustrations of Political Economy* (1833) pp. 42, 45–6, 106; and *Thirty Years' Peace*, vol. II, p. 313 and following.

47. Martineau, *Thirty Years' Peace*, vol. III, pp. 92–3; *Memorials*, p. 551.

48. Ibid., p. 351; Martineau, *Society in America*, vol. III, pp. 182–8, and *Retrospect of Western Travel*, 2 vols (London: Saunders & Otley, 1838) pp. 123–39 (on prisons).

49. Martineau to her family, 12 Dec 1834, in *Memorials*, pp. 246–8. After her trip to America she was considered an authority on prisons and the Inspector of Prisons sought her advice on the appointment of a new prison governor (ibid., p. 346).

50. Martineau, *Thirty Years' Peace*, vol. II, p. 239. Her figure for the value of game wantonly destroyed by the rich is £5 million a year.

51. Chester Kirby, 'The English Game Law System', *American Historical Review*, vol. XXXVIII (Jan 1933) pp. 240–62, and 'The Attack on the English Game Laws in the Forties', *Journal of Modern History*, vol. IV (Mar 1932) pp. 18–37; Martineau, *Thirty Years' Peace*, vol. IV, pp. 303–7.

52. Martineau, *Autobiography*, vol. I, p. 521.

53. Ibid., pp. 523–6. Martineau took a good bit of credit for the repeal of the Corn Laws by reasoning that she effected the detente between Cobden and Peel which made political victory possible.

54. *Memorials*, p. 493.

55. Martineau, *Society in America*, vol. II, pp. 51–2.

56. Martineau, *Thirty Years' Peace*, vol. IV, p. 216; Betty Fladeland, *Men and*

*Brothers: Anglo-American Antislavery Co-operation* (Urbana: Univ. of Illinois Press, 1972) p. 305.

57. *Memorials*, pp. 489, 491.

58. Against tithes she wrote her tale 'The Tenth Haycock'. 'The Jerseymen Meeting' and 'The Jerseymen Parting' incorporated her advice on excise taxes: Martineau, *Autobiography*, vol. I, pp. 196–200.

59. *Memorials*, p. 315; Martineau, *Thirty Years' Peace*, vol. II, p. 506.

60. *Memorials*, p. 534.

61. Ibid., pp. 534–41. Several other well-known women in the antislavery movement joined Martineau in signing the protest. They included Martha Baines, Ursula Bright, Eliza Wigham, Jane Wigham, Elizabeth Pease Nichol and Mary Estlin. Florence Nightingale's activity in this movement is interesting in view of the fact that several years earlier she had written in a tone disdainful of 'women's missionaries', and confessed, 'I am brutally indifferent to the wrongs or rights of my sex – and I should have been equally so to any controversy as to whether women ought or ought not to have done what I have done for the army – though a woman having the opportunity & *not* doing it, ought, I think to be burnt alive' – Nightingale to Martineau, 30 Nov 1858, Nightingale Papers, Add. MS 45788, BL.

62. Martineau, *Autobiography*, vol. I, p. 451.

63. Martineau, *Society in America*, vol. I, pp. 199–201, 204–7; vol. II, p. 310; vol. III, pp. 105–18 ('Women').

64. Letter from Martineau to Mrs Frances D. Gage, 2 Jan 1852, Literary MSS, Huntington Library, San Merino, Calif.; also printed in the *Anti-Slavery Bugle* (Salem, Ohio), 31 July 1852.

65. *Memorials*, pp. 321–4, 552.

66. Martineau, *Autobiography*, vol. I, p. 159. George Jacob Holyoake in *John Stuart Mill as Some of the Working Classes Knew Him* (London: Trübner, 1873) p. 3, credits Harriet Martineau with being the first public writer on co-operatives. For her position on savings banks and Friendly Societies, see *Thirty Years' Peace*, vol. I, pp. 116–17, 122–3.

67. Martineau, *Society in America*, vol. I, p. x, and vol. II, pp. 250–3, 352–9. It should be noted that, while Martineau was pleased with the lack of class insolence in America and saw 'invariable respect paid to man as man' among whites, yet she deplored that all of that was spoiled by contempt for blacks. See ibid., vol. III, pp. 27–8.

68. Martineau: *Autobiography*, vol. II, pp. 1–4; and *Thirty Years' Peace*, vol. III, pp. 262–3. In Ambleside, living in the same area as Wordsworth, Martineau wrote of him, 'I, deaf, can hardly conceive how he with eyes & ears & a heart which leads him to converse with the poor in his incessant walks can be so unaware of their social state' – Martineau to H. Crabb Robinson, 8 Feb 1846, in *The Correspondence of Henry Crabb Robinson with the Wordsworth Circle 1808–1866*, ed. Edith J. Morley, 2 vols (Oxford: Clarendon Press, 1927) vol. II, no. 429, pp. 620–2.

69. Martineau, *Thirty Years' Peace*, vol. III, p. 485.

70. Ibid., pp. 91–2, 263–4.

71. Ibid., pp. 489–90.

72. Martineau to R. M. Bacon [Editor of the Norwich *Mercury*], Tynemouth, 14 Nov [?], Add. MS 6247 (87), University Library, Cambridge.

73. Martineau, *Thirty Years' Peace*, vol. III, pp. 264–6, 488–93.
74. The quotations are from Martineau to Charles Buller, MP, 21 Aug 1841, reproduced in *Autobiography*, vol. I, Appendix D, pp. 587–94. See also the *Nonconformist*, 26 Oct 1842. The *Nonconformist* for 13 Dec 1843 reported that when she refused the pension her friends made up a testimonial fund of £1358 8s. 10d. in her honour. In 1842 the Radicals held a meeting in London, chaired by colonel T. Perronet Thompson, to thank her for standing firm on principle (*Memorials*, pp. 364–5). In 1872 she again refused a pension, offered to her by Gladstone (ibid., pp. 548–9).
75. Webb, *Martineau*, pp. 257, 268–9.
76. Martineau, *Autobiography*, vol. II, pp. 6–10; *Memorials*, pp. 402–3, 443–5. The quotation is from Martineau, *Household Education* (Boston: James R. Osgood, 1877) p. 10 (first published 1848).
77. A. R. Schoyen, *The Chartist Challenge: A Portrait of George Julian Harney* (London: William Heinemann, 1958) p. 163; Wheatley, *Martineau*, p. 276; Bosanquet, *Martineau*, pp. 111–12, 208.
78. *People's Journal*, esp. issues of 30 May 1846 and throughout that year. Two years later the Howitts took over the journal and its name changed to *People's and Howitt's Journal*.
79. In Apr 1859 Martineau was hired as a regular contributor to the *Anti-Slavery Standard* with a remuneration of £50 a year. See Garrison to Oliver Johnson, 16 Apr 1859, Garrison Papers, BPL. Martineau to 'Dear Friend', 17 Sep 1862 and 27 Nov 1862, Martineau Papers, Archives Department, Record Office, Cumbria County; *Memorials*, pp. 449–53, 495–8.
80. Ibid., pp. 562–73.
81. Florence Nightingale to Maria Weston Chapman, 29 Sep 1876, ibid., pp. 581–2.
82. Ibid., pp. 591–2.

## NOTES TO CHAPTER FIVE: T. PERRONET THOMPSON

1. Horace White to Thompson, 1 May 1866, Thompson Papers, University of Hull. White had been active in the struggle to keep slavery out of Kansas and was a war correspondent for the *Chicago Tribune* during the Civil War.
2. Thompson to P. T. E. Thompson, 7 July 1840, Thompson Papers.
3. L. G. Johnson, *General T. Perronet Thompson 1783–1869. His Military, Literary and Political Campaigns* (London: George Allen and Unwin, 1957) pp. 11, 24–5, 39. His mother was the daughter of the Vicar of Shoreham in Kent, and her grandfather, the Revd Vincent Perronet, was connected with John Wesley in his early work. See William Howitt, 'T. P. Thompson', *Howitt's Journal*, vol. II, no. 31 (31 July 1847) pp. 65–8.
4. Johnson, *Thompson*, p. 26; *Autobiographical Recollections of Sir John Bowring. With a Brief Memoir by Lewin B. Bowring* (London: Henry S. King, 1877) p. 70.
5. For the beginnings of the Sierra Leone colony see E. M. Howse, *Saints in Politics, The 'Clapham Sect' and the Growth of Freedom* (Toronto: Univ. of Toronto Press, 1952) pp. 45–57; also Ellen Gibson Wilson, *The Loyal Blacks* (New York: G. P. Putnam's Sons, 1976).

6. Henry James Robinson, 'Thomas Perronet Thompson, 1783–1869', *DNB*, vol. xix, pp. 704–6.

7. Johnson, *Thompson*, pp. 36–7.

8. Ibid., pp. 261–3, 281; *London Dispatch and People's Political and Social Reformer*, 26 Mar 1837; Broadside, 'Sunderland Election' [23 July 1845], and Thompson to Bowring, 18 Feb 1841, Thompson Papers. Although Thompson worked with James Silk Buckingham in reform, he did not like him very much personally. He thought Buckingham too 'saintly' and 'time-serving'.

9. 'Sunderland Election' Broadside and undated election card, ibid.; Thompson to Bowring, 23 May 1841, ibid.

10. Johnson, *Thompson*, pp. 65–6; Wilson, *The Loyal Blacks*, pp. 405–6.

11. Johnson, *Thompson*, pp. 98–100. It was in the same period, 1819–20, that the US Congress passed laws declaring the slave trade to be piracy, and during the same time that Great British was trying to get an anti-slave-trade treaty with the United States. See Betty Fladeland, *Men and Brothers: Anglo-American Antislavery Co-operation* (Urbana: Univ. of Illinois Press, 1972) chs 5 and 6.

12. Thompson to Bowring, 13 Dec 1831 and 3 Jan 1832, Thompson Papers. Bowring was a close friend of Jeremy Bentham and was his executor. He was also an active abolitionist.

13. Bowring, *Autobiographical Recollections*, pp. 70–2; Wilson, *The Loyal Blacks*, pp. 405–6; *Northern Liberator*, 19 Sep 1840.

14. Thompson was retired from active service in the Army in 1821 with a reprimand for bad judgement in the ordering of an expedition against the Arabs. Nevertheless he received his promotions: in 1829 to Lieutenant-Colonel, in 1846 to Colonel, in 1854 to Major-General, in 1860 to Lieutenant-General, and in 1868 (a year before his death) to General. His letters are full of embittered complaints about the delays in promotions. Between 1835 and 1837 he represented Hull in Parliament; from 1847 to 1852 and again from 1857 to 1859 he represented Bradford. See *DNB*, vol. xix, pp. 704–6.

15. Thompson to Bowring, 1 Feb 1837, and Thompson to the Bradford Reform Association, 27 Mar 1848, Thompson Papers; Johnson, *Thompson*, pp. 261–3. Later Thompson stood with Cobden against British military operations in China. This stand estranged him from his friend of long standing, John Bowring, who was one of the British officials involved in the China operations.

16. Thompson to the Bradford Reform Association, 28 June and 3 July 1848, Thompson Papers. For the debates see the *British and Foreign Anti-Slavery Reporter* throughout 1844, 1845 and 1846. Also, C. Duncan Rice, '"Humanity Sold for Sugar!" The British Abolitionist Response to Free Trade in Slave-Grown Sugar', *Historical Journal*, vol. xiii, no. 3 (1970) pp. 402–18.

17. Johnson, *Thompson*, pp. 286–7.

18. Ibid., pp. 121, 143; Bowring, *Autobiographical Recollections*, pp. 7–8, 72; Thompson to Bowring, 8 Sep 1831, Thompson Papers.

19. Thompson to Bowring, 13 and 20 Dec 1831, ibid.

20. Johnson, *Thompson*, pp. 145–6, 170–1.

21. See, for example, Thompson to John R. Roebuck, 19 Dec 1831 and 21 Jan 1935, Thompson Papers.

22. Thompson to Bowring, 2 Aug 1834. In 1826 Thompson had written an article for the *Quarterly Review* in which he attacked Mill, but for some reason it was lost *en route* to the publisher. Thompson to [John Gibson] Lockhart, 16 Mar and 9 Oct 1826, Thompson Papers. Mill was a contributor to the *Westminster Review* and there were hard feelings on his part when Bowring sold the periodical to Thompson without consulting him. See Johnson, *Thompson*, p. 143.

23. Thompson to Bowring, 13 Dec 1831, Thompson Papers.

24. The quotation on the pimple and the pox was in regard to Oastler's work and is found in Thompson to Bowring, 22 June 1841, ibid. Johnson, *Thompson*, p. 187; 'Condition of the Working Classes and the Factory Bill', *Westminster Review*, vol. XVIII (Apr 1833) pp. 380–404. Since book reviews were not signed, one cannot always be positive of the authorship of each one, but while Thompson was the editor they certainly reflected his opinions. Although the Factory Act of 1833 provided for education for factory children, the expense for such a programme could be taken out of the children's wages.

25. Johnson, *Thompson*, pp. 203, 204, 212, 264. In 1848 he did not oppose a bill to reduce the hours for journeymen bakers, but it is not clear whether he voted for it or abstained. See Thompson to Bradford Reform Association, 31 May 1848, and to Bowring, 17 July 1832, Thompson Papers.

26. *Westminster Review*, XVIII, pp. 380–404; Johnson, *Thompson*, p. 187.

27. *Westminster Review*, XVIII, pp. 380–404.

28. 'The Suffering Rich', ibid., vol. XX (Apr 1834) pp. 265–74.

29. 'Machine Breaking', ibid., vol. XIV (Jan 1831) pp. 191–210.

30. 'On the Instrument of Exchange', ibid., vol. I (Jan 1824) pp. 171–205; 'Aristocratic Taxation', ibid., vol. XXI (July 1834) pp. 140–85; clippings from the *Bradford Advertiser*, 10 Apr 1862 and 18 Mar 1865, Thompson Papers; Thompson to Harriet Martineau, 9 Nov 1842, to J. T. Dexter, 14 July 1868, and to Secretary of the Bradford Reform Association, 11 Aug 1851, ibid.

31. *London Dispatch and People's Political and Social Reformer*, 11 Dec 1836; review article on 'Society for the Diffusion of Useful Knowledge', *Westminster Review*, vol. XIV (Apr 1831) pp. 365–94; ibid., vol. XXI, pp. 140–85. For Brougham on education see Chester W. New, *The Life of Henry Brougham to 1830* (Oxford: Clarendon Press, 1961) pp. 198–226, 328–51.

32. *Westminster Review*, vol. XXI, pp. 140–85; Johnson, *Thompson*, pp. 202, 229; Thompson to Bowring, 26 Oct 1830, 21 Jan and 23 Mar 1835, and 23 May 1841, and to the Bradford Reform Association, 10 Mar 1851, Thompson Papers. In 1852, when Thompson lost his seat in Parliament by six votes, he blamed the Catholics. See Johnson, *Thompson*, p. 274; Bowring, *Autobiographical Recollections*, pp. 70–2; and Howitt, in *Howitt's Journal*, vol. II, no. 31. A question of interest is whether or not abolitionists had a heritage of anti-Catholicism. An undated campaign flyer for one of Wilberforce's campaigns begins, 'Slave Trade / Popery with a Vengeance / Popery and Slavery Always Have and Always Will Go Hand-in-Hand', and ends with 'No Popery! No Slavery! Wilberforce and Lascelles Forever!'

33. Thompson to Bowring, 10 May 1833, Thompson Papers.
34. He gave serious consideration to Malthus's ideas of population limitation, and proposed that the birth-control issue should be placed in the hands of able women such as Martineau and the popular novelist Mrs Marcet. He said that the woman who assumed the leadership would immortalize herself and 'We should have such a *propaganda* as never was before' (Thompson to Bowring, 2 [Nov] 1834, ibid.).
35. Thompson to Bowring, 10 May 1833 and 2 Aug 1834, and to Professor Pryme [MP] from *Westminster Review*, XIX (July 1833), ibid.
36. [Thompson], *A Catechism on the Corn Laws; with a List of Fallacies and the Answers. By a Member of the University of Cambridge* (London, 1827). It went through twenty editions.
37. See, for example, Thompson to Bowring, 24 Aug and 26 Oct 1830, and 5 Dec 1831, Thompson Papers.
38. Thompson to Bowring, 13 Dec 1831, ibid.
39. Thompson to Bowring, 12 Apr 1853, ibid.
40. Thompson to Bowring, 10 May 1833, ibid.
41. Johnson, *Thompson*, pp. 192–6; *DNB*, vol. XIX, p. 705. In his *Autobiographical Recollections* Bowring claimed that Thompson's father was ready to pay £5000 for a rotten-borough seat in Parliament for his son, and that he – Bowring – was charged with 'the negotiation'. But the plan was dropped because the Radicals backed and elected Thompson.
42. Dorothy Thompson, *The Early Chartists* (Columbia: Univ. of South Carolina Press, 1971) pp. 6–7.
43. Thompson to Bowring, 11 Jan, 3 and 20 Feb 1840, Thompson Papers.
44. Thompson to Bowring, 7 Feb 1840, ibid.
45. Thompson to Bowring, 24 Nov 1837, ibid.
46. Thompson to Bowring, 16 Mar 1840, ibid.
47. Thompson to Bowring, 21 Mar and 1 Apr 1840, ibid.
48. *Westminster Review*, vol. XX, pp. 265–74.
49. Johnson, *Thompson*, pp. 213, 221, 224. Johnson says that Thompson identified himself with the Chartists from the beginning. Ebenezer Elliott, famous as the 'Corn Law Rhymer', wrote a poem entitled 'Colonel Thompson in Palace Yard':

> Who is that small Napoleon-featured pleader?
> The sage, whose metaphors are demonstrations;
> The bard, whose music yet shall teach all nations
> That ignorance is want, war, waste and treason;
> Thompson, the Haydn and Moliere of reason
> Clear-voiced as evening's throstle, o'er the booming
> Of conscious forests heard when storms are coming
> He stills those thousands, like a people's leader.

50. Thompson to Bowring, 7 and 28 May 1841, Thompson Papers.
51. Thompson to Bowring, 26 May 1841, ibid.
52. See essay on Sturge in this volume.
53. Thompson to Richard Cobden, 25 Sep 1842, Thompson Papers.
54. Thompson to Bowring, 12 Oct 1841 and 6 Oct 1843, ibid. His use of the term 'bump of' instead of 'aptitude for' reflects the popularity of phrenology

in the mid nineteenth century. Thompson wrote to Cobden, 25 Nov 1842, 'I see that Feargus's rod (like Moses's) has swallowed up Joseph's at Birmingham, which I am rather glad of, than otherwise. It just shows the profundity of Joseph's miscalculation' (ibid.).

55. The flyer is in the BL catalogue under the heading 'Chartist League Agitators'. It is undated.
56. W. J. Linton, *Threescore and Ten Years 1820 to 1890, Recollections* (New York: Charles Scribner's Sons, 1894) pp. 158–9.
57. At his father's death Thompson inherited a substantial fortune and a country estate, but eschewed the life of a country gentleman to live in London and spend money on his reform causes (Johnson, *Thompson*, p. 142).
58. See letters from Thompson to Cobden throughout 1842, Thompson Papers. The London *Times* attacked Thompson for his socialism, although Thompson maintained that his Chartist and socialist friends knew very well that he was not one.
59. Thompson to the Bradford Reform Association, 10 Apr 1848, Thompson Papers.
60. Thompson to the Bradford Reform Association, 5 May and 11 Aug 1851, and to J. T. Dexter, 14 July 1868, ibid. Thompson, *Catechism of the Ballot; or, a List of Fallacies and the Answers*, 3rd edn (London: G. Brown, 1859).
61. Letter of Thompson, 10 Apr 1862, clipping from *Bradford Advertiser*, Thompson Papers.
62. Thompson to Bradford Reform Association, 12 June 1848, ibid.
63. Thompson to Bowring, 26 Jan 1840, ibid.
64. Thompson to the Electors of Bradford, 9 Mar 1857, ibid.
65. Johnson, *Thompson*, p. 279; George Thompson Papers, John Rylands Library, for his participation in the British India Society and the Aborigines Protection Society.
66. *Daily News* (London), 17 May 1853.
67. Johnson, *Thompson*, pp. 282–3.
68. Ibid., p. 285 to end; Bowring, *Autobiographical Recollections*, pp. 70–2.
69. *DNB*, vol. xix, p. 705; see the BL catalogue for these publications.
70. Johnson, *Thompson*, p. 286.

## NOTES TO CHAPTER SIX: PATRICK BREWSTER AND HENRY SOLLY

1. Alexander Wilson, *The Chartist Movement in Scotland* (Manchester: Manchester Univ. Press, 1970) pp. 32, 202; Solly, *These Eighty Years, or, The Story of an Unfinished Life*, 2 vols (London: Simpkin, Marshall, 1893) vol. i, pp. 398–9.
2. Arthur Henry Grant, 'Patrick Brewster', and Robert Hunt, 'Sir David Brewster', *DNB*, vol. ii, pp. 1207–12; W. H. Marwick, 'Patrick Brewster', *Scottish Educational Journal*, 10 Oct 1930, pp. 1048–9.
3. Solly, *These Eighty Years*, vol. i, pp. 1–4, 36, 244, 299, 315, 328, 343.
4. Thomas Johnson in Introduction to Brewster, *Chartist and Socialist*

*Sermons* (Glasgow: Forward [n.d.]) p. iii. Although there is no date of printing, this edn must have appeared in the late nineteenth or early twentieth century, because an advertisement in the back includes works by Sidney Webb. The frontispiece is a portrait of Brewster.

5. Brewster: *Chartist and Socialist Sermons*; and *The Seven Chartist and Military Discourses Libelled by the Marquis of Abercorn, and Other Heritors of the Abbey Parish. To Which are Added, Four Other Discourses Formerly Published, with One or Two More as a Specimen of the Author's Mode of Treating Other Scripture Topics* (Paisley: published by the author, 1843). The Chartist Sermons are the same in both pamphlets. The texts are from the Authorized (King James) version of the Bible.

6. Brewster, *Chartist and Socialist Sermons*, pp. 1–15 (Chartist Sermon I: 'The Spoiling of the Masses in the Name of God' and 83–90 ('An Essay on Passive Obedience in Connection with the Principles of Christianity, the Rights of Subjects and the Duty of Rulers'). The simile about peeling the layers of hypocrisy as one would peel an onion was Brewster's.

7. Ibid., pp. 15–29 (Chartist Sermon II), and Selections from Military Sermons, pp. 76, 81–2.

8. Brewster, *Chartist and Socialist Sermons*, vol. II, pp. 17, 20–1, and vol. III, pp. 32–3.

9. Brewster, *Seven Chartist and Military Discourses*, pp. 1–34 (Chartist Sermon I), 35–67 (II) and 68–111 (III), and *The Duties of the Present Crisis with a Special Reference to the Liberated Negroes in the British Colonies: A Sermon Preached on the First of August, 1838, in the Abbey Church* (Paisley: Joseph Murray, 1838).

10. Brewster, *Seven Chartist and Military Discourses*, pp. 68–111 (Chartist Sermon III: 'The Bondage of the Working Class').

11. Ibid., pp. 112–41 (Chartist Sermon IV: 'Land and Capital'). There are interesting comments on Brewster's attack on the Poor Laws in the manuscript Journal and Commonplace Book of Henry C. Wright, entry for 18 June 1845, Wright Papers, BPL. Wright was an American abolitionist, also sympathetic to the working class. See also Marwick, in *Scottish Educational Journal*, 10 Oct 1930.

12. Brewster: *Seven Chartist and Military Discourses*, pp. 142–81 (Military Sermon I) and 182–200 (II); and *Chartist and Socialist Sermons*, Selections from Military Sermons, pp. 69–73.

13. Ibid., Chartist Sermon II, p. 17; Brewster, *Seven Chartist and Military Discourses*, pp. 222–41 (Military Sermon IV), and Appendix, p. 416. The other Military Sermons continue in the same vein.

14. Brewster, *Chartist and Socialist Sermons*, Selections from Military Sermons, pp. 75–8.

15. Ibid., Chartist Sermon II, p. 40, and IV, pp. 52–4. A note by the editor says that when Brewster uttered these lines he was specifically looking out at his own Superintendent and Overseers of the Abbey Church. See also Marwick, in *Scottish Educational Journal*, 10 Oct 1930.

16. Brewster: *Chartist and Socialist Sermons*, Chartist Sermon I, p. 3, and II, p. 24; and *Seven Chartist and Military Discourses*, Chartist Sermon II, pp. 40–3, and Military Sermon II.

17. According to Alexander Wilson, Brewster's joining the Chartists was the most important event for Scottish labour since the visit of Thomas Attwood in 1835 (*The Chartist Movement in Scotland*, p. 260).

18. Ibid., pp. 62–3.

19. Brewster, *Chartist and Socialist Sermons*, Chartist Sermon II, p. 17.

20. Wilson, *Chartist Movement in Scotland*, pp. 32, 75, 202. By 1841 there were at least twenty Chartist churches in Scotland. See ibid., pp. 124–5. Wilson says another act which brought retaliation against Brewster to a head was his attendance at a Glasgow dinner to honour Daniel O'Connell.

21. Brewster: *Chartist and Socialist Sermons*, p. iv; and *Seven Chartist and Military Discourses*, Appendix, pp. 409–16. W. H. Marwick, in *Scottish Educational Journal*, 10 Oct 1930, says that the Marquis of Abercorn, Brewster's patron, instituted the prosecution against him, 'apparently resentful at the misuse of his patronage in his minority'.

22. J. A. Collins to Garrison, 27 [or 7?] Dec 1840, Garrison Papers, BPL.

23. *Slavery and 'the Woman Question'. Lucretia Mott's Diary of her Visit to Great Britain to Attend the World's Anti-Slavery Convention of 1840*, ed. Frederick B. Tolles (Haverford, Pa: Friends Historical Association, 1952) pp. 70, 72.

24. *Glasgow Argus*, 19 Apr 1841; GES Minute Book III, entries for 10, 16, 25, 29 Mar and 13 Apr 1841, Mitchell Library, Glasgow; Robert L. Bingham, 'The Glasgow Emancipation Society 1833–76' (unpublished thesis, University of Glasgow, 1973) p. 151.

25. GES Minute Book III, 27 Apr 1841.

26. Ibid., 31 May 1841. For more on Collins and the GES, see C. Duncan Rice, *The Scots Abolitionists 1833–1861* (Baton Rouge: Louisiana State Univ. Press, 1981) pp. 108–13.

27. GES Minute Book III, entry for 3 Aug 1841. This minute says that Thompson's motion with Brewster's amendment carried by a 'large majority', but the *Annual Report* of the GES implies that the audience was impatient with Brewster and passed only the Thompson resolution. See *Seventh Annual Report of the Glasgow Emancipation Society* (Glasgow: Aird & Russell, 1841) pp. 51–6. Brewster and Thompson were both members of the Anti-Corn Law League, but Thompson did not come out openly for Chartism until May 1842.

28. *Nonconformist* (London), 21 July 1841; *Scotsman* (Edinburgh), 21 July 1841.

29. Ibid., 21 Aug 1841; *Nonconformist*, 18 and 25 Aug 1841.

30. Solly, *These Eighty Years*, vol. I, pp. 170–2, 236, 299, 328.

31. Garrison to S. J. May, 19 Dec 1846, Garrison Papers; *Inquirer* (London), 22 Aug 1846; Solly, *These Eighty Years*, vol. II, p. 117.

32. Ibid., vol. I, p. 329; Solly, *James Woodford, Carpenter and Chartist*, 2 vols (London: Sampson Law, Marston, Searle & Rivington, 1881) pp. 147, 171, 201–2.

33. The quotations are from Solly to Frederick H. Janson, 30 Sep 1840, Solly Collection, vol. I, N77, British Library of Political and Economic Science, London; Solly, *These Eighty Years*; vol. I, pp. 343–6.

34. Solly, *The Midnight Cry. A Sermon Preached before the Somerset and*

*Dorset Association, at their Annual Meeting, Held at Dorchester, June, 1845* (London; Chapman Bros; Bristol: H. C. Evans; and Wortley, Yorks: J. Barker, 1846). The last-named publisher is the subject of the following essay in this volume.

35. Solly, *These Eighty Years*, vol. i, pp. 349–50, 398–9.

36. Ibid., pp. 369–70.

37. *Nonconformist*, 18 and 25 Aug 1841.

38. Solly, *These Eighty Years*, vol. i, pp. 375–82.

39. *Nonconformist*, 16 Apr and 18 May 1842. The *Nonconformist* was the organ of the Complete Suffrage Union. See essay on Joseph Sturge in this volume.

40. Solly, *These Eighty Years*, vol. i, pp. 389, 400–6.

41. *Nonconformist*, 21 Sep, 5 and 12 Oct 1842.

42. Ibid., 28 Dec 1842; Solly, *These Eighty Years*, vol. i, pp. 406–9. Bronterre O'Brien's paper the *British Statesman* (London), 31 Dec 1842, specifically named Brewster as a strong opponent of using the name 'The Charter'.

43. Solly, *These Eighty Years*, vol. i, p. 419.

44. Letter to J. R. Seeley, Regius Professor of Modern History at Cambridge, May 1881, which appears as the introduction to Solly's *James Woodford*. See also the advertisement for the novel which is included at the end of vol. i of *These Eighty Years*. Quotation from *James Woodford*, p. 19.

45. Solly, *Gonzaga: A Tale of Florence. A Drama in Five Acts: Adapted from the Original Dramatic Poem, 'Gonzaga Di Capponi'* (London: Samuel French, 1877); playbill for performance on 28 Apr 1877, Solly Collection, vol. i, N94 and N146; *Reasoner and London Tribune*, 22 June 1856.

46. Clippings advertising *The Shepherd's Dream*, Solly Collection, vol. i, N148 and N149, and Joseph H. Hutton to Solly, 16 Feb 1882, ibid., N150, in which Hutton expresses great disappointment in the play because it is too unrealistic. He can't believe that a woman of refinement would marry a working man and raise him to her level; he would draw her down to his.

47. Solly tried to persuade Sturge to stand for Tavistock in the 1843 parliamentary election. Sturge declined but sent Vincent there to lecture. Vincent was such a success that he was put in nomination, but lost. Solly attributed the defeat to the Duke of Bedford who rounded up tenant farmers to vote against the 'Chartist menace'. See *These Eighty Years*, vol. i, pp. 416–17. For Solly's co-operation in the Anti-Slavery League, see the *Nonconformist*, 12 Aug 1846, and *Inquirer*, 22 Aug 1846.

48. Solly, *Working Men's Clubs and Institutes: An Answer to the Question, Why Are They Wanted?*, 2nd edn (London: Council of the Working Men's Club and Institute Union, 1865) p. 16.

49. Solly, *These Eighty Years*, vol. ii, pp. 72, 82–5, 186.

50. Quoted from Introduction to Solly, *James Woodford*, p. vii.

51. Solly, *A Few Thoughts on How to Deal with the Unemployed Poor of London, and with its 'Roughs' and Criminal Classes?* ([London]: Social Science Association, 1868) pp. 7–10.

52. The quotation is from ibid., p. 10. Solly: *Working Men's Social Clubs and Educational Institutes* (London: Working Men's Club and Institute Union, 1867); *Working Men's Clubs and Institutes: An Answer to the Question,*

*Why Are They Wanted?; Working Men; A Glance at Some of their Wants; with Reasons and Suggestions for Helping them to Help Themselves*, 4th edn (London: Jerrold, 1865); *Working Men's Clubs and Alcoholic Drinks: Is the Prohibitory Policy Necessary or Expedient?* (London: Samuel Palmer, 1872).

53. R. D. Taylor to Solly, 9 Aug 1849, the Revd Henry W. Crosskey to Solly, 2 Oct 1849, George Dawson to Solly, 20 Sep [no year], flyer for 'The Society of Christian Disciples', Dec 1849, and 'Scheme for a Free Christian Union' [n.d.], all in Solly Collection, vol. VIII, I16, I121, I146, I171, I172, I199 and I1157. In questioning the practicality of Solly's idea, R. D. Taylor said such a venture would require 'the supervision of so energetic a mind as [Joseph] Barker's', who had succeeded with his 'Barkerites'. See following essay in this volume. On George Dawson see Alexander Ireland, *Recollections of George Dawson and his Lectures in Manchester in 1846–7* (Manchester), repr. from *Manchester Quarterly*, no. II, Apr 1882. In 1846 Bishop Samuel Wilberforce refused to sit on the same platform with Dawson because of his free-thinking ideas (ibid., 12).

54. Solly: *James Woodford*, pp. 209–11; *These Eighty Years*, vol. I, p. 416, and vol. II, pp. 110, 566; *Home Colonization. Re-housing of the Industrial Classes, or, Village Communities vs. Town Rookeries* (London: W. Swan Sonnenschein, 1884). An early abolitionist who had much the same idea for home colonies was the Quaker William Allen. See [William Allen], *Colonies at Home: Or, The Means for Rendering the Industrious Labourer Independent of Parish Relief; and for Providing for the Poor Population of Ireland, by the Cultivation of the Soil* (Lindfield, Sussex: C. Greene [1827]). All of vol. XIV in the Solly Collection is devoted to temperance.

55. The phrase comes from *Five Hundred Thousand Strokes for Freedom. A Series of Anti-Slavery Tracts. Of Which Half a Million Are Now First Issued by the Friends of the Negro*, ed. Wilson Armistead (London: E. & F. Cash, 1853).

56. Baron Lyttleton to Solly, 14 May 1875, Solly Collection, vol. I, N41. See other letters from patrons throughout the correspondence in the Collection.

57. Prospectus for the *Bee-Hive*, Solly Collection, vol. V, F10; Jack R. Pole, *Abraham Lincoln and the Working Classes of Britain* (London: Commonwealth–American Current Affairs Unit of the British Speaking Union [1959]). Prospectuses for the other publications and letters regarding them are in the Solly Collection, vol. V, F10, F18, F33, F59, F238 and F253. *Our Magazine*, complete for 1891, is in the BL.

58. Solly Collection, vol. I, N86, but particularly lecture notes and notices throughout vol. II.

59. Sidney Webb to Solly, 6 Nov 1896, ibid., vol. I, N62, and notes at end of vol. II.

60. Joseph Hartley Wicksteed to 'Grandpapa', undated, ibid., vol. I, N68.

61. Thomas Solly to Solly, 21 May 1867, ibid., N10. Another letter from Thomas (ibid., N12) contains advice on Solly's proposal for his play *Gonzaga*.

62. Brewster, *Chartist and Socialist Sermons*, Introduction, pp. iv–v.

63. Robert Applegarth to Solly [1868], Solly Collection, vol. I, N21.

NOTES TO CHAPTER SEVEN: JOSEPH BARKER

1.  Letter from Barker, 22 Nov 1856, repr. in *What Joseph Barker Thought of the Southern Statesmen When He Lived Near Them* [1863] Broadside, Anti-Slavery Collection, John Rylands Library, Manchester.
2.  I have included more biographical data on Barker than on the other essay subjects in this volume because there is no full biography of him in print and he is known hardly at all. His diary, covering the years 1865 to 1875, is filled with reminiscences of the hardships of his early life, which may have become exaggerated as he grew older. See entries for 26 May 1865, 9 and 21 Feb and 2 Sep 1866, 17 Apr and 1 Dec 1868, and 3 Nov 1869. There are also many others, esp. from p. 1017 of Reel 2 of the microfilm, Barker Collection, Nebraska State Historical Society, Lincoln, Neb. Unless otherwise stated, I have taken material on his private life from the Diary; a typescript without author, 'Rev. Joseph Barker', and a typescript by Francis T. B. Martin, a descendant, 'The Barker Family of Keighley, and Later of Bramley, Near Leeds, Yorkshire, England, 1957', all in the Barker Collection; and from three of Barker's own accounts: *Lessons I Have Learned on my Way through Life* (London: James Beveridge, 1869); *Modern Skepticism: A Journey through the Land of Doubt and Back Again* (Philadelphia: Smith, English, 1874); and the *Life of Joseph Barker. Written by Himself. Edited by his Nephew, John Thomas Barker* (London: Hodder and Stoughton, 1880). All of these memoirs are coloured by Barker's age and by his desire to put himself in a good light and must be used carefully. Modern printed accounts with brief material on Barker's early life include Arthur F. Grant, 'Joseph Barker', *DNB*, vol. I, pp. 1124–7; and J. F. C. Harrison, 'Chartism in Leeds', in *Chartist Studies*, ed. Asa Briggs (London: Macmillan, 1959) pp. 65–98.
3.  Autobiographical bits in 'How Did You Become an Infidel?', pp. 1–10, and 'Books I Have Read', Barker Collection.
4.  'How Did You Become an Infidel?' pp. 12–19, ibid.; Barker, *Life*, pp. 35–6; *DNB*, vol. I, pp. 1124–7. 'Books I Have Read', Barker Collection, contains the information on how he was taught to read. The family fortune improved to the point that by 1869 Barker could write in his diary (28 Feb 1869) that his relatives then owned most of Bramley.
5.  The Barker Collection has vol. I (Dec 1837 – July 1838) of the *Evangelical Reformer*. It was published until 1840. For Barker on Quakerism see his *Life*, pp. 254, 273, 280–1; 'How Did You Become an Infidel?' p. 30, Barker Collection; and Barker, *Letter to J. J. Gurney, Containing Remarks on his Views of the Atonement, Imputed by Righteousness, &c.* (Newcastle: J. Barker [n.d.]).
6.  The quotation about Wesley's works is from Barker, *Life*, p. 58.
7.  R. D. Webb to S. J. May, 8 Mar 1854, May Papers, BPL; *Memoir of James Haughton*, ed. Samuel Haughton (Dublin: E. Ponsonby) Appendix H, pp. 302–4.
8.  George J. Holyoake, *The History of Co-operation* (New York: E. P. Dutton, 1906) vol. I, p. 205. It should be remembered that Holyoake and Barker had had an altercation over Holyoake's criticism of Garrison's extremism.

9. Letter from Barker, no. II, 9 June 1854, in *Anti-Slavery Bugle* (Salem, Ohio), 8 July 1854 (on microfilm at Ohio State University).

10. Review of Barker's *Teachings of Experience* with pencil annotation ascribing it to the *Methodist Quarterly*, undated, Barker Collection.

11. Barker: *Mercy Triumphant; or Teaching the Children of the Poor to Write on the Sabbath Day, Proved to Be in Perfect Agreement with the Oracle of God* (Manchester: Cave and Sever, n.d.) Barker Collection; and *Life*, pp. 245, 247. One of the ministers with whom Barker found himself in conflict was the Revd John Angell James, a prominent Birmingham clergyman and also an abolitionist. See the *Christian*, 1 Nov 1847.

12. Barker: *The Gospel Triumphant: or, a Defense of Christianity against the Attacks of the Socialists; and an Exposure of the Infidel Character and Mischievous Tendency of the Social System of R. Owen* (Newcastle: J. Blackwell, 1839); and *Conversation between a Socialist and a Christian* (Newcastle: J. Barker [n.d.]). The letter to the *Gateshead Observer* is quoted in Edward Royle, *Victorian Infidels: The Origins of the British Secularist Movement 1791–1866* (Manchester: Manchester Univ. Press, 1974) p. 65. See the *Reasoner* and *Secular Gazette*, vol. XIV (Spring and Summer 1853), for the running argument and then reconciliation between Barker and George Holyoake over Owenite socialism. See also the *Christian*, vol. III, no. lxii, (Feb 1847 [NB: in vols I and II and part of III there are no specific dates for each issue; for subsequent issues reference is by issue date, not vol.]); and Michael Brook, *Joseph Barker and the People, the True Emigrant's Guide* (Leeds, 1963), repr. from *Publications of the Thoresby Society* (Leeds), Miscellany, vol. 13, pt 3 (1961) pp. 331–78.

13. *Christian*, 14 Feb 1848.

14. Barker, *The Cause of the Present Distress at Present Prevailing in Great Britain and Ireland, and the Means by Which the Distress May Be Cured, and the Recurrence of Similar Calamities for the Future Prevented* [Wortley, 1845]. The pamphlets printed without place during this period were from Barker's own press at Wortley. See also the *Christian*, 1 Sep 1847, 14 Mar, 1 and 14 Apr 1848.

15. *Autobiographical Recollections of Sir John Bowring. With a Brief Memoir by Lewin B. Bowring* (London: Henry S. King, 1877) p. 65.

16. Ibid., pp. 5–7.

17. Ibid., p. 61. For more background see Betty Fladeland, 'Abolitionist Pressures on the Concert of Europe, 1814–1822', *Journal of Modern History*, vol. 38 (Dec 1966) pp. 355–73.

18. Bowring, *The Press (Written for the Occasion of the Opening of the Barker Steam Press,) and Other Poetry* [Wortley, 1846]. Barker: *Proposal for a New Library, of Three Hundred Volumes, the Cheapest Collection of Works Ever Published* [Wortley, 1846]; and *The Press and the People, or A Report of the Proceedings Connected with the Opening of the Barker Steam Press, on Monday, July 6, 1846, and of the Speeches Delivered on the Occasion by Dr Bowring, MP, Mr Barker, C. Larken, Esq., and Others* [Wortley, 1846].

19. *DNB*, vol. I, pp. 1124–7.

20. Bowring: *Autobiographical Recollections*, pp. 27, 65, 79, 291; and *On*

*Remunerative Prison Labour, as an Instrument for Promoting the Reformation and Diminishing the Cost of Offenders* (Exeter: William Clifford; and London: W. Kent [1865]).

21. Barker, *The Cause of the Present Distress*.

22. [Barker], *Slander Refuted* [Wortley, 1845]; *Christian*, 14 June 1847.

23. *Mary Howitt, An Autobiography*, ed. Margaret Howitt, 2 vols (London: William Isbister, 1889) vol. II, p. 38; Barker, *Letter to J. J. Gurney*.

24. Mary Howitt, *Autobiography*, vol. II, pp. 33–42; *People's Journal, Howitt's Journal* and *People's and Howitt's Journal* from 1846 to 1849. The Howitts first wrote for the *People's Journal* while it was under the editorship of John Saunders and then took it over. Among the many things William Howitt wrote was a series, 'Letters on Labour to the Working Man of England', in which he stressed not only the dignity of labour but also the political power of labour, especially through co-operative associations. See *People's Journal*, 11 Apr – 20 June 1846.

25. *Howitt's Journal*, 20 Mar 1847; *Christian*, vol. II, p. 557.

26. William James to S. J. May, Jr, 26 June 1844, May Papers.

27. In his diary, 28 June 1865, Barker pinpoints the beginning of his antislavery lectures as in 1828. 'History and Confessions of a Man', *Christian*, 1 Aug 1847. This was still another autobiographical account which Barker ran serially in the paper. The Quakers named gave Barker money and lent him rooms for his lectures on peace. See Barker, *Life*, pp. 273–4.

28. Garrison to Elizabeth Pease, 28 Feb 1843, in *The Letters of William Lloyd Garrison*, ed. Walter M. Merrill, vol. III: *No Union with Slaveholders 1841–1849* (Cambridge, Mass.: Belknap Press, 1973) pp. 123–7; letters from Wright in the *Liberator*, 7 and 28 Apr, 5 May and 23 June 1843. Elizabeth Pease's donation to the Barker Press is mentioned in Barker, *Modern Skepticism*, p. 179.

29. The quotation is in Wright's letter in the *Liberator*, 23 June 1843, in which he also states that he would like to level to the ground all the castles and cathedrals of England because they are symbols of the oppression of the people. For Barker's anarchistic expressions see *Non-Resistance. In Two Letters, the First from H. C. Wright, of America, and the Second from J. Barker, of England, with an Appendix, Containing Answers to Questions on the Subject* [Wortley, 1843]. Wright's letter is dated Dublin, 26 Nov 1842, and Barker's Newcastle-on-Tyne, 7 Dec 1842.

30. Garrison to Helen Garrison, 10 Sep 1846, Garrison Papers, BPL; Garrison to R. D. Webb, 12 Sep 1846, in *Letters of Garrison*, vol. III, pp. 408–10. The Anti-Slavery League, organised in 1846, hoped to bring the various local Garrisonian bodies under a central organisation, playing the role that the British and Foreign Anti-Slavery Society did for the non-Garrisonians.

31. *Liberator*, 17 Dec 1847, 22 Dec 1848 for the quotations; *Christian*, 1 July 1847.

32. Barker, *Life*, p. 309; Brook, *Joseph Barker and the People*, p. 354; R. D. Webb to [Maria Weston Chapman], 8 July 1849, Weston Papers, BPL. Years later, when Barker had become critical of the Garrisonians, he denounced their treatment of Frederick Douglass, saying that in public

meetings they 'baited him like a bull', and said all manner of evil about him. See *Barker's Review of Politics, Literature, Religion, and Morals, and Journal of Education, Science, and Co-operation*, 5 Apr 1862.

33. Barker to P. P. Carpenter and Wright to P. P. Carpenter in the *Christian*, vol. III, pp. 133–41.

34. Barker, *Life*, p. 312; *Anti-Slavery Bugle*, 15 Nov 1851.

35. For Barker on women's rights see the account of his speech to the Ohio Women's Rights Association, *Anti-Slavery Bugle*, 11 June 1853. For the Howitts' efforts to change the property laws for married women see Mary Howitt, *Autobiography*, vol. II, pp. 114–17. For background on the World Anti-Slavery Convention see C. Duncan Rice, *The Scots Abolitionists 1833–1861* (Baton Rouge and London: Louisiana State Univ. Press, 1981) ch. 4; Howard Temperley, *British Antislavery 1833–1870* (Columbia: Univ. of South Carolina Press, 1972) pp. 85–92.

36. Barker, *Blessings of Free Trade, and How They May Be Increased and Made Lasting, A Speech Delivered at the Wortley Free Trade Rejoicing Dinner, on Monday, July 27, 1846* [Wortley, 1846].

37. Betty Fladeland, '"Our Cause Being One and the same": Abolitionists and Chartism', in *Slavery and British Society 1776–1846*, ed. James Walvin (London: Macmillan, 1982) pp. 69–99.

38. *Inquirer* (London), 5 Sep 1846.

39. *Anti-Slavery Bugle*, 10 Sep 1853 and 27 Oct 1855.

40. *Christian*, vol. III (1847), e.g. pp. 358–59, 381.

41. Ibid., 14 Feb 1848. Barker uses the term 'Christian Brethren' as synonymous with 'Barkerites', whom Arthur Grant in the *DNB* identifies as those adherents of Barker who left the New Connexion of Methodists with him in 1841. Arthur O'Neil was an abolitionist as well as a Chartist and co-operated with Sturge in Birmingham, where they both lived.

42. *Christian*, 14 Feb 1848. I have found no evidence that Solly and Barker ever acted together, but advertisements for Solly's sermons appear in the *Christian*. See vol. III (1847) p. 456, for example.

43. Brook, *Joseph Barker and the People*, p. 336; Harrison, in *Chartist Studies*, ed. Briggs, pp. 65–98; Barker, *The Reformer's Almanac, and Companion to the Almanacs, for 1848* (Wortley: J. Barker, 1848) pp. 64–9, 229–37, 255–6; Royle, *Victorian Infidels*, p. 146.

44. *People* (Wortley, near Leeds), 27 May 1848. The paper sold for one penny.

45. Ibid., vol. I, no. 37. In this paper Barker switched from dates for issues to vol. and no.

46. *DNB*, vol. I, pp. 1124–7; *Reformer's Almanac*, Jan 1848 and June 1848. Allowance should be made for the fact that the number for the crowd at the West Riding meeting was Barker's own estimate.

47. E[manuel] W[arewoods] to Mrs Barker, 27 Aug 1848, and Barker Diary, 6 Oct 1873, Barker Collection.

48. Barker: 'The Triumph of Right over Might; or A Full Account of the Attempt Made by the Manchester Magistrates and the Whig Government to Rob J. Barker of his Liberty, and Suppress his Publications, and of the Signal Failure of That Attempt', *People*, end of vol. I (1848); *Modern Skepticism*, pp. 245–52; *Life*, pp. 291–7. See also the *Spirit of the Age*

(London), 14 Oct 1848; Harrison, in *Chartist Studies*, ed. Briggs, pp. 65–98.

49. Frederick Douglass to Barker, 16 Oct 1847, and James W. Walker to Barker, 6 Sep 1847, in the *Christian*, 1 Nov 1847.

50. See issues of the *People* throughout 1848, and the *Reformer's Almanac* and *Companion to the Almanacs* for 1848 and 1849; Barker, *Life*, pp. 308–9.

51. Quoted in Brook, *Joseph Barker and the People*, p. 339.

52. R. D. Webb to 'Dear Miss Hateful Perkins', 11 Dec 1849, Weston Papers; Brook, *Joseph Barker and the People*, pp. 342–6, 355, Ray Boston, *British Chartists in America 1839–1900* (Manchester: Manchester Univ. Press, 1971) p. xiii and ch. 2.

53. Louis Billington, 'Some Connections between British and American Reform Movements 1830–1860. With Special Reference to the Anti-Slavery Movement' (unpublished MA thesis, University of Bistol, 1966) p. 261; Boston, *British Chartists in America*, pp. 7–8.

54. *People*, 27 May 1848; Brook, *Joseph Barker and the People*, pp. 355–6.

55. *People*, vol. I, nos. 17 and 20, for an exchange between James Haughton and Barker on the subject.

56. Barker's *Life*, p. 308, says that he visited the United States in 1847, and several writers since then, including Grant in the *DNB* article, have repeated what was probably a printer's error in substituting a '7' for a '9', because he actually made his first visit in 1849. See the *People*, vol. II (1849); Barker, *Modern Skepticism*, pp. 254–5; Brook, *Joseph Barker and the People*, pp. 368–73; Martin, 'The Barker Family', Barker Collection.

57. Under the old Fugitive Slave Law the burden of proof was on the slave-holder. In the new act, the burden was on the captured person to prove that he was not a fugitive slave. Moreover, when a claimant took the captured person to a judge or justice of the peace for a decision, the judge received a fee of $5 if he set the captive free, but $10 if he remanded him to slavery. The quotation is in 'American Reminiscences', *Barker's Review*, 28 Sep 1861.

58. Barker to Garrison, 24 Oct 1850, Garrison Papers; printed in *Anti-Slavery Bugle*, 18 Jan 1851. Barker to Sydney Howard Gay, 24 Oct 1850, Gay Collection, Columbia University, New York. He told Gay he would bring his wife and children to the United States to get their opinion before he decided whether or not to settle.

59. Boston, *British Chartists in America*, pp. 21–2.

60. Barker to Garrison, 9 May 1849, in the *People*, vol. I, no. 52; Barker, *Life*, pp. 311–12.

61. *Anti-Slavery Bugle*, 15 Nov 1851. For background see Douglas Gamble: 'The Western Anti-Slavery Society: Garrisonian Abolitionism in Ohio' (unpublished MA thesis, Ohio State University, 1970); and 'Moral Suasion in the West: Garrisonian Abolitionism, 1831–1861' (unpublished Ph D dissertation, Ohio State University, 1973).

62. Letter from Barker in *Anti-Slavery Bugle*, 15 Nov 1851.

63. Barker, *Modern Skepticism*, pp. 259–65.

64. *Anti-Slavery Bugle*, 29 May 1852.

65. 'The Bible and Slavery' (letter from Barker), ibid., 31 Jan 1852.

66. Ibid., 30 Oct 1852; Barker, *Modern Skepticism*, pp. 293–4.

67. *Anti-Slavery Bugle*, 9, 16 and 23 July 1853; *Liberator*, 10 Feb 1854.

68. Barker, *Modern Skepticism*, pp. 294–5. Barker says that he was chosen President, but the accounts in the *Liberator*, 17 June 1853, have Garrison presiding. Barker's account was written later in life and both his memory and his ego were probably playing tricks on him. But Royle in *Victorian Infidels*, p. 173, says that Barker was the most important link between British and American secularists.

69. Barker, *Modern Skepticism*, pp. 295–300; *Liberator*, 20 and 27 Jan, 10, 17 and 24 Feb, and 3 and 10 Mar 1854.

70. S. J. May, Jr, to R. D. Webb, 12 Feb 1854, Webb to May, 8 Mar 1854, May Papers; also Webb to [M. W. Chapman], 31 Dec 1851, Weston Papers. *Liberator*, 10 Feb 1854, carried a notice of Barker's Boston lectures but they were not reported.

71. The letter debate with the Wilsons is first mentioned in the *Anti-Slavery Bugle*, 31 Jan 1852. See the *Liberator*, 25 Mar, 1 and 22 Apr 1853. In the issue of 28 Apr 1854, Garrison announced that he had received still another letter from Mrs Wilson, reopening the debate; but since the argument had already run on 'to a wearisome length', and since Barker was about to leave for England, he would suspend publication until Barker's return.

72. *Liberator*, 25 Mar and 25 Nov 1853.

73. *Anti-Slavery Bugle*, 11 June and 8 Oct 1853 for Barker's speeches to the Ohio Women's Rights Convention and to the Yearly Meeting of Progressive Friends; Barker, *Seven Lectures on the Supernatural Origin and Divine Authority of the Bible* (Stoke-on-Trent: George Turner, 1854) p. 16.

74. Undated fragment, Barker Collection.

75. Letter from Barker in the *Liberator*, 18 July 1851. In 'American Reminiscences', which appeared regularly in *Barker's Review* during 1861, there are interesting descriptions of the American landscape, people, farming, products and folk ways.

76. Undated fragment on temperance, Martin's typescript 'The Barker family', and numerous entries on alcohol and tobacco throughout the Diary, Barker Collection. On his spiritualism see *Liberator*, 7 and 21 Jan 1853, for letters from Wright and Barker; Lewis Perry, *Childhood, Marriage and Reform: Henry Clarke Wright, 1797–1870* (Chicago: University of Chicago Press, 1980) pp. 158–9.

77. Letter from Wright in *Anti-Slavery Bugle*, 8 Jan 1853; Wright to *Liberator*, 21 Jan 1853; *National Reformer*, 2 June 1860. This last was a paper edited by Barker after his return to England in 1860.

78. *Anti-Slavery Bugle*, 8 Jan and 29 Oct 1853; Barker to Garrison, 21 Dec 1852, Garrison Papers.

79. R. D. Webb to A. W. Weston, 11 Mar 1851, Weston Papers. This letter is filed under the date 11 Mar 1857, but I think that what appears to be the beginning stroke of the '7' is actually the top stroke of the '5' and that Webb failed to lift his pen before adding the '1'. Internal evidence shows that the letter was written as the Barker family was about to leave England for America (1851). It also refers to Webster and Fillmore as the villains of

the new 'diabolical' Fugitive Slave Law which Webb had just read about in the *Liberator*, an obvious reference to the Fugitive Slave Law of 1850.

80. *Anti-Slavery Bugle*, 8 Jan and 29 Oct 1853; Barker Diary, 8 Nov 1867, Barker Collection; *Christian*, vol. ii, pp. 522–3 and 1 Nov 1847. The Hutchinsons and Barker had first met in England and their paths crossed again when Barker landed in New York in 1851. See Barker, *Modern Skepticism*, p. 257; Barker to Garrison, *Liberator*, 27 Dec 1853. In 1854 Suliot planned to start classes in Salem which would be open to women and blacks, but I have no evidence that his plan materialised. See Joseph Barker, Jr, to Garrison, 2 Oct 1854, Garrison Papers.

81. Barker, *Life*, pp. 316–18.

82. Barker to [Ernest Charles Jones], [1853], Seligman/Jones Collection, Columbia University, New York.

83. 'Remarks of Jos. Barker at 11th Anniversary of the Western Anti-Slavery Society in Salem on Aug. 27, 1853', *Anti-Slavery Bugle*, 10 Sep 1853; *Liberator*, 30 Sep 1853.

84. Report of Barker speech to the Massachusetts Anti-Slavery Society, *Liberator*, 17 Feb 1854; letter from Barker, *Liberator*, 24 Feb 1854.

85. Barker article on rights of labour, *Anti-Slavery Bugle*, 8 Oct 1853; speech to the Massachusetts Anti-Slavery Society, *Liberator*, 17 Feb 1854.

86. Barker wrote a series of letters from England that were published in the *Anti-Slavery Bugle* and also in the *Liberator*. They began in the June 1854 issues and ran through September.

87. For the quotations see Letter no. ii from Barker, *Anti-Slavery Bugle*, 8 July 1854, and *Liberator*, 7 July 1854; also Barker to *Liberator*, 5 Jan 1855.

88. Barker to Editor of the *Leader* (London), repr. in the *Anti-Slavery Bugle* and copied in the *Liberator*, 24 Nov 1854.

89. The Revd [Francis] Bishop to Mary E. Estlin, 1 Aug 1854, Weston Papers; Barker to Garrison, 23 Aug 1854, Garrison Papers; Alfred Steinthal to S. J. May, Jr, 17 Aug 1854, and Parker Pillsbury to S. J. May, 5 Oct 1854, May Papers.

90. Eliza Wigham to S. J. May, Jr, 7 Mar 1856, ibid.

91. *Anti-Slavery Bugle*, 27 Oct and 3 Nov 1855; Parker Pillsbury to S. J. May, Jr, 22 Nov 1855 and 14 Feb 1856, and R. D. Webb to S. J. May, Jr, 21 Dec 1855, May Papers. While critical of Barker, saying that his 'fluency of language tempted him to extremes', Webb also praised him for his courage. For an excellent treatment of Stephen S. Foster see Jane H. Pease and William H. Pease, *Bound with Them in Chains: A Biographical History of the Antislavery Movement* (Westport, Conn.: Greenwood, 1972) pp. 191–217. Barker claimed that after the debate with Foster the Garrisonians began to slander him as they had Frederick Douglass (*Barker's Review*, 5 Apr 1862).

92. Barker: 'American Reminiscences', *Barker's Review*, 19 Apr 1862; and *Modern Skepticism*, p. 267.

93. Barker to Garrison, 22 Oct 1856, *Liberator*, 14 Nov 1856; unidentified review of Barker, *Teachings of Experience; or Lessons I Have Learned on my Way through Life* (London: James Beveridge, 1869); Barker, *Modern Skepticism*, pp. 311–23; *Barker's Review*, 3 May 1862; Barker, *Life*, pp. 331–2; Martin, 'The Barker Family', Barker Collection. In moving to

Nebraska Barker lost all of his library, about 1000 volumes, when the Ohio River boat carrying them capsized.

94. Barker to Garrison, 22 Oct 1856, and to Wright, 8 Jan 1857, *Liberator*, 14 Nov 1856 and 6 Feb 1857. The letter to Garrison describes the conditions of the sailors on the river boats.

95. Barker: *Modern Skepticism*, pp. 318, 325–30; *Life*, pp. 338–41; Diary, 24 Aug 1866.

96. *National Reformer*, 1 Sep 1860.

97. Ibid., 2 June 1860; *The Belief in a Personal God and a Future Life. Six Nights Discussion between Thomas Cooper and Joseph Barker, Held in St George's Hall, Bradford, September 1860* (London: Ward, [1860]); *What Atheism Can Say for Itself, By Mr Joseph Barker. Extracted from a Dicussion between Himself and Mr Thomas Cooper, at St George's Hall, Bradford, September, 1860* (Leicester: Ward, 1870). On the flyleaf of the latter, in the Barker Collection, Barker has written, 'Cooper never forgave me'. See also Barker Diary, 1 June 1867, ibid.

98. Reviews of Barker's *Teachings of Experience*, one from the *Methodist Quarterly*, undated, one from the *North Londoner*, 22 Jan 1870, and one from the *Record*, undated; excerpts from reviews of *Modern Skepticism*, Barker Collection. The book which had so disgusted him was *The Elements of Social Science; or, Physical, Sexual, and Natural Religion*, published in 1854 and identified in Royle, *Victorian Infidels*, p. 277.

99. Barker, *Life*, pp. 352–3, 359–60; *Barker's Review*, 12 and 19 Dec 1863. He always credited his wife and sons, too, for his return to Christianity.

100. One must follow *Barker's Review* from 1861 to 1863 to get the whole picture of his thoughts and reactions. On tariff, see the issues of 7 Sep, 23 Nov, 7 and 21 Dec, and 29 Nov 1862.

101. *Barker's Review* with reprint of *Times* article, 13 June 1863. For more on British sympathies during the Civil War see, Temperley, *British Antislavery*, ch. 12; Betty Fladeland, *Men and Brothers: Anglo-American Antislavery Co-operation* (Urbana: Univ. of Illinois Press, 1972) ch. 16; and Christine Bolt, *The Anti-Slavery Movement and Reconstruction* (London: Oxford Univ. Press, 1969).

102. Quotation from *Barker's Review*, 6 Sep 1862.

103. Ibid., also 12 July 1862; Barker Diary, 12 May 1865, Barker Collection. Barker gave three speeches, published separately, but all under the title *The American Question* and all published in London by Barker & Co. in 1863. The three subtitles are: 'A Lecture Delivered in the Corn Exchange, Manchester, in Answer to the Speeches Delivered by the Hon. and Rev. B. Noel, Dr Massey [sic], and Others, in the Free Trade Hall, on June 3'; 'A Speech Delivered at a Public Meeting, at Burnley, in Reply to Messrs Dennison and Sinclair'; and 'Moderation, Intervention, Recognition. A Lecture by Mr Barker at Mossley'. Hereinafter referred to as I, II, and III.

104. Barker Diary, 1 Aug 1872, Barker Collection; *Barker's Review*, 8 and 22 Feb, 6 Sep 1862, and 1 Aug 1863.

105. Ibid., 8, 15, 22, 29 Nov and 6 Dec 1862; Barker Diary, 13 May 1865, Barker Collection.

106. *Barker's Review*, 5, 12, 19, 26 Oct, 23 Nov and 20 Dec 1862, 28 Jan 1863; Barker, *American Question*, III.

107. *Barker's Review*, 13 Dec 1863; Barker, *American Question*, II.

108. *Barker's Review*, 22 Feb, 12 July and 6 Sep 1862; Barker, *American Question*, I.

109. Barker Diary, 24 July 1865, 21 Jan 1873 and 3 Mar 1874, Barker Collection.

110. *Barker's Review*, 8 Nov 1862, 24 Jan, 7 Feb, 16 Apr and 18 and 25 July 1863; George Thompson to Amelia, 19 JUNE 1861, excerpt kindly furnished me by Nicolas Spence, a descendant of Thompson who is currently working on a biography of him.

111. The label 'Copperhead' derived from snakes of that name. Some Copperheads simply refused to aid the Northern war effort, while others engaged in sabotage, thus giving aid and support to the enemy.

112. Barker, *American Question*, I.

113. Ibid., I, II, and III.

114. Ibid., III; Barker Diary, 13 May 1865, Barker Collection.

115. 'English Sentiment on the American Question', *Liberator*, 23 Sep 1864. In the same issue there is a bit from the *Boston Investigator*, an 'infidel' publication which Barker had formerly supported. It also accused him of advocating any cause which would bring him money and make him rich.

116. Repr. from London *Morning Star*, *Liberator*, 6 Nov 1863; Broadside, John Rylands Library, Manchester.

117. *Liberator*, 4 Nov 1864.

118. *Barker's Review*, 22 Feb, 21 June and 25 Oct 1862.

119. One really must follow all of *Barker's Review*; see esp. issues of 28 Sep and 2 Nov 1861.

120. Ibid., 11 Jan, 12 Apr, 22 Mar, 10 and 17 May 1862. After 1865 one must follow the Diary to get the transitions. See esp. entries for 13 and 15 May 1865, 27 July and 2 Dec 1866, 8 June and 30 July 1867, 7 Mar and 4 May 1870, 25 Feb and 18 Apr 1871, 4 Sep 1872, Barker Collection.

121. Ibid., 5, 16 and 22 July 1865, 3 Mar and 6 May 1866, 1, 13 and 16 June and 2 Nov 1867, 13 July 1868, 19 Nov 1869, 17 Feb 1874.

122. Ibid., 16 May 1865 for quotations on Lincoln; 28 June and 19 Sep 1865 for quotations on abolitionists.

123. Barker's diary is filled with his comments on family relationships. After his wife's death his happy family life fell apart, and in the last years he compared himself to King Lear, constantly complaining that his children were conniving to deprive him of his property. In the entry for 6 June (should be July) 1874 he threatened to go to a poorhouse or an insane asylum where he could pay for an attendant. He interpreted his misfortune as God's punishment of him for having been an overindulgent, doting father.

124. Barker Diary, 3 Oct 1873 and 9 July 1870, Barker Collection. He wrote that 'Even those who fell into vice were not entirely without excuse.' In several Diary entries as well as in his *Life* (p. 314), Barker hints at the 'immoral habits' of some abolitionists. The only ones he names outright are Wright and Salmon P. Chase (Diary, 8 May 1873).

125. Ibid., 21 Feb 1874.

126. Ibid., 26 Mar and 6 Apr 1874.

127. Ibid., 8 Apr 1872.

128. One must read the whole diary to get the picture. Some references are: 11, 12, 16 and 22 July and 9 Sep 1865, 5 Jan, 9 Feb and 6 Aug 1866, 1 June 1867, 24 Oct 1869 and 6 Sep 1872. The diary is a mine of information on his dreams and his phobias and is very frank on his sexual life. In 1873–4, when he was considering remarriage to a young widow in Philadelphia, he used a shorthand code for a few of his entries. There are also several fragments in the Barker Collection that contain bits of self-analysis. After moving to Nebraska, Barker grew much more sensitive to the wrongs against the Indians. There are many entries in his diary on his good relationships with them, although, as was his custom, he freely pointed out their faults as well.

129. Quotations from Barker Diary, 17 Feb 1871 and 18 Mar 1875, Barker Collection.

130. Ibid., 2 Jan 1869.

## EPILOGUE

1. Letter from Solly 'To the Members of the Trade Societies of the United Kingdom', June 1866, in Solly, *Working Men's Social Clubs and Educational Institutes* (London: Working Men's Club and Institute Union, 1867) pp. 197–207; Solly, *These Eighty Years, or, The Story of an Unfinished Life*, 2 vols (London: Sunplain Marshall, 1893) ch. 10.

2. David Donald, 'Toward a Reconsideration of Abolitionists', in *Lincoln Reconsidered* (New York: Alfred A. Knopf, 1956) pp. 19–36; Martin Duberman, 'The Abolitionists and Psychology', *Journal of Negro History*, vol. XLVII (July 1962) pp. 183–91; Betty Fladeland, 'Who Were the Abolitionists?', ibid., vol. XLIX (Apr 1964) pp. 99–115; Larry Gara, 'Who Was an Abolitionist?' in *The Antislavery Vanguard*, ed. Martin Duberman (Princeton, NJ: Princeton Univ. Press, 1965) pp. 32–51.

# Index

# THE MORAL LAW

# THE MORAL LAW

*or*

KANT'S *GROUNDWORK OF THE METAPHYSIC OF MORALS*

A NEW TRANSLATION

WITH

ANALYSIS AND NOTES

*by*

## H. J. PATON

*White's Professor of Moral Philosophy in the University of Oxford
Fellow of the British Academy*

## HUTCHINSON'S UNIVERSITY LIBRARY

47 Princes Gate, London

*New York*      *Melbourne*      *Sydney*      *Cape Town*

Printed in Great Britain by
William Brendon and Son, Ltd.
The Mayflower Press (late of Plymouth)
at Bushey Mill Lane
Watford, Herts.

# CONTENTS

# TRANSLATOR'S PREFACE

IN spite of its horrifying title Kant's *Groundwork of the Metaphysic of Morals* is one of the small books which are truly great: it has exercised on human thought an influence almost ludicrously disproportionate to its size. In moral philosophy it ranks with the *Republic* of Plato and the *Ethics* of Aristotle; and perhaps—partly no doubt through the spread of Christian ideals and through the long experience of the human race during the last two thousand years—it shows in some respects a deeper insight even than these. Its main topic—the supreme principle of morality—is of the utmost importance to all who are not indifferent to the struggle of good against evil. Written, as it was, towards the end of the eighteenth century, it is couched in terms other than those that would be used to-day; but its message was never more needed than it is at present, when a somewhat arid empiricism is the prevailing fashion in philosophy. An exclusively empirical philosophy, as Kant himself argues, can have nothing to say about morality: it can only encourage us to be guided by our emotions, or at the best by an enlightened self-love, at the very time when the abyss between unregulated impulse or undiluted self-interest and moral principles has been so tragically displayed in practice. In the face of all this Kant offers us a defence of reasonableness in action: he reminds us that, however much the applications of morality may vary with varying circumstances, a good man is one who acts on the supposition that there is an unconditioned and objective moral standard holding for all men in virtue of their rationality as human beings. His claim to establish this is worth the serious consideration of all who are not content to regard themselves as victims of instinctive movements over which they have no intelligent control. Even if they do not agree with his doctrine, there is no doubt that they will see more in it the more they study it.

Unfortunately most readers in this country—and I fear even many teachers of philosophy—feel insufficiently at home in German to read this work most easily in the original. Kant has on the whole not been so fortunate in his translators as Hegel, and his English students may easily get the impression that he was a fumbler. He

7

is very far indeed from being a fumbler, though he does expect too much from his readers: for example, he expects them to recognize at once in his long sentences the particular noun to which his excessive number of pronouns refer. I have kept in the main the structure of his sentences, which are, as it were, hewn out of the rock, but I have made no attempt to give a word for word translation. Every translation must to some extent be a veil, but it need not be an unbecoming one. I have striven to make his thought move in an English dress with some ease and even—if it were possible—with some elegance. Contrary to the usual opinion, what has struck me most in the course of my undertaking is how well he can write. And it is my hope that through this English rendering there may loom at least something of his liveliness of mind, his suppressed intellectual excitement, his moral earnestness, his pleasure in words, and even, it may be, something of his peculiar brand of humour, which is so dry that it might have come directly out of Scotland itself.

I have prefaced my translation by an analysis of the argument, and I have also added some notes. All this, I hope, may be of help to the inexperienced reader beginning the study of moral philosophy, and I trust that those who are more advanced will forgive me if at times I appear to underline the obvious. For more serious difficulties connected with the Critical Philosophy as a whole, I must refer readers to my commentary, *The Categorical Imperative*, and also—on the purely theoretical side of Kant's philosophy—to *Kant's Metaphysic of Experience*.

For ease of reference and in order to facilitate grasp of the structure of the argument I have inserted into the text some cross-headings. These, in distinction from Kant's own headings, are contained in square brackets. It should also be noted that Kant's own parentheses are in brackets. Parentheses between dashes are in all cases mine and are intended to make the main line of the argument easier to follow.

In the margin the numbers from i to xiv and from 1 to 128 give the pages of the *second* edition, which is the best published in Kant's lifetime, and I use these everywhere in my references. Unfortunately I did not use them in *The Categorical Imperative*, and, as they are not yet commonly accessible (though they ought to be), I have also given in the margin the pages of the edition issued by the Royal Prussian Academy in Berlin. The numbering of these pages begins with 387 so that there is no danger of confusion.

The only abbreviations I have used are *T.C.I.* and *K.M.E.* for my two books on Kant already mentioned.

I must in conclusion express my thanks to the many friends and pupils whom I have bothered on small points of translation, but especially to Dr. H. W. Cassirer for assuring me that my version is—or at least was—free from howlers; to Mr. W. H. Walsh for reading the proofs; and to Miss M. J. Levett, whose fierce sense of English usage has saved me from some of the Teutonisms into which a translator from the German can so easily fall. Above all I must thank my wife for typing the whole of my manuscript in these difficult days by an almost super-human effort which must surely have been inspired by the motive of duty for duty's sake.

H. J. PATON.

Corpus Christi College,
    Oxford.
*August,* 1947.

# ANALYSIS
## OF THE
# ARGUMENT

# ANALYSIS OF THE ARGUMENT

## PREFACE

Pages i–iii.—*The different branches of philosophy.*

THE three main branches of philosophy are logic, physics, and ethics. Of these *logic* is formal: it abstracts from all differences in the objects (or matter) about which we think and considers only the necessary laws (or forms) of thinking as such. Since it borrows nothing from our sensuous experience of objects, it must be regarded as a wholly non-empirical or *a priori* science. *Physics* deals with the laws of nature, and *ethics* with the laws of free moral action. These two philosophical sciences deal therefore with objects of thought which are sharply distinguished from one another.

Unlike logic, both physics and ethics must have an *empirical* part (one based on sensuous experience) as well as a non-empirical or *a priori* part (one not so based); for physical laws must apply to nature as an object of experience, and ethical laws must apply to human wills as affected by desires and instincts which can be known only by experience.

A philosopher of to-day would have to argue that these sciences have an *a priori* part rather than that they have an empirical part; and indeed many philosophers would deny the first possibility altogether. Nevertheless, if we take physics in a wide sense as the philosophy of nature, it appears to proceed in accordance with certain principles which are more than mere generalizations based on such data as are given to our senses. The task of formulating and, if possible, justifying these principles Kant regards as the *a priori* or pure part of physics (or as *a metaphysic of nature*). Among these principles he includes, for example, the principle that every event must have a cause, and this can never be proved (though it may be confirmed) by experience. He holds that it states a condition without which experience of nature, and so physical science itself, would be impossible.

It should be obvious that from experience of what men in fact do we are unable to prove what they ought to do; for we must admit that they often do what they ought not to do—provided we allow that there is such a thing as a moral 'ought' or a moral duty. Hence if there are moral principles in accordance with which men ought to act, knowledge of these principles must be *a priori* knowledge: it cannot be based on sensuous experience. The *a priori* or pure part of ethics is concerned with the *formulation* and *justification* of moral principles—with such terms as 'ought', 'duty', 'good' and 'evil', 'right' and 'wrong'. This *a priori* part of ethics may be called *a metaphysic of morals* (though at other times 'justification'—as opposed to 'formulation'—is reserved by Kant for a *critique of practical reason*). For detailed knowledge of particular human duties we require experience of human nature (and indeed of many other things). This belongs to the empirical part of ethics and is called by Kant '*practical anthropology*', though his use of the term is not altogether clear.

Kant's doctrine of *a priori* knowledge rests mainly on the assumption that mind—or reason, as he calls it—functions actively in accordance with principles which it can know and understand. He holds that such rational principles can be manifested, not only in thinking as such (which is studied in logic), but also in scientific knowledge and in moral action. We can separate out these rational principles, and we can understand how they are necessary for any rational being so far as he seeks to think rationally about the world and to act rationally in the world. If we believe that reason has no activity and no principles of its own and that mind is merely a bundle of sensations and desires, there can be for us no *a priori* knowledge; but we are hardly entitled to assert this without considering the arguments on the other side.

Pages iii–ix.—*The need for pure ethics.*

If the distinction between *a priori* and empirical ethics is sound, it is desirable to treat each part separately. The result of mixing them up is bound to be intellectual confusion, but it is also likely to lead to moral degeneration. If actions are to be morally good they must be done for the sake of duty, and only the *a priori* or pure part of ethics can show us what the nature of duty is. By mixing up the different parts of ethics we may easily begin to confuse duty with self-interest, and this is bound to have disastrous effects in practice.

### Pages ix–xi.—*The philosophy of willing as such.*

The *a priori* part of ethics is not to be confused with a philosophy of willing *as such*, since it deals, not with all willing, but with a particular *kind* of willing—namely, with willing that is morally good.

### Pages xi–xiii.—*The aim of the* Groundwork.

The aim of the *Groundwork* is not to give us a complete exposition of the *a priori* part of ethics—that is, a complete metaphysic of morals. Its aim is rather to lay the *foundations* for such a metaphysic of morals, and so to separate out the really difficult part. Even as regards these foundations the *Groundwork* does not pretend to be complete: we require a full 'critique of practical reason' for this purpose. The need for such a critique of reason is, however, less pressing in practical matters than in theoretical, since ordinary human reason is a far safer guide in morals than it is in speculation; and Kant is anxious to avoid the complications of a full critique.

The essential point in all this is that the *Groundwork* has the limited, and yet all-important, aim of establishing the *supreme principle of morality*. It excludes all questions concerned with the *application* of this principle (although it occasionally gives illustrations of the way in which such applications may be made). Hence we should not expect from this book any detailed account of the application of moral principles, nor should we blame Kant for failing to supply it—still less should we invent theories of what he must have thought on this subject. If we want to know how he applied his supreme principle, we must read his neglected *Metaphysic of Morals*. In the *Groundwork* itself the only question to be considered is whether Kant has succeeded or failed in establishing the supreme principle of morality.

### Page xiv.—*The method of the* Groundwork.

Kant's method is to start with the provisional assumption that our ordinary moral judgements may legitimately claim to be true. He then asks what are the *conditions* which must hold if these claims are to be justified. This is what he calls an *analytic* (or regressive) argument, and by it he hopes to discover a series of conditions till he comes to the ultimate condition of all moral judgements— the supreme principle of morality. He attempts to do this in Chapters I and II. In Chapter III his method is different. There he starts with the insight of reason into its own activity and attempts to derive from this the supreme principle of morality. This is what he calls a *synthetic* (or progressive) argument. If it were successful, we could reverse the direction of the argument in the first two chapters: beginning with the insight of reason into the principle of its own activity we could pass to the supreme principle of morality and from this to the ordinary moral judgements with which we started. In this way we should be able to justify our provisional assumption that ordinary moral judgements may legitimately claim to be true.

Chapter I attempts to lead us by an analytic argument from ordinary moral judgement to a philosophical statement of the first principle of morality. Chapter II, after dismissing the confusions of a 'popular' philosophy which works with examples and mixes the empirical with the *a priori*, proceeds (still by an analytic argument) to *formulate* the first principle of morality in different ways: it belongs to a metaphysic of morals. Chapter III attempts (in a synthetic argument) to *justify* the first principle of morality by deriving it from its source in pure practical reason: it belongs to a critique of pure practical reason.

## CHAPTER I

# THE APPROACH TO MORAL PHILOSOPHY

### Pages 1-3.—*The good will.*

THE only thing that is good without qualification or restriction is a good will. That is to say, a good will alone is good *in all circumstances* and in that sense is an absolute or unconditioned good. We may also describe it as the only thing that is good *in itself*, good independently of its relation to other things.

This does not mean that a good will is the only good. On the contrary, there are plenty of things which are good in many respects. These, however, are not good in all circumstances, and they may all be thoroughly bad when they are used by a bad will. They are therefore only conditioned goods—that is, good under certain conditions, not good absolutely or in themselves.

### Pages 3-4.—*The good will and its results.*

The goodness of a good will is not derived from the goodness of the results which it produces. The conditioned goodness of its products cannot be the source of the unconditioned goodness which belongs to a good will alone. Besides, a good will continues to have its own unique goodness even where, by some misfortune, it is unable to produce the results at which it aims.

There is nothing in this to suggest that for Kant a good will does not aim at producing results. He holds, on the contrary, that a good will, and indeed any kind of will, must aim at producing results.

### Pages 4-8.—*The function of reason.*

Ordinary moral consciousness supports the view that a good will alone is an unconditioned good. Indeed this is the presupposition (or condition) of all our ordinary moral judgements.

17

Nevertheless the claim may seem to be fantastic, and we must seek further corroboration by considering the function of reason in action.

In order to do this we have to presuppose that in organic life every organ has a purpose or function to which it is well adapted. This applies also to mental life; and in human beings reason is, as it were, the organ which controls action, just as instinct is the organ which controls action in animals. If the function of reason in action were merely to attain happiness, this is a purpose for which instinct would have been a very much better guide. Hence if we assume that reason, like other organs, must be well adapted to its purpose, its purpose cannot be merely to produce a will which is good as a means to happiness, but rather to produce a will which is good in itself.

Such a purposive (or teleological) view of nature is not readily accepted to-day. We need only note that Kant does hold this belief (though by no means in a simple form) and that it is very much more fundamental to his ethics than is commonly supposed. In particular we should note that reason in action has for him two main functions, the first of which has to be subordinated to the second. The first function is to secure the individual's own happiness (a conditioned good), while the second is to manifest a will good in itself (an unconditioned good).

### Page 8.—*The good will and duty.*

*Under human conditions*, where we have to struggle against unruly impulses and desires, a good will is manifested in acting *for the sake of duty*. Hence if we are to understand human goodness, we must examine the concept of duty. Human goodness is most conspicuous in struggling against the obstacles placed in its way by unruly impulses, but it must not be thought that goodness as such consists in overcoming obstacles. On the contrary, a perfectly good will would have no obstacles to overcome, and the concept of duty (which involves the overcoming of obstacles) would not apply to such a perfect will.

### Pages 8–13.—*The motive of duty.*

*A human action is morally good, not because it is done from immediate inclination—still less because it is done from self-interest—but because it is done for the sake of duty.* This is Kant's first proposition about duty, though he does not state it in this general form.

An action—even if it accords with duty and is in that sense right—is not commonly regarded as morally good if it is done solely out of self-interest. We may, however, be inclined to attribute moral goodness to right actions done solely from some immediate inclination—for example, from a direct impulse of sympathy or generosity. In order to test this we must *isolate* our motives: we must consider first an action done solely out of inclination and *not* out of duty, and then an action done solely out of duty and *not* out of inclination. If we do this, then, we shall find—to take the case most favourable to immediate inclination—that an action done solely out of natural sympathy may be right and praise-worthy, but that nevertheless it has no distinctively moral worth. The same kind of action done solely out of duty does have dis-tinctively moral worth. The goodness shown in helping others is all the more conspicuous if a man does this for the sake of duty at a time when he is fully occupied with his own troubles and when he is not impelled to do so by his natural inclinations.

Kant's doctrine would be absurd if it meant that the presence of a natural inclination to good actions (or even of a feeling of satisfaction in doing them) detracted from their moral worth. The ambiguity of his language lends some colour to this interpreta-tion, which is almost universally accepted. Thus he says that a man shows moral worth if he does good, not from inclination, but from duty. But we must remember that he is here contrasting two motives taken in *isolation* in order to find out which of them is the source of moral worth. He would have avoided the ambiguity if he had said that a man shows moral worth, not in doing good from inclination, but in doing it for the sake of duty. It is the motive of duty, not the motive of inclination, that gives moral worth to an action.

Whether these two kinds of motive can be present in the same moral action and whether one can support the other is a question which is not even raised in this passage nor is it discussed at all in the *Groundwork*. Kant's assumption on this subject is that if an action is to be morally good, the motive of duty, while it may be present *at the same time* as other motives, must by itself be sufficient to determine the action. Furthermore, he never wavers in the belief that generous inclinations are a help in doing good actions, that for this reason it is a duty to cultivate them, and that without them a great moral adornment would be absent from the world.

It should also be observed that, so far from decrying happiness, Kant holds that we have at least an indirect duty to seek our own happiness.

### Pages 13-14.—*The formal principle of duty.*

Kant's second proposition is this: *An action done from duty has its moral worth, not from the results it attains or seeks to attain, but from a formal principle or maxim—the principle of doing one's duty whatever that duty may be.*

This re-states the first proposition in a more technical way. We have already seen that a good will cannot derive its uncon-ditioned goodness from the conditioned goodness of the *results* at which it aims, and this is true also of the morally good actions in which a good will acting for the sake of duty is manifested. What we have to do now is to state our doctrine in terms of what Kant calls 'maxims'.

A maxim is a principle upon which we act. It is a purely personal principle—not a copy-book maxim—and it may be good or it may be bad. Kant calls it a 'subjective' principle, meaning by this a principle on which a rational agent (or subject of action) *does* act—a principle manifested in actions which are in fact performed. An 'objective' principle, on the other hand, is one on which every rational agent *would necessarily* act if reason had full control over his actions, and therefore one on which he *ought* to act if he is so irrational as to be tempted to act otherwise. Only when we act on objective principles do they become *also* subjective, but they continue to be objective whether we act on them or not.

We need not formulate in words the maxim of our action, but if we know what we are doing and will our action as an action of a particular *kind*, then our action has a maxim or subjective principle. A maxim is thus always some sort of *general* principle under which we will a particular action. Thus if I decide to commit suicide in order to avoid unhappiness, I may be said to act on the principle or maxim 'I will kill myself *whenever* life offers more pain than pleasure'.

All such maxims are *material* maxims: they generalize a particular action with its particular motive and its intended result. Since the moral goodness of an action cannot be derived from its intended results, it manifestly cannot be derived from a material maxim of this kind.

The maxim which gives moral worth to actions is the maxim or principle of doing one's duty whatever one's duty may be. Such a maxim is empty of any particular matter: it is not a maxim of satisfying particular desires or attaining particular results. In Kant's language it is a *formal* maxim. To act for the sake of duty is to act on a formal maxim 'irrespective of all objects of the faculty of desire'. A good man adopts or rejects the material maxim of any proposed action according as it harmonizes or conflicts with the controlling and formal maxim of doing his duty for its own sake. Only such 'dutiful' actions can be morally good.

### Pages 14–17.—*Reverence for the law.*

A third proposition is alleged to follow from the first two. It is this: *Duty is the necessity to act out of reverence for the law.*

This proposition cannot be derived from the first two unless we can read into them a good deal more than has been explicitly stated: both 'reverence' and 'the law' appear to be terms which we have not met in the premises. Furthermore the proposition itself is not altogether clear. Perhaps it would be better to say that to act on the maxim of doing one's duty for its own sake is to act out of reverence for the law.

It is not altogether easy to follow Kant's argument. He appears to hold that if the maxim of a morally good action is a *formal* maxim (not a material maxim of satisfying one's desires), it must be a maxim of acting reasonably—that is, of acting on a law valid for all rational beings as such independently of their particular desires. Because of our human frailty such a law must appear to us as a law of duty, a law which commands or compels obedience. Such a law, considered as *imposed* upon us, must excite a feeling analogous to fear. Considered, on the other hand, as self-imposed (since it is imposed by our own rational nature), it must excite a feeling analogous to inclination or attraction. This complex feeling is *reverence* (or respect)—a unique feeling which is due,

CHAPTER II

## OUTLINE OF A METAPHYSIC OF MORALS

Pages 25–30.—*The use of examples.*

ALTHOUGH we have extracted the supreme principle of morality from ordinary moral judgements, this does not mean that we have arrived at it by generalizing from examples of morally good actions given to us in experience. Such an empirical method would be characteristic of a 'popular' philosophy, which depends on examples and illustrations. In actual fact we can never be sure that there are any examples of 'dutiful' actions (actions whose determining motive is that of duty). What we are discussing is not what men in fact do, but what they ought to do.

Even if we had experience of dutiful actions, this would not be enough for our purposes. What we have to show is that there is a moral law valid for all rational beings as such and for all men in virtue of their rationality—a law which rational beings as such ought to follow if they are tempted to do otherwise. This could never be established by any experience of actual human behaviour.

Furthermore, examples of morally good action can never be a substitute for moral principles nor can they supply a ground on which moral principles can be based. It is only if we already possess moral principles that we can judge an action to be an example of moral goodness.

Morality is not a matter of blind imitation, and the most that examples can do is to encourage us to do our duty: they can show that dutiful action is possible, and they can bring it more vividly before our minds.

Pages 30–34.—*Popular philosophy.*

Popular philosophy, instead of separating sharply the *a priori* and empirical parts of ethics, offers us a disgusting hotch-potch in which *a priori* and empirical elements are hopelessly intermingled. Moral principles are confused with principles of self-interest, and this has the effect of weakening the claims of morality in a misguided effort to strengthen them.

### Pages 34–36.—*Review of conclusions.*

Moral principles must be grasped entirely *a priori*. To mix them up with empirical considerations of self-interest and the like is not merely a confusion of thought but an obstacle in the way of moral progress. Hence before we attempt to apply moral principles we must endeavour to formulate them precisely in a pure metaphysic of morals from which empirical considerations are excluded.

### Pages 36–39.—*Imperatives in general.*

We must now try to explain what is meant by words like 'good' and 'ought', and in particular what is meant by an 'imperative'. There are different kinds of imperative, but we have to deal first with imperatives *in general* (or what is common to all kinds of imperative): we are not concerned merely with the moral imperative (though we may have this particularly in mind). This is a source of difficulty on a first reading, especially as the word 'good' has different senses when used in connection with different kinds of imperative.

We begin with the conception of a rational agent. A rational agent is one who has the power to act in accordance with his idea of laws—that is, to act in accordance with *principles*. This is what we mean when we say that he has a *will*. 'Practical reason' is another term for such a will.

We have already seen that the actions of rational agents have a *subjective* principle or maxim, and that in beings who are only imperfectly rational such subjective principles must be distinguished from *objective* principles—that is, from principles on which a rational agent would necessarily act if reason had full control over passion. So far as an agent acts on objective principles, his will and his actions may be described as *in some sense* 'good'.

Imperfectly rational beings like men do not always act on objective principles: they may do so or they may not. This is expressed more technically by saying that for men actions which are objectively necessary are subjectively contingent.

To imperfectly rational beings objective principles seem almost to *constrain* or (in Kant's technical language) to *necessitate* the will —that is, they seem to be imposed upon the will from without instead of being its *necessary* manifestation (as they would be in the case of a wholly rational agent). There is in this respect a sharp difference between being *necessary*, and being *necessitating*, for a rational will.

Where an objective principle is conceived as *necessitating* (and not merely as necessary), it may be described as a *command*. The formula of such a command may be called an *imperative* (though Kant does not in practice distinguish sharply between a command and an imperative).

All imperatives (not merely moral ones) are expressed by the words '*I ought*'. '*I ought*' may be said to express from the side of the subject the relation of *necessitation* which holds between a principle recognized as objective and an imperfectly rational will. When I say that '*I ought*' to do something, I mean that I recognize an action of this kind to be imposed or necessitated by an objective principle valid for any rational agent as such.

Since imperatives are objective principles considered as necessitating, and since action in accordance with objective principles is good action (in some sense), all imperatives command us to do *good* actions (not merely—as some philosophers hold—actions that are obligatory or right).

A perfectly rational and wholly good agent would *necessarily* act on the same objective principles which for us are imperatives, and so would manifest a kind of goodness just as we do when we obey these imperatives. But for him such objective principles would not be imperatives: they would be necessary but not necessitating, and the will which followed them could be described as a 'holy' will. Where we say 'I ought', an agent of this kind would say 'I will'. He would have no duties nor would he feel reverence for the moral law (but something more akin to love).

In an important footnote Kant explains, if somewhat obscurely, what he means by such terms as 'inclination' and 'interest', and he distinguishes between 'pathological' (or sensuous) interest and 'practical' (or moral) interest. For this *see* the analysis of pages 121–123.

## Pages 39–44.—*Classification of imperatives*

There are three different kinds of imperatives. Since imperatives are objective principles considered as necessitating, there must equally be three corresponding kinds of objective principle and three corresponding kinds (or senses) of 'good'.

Some objective principles are *conditioned* by a will for some end—that is to say, they would necessarily be followed by a fully rational agent *if* he willed the end. These principles give rise to *hypothetical* imperatives, which have the general form '*If* I will this end, I ought to do such and such'. They bid us do actions which are *good as means* to an end that we already will (or might will).

When the end is merely one that we might will, the imperatives are *problematic* or *technical*. They may be called imperatives of skill, and the actions they enjoin are good in the sense of being '*skilful*' or '*useful*'.

Where the end is one that every rational agent wills by his very nature, the imperatives are *assertoric* or *pragmatic*. The end which every rational agent wills by his very nature is his own happiness, and the actions enjoined by a pragmatic imperative are good in the sense of being '*prudent*'.

Some objective principles are *unconditioned*: they would necessarily be followed by a fully rational agent but are not based on the previous willing of some further end. These principles give rise to *categorical* imperatives, which have the general form 'I ought to do such and such' (without any '*if*' as a prior condition). They may also be called 'apodeictic'—that is, necessary in the sense of being unconditioned and absolute. These are the unconditioned imperatives of morality, and the actions they enjoin are *morally good*—good in themselves and not merely good as a means to some further end.

The different kinds of imperative exercise a different kind of *necessitation*. This difference may be marked by describing them as *rules* of skill, *counsels* of prudence, *commands* (or *laws*) of morality. Only commands or laws are absolutely binding.

## Pages 44-50.—*How are imperatives possible?*

We have now to consider how these imperatives are 'possible'—
that is, how they can be *justified*. To justify them is to show that
the principles on which they bid us act are *objective* in the sense
of being valid for any rational being as such. Kant always assumes
that a principle on which a fully rational agent as such would
*necessarily* act is also one on which an imperfectly rational agent
*ought* to act if he is tempted to do otherwise.

In order to understand the argument we must grasp the
distinction between analytic and synthetic propositions.

In an *analytic* proposition the predicate is contained in the subject-
concept and can be derived by analysis of the subject-concept.
Thus 'Every *effect* must have a cause' is an analytic proposition;
for it is impossible to conceive an effect without conceiving it as
having a cause. Hence in order to justify an analytic proposition
we do not need to go beyond the concept of the subject. In a
*synthetic* proposition the predicate is *not* contained in the subject-
concept and cannot be derived by analysis of the subject-concept.
Thus 'Every *event* must have a cause' is a synthetic proposition;
for it is possible to conceive an event without conceiving that it
has a cause. In order to justify any synthetic proposition we have
to go beyond the concept of the subject and discover some 'third
term' which will entitle us to attribute the predicate to the subject.

*Any fully rational agent who wills an end necessarily wills the
means to the end.* This is an analytic proposition; for to will (and
not merely to wish) an end is to will the action which is a means
to this end. Hence any rational agent who wills an end *ought* to
will the means to this end if he is irrational enough to be tempted
to do otherwise. There is thus no difficulty in justifying *imperatives
of skill*.

It should be noted that in finding out what are in fact the
means to our ends we make use of synthetic propositions: we
have to discover what causes will produce certain desired effects,
and it is impossible to discover the cause of any effect by a mere
analysis of the concept of the effect by itself. These synthetic
propositions, however, are theoretical only: when we know what
cause will produce the desired effect, the principle determining our
will as rational beings is the analytic proposition that any fully

rational agent who wills an end necessarily wills the known means to that end.

When we come to consider *imperatives of prudence*, we meet a special difficulty. Although happiness is an end which we all in fact seek, our concept of it is unfortunately vague and indeterminate: we do not know clearly what our end is. At times Kant himself speaks as if the pursuit of happiness were merely a search for the means to the maximum possible amount of pleasant feeling throughout the whole course of life. At other times he recognizes that it involves the choice and harmonizing of ends as well as of the means to them. Apart from these difficulties, however, imperatives of prudence are justified in the same way as imperatives of skill. They rest on the analytic proposition that any fully rational agent who wills an end must necessarily will the known means to that end.

This kind of justification is not possible in the case of *moral or categorical imperatives*; for when I recognize a moral duty by saying 'I ought to do such and such', this does not rest on the presupposition that some further end is already willed. To justify a categorical imperative we have to show that a fully rational agent would necessarily act in a certain way—not *if* he happens to want something else, but simply and solely as a rational agent. A predicate of this kind, however, is not contained in the concept 'rational agent' and cannot be derived by analysis of this concept. The proposition is not analytic but synthetic, and yet it is an assertion of what a rational agent as such would *necessarily* do. Such an assertion can never be justified by experience of examples nor, as we have seen, can we be sure that we have any such experience. The proposition is not merely synthetic, but also *a priori*, and the difficulty of justifying such a proposition is likely to be very great. This task must be postponed till later.

## Pages 51–52.—*The Formula of Universal Law.*

Our first problem is to *formulate* the categorical imperative—that is, to state what it commands or enjoins. This topic is pursued ostensibly for its own sake, and we are given a succession of formulæ; but in all this the analytic argument to the supreme principle or morality (the principle of autonomy) is still being carried on;

and we shall find later that it is the principle of autonomy which enables us to connect morality with the Idea of freedom as expounded in the final chapter.

A categorical imperative, as we have already seen, merely bids us act in accordance with universal law as such—that is, it bids us act on a principle valid for all rational beings as such, and not merely on one that is valid *if* we happen to want some further end. Hence it bids us accept or reject the *material* maxim of a contemplated action according as it can or cannot be willed also as a universal law. We may express this in the formula '*Act only on that maxim through which you can at the same time will that it should become a universal law*'.

There is thus only one categorical imperative. We may also more loosely describe as categorical imperatives the various particular moral laws in which the one general categorical imperative is applied—as, for example, the law 'Thou shalt not kill'. Such laws are all 'derived' from the one categorical imperative as their principle. In the *Groundwork* Kant appears to think that they can be derived from this formula by itself, but in the *Critique of Practical Reason* he holds that for this purpose we require to make use of the formula which immediately follows.

### Page 52.—*The Formula of the Law of Nature.*

'*Act as if the maxim of your action were to become through your will a* universal law of nature'.

This formula, though subordinate to the previous one, is entirely distinct from it: it refers to a law of nature, not of freedom, and it is the formula which Kant himself uses in his illustrations. He gives no explanation of why he does so beyond saying—on page 81—that there is an *analogy* between the universal law of morality and the universal law of nature. The subject is a highly technical one and is expounded further in the *Critique of Practical Reason*, but for this I must refer to my book, *The Categorical Imperative*, especially pages 157–164.

A law of nature is primarily a law of cause and effect. Nevertheless, when Kant asks us to consider our maxims *as if* they were laws of nature, he treats them as purposive (or teleological) laws. He is already supposing that nature—or at least human nature—

is teleological or is what he later calls a kingdom of nature and not a mere mechanism.

In spite of these difficulties and complications Kant's doctrine is simple. He holds that a man is morally good, not so far as he acts from passion or self-interest, but so far as he acts on an impersonal principle valid for others as well as for himself. This is the *essence* of morality; but if we wish to *test* the maxim of a proposed action we must ask whether, if universally adopted, it would further a systematic harmony of purposes in the individual and in the human race. Only if it would do this can we say that it is fit to be willed as a universal moral law.

The *application* of such a test is manifestly impossible without empirical knowledge of human nature, and Kant takes this for granted in his illustrations.

### Pages 52–57.—*Illustrations.*

Duties may be divided into duties towards self and duties towards others, and again into perfect and imperfect duties. This gives us four main *types* of duty, and Kant gives us one illustration of each type in order to show that his formula can be applied to all four.

A perfect duty is one which admits of no exception in the interests of inclination. Under this heading the examples given are the ban on suicide and on making a false promise in order to receive a loan. We are not entitled to commit suicide because we have a strong inclination to do so, nor are we entitled to pay our debt to one man and not to another because we happen to like him better. In the case of imperfect duties the position is different: we are bound only to adopt the *maxim* of developing our talents and of helping others, and we are to some extent entitled to decide arbitrarily *which* talents we will develop and *which* persons we will help. There is here a certain 'latitude' or 'playroom' for mere inclination.

In the case of duties towards self Kant assumes that our various capacities have a natural function or purpose in life. It is a perfect duty *not* to thwart such purposes; and it is also a positive, but imperfect, duty to further such purposes.

In the case of duties towards others we have a perfect duty

*not* to thwart the realization of a possible systematic harmony of purposes among men; and we have a positive, but imperfect, duty to further the realization of such a systematic harmony.

The qualifications to be attached to such principles are necessarily omitted in such a book as the *Groundwork*.

### Pages 57–59.—*The canon of moral judgement.*

The general canon of moral judgement is that we should be able to *will* that the maxim of our action should become a universal law (of *freedom*). When we consider our maxims as possible (teleological) laws of *nature*, we find that some of them cannot even be *conceived* as such laws: for example, a law that self-love (which considered as falling under a law of nature becomes something like a feeling—or instinct—of self-preservation) should both further and destroy life is inconceivable. In such a case the maxim is opposed to perfect or strict duty. Other maxims, though not inconceivable as possible (teleological) laws of nature, yet cannot be consistently *willed* as such laws: there would be inconsistency or inconsequence in willing, for example, that men should possess talents, and yet should never use them. Maxims of this kind are opposed to imperfect duty.

Whatever may be thought of the details of Kant's argument—and the argument against suicide is particularly weak—we have to ask ourselves whether a teleological view of human nature is not necessary to ethics, just as some sort of teleological view of the human body is necessary to medicine. It should also be observed that on Kant's view moral questions are not merely questions of what we can *think* but of what we can *will*, and that bad action involves, not a theoretical contradiction, but an opposition (or antagonism) of inclination to a rational will supposed to be in some sense actually present in ourselves.

### Pages 59–63.—*The need for pure ethics.*

Kant re-emphasizes his previous contentions on this subject.

### Pages 63–67.—*The Formula of the End in Itself.*

*Act in such a way that you always treat humanity, whether in your own person or in the person of any other, never simply as a means, but always at the same time as an end.*

This formula brings in a second aspect of all action; for all rational action, besides having a principle, must also set before itself an end. Ends—like principles—may be merely *subjective*: they may be arbitrarily adopted by an individual. Subjective or relative ends which a particular agent seeks to produce are, as we have seen, the ground only of *hypothetical* imperatives, and their value is relative and conditioned. If there were also *objective* ends given to us by reason, ends which in all circumstances a fully rational agent would necessarily pursue, these would have an absolute and unconditioned value. They would also be ends which an imperfectly rational agent *ought* to pursue if he were irrational enough to be tempted to do otherwise.

Such ends could not be mere products of our actions, for—as we have seen all along—no mere product of our action can have an unconditioned and absolute value. They must be already existent ends; and their mere existence would impose on us the duty of pursuing them (so far as this was in our power). That is to say, they would be the *ground* of a *categorical* imperative in somewhat the same way as merely subjective ends are the ground of hypothetical imperatives. Such ends may be described as ends in themselves—not merely as ends relative to particular rational agents.

Only rational agents or *persons* can be ends in themselves. As they alone can have an unconditioned and absolute value, it is wrong to use them simply as means to an end whose value is only relative. Without such ends in themselves there would be no unconditioned good, no supreme principle of action, and so—for human beings—no categorical imperative. Thus, like our first formula, the Formula of the End in Itself follows from the very essence of the categorical imperative—provided we remember that all action must have an end as well as a principle.

Kant adds that every rational agent necessarily conceives his own existence in this way on grounds valid for every rational agent as such. The justification for this depends, however, on his account of the Idea of freedom, which is reserved till later.

The new formula, like the first one, must give rise to particular categorical imperatives when applied to the special nature of man.

c

## Pages 67–68.—*Illustrations*.

The same set of examples brings out even more clearly the teleological presuppositions necessary for any *test* by which the categorical imperative can be applied. We have a perfect duty *not* to use ourselves or others *merely* as a means to the satisfaction of our inclinations. We have an imperfect, but *positive*, duty to further the ends of nature in ourselves and in others—that is, to seek our own perfection and the happiness of others.

As Kant himself indicates in one passage, we are concerned only with very general *types* of duty. It would be quite unfair to complain that he does not deal with all the qualifications that might be necessary in dealing with special problems.

## Pages 69–71.—*The Formula of Autonomy*.

*So act that your will can regard itself at the same time as making universal law through its maxim.*

This formula may seem at first sight to be a mere repetition of the Formula of Universal Law. It has, however, the advantage of making explicit the doctrine that the categorical imperative bids us, not merely to follow universal law, but to follow a universal law which we ourselves make as rational agents and one which we ourselves particularize through our maxims. This is for Kant the most important formulation of the supreme principle of morality, since it leads straight to the Idea of freedom. We are subject to the moral law only because it is the necessary expression of our own nature as rational agents.

The Formula of Autonomy—though the argument is obscurely stated—is derived from combining the Formula of Universal Law and the Formula of the End in Itself. We have not only seen that we are bound to obey the law in virtue of its universality (its objective validity for all rational agents); we have also seen that rational agents as subjects are the *ground* of this categorical imperative. If this is so, the law which we are bound to obey must be the product of our own will (so far as we are rational agents)—that is to say, it rests on 'the Idea of the will of every rational being as a will which makes universal law'.

Kant puts his point more simply later—page 83—when he says of a rational being 'it is precisely the fitness of his maxims to make universal law that marks him out as an end in himself'. If a rational agent is truly an end in himself, he must be the author of the laws which he is bound to obey, and it is this which gives him his supreme value.

## Pages 71–74.—*The exclusion of interest.*

A categorical imperative excludes interest: it says simply 'I ought to do this', and it does *not* say 'I ought to do this *if* I happen to want that'. This was implicit in our previous formulae from the mere fact that they were formulae of an imperative recognized to be categorical. It is now made explicit in the Formula of Autonomy. A will may be subject to laws because of some interest (as we have seen in hypothetical imperatives). A will which is not subject to law because of any interest can be subject only to laws which it itself makes. Only if we conceive the will as making its own laws can we understand how an imperative can exclude interest and so be categorical. The supreme merit of the Formula of Autonomy is this: by the express statement that a rational will makes the laws which it is bound to obey the essential character of the categorical imperative is for the first time made fully explicit. Hence the Formula of Autonomy follows directly from the character of the categorical imperative itself.

All philosophies which seek to explain moral obligation by any kind of interest make a categorical imperative inconceivable and deny morality altogether. They may all be said to propound a doctrine of *heteronomy*—that is, they portray the will as bound only by a law which has its origin in some object or end *other* than the will itself. Theories of this kind can give rise only to hypothetical, and so non-moral, imperatives.

## Pages 74–77.—*The Formula of the Kingdom of Ends.*

*So act as if you were through your maxims a law-making member of a kingdom of ends.*

This formula springs directly from the Formula of Autonomy. So far as rational agents are all subject to universal laws which they themselves make, they constitute a kingdom—that is, a state or commonwealth. So far as these laws bid them treat each other as ends in themselves, the kingdom so constituted is a kingdom of ends. These ends cover, not only persons as ends in themselves, but also the personal ends which each of these may set before himself in accordance with universal law. The concept of the kingdom of ends is connected with the Idea of an intelligible world in the final chapter.

We must distinguish between the *members* of such a kingdom (all finite rational agents) and its supreme *head* (an infinite rational agent). As law-making members of such a kingdom rational agents have what is called 'dignity'—that is, an intrinsic, unconditioned, incomparable worth or worthiness.

### Pages 77-79.—*The dignity of virtue.*

A thing has a *price* if any substitute or equivalent can be found for it. It has *dignity* or worthiness if it admits of no equivalent.

Morality or virtue—and humanity so far as it is capable of morality—alone has dignity. In this respect it cannot be compared with things that have economic value (a market price) or even with things that have an æsthetic value (a fancy price). The incomparable worth of a good man springs from his being a law-making member in a kingdom of ends.

### Pages 79-81.—*Review of the Formulae.*

In the final review three formulae only are mentioned: (1) the Formula of the Law of Nature, (2) the Formula of the End in Itself, and (3) the Formula of the Kingdom of Ends. The first formula is said to be concerned with the form of a moral maxim—that is, with universal law; the second with its matter—that is, with its ends; while the third combines both form and matter. In addition, however, the Formula of Universal Law is mentioned as the strictest test to apply (presumably because it is concerned primarily with the motive of moral action). The purpose of the others is to bring the Idea of duty closer to intuition (or imagination).

A new version is given for the Formula of the Kingdom of Ends. '*All maxims as proceeding from our own making of laws ought to harmonize with a possible kingdom of ends as a kingdom of nature.*'

The kingdom of nature has not been mentioned before, and it seems to stand to the kingdom of ends in the same sort of relation as the universal law of nature stands to the universal law of freedom. Kant makes it perfectly clear that when he regards nature as offering an analogy for morality, nature is considered to be teleological.

The Formula of Autonomy is here amalgamated with the Formula of the Kingdom of Ends.

### Pages 81–87.—*Review of the whole argument.*

The final review summarizes the whole argument from beginning to end—from the concept of a good will to the concept of the dignity of virtue and the dignity of man as capable of virtue. The transitions from one formula to another are simplified and in some ways improved. The most notable addition is, however, the account given of the kingdom of nature. The kingdom of ends can be realized only if *all* men obey the categorical imperative, but even this would not be enough: unless nature itself also *co-operates* with our moral strivings, this ideal can never be attained. We cannot be confident of co-operation either from other men or from nature, but in spite of this the imperative which bids us act as law-making members of a kingdom of ends remains categorical. We ought to pursue this ideal whether or not we can expect to secure results, and this disinterested pursuit of the moral ideal is at once the source of man's dignity and the standard by which he must be judged.

### Pages 87–88.—*Autonomy of the will.*

We have shown by an analytic argument that the principle of the autonomy of the will (and consequently also a categorical imperative enjoining action in accordance with such autonomy) is a necessary condition of the validity of moral judgements. If, however, we wish to establish the validity of the principle of autonomy, we must pass beyond our judgements about moral actions to a critique of pure practical reason.

### Pages 88–89.—*Heteronomy of the will.*

Any moral philosophy which rejects the principle of autonomy has to fall back on a principle of heteronomy: it must make the

law governing human action depend, not on the will itself, but on
objects other than the will. Such a view can give rise only to
hypothetical and so non-moral imperatives.

### Pages 89–90.—*Classification of heteronomous principles.*

Heteronomous principles are either *empirical* or *rational*. When
they are empirical, their principle is always the pursuit of *happiness*,
although some of them may be based on natural feelings of pleasure
and pain, while others may be based on a supposed moral feeling
or moral sense. When they are rational, their principle is always
the pursuit of *perfection*, either a perfection to be attained by our
own will or one supposed to be already existent in the will of God
which imposes certain tasks upon our will.

### Pages 90–91.—*Empirical principles of heteronomy.*

Since all empirical principles are based on sense and so lack
universality, they are quite unfitted to serve as a basis for moral
law. The principle of seeking one's own happiness is, however,
the most objectionable. We have a right (and even an indirect
duty) to seek our own happiness so far as this is compatible with
moral law; but to be happy is one thing and to be good is another;
and to confuse the two is to abolish the specific distinction between
virtue and vice.

The doctrine of moral sense has at least the merit of finding
a direct satisfaction in virtue and not merely satisfaction in its
alleged pleasant results. Kant always recognizes the reality of moral
feeling, but he insists that it is a consequence of our recognition of
the law: it cannot itself provide any uniform standard for ourselves
and still less can it legislate for others. The doctrine of moral sense
must in the last resort be classed with doctrines which regard
pleasure or happiness as the only good, since it too finds the good
in the satisfaction of a particular kind of feeling.

### Pages 91–93.—*Rational principles of heteronomy.*

The rational principle of perfection as an end to be attained by
us is the best of the proposed heteronomous principles of morality
since it at least appeals to reason for a decision. So far, however,

as it merely bids us aim at the maximum reality appropriate to us, it is utterly vague; and if it includes moral perfection, it is obviously circular. Kant himself holds that the moral law bids us cultivate our natural perfection (the exercise of our talents) and our moral perfection (the doing of duty for duty's sake). His objections are directed against the view that we should obey the moral law for the sake of realizing our own perfection.

The theological principle that to be moral is to obey the perfect will of God must be utterly rejected. If we suppose that God is good, this can only be because we already know what moral goodness is, and our theory is a vicious circle. If, on the other hand, we exclude goodness from our concept of God's will and conceive Him merely as all-powerful, we base morality on fear of an arbitrary, but irresistible, will. A moral system of this kind is in direct opposition to morality. Although morality on Kant's view must lead to religion, it cannot be derived from religion.

## Pages 93-95.—*The failure of heteronomy*.

All these doctrines suppose that moral law has to be derived, not from the will itself, but from some object of the will. In being thus heteronomous they can give us no moral or categorical imperative and must consider morally good action to be good, not in itself, but merely as a means to an anticipated result. They thus destroy all *immediate* interest in moral action, and they place man under a law of nature rather than under a law of freedom.

## Pages 95-96.—*The position of the argument*.

All Kant claims to have done is to have shown by an analytic argument that the principle of autonomy is the necessary condition of all our moral judgements. If there is such a thing as morality, and if our moral judgements are not merely chimerical, then the principle of autonomy must be accepted. Many thinkers might take this as sufficient proof of the principle, but Kant does not regard such an argument as a proof. He has not even asserted the truth of the principle, still less pretended to prove it.

The principle of autonomy and the corresponding categorical imperative are synthetic *a priori* propositions: they assert that a rational agent—if he had full control over passion—would necessarily act only on maxims by which he can regard himself as making universal law, and that he ought so to act if he is irrational enough to be tempted to act otherwise. Such a proposition requires a synthetic use of pure practical reason, and on this we cannot venture without a critique of this power of reason itself.

# ANALYSIS OF THE ARGUMENT

## CHAPTER III

## OUTLINE OF A CRITIQUE OF PRACTICAL REASON

Pages 97–99.—*Freedom and autonomy*.

When we consider *will* (or practical reason), we may define it as a kind of causality (a power of causal action) belonging to living beings so far as they are rational. To describe such a will as *free* would be to say that it can act causally *without* being caused to do so by something other than itself. Non-rational beings can act causally only so far as they are caused to do so by something other than themselves, and this is what is meant by natural *necessity* as opposed to freedom: if one billiard ball causes another to move, it does so only because it has itself been caused to move by something else.

So far our description of freedom is negative. But a lawless free will would be self-contradictory, and we must make our description positive by saying that a free will would act under laws, but that these laws could not be imposed on it by something other than itself; for, if they were, they would merely be laws of natural necessity. If the laws of freedom cannot be other-imposed (if we may use such an expression), they must be self-imposed. That is to say, freedom would be identical with autonomy; and since autonomy is the principle of morality, a free will would be a will under moral laws.

If then we could presuppose freedom, autonomy, and therefore morality, would follow by mere analysis of the concept of freedom. Nevertheless, as we have seen, the principle of autonomy is a synthetic *a priori* proposition and so can be justified only by bringing in a third term to connect the subject and the predicate of the proposition. The positive concept of freedom furnishes, or directs us to, this third term; but we require further preparation if we are to show what this third term is and to deduce freedom from the concept of pure practical reason.

Pages 99–100.—*Freedom as a necessary presupposition.*

If morality is to be derived from freedom, and if—as we have maintained—morality must be valid for all rational beings as such, it looks as if we have got to prove that the will of a rational being as such is necessarily free. This can never be proved by any experience of merely human action, nor indeed can it be proved at all from the point of view of philosophical theory. For purposes of action, however, it would be enough if we could show that a rational being can act only under the *presupposition* of freedom; for if this were so, the moral laws bound up with freedom would be valid for him just as much as if he were *known* to be free.

Reason as such must necessarily function under the presupposition that it is free both negatively and positively: it must presuppose that it is not determined by outside influences and that it is the source of its own principles. If a rational subject supposed his judgements to be determined, not by rational principles, but by external impulsions, he could not regard these judgements as his own. This must be equally true of practical reason: a rational agent must regard himself as capable of acting on his own rational principles and only so can he regard his will as his own. That is to say, from a practical point of view every rational agent must presuppose his will to be free. Freedom is a necessary presupposition of all action as well as of all thinking.

Pages 101–105.—*Moral interest and the vicious circle.*

We have argued that in action rational beings must presuppose their own freedom and that from this presupposition there necessarily follows the principle of autonomy and consequently the corresponding categorical imperative. In this way we have at least formulated the principle of morality more precisely than has been done before. But why should I simply as a rational being subject myself, and so also other rational beings, to this principle? Why should I attach such supreme value to moral action and feel in this a personal worth in comparison with which pleasure is to count as nothing? Why should I take an interest in moral excellence for its own sake? Have we really given a convincing answer to these difficult questions?

It is no doubt true that we do in fact take an interest in moral excellence, but this interest arises only because we assume that the moral law is binding. We do not as yet see how the moral law can be binding. It may seem that we have fallen into a vicious circle: we have argued that we must suppose ourselves to be free because we are under moral laws and have then argued that we must be under moral laws because we have supposed ourselves to be free. To do this is very far from giving us any justification of the moral law.

Pages 105–110.—*The two standpoints.*

In order to escape from such a vicious circle we must ask ourselves whether we have not two different standpoints (or points of view) from which we may regard our actions. Do we have one standpoint when we conceive ourselves as acting freely and another when we contemplate our actions as observed events?

This doctrine of the two standpoints is an essential part of Kant's Critical Philosophy, which has hitherto been kept in the background. In dealing with it he has to face a difficulty: he cannot assume the elaborate arguments of the *Critique of Pure Reason* to be familiar to his readers nor can he attempt to repeat these elaborate arguments in a short treatise on ethics. He consequently falls back on some rather elementary considerations which, taken by themselves, cannot be very convincing.

All the ideas that are given to our senses come to us without any volition of our own. We assume that these ideas come to us from objects, but by means of ideas so given we can know objects only as they affect ourselves: what these objects are in themselves we do not know. This gives rise to a distinction between things as they appear to us and things as they are in themselves—or again between *appearances* and *things in themselves*. Only appearances can be known by us; but behind appearances we must assume things in themselves, although these things can never be known as they are in themselves, but only as they affect us. This gives us a rough distinction—it is only rough—between a *sensible* world (a world given to sense or at least through sense) and an *intelligible* world (one which we can conceive but never know, since all human knowledge requires a combination of sensing and conceiving).

This distinction applies also to man's knowledge of himself.

By inner sense (or introspection) he can know himself only as he appears, but behind this appearance he must assume that there is an Ego as it is in itself. So far as he is known by inner sense, and indeed so far as he is capable of receiving sensations passively, man must regard himself as belonging to the sensible world. So far, however, as he may be capable of pure activity apart from sense, he must regard himself as belonging to the intelligible world. The intelligible world is here described as an 'intellectual' world—a world which is intelligible because it is intelligent—although it is added that of this world we can know nothing further.

Now man actually finds in himself a pure activity apart from sense. He finds in himself a power of reason. Here, it should be noted, Kant appeals first, as he did before, to theoretical reason, although he now takes reason in his own special Critical sense. We have a spontaneous power of 'understanding' which (no doubt along with other factors) produces from itself such concepts (or *categories*) as that of cause and effect and uses these concepts to bring the ideas of sense under rules. Thus in spite of its genuine spontaneity understanding is still bound up with sense, and apart from sense it would think nothing at all. 'Reason', on the other hand, is a power of *Ideas*—that is, it produces concepts (of the unconditioned) which go beyond sense altogether and can have no examples given to sense. Unlike understanding, reason shows a pure spontaneity which is entirely independent of sense.

In virtue of this spontaneity man must conceive himself as belonging, *qua* intelligence, to the intelligible world and as subject to laws which have their ground in reason alone. So far as he is sensuous and is known to himself by means of inner sense he must regard himself as belonging to the sensible world and as subject to the laws of nature. These are the two standpoints from which a finite rational being must view himself.

This doctrine applies equally to pure practical reason. Since from one standpoint man, as a finite rational being, must conceive himself as belonging to the intelligible world, he must conceive his will as free from determination by sensuous causes and as obedient to laws having their ground in reason alone. To say this is to say that he can never conceive the causal action of his own will except under the Idea of freedom. Thus he must, as a rational being, act only on the presupposition of freedom, and from this there follows, as we have seen, the principle of autonomy and the categorical imperative.

The suspicion of a vicious circle is now removed. From the standpoint of a rational agent who conceives himself as free and as a member of the intelligible world, man must recognize the principle of autonomy. When he thinks of himself as a member of both the intelligible and the sensible world, he must recognize the principle of autonomy as a categorical imperative.

In all this Kant does not make it wholly clear whether his inference is from membership of the intelligible world to freedom or *vice versa*. It might well be suggested that we conceive ourselves as free in action and so as members of the intelligible world only because we already recognize the principle of autonomy and the categorical imperative; and indeed this appears to be Kant's own view in the *Critique of Practical Reason*. Nevertheless, his comparison between pure theoretical reason and pure practical reason is of very great interest; and we must remember that just as pure theoretical reason conceives Ideas of the unconditioned, so pure practical reason seeks in action to realize the Idea of an unconditioned law.

Pages 110–112.—*How is a categorical imperative possible?*

As a finite rational agent man must regard himself from two standpoints—first as a member of the intelligible world, and secondly as a member of the sensible world. If I were solely a member of the intelligible world, all my actions would necessarily accord with the principle of autonomy; if I were solely a part of the sensible world, they would necessarily be entirely subject to the law of nature. At this point unfortunately we come to an argument which may be new but is certainly confused in expression and hard to interpret. *The intelligible world contains the ground of the sensible world and also of its laws.* From this premise (which itself demands considerable expansion) Kant appears to infer that the law governing my will as a member of the intelligible world *ought* to govern my will in spite of the fact that I am also (from another point of view) a member of the sensible world.

This looks like a metaphysical argument from the superior reality of the intelligible world and so of the rational will, but such an interpretation seems to be immediately repudiated by

Kant. The categorical 'I ought', we are told, is a synthetic *a priori* proposition; and the third term which connects this 'ought' with the will of an imperfectly rational agent like myself is the *Idea* of the same will, viewed, however, as a pure will belonging to the intelligible world. This *Idea* is apparently the third term to which freedom was said to direct us at the end of the first section of the present chapter: it may indeed be described as a more precise Idea of freedom—that is, of a free will. Its function is said to be roughly similar to that played by the categories in the synthetic *a priori* propositions which are necessary for our experience of nature.

This doctrine is confirmed by an appeal to our ordinary moral consciousness as present even in a bad man. The moral 'I ought' is really an 'I will' for man regarded as a member of the intelligible world. It is conceived as an 'I ought' only because he considers himself to be also a member of the sensible world—and so subject to the hindrances of sensuous desires.

Pages 113–115.—*The antinomy of freedom and necessity.*

Kant's argument obviously raises the problem of freedom and necessity. This problem constitutes what Kant calls an 'antinomy'— that is to say, we are faced with mutually conflicting propositions each of which appears to be the necessary conclusion of an irrefutable argument.

The concept of freedom is an Idea of reason without which there could be no moral judgements, just as the concept of natural necessity (or of cause and effect) is a category of the understanding without which there could be no knowledge of nature. Yet the two concepts are apparently incompatible with each other. According to the first concept our actions must be free; and according to the second concept our actions (as events in the known world of nature) must be governed by the laws of cause and effect. Reason has to show that there is no genuine contradiction between the two concepts or else to abandon freedom in favour of natural necessity, which has at least the advantage of being confirmed in experience.

Pages 115-118.—*The two standpoints.*

It would be impossible to resolve the contradiction if we conceived of ourselves as free and as determined in the same sense and
in the same relationship. We have to show that the contradiction
arises from conceiving ourselves in two different senses and relationships and that from this double standpoint these two characteristics
not only can, but must, be combined in the same subject. This task
is incumbent on speculative philosophy if practical (or moral)
philosophy is to be freed from damaging external attacks.

The two standpoints in question are those we have already
encountered. Man must—from different points of view—consider
himself both as a member of the intelligible world and as a part
of the sensible world. Once this is grasped the contradiction dis-
appears. Man can, and indeed must, consider himself to be free as
a member of the intelligible world and determined as a part of
the sensible world; nor is there any contradiction in supposing
that as an *appearance* in the sensible world he is subject to laws
which do not apply to him as a *thing in itself*. Thus man does not
consider himself responsible for his desires and inclinations, but
he does consider himself responsible for indulging them to the
detriment of the moral law.

In this passage Kant speaks as if we *know* the intelligible world
to be governed by reason. This unguarded statement he immediately
proceeds to qualify.

Pages 118-120.—*There is no knowledge of the intelligible world.*

In thus *conceiving* the intelligible world and so *thinking itself
into* the intelligible world practical reason does not overstep its
limits: it would do this only if it claimed to *know* the intelligible
world and so to *intuit itself into* the intelligible world (since all
human knowledge requires sensuous intuition as well as concepts).
Our thought of the intelligible world is negative—that is to say,
it is only the thought of a world which is *not* known through sense.
It enables us, however, not only to conceive the will as negatively
free (free from determination by sensuous causes), but also to
conceive it as positively free (free to act on its own principle of
autonomy). Without this concept of the intelligible world we
should have to regard our will as completely determined by

sensuous causes, and consequently this concept (or point of view) is necessary if we are to regard our will as rational and so far as free. Admittedly when we think ourselves into the intelligible world our thought carries with it the Idea of an order and a law different from that of the world of sense: it becomes necessary for us to conceive the intelligible world as the totality of rational beings considered as ends in themselves. Nevertheless this is not a claim to knowledge of the intelligible world: it is merely a claim to conceive it as compatible with the formal condition of morality—the principle of autonomy.

### Pages 120–121.—*There is no explanation of freedom.*

Reason would overstep all its limits if it pretended to explain how freedom is possible or, in other words, to explain how pure reason can be practical.

The only things we can explain are objects of experience, and to explain them is to bring them under the laws of nature (the laws of cause and effect). Freedom, however, is merely an Idea: it does not supply us with examples which can be known by experience and can be brought under the law of cause and effect. We obviously cannot explain a free action by pointing out its cause, and this means that we cannot explain it at all. All we can do is to *defend* freedom against the attacks of those who claim to know that freedom is impossible. Those who do this very properly apply the laws of nature to man considered as an appearance; but they continue to regard him as an appearance when they are asked to conceive him, *qua* intelligence, as also a thing in himself. To insist on considering man only from one point of view is admittedly to exclude the possibility of regarding him as both free and determined; but the seeming contradiction would fall away if they were willing to reflect that things in themselves must lie behind appearances as their ground and that the laws governing things in themselves need not be the same as the laws governing their appearances.

### Pages 121–123.—*There is no explanation of moral interest.*

To say that we cannot explain how freedom is possible is also to say that we cannot explain how it is possible to take an interest in the moral law.

An interest arises only through a combination of feeling and reason. A sensuous impulse becomes an interest only when it is conceived by reason, and consequently interests are found only in finite rational agents who are also sensuous. Interests may be regarded as the motives of human action, but we must remember that there are two kinds of interest. When the interest is based on the feeling and desire aroused by some object of experience, we may be said to have a mediate (or pathological) interest in the action appropriate to attain the object. When the interest is aroused by the Idea of the moral law, we may be said to take an immediate (or practical) interest in the action willed in accordance with this Idea.

The basis of the interest we take in moral action is what is called 'moral feeling'. This feeling is the result of recognizing the binding character of the moral law and not—as is often held—the gauge of our moral judgements.

This means that pure reason by its Idea of the moral law must be the cause of a moral feeling which can be regarded as the sensuous motive of moral action. We have here a special kind of causality—the causality of a mere Idea—and it is always impossible to know a priori what cause will produce what effect. In order to determine the cause of any effect we must have recourse to experience; but experience can discover the relation of cause and effect only between two objects of experience; and in this case the cause is not an object of experience, but is, on the contrary, a mere Idea which can have no object in experience. Hence it is impossible to explain moral interest—that is, to explain why we should take an interest in the universality of our maxim as a law. This doctrine, it may be added, does not appear to be self-consistent, and a different view is taken in the Critique of Practical Reason.

The really important point is that the moral law is not valid merely because it interests us. On the contrary, it interests us because we recognize it to be valid.

Kant concludes by saying that the moral law is valid because it springs from our own will as intelligence and so from our proper self; 'but what belongs to mere appearance is necessarily subordinated by reason to the character of the thing in itself'.

This looks like a metaphysical argument for morality, one based on the superior reality of the intelligible world and so of

D

the rational will. This type of argument seemed to be suggested also (although immediately repudiated) in the section 'How is a categorical imperative possible?' In the main, however, Kant's metaphysics rests on his ethics rather than *vice versa*.

## Pages 124–126.—*General review of the argument.*

We must now turn back to our main question 'How is a categorical imperative possible?' We have answered this question so far as we have shown that it is possible only on the presupposition of freedom and that this presupposition is one which is necessary for rational agents as such. From this presupposition there follows the principle of autonomy and so of the categorical imperative; and this is sufficient for purposes of action—sufficient to convince us of the validity of the categorical imperative as a principle of action. We have also shown that it is not only possible to presuppose freedom without contradicting the necessity which must prevail in the world of nature, but that it is also objectively necessary for a rational agent conscious of possessing reason and a will to make this presupposition the condition of all his actions. We cannot, however, explain how freedom is possible, how pure reason by itself can be practical, or how we can take a moral interest in the mere validity of our maxims as universal laws.

We can explain things only by showing them to be the effects of some cause, and this kind of explanation is here excluded. Kant is careful to insist that it is impossible to use the intelligible world as the basis for the required explanation. He is so often charged with doing precisely this that his statement here is worthy of very close attention. I have a necessary Idea of the intelligible world, but it is only an Idea: I can have no knowledge of this world since I have, and can have, no *acquaintance* with such a world (by means of intuition). My Idea of it signifies only a world *not* accessible to our senses—a 'something more' beyond the world of sense: if we could not conceive this 'something more', we should have to say that all action is determined by sensuous motives. Even of the *pure reason* which conceives the Idea or Ideal of the intelligible world (and which also conceives itself as a member of such a world) we have still only an *Idea*: we have only a concept of its form (the principle of autonomy) and a corresponding concept of it as causing actions solely in virtue of its form. Here all sensuous motives are removed, and a mere Idea would itself have to be the motive of moral action. To make this intelligible *a priori* is altogether beyond our powers.

### Pages 126–127.—*The extreme limit of moral enquiry.*

With this Idea of an intelligible world as a something more and other than the sensible world we come to the extreme limit of all moral enquiry. To fix this limit is, however, of the utmost practical importance. Unless we see that the world of sense is not the whole of reality, reason will never be kept from trying to discover empirical interests as a basis for morality—a proceeding fatal to morality itself. And unless we see that we can have no knowledge of the 'something more' beyond the world of sense, reason will never be kept from fluttering about impotently in a space which for it is empty—the space of transcendent concepts known to it as 'the intelligible world'—and so from getting lost among mere phantoms of the brain. Empirical and mystical theories of morality can alike be got rid of only when we have determined the limit of moral enquiry.

Yet although all *knowledge* ends when we come to the limit of the sensible world, the Idea of the intelligible world as a whole of all intelligences may serve the purpose of a rational *belief*; and it may arouse a lively interest in the moral law by means of the splendid ideal of a universal kingdom of ends.

### Pages 127–128.—*Concluding note.*

In his final note Kant gives some indication of the character of 'reason' in his own technical sense. Reason cannot be satisfied with the merely contingent and always seeks for knowledge of the necessary. But it can grasp the necessary only by finding its condition. Unless the condition is itself necessary reason must still be unsatisfied, so it must seek the condition of the condition and so on *ad infinitum*. Thus it is bound to conceive the Idea of the *totality* of conditions—a totality which, if it is a totality, can have no further conditions and so must be *unconditionally necessary* if there is to be anything necessary at all. Such an Idea of the unconditionally necessary cannot, however, give us knowledge since it has no corresponding sensible object.

We have seen that pure practical reason must similarly conceive a law of action which is unconditionally necessary and is therefore a categorical imperative (for imperfectly rational agents). If we can comprehend a necessity only by discovering its condition, an unconditioned necessity must be incomprehensible. Hence Kant concludes—with an unnecessary appearance of paradox—that the unconditioned necessity of the categorical imperative must be incomprehensible, but that we can comprehend its incomprehensibility.

The practical point of all this is that it is absurd to ask why we should do our duty (or obey the categorical imperative) and to expect as an answer that we should do so because of *something else*—some interest or satisfaction of our own in this world or the next. If such an answer could be given, it would mean that no imperatives were categorical and that duty is a mere illusion.

# GROUNDWORK

## OF THE

# METAPHYSIC OF MORALS

### BY

# IMMANUEL KANT

## [*The different branches of philosophy*.]

ANCIENT Greek philosophy was divided into three sciences: **physics, ethics,** and **logic.** This division fits the nature of the subject perfectly, and there is no need to improve on it—except perhaps by adding the principle on which it is based. By so doing we may be able on the one hand to guarantee its completeness and on the other to determine correctly its necessary subdivisions.

All rational knowledge is either *material* and concerned with some object, or *formal* and concerned solely with the form of understanding and reason themselves—with the universal rules of thinking as such without regard to differences in its objects. Formal philosophy is called **logic**; while material philosophy, which has ii to do with determinate objects and with the laws to which they are subject, is in turn divided into two, since the laws in question are laws either of **nature** or of **freedom.** The science of the first is called **physics,** that of the second **ethics.** The former is also called natural philosophy, the latter moral philosophy.

Logic can have no empirical part[1]—that is, no part in which the universal and necessary laws of thinking are based on grounds taken from experience. Otherwise it would not be logic—that is, it would not be a canon for understanding and reason, valid for all thinking and capable of demonstration. As against this, both natural and moral philosophy can each have an empirical part, since the former has to formulate its laws for nature as an object of experience, and the latter for the will of man so far as affected by nature—the first set of laws being those in accordance with which everything happens, the second being those in accordance 388] iii with which everything ought to happen, although they also take into account the conditions under which what ought to happen very often does not happen.

All philosophy so far as it rests on the basis of experience can be called *empirical* philosophy. If it sets forth its doctrines as depending entirely on *a priori* principles, it can be called *pure* philosophy. The latter when wholly formal is called *logic*; but if it is confined to determinate objects of the understanding, it is then called *metaphysics*.

In this way there arises the Idea of a two-fold metaphysic—
*a metaphysic of nature* and *a metaphysic of morals*. Thus physics will
have its empirical part, but it will also have a rational one; and
likewise ethics—although here the empirical part might be called
specifically *practical anthropology*, while the rational part might
properly be called *morals*.

[*The need for pure ethics.*]

All industries, arts, and crafts have gained by the division of
iv labour—that is to say, one man no longer does everything, but
each confines himself to a particular task, differing markedly from
others in its technique, so that he may be able to perform it with
the highest perfection and with greater ease. Where tasks are not
so distinguished and divided, where every man is a jack of all
trades, there industry is still sunk in utter barbarism. In itself it
might well be a subject not unworthy of examination, if we asked
whether pure philosophy in all its parts does not demand its own
special craftsman, and whether it would not be better for the whole
of this learned industry if those accustomed to purvey, in accordance
with the public taste, a mixture of the empirical and the rational
in various proportions unknown to themselves—the self-styled
'creative thinkers' as opposed to the 'hair-splitters' who attend to
the purely rational part—were to be warned against carrying on
at once two jobs very different in their technique, each perhaps
v requiring a special talent and the combination of both in one
person producing mere bunglers. Here, however, I confine myself
to asking whether the nature of science does not always require
that the empirical part should be scrupulously separated from the
rational one, and that (empirical) physics proper should be prefaced
by a metaphysic of nature, while practical anthropology should be
prefaced by a metaphysic of morals—each metaphysic having to
be scrupulously cleansed of everything empirical if we are to know
389 how much pure reason can accomplish in both cases and from
what sources it can by itself draw its own *a priori* teaching. I leave
it an open question whether the latter business[1] is to be conducted
by all moralists (whose name is legion) or only by some who feel
a vocation for the subject.

Since my aim here is directed strictly to moral philosophy, I limit my proposed question to this point only—Do we not think it a matter of the utmost necessity to work out for once a pure moral philosophy completely cleansed of everything that can only **vi** be empirical and appropriate to anthropology?[1] That there must be such a philosophy is already obvious from the common Idea[2] of duty and from the laws of morality. Every one must admit that a law has to carry with it absolute necessity if it is to be valid morally—valid, that is, as a ground of obligation; that the command 'Thou shalt not lie' could not hold merely for men, other rational beings having no obligation to abide by it—and similarly with all other genuine moral laws; that here consequently the ground of obligation must be looked for, not in the nature of man nor in the circumstances of the world in which he is placed, but solely *a priori* in the concepts of pure reason; and that every other precept based on principles of mere experience—and even a precept that may in a certain sense be considered universal, so far as it rests in its slightest part, perhaps only in its motive, on empirical grounds[3] —can indeed be called a practical rule, but never a moral law.

Thus in practical knowledge as a whole, not only are moral **vii** laws, together with their principles, essentially different from all the rest in which there is some empirical element, but the whole of moral philosophy is based entirely on the part of it that is pure. When applied to man it does not borrow in the slightest from acquaintance with him (in anthropology), but gives him laws *a priori* as a rational being.[1] These laws admittedly require in addition a power of judgement sharpened by experience, partly in order to distinguish the cases to which they apply, partly to procure for them admittance to the will of man and influence over practice; for man, affected as he is by so many inclinations,[2] is capable of the Idea of a pure practical reason, but he has not so easily the power to realize the Idea *in concreto* in his conduct of life.

A metaphysic of morals is thus indispensably necessary, not merely in order to investigate, from motives of speculation, the source of practical principles which are present *a priori* in our 390] **viii** reason, but because morals themselves remain exposed to corruption of all sorts as long as this guiding thread is lacking, this ultimate norm for correct moral judgement. For if any action is to be morally good, it is not enough that it should *conform* to the moral law—

it must also be done *for the sake of the moral law*: where this is not so, the conformity is only too contingent and precarious, since the non-moral ground at work will now and then produce actions which accord with the law, but very often actions which transgress it. Now the moral law in its purity and genuineness (and in the field of action it is precisely this that matters most) is to be looked for nowhere else than in a pure philosophy. Hence pure philosophy (that is, metaphysics[1]) must come first, and without it there can be no moral philosophy at all. Indeed a philosophy which mixes up these pure principles with empirical ones does not deserve the name of philosophy (since philosophy is distinguished from ordinary rational knowledge precisely because it sets forth in a separate science what the latter apprehends only as confused with other ix things). Still less does it deserve the name of moral philosophy, since by this very confusion it undermines even the purity of morals themselves and acts against its own proper purpose.

## [*The philosophy of willing as such.*]

It must not be imagined that in the propaedeutics prefixed to his moral philosophy by the celebrated *Wolff*—that is, in the '*Universal Practical Philosophy*',[1] as he called it—we already have what is here demanded and consequently do not need to break entirely new ground. Precisely because it was supposed to be a universal practical philosophy, it has taken into consideration, not a special kind of will—not such a will as is completely determined by *a priori* principles apart from any empirical motives and so can be called a pure will—but willing as such, together with all activities and conditions belonging to it in this general sense. Because of this it differs from a metaphysic of morals in the same way as general x logic differs from transcendental philosophy, the first of which sets forth the activities and rules of thinking *as such*, while the second expounds the special activities and rules of **pure** thinking— that is, of the thinking whereby objects are known completely *a priori*;[1] for a metaphysic of morals has to investigate the Idea and principles of a possible *pure* will, and not the activities and conditions of human willing as such, which are drawn for the most part from 391 psychology. The fact that in this 'universal practical philosophy' there is also talk (though quite unjustifiably) about moral laws and duty is no objection to what I say. For the authors of this science remain true to their Idea of it on this point as well: they do not distinguish motives which, as such, are conceived completely *a priori* by reason alone and are genuinely moral, from empirical motives which understanding raises to general concepts by the mere comparison of experiences. On the contrary, without taking into account differences in their origin they consider motives only **xi** as regards their relative strength or weakness (looking upon all of them as homogeneous) and construct on this basis their concept of *obligation*. This concept is anything but moral; but its character is only such as is to be expected from a philosophy which never decides, as regards the *source* of all practical concepts, whether they arise only *a posteriori* or arise *a priori* as well.

## [*The aim of the* Groundwork.]

Intending, as I do, to publish some day a metaphysic of morals, I issue this *Groundwork* in advance. For such a metaphysic there is strictly no other foundation than a critique of *pure practical reason*, just as for metaphysics[1] there is no other foundation than the critique of pure speculative reason which I have already published. Yet, on the one hand, there is not the same extreme necessity for the former critique as for the latter, since human reason can, in matters of morality, be easily brought to a high degree of accuracy and precision even in the most ordinary intelligence, whereas in its theoretical, but pure, activity it is, on the contrary, out and out dialectical;[1] and, on the other hand, a critique **xii** of practical reason, if it is to be complete, requires, on my view, that we should be able at the same time to show the unity of practical and theoretical reason in a common principle, since in the end there can only be one and the same reason, which must be differentiated solely in its application. Here, however, I found myself as yet unable to bring my work to such completeness without introducing considerations of quite another sort and so confusing the reader. This is why, instead of calling it a 'Critique of Pure Practical Reason', I have adopted the title 'Groundwork of the Metaphysic of Morals'.

But, in the third place, since a metaphysic of morals, in spite of its horrifying title, can be in a high degree popular and suited

to the ordinary intelligence, I think it useful to issue separately
this preparatory work on its foundations so that later I need not
insert the subtleties inevitable in these matters into doctrines more
392] **xiii** easy to understand.

The sole aim of the present Groundwork is to seek out and
establish *the supreme principle of morality*. This by itself is a business
which by its very purpose constitutes a whole and has to be separated
off from every other enquiry. The application of the principle to
the whole system would no doubt throw much light on my
answers to this central question, so important and yet hitherto so
far from being satisfactorily discussed; and the adequacy it manifests
throughout would afford it strong confirmation. All the same, I
had to forego this advantage, which in any case would be more
flattering to myself than helpful to others, since the convenience
of a principle in use and its seeming adequacy afford no completely
safe proof of its correctness. They rather awaken a certain bias
against examining and weighing it in all strictness for itself without
any regard to its consequences.

### [*The method of the* Groundwork.]

**xiv**　　The method I have adopted in this book is, I believe, one which
will work best if we proceed analytically from common knowledge to the formulation of its supreme principle and then back
again synthetically from an examination of this principle and its
origins to the common knowledge in which we find its application.
Hence the division turns out to be as follows:—

1. *Chapter I:* Passage from ordinary rational knowledge of
   morality to philosophical.
2. *Chapter II:* Passage from popular moral philosophy to a
   metaphysic of morals.
3. *Chapter III:* Final step from a metaphysic of morals to a
   critique of pure practical reason.

## PASSAGE FROM ORDINARY RATIONAL KNOWLEDGE OF MORALITY TO PHILOSOPHICAL

### [*The good will.*]

IT is impossible to conceive anything at all in the world, or even out of it, which can be taken as good without qualification, except a **good will.** Intelligence, wit, judgement, and any other *talents* of the mind we may care to name, or courage, resolution, and constancy of purpose, as qualities of *temperament,* are without doubt good and desirable in many respects; but they can also be extremely bad and hurtful when the will is not good which has to make use of these gifts of nature, and which for this reason has the term '*character*' applied to its peculiar quality. It is exactly the same with *gifts of fortune.* Power, wealth, honour, even health and that complete well-being and contentment with one's state which goes by the name of '*happiness*', produce boldness, and as a consequence 2 often over-boldness as well, unless a good will is present by which their influence on the mind—and so too the whole principle of action—may be corrected and adjusted to universal ends; not to mention that a rational and impartial spectator can never feel approval in contemplating the uninterrupted prosperity of a being graced by no touch of a pure and good will, and that consequently a good will seems to constitute the indispensable condition of our very worthiness to be happy.

Some qualities are even helpful to this good will itself and can make its task very much easier.[1] They have none the less no inner unconditioned worth, but rather presuppose a good will which 394 sets a limit to the esteem in which they are rightly held[2] and does not permit us to regard them as absolutely good. Moderation in affections and passions,[3] self-control, and sober reflexion are not only good in many respects: they may even seem to constitute part of the *inner* worth of a person. Yet they are far from being properly described as good without qualification (however unconditionally they have been commended by the ancients). For with-

out the principles of a good will they may become exceedingly
3 bad; and the very coolness of a scoundrel makes him, not merely
more dangerous, but also immediately more abominable in our
eyes than we should have taken him to be without it.

### [The good will and its results.]

A good will is not good because of what it effects or accomplishes—because of its fitness for attaining some proposed end:
it is good through its willing alone—that is, good in itself. Considered in itself it is to be esteemed beyond comparison as far
higher than anything it could ever bring about merely in order to
favour some inclination or, if you like, the sum total of inclinations.
Even if, by some special disfavour of destiny or by the niggardly
endowment of step-motherly nature, this will is entirely lacking
in power to carry out its intentions; if by its utmost effort it still
accomplishes nothing, and only good will is left (not, admittedly,
as a mere wish, but as the straining of every means so far as they
are in our control); even then it would still shine like a jewel for
its own sake as something which has its full value in itself. Its usefulness or fruitlessness can neither add to, nor subtract from, this
value. Its usefulness would be merely, as it were, the setting which
enables us to handle it better in our ordinary dealings or to attract
4 the attention of those not yet sufficiently expert, but not to
commend it to experts or to determine its value.

### [The function of reason.]

Yet in this Idea of the absolute value of a mere will, all useful
results being left out of account in its assessment, there is something
so strange that, in spite of all the agreement it receives even from
ordinary reason, there must arise the suspicion that perhaps its
secret basis is merely some high-flown fantasticality, and that we
may have misunderstood the purpose of nature in attaching reason
395 to our will as its governor. We will therefore submit our Idea to
an examination from this point of view.

In the natural constitution of an organic being—that is, of one
contrived for the purpose of life—let us take it as a principle that
in it no organ is to be found for any end unless it is also the most
appropriate to that end and the best fitted for it. Suppose now

that for a being possessed of reason and a will the real purpose of nature were his *preservation*, his *welfare*, or in a word his *happiness*. In that case nature would have hit on a very bad arrangement by choosing reason in the creature to carry out this purpose. For all the actions he has to perform with this end in view, and the whole 5 rule of his behaviour, would have been mapped out for him far more accurately by instinct; and the end in question could have been maintained far more surely by instinct than it ever can be by reason. If reason should have been imparted to this favoured creature as well, it would have had to serve him only for contemplating the happy disposition of his nature, for admiring it, for enjoying it, and for being grateful to its beneficent Cause—not for subjecting his power of appetition to such feeble and defective guidance or for meddling incompetently with the purposes of nature. In a word, nature would have prevented reason from striking out into a *practical use* and from presuming, with its feeble vision, to think out for itself a plan for happiness and for the means to its attainment. Nature would herself have taken over the choice, not only of ends, but also of means, and would with wise precaution have entrusted both to instinct alone.

In actual fact too we find that the more a cultivated reason concerns itself with the aim of enjoying life and happiness, the farther does man get away from true contentment. This is why there arises in many, and that too in those who have made most trial of this use of reason, if they are only candid enough to admit 6 it, a certain degree of *misology*—that is, a hatred of reason;[1] for when they balance all the advantage they draw, I will not say from thinking out all the arts of ordinary indulgence, but even from science (which in the last resort seems to them to be also an indulgence of the mind), they discover that they have in fact only brought more trouble on their heads than they have gained in the 396 way of happiness. On this account they come to envy, rather than to despise, the more common run of men, who are closer to the guidance of mere natural instinct, and who do not allow their reason to have much influence on their conduct. So far we must admit that the judgement of those who seek to moderate—and even to reduce below zero—the conceited glorification of such advantages as reason is supposed to provide in the way of happiness and contentment with life is in no way soured or ungrateful to the goodness with which the world is governed. These judgements rather have as their hidden ground the Idea of another and much more worthy purpose of existence, for which, and not for happiness, reason is quite properly designed, and to which, therefore, as a supreme condition the private purposes of man must for the most part be subordinated.

For since reason is not sufficiently serviceable for guiding the 7 will safely as regards its objects and the satisfaction of all our needs (which it in part even multiplies)—a purpose for which an implanted natural instinct would have led us much more surely; and since none the less reason has been imparted to us as a practical power—that is, as one which is to have influence on the *will*; its true function must be to produce a *will* which is *good*, not as a *means* to some further end, but *in itself*; and for this function reason was absolutely necessary in a world where nature, in distributing her aptitudes, has everywhere else gone to work in a purposive manner. Such a will need not on this account be the sole and complete good,[1] but it must be the highest good and the condition of all the rest, even of all our demands for happiness. In that case we can easily reconcile with the wisdom of nature our observation that the cultivation of reason which is required for the first and unconditioned purpose may in many ways, at least in this life, restrict the attainment of the second purpose—namely, happiness—which is always conditioned; and indeed that it can even reduce happiness to less than zero without nature proceeding contrary to its purpose; for reason, which recognizes as its highest practical function the establishment of a good will, in attaining this end is capable only of its own peculiar kind of contentment[2] —contentment in fulfilling a purpose which in turn is determined 8 by reason alone, even if this fulfilment should often involve interference with the purposes of inclination.

## [*The good will and duty.*]

397     We have now to elucidate the concept of a will estimable in itself and good apart from any further end. This concept, which is already present in a naturally sound understanding and requires not so much to be taught as merely to be clarified, always holds the highest place in estimating the total worth of our actions and

constitutes the condition of all the rest. We will therefore take up the concept of **duty,** which includes that of a good will, exposed, however, to certain subjective limitations and obstacles. These, so far from hiding a good will or disguising it, rather bring it out by contrast and make it shine forth more brightly.[1]

## [*The motive of duty.*]

I will here pass over all actions already recognized as contrary to duty, however useful they may be with a view to this or that end; for about these the question does not even arise whether they could have been done *for the sake of duty* inasmuch as they are directly opposed to it. I will also set aside actions which in fact accord with duty, yet for which men have *no immediate inclination,* but perform them because impelled to do so by some other inclination. For there it is easy to decide whether the action **9** which accords with duty has been done *from duty* or from some purpose of self-interest. This distinction is far more difficult to perceive when the action accords with duty and the subject has in addition an *immediate* inclination to the action. For example,[1] it certainly accords with duty that a grocer should not overcharge his inexperienced customer; and where there is much competition a sensible shopkeeper refrains from so doing and keeps to a fixed and general price for everybody so that a child can buy from him just as well as anyone else. Thus people are served *honestly;* but this is not nearly enough to justify us in believing that the shopkeeper has acted in this way from duty or from principles of fair dealing; his interests required him to do so. We cannot assume him to have in addition an immediate inclination towards his customers, leading him, as it were out of love, to give no man preference over another in the matter of price. Thus the action was done neither from duty nor from immediate inclination, but solely from purposes of self-interest.

On the other hand, to preserve one's life is a duty, and besides this every one has also an immediate inclination to do so. But on account of this the often anxious precautions taken by the greater part of mankind for this purpose have no inner worth, and the maxim[2] of their action is without moral content. They do **398** protect their lives *in conformity with duty,* but not *from the motive* **10** *of duty.* When, on the contrary, disappointments and hopeless

E

misery have quite taken away the taste for life; when a wretched
man, strong in soul and more angered at his fate than faint-hearted
or cast down, longs for death and still preserves his life without
loving it—not from inclination or fear but from duty; then indeed
his maxim has a moral content.

To help others where one can is a duty, and besides this there
are many spirits of so sympathetic a temper that, without any
further motive of vanity or self-interest, they find an inner pleasure
in spreading happiness around them and can take delight in the
contentment of others as their own work. Yet I maintain that
in such a case an action of this kind, however right and however
amiable it may be, has still no genuinely moral worth. It stands
on the same footing as other inclinations[1]—for example, the
inclination for honour, which if fortunate enough to hit on something beneficial and right and consequently honourable, deserves
praise and encouragement, but not esteem; for its maxim lacks
moral content, namely, the performance of such actions, not from
inclination, but *from duty*. Suppose then that the mind of this
friend of man was overclouded by sorrows of his own which
ɪɪ extinguished all sympathy with the fate of others, but that he still
had power to help those in distress, though no longer stirred by
the need of others because sufficiently occupied with his own;
and suppose that, when no longer moved by any inclination, he
tears himself out of this deadly insensibility and does the action
without any inclination for the sake of duty alone; then for the
first time his action has its genuine moral worth. Still further:
if nature had implanted little sympathy in this or that man's heart;
if (being in other respects an honest fellow) he were cold in
temperament and indifferent to the sufferings of others—perhaps
because, being endowed with the special gift of patience and
robust endurance in his own sufferings, he assumed the like in
others or even demanded it; if such a man (who would in truth
not be the worst product of nature) were not exactly fashioned
by her to be a philanthropist, would he not still find in himself
a source from which he might draw a worth far higher than any
that a good-natured temperament can have? Assuredly he would.
It is precisely in this that the worth of character begins to show
399 —a moral worth and beyond all comparison the highest—namely
that he does good, not from inclination, but from duty.

To assure one's own happiness is a duty (at least indirectly); for discontent with one's state, in a press of cares and amidst unsatis- 12 fied wants, might easily become a great *temptation to the transgression of duty*. But here also, apart from regard to duty, all men have already of themselves the strongest and deepest inclination towards happiness, because precisely in this Idea of happiness there is combined the sum total of inclinations.[1] The prescription for happiness is, however, often so constituted as greatly to interfere with some inclinations, and yet men cannot form under the name of 'happiness' any determinate and assured conception of the satisfaction of all inclinations as a sum. Hence it is not to be wondered at that a single inclination which is determinate as to what it promises and as to the time of its satisfaction may outweigh a wavering Idea; and that a man, for example, a sufferer from gout, may choose to enjoy what he fancies and put up with what he can—on the ground that on balance he has here at least not killed the enjoyment of the present moment because of some possibly groundless expectations of the good fortune supposed to attach to soundness of health. But in this case also, when the universal inclination towards happiness has failed to determine his will, when good health, at least for him, has not entered into his calculations as so necessary, what remains over, here as in other cases, is a law—the law of furthering his happiness, not from inclination, 13 but from duty—and in this for the first time his conduct has a real moral worth.

It is doubtless in this sense that we should understand too the passages from Scripture in which we are commanded to love our neighbour and even our enemy. For love out of inclination cannot be commanded; but kindness done from duty—although no inclination impels us, and even although natural and unconquerable disinclination stands in our way—is *practical*, and not *pathological*, love, residing in the will and not in the propensions of feeling, in principles of action and not of melting compassion; and it is this practical love alone which can be an object of command.

## [*The formal principle of duty.*]

Our second proposition[1] is this: An action done from duty has its moral worth, *not in the purpose* to be attained by it, but in

the maxim in accordance with which it is decided upon; it depends
400 therefore, not on the realization of the object of the action, but
solely on the *principle* of *volition* in accordance with which,
irrespective of all objects of the faculty of desire,[2] the action has
been performed. That the purposes we may have in our actions,
and also their effects considered as ends and motives of the will,
can give to actions no unconditioned and moral worth is clear
from what has gone before. Where then can this worth be found
14 if we are not to find it in the will's relation to the effect hoped for
from the action? It can be found nowhere but *in the principle of
the will*, irrespective of the ends which can be brought about by
such an action; for between its *a priori* principle, which is formal,
and its *a posteriori* motive, which is material, the will stands, so to
speak, at a parting of the ways; and since it must be determined
by some principle, it will have to be determined by the formal
principle of volition when an action is done from duty, where,
as we have seen, every material principle is taken away from it.

## [*Reverence for the law.*]

Our third proposition, as an inference from the two preceding,
I would express thus: *Duty is the necessity to act out of reverence
for the law*. For an object as the effect of my proposed action I can
have an *inclination*, but *never reverence*, precisely because it is merely
the effect, and not the activity, of a will. Similarly for inclination
as such, whether my own or that of another, I cannot have
reverence: I can at most in the first case approve, and in the second
case sometimes even love—that is, regard it as favourable to my
own advantage. Only something which is conjoined with my
will solely as a ground and never as an effect—something which
does not serve my inclination, but outweighs it or at least leaves
15 it entirely out of account in my choice—and therefore only bare
law for its own sake, can be an object of reverence and therewith
a command. Now an action done from duty has to set aside
altogether the influence of inclination, and along with inclination
every object of the will; so there is nothing left able to determine
the will except objectively the *law* and subjectively *pure reverence*

for this practical law, and therefore the maxim* of obeying this law even to the detriment of all my inclinations. 401

Thus the moral worth of an action does not depend on the result expected from it, and so too does not depend on any principle of action that needs to borrow its motive from this expected result. For all these results (agreeable states and even the promotion of happiness in others) could have been brought about by other causes as well, and consequently their production did not require the will of a rational being, in which, however, the highest and unconditioned good can alone be found. Therefore nothing but the *idea of the law* in itself, *which admittedly is present only in a rational* 16 *being*—so far as it, and not an expected result, is the ground determining the will—can constitute that pre-eminent good which we call moral, a good which is already present in the person acting on this idea and should not be awaited merely from the result.**

## [*The categorical imperative.*]

But what kind of law can this be the thought of which, even 402 without regard to the results expected from it, has to determine the will if this is to be called good absolutely and without qualifi-

*A *maxim* is the subjective principle of a volition: an objective principle (that 15 is, one which would also serve subjectively as a practical principle for all rational beings if reason had full control over the faculty of desire) is a practical *law.*

**It might be urged against me that I have merely tried, under cover of the word 16 ' *reverence*', to take refuge in an obscure feeling instead of giving a clearly articulated answer to the question by means of a concept of reason. Yet although reverence is a feeling, it is not a feeling *received* through outside influence, but one *self-produced* by a rational concept, and therefore specifically distinct from feelings of the first kind, all of which can be reduced to inclination or fear. What I recognize immediately as law for me, I recognize with reverence, which means merely consciousness of the *subordination* of my will to a law without the mediation of external influences on my senses. Immediate determination of the will by the law and consciousness of this determination is called '*reverence*', so that reverence is regarded as the *effect* of the law on the subject and not as the *cause* of the law. Reverence is properly the idea of a value which demolishes my self-love. Hence there is something which is regarded neither as an object of inclination nor as an object of fear, though it has at the same time some analogy with both. The *object* of reverence is the *law* alone—that law which we impose *on ourselves* but yet as necessary in itself. Considered as a law, we are subject to it without any consultation of self-love; considered as self-imposed it is a consequence of our will. In the first respect it[1] is analogous to fear, in the second to inclination. All reverence for a person is properly only 17 reverence for the law (of honesty and so on) of which that person gives us an example. Because we regard the development of our talents as a duty,[1] we see too in a man of talent a sort of *example of the law* (the law of becoming like him by practice), and this is what constitutes our reverence for him. All moral *interest*, so-called, consists solely in *reverence* for the law.

cation? Since I have robbed the will of every inducement that might arise for it as a consequence of obeying any particular law, nothing is left but the conformity of actions to universal law as such, and this alone must serve the will as its principle. That is to say, I ought never to act except in such a way *that I can also will that my maxim should become a universal law*. Here bare conformity to universal law as such (without having as its base any law prescribing particular actions) is what serves the will as its principle, and must so serve it if duty is not to be everywhere an empty delusion and a chimerical concept. The ordinary reason of mankind also agrees with this completely in its practical judgements and always has the aforesaid principle before its eyes.

18    Take this question, for example. May I not, when I am hard pressed, make a promise with the intention of not keeping it? Here I readily distinguish the two senses which the question can have—Is it prudent, or is it right, to make a false promise? The first can doubtless often be the case. I do indeed see that it is not enough for me to extricate myself from present embarrassment by this subterfuge: I have to consider whether from this lie there may not subsequently accrue to me much greater inconvenience than that from which I now escape, and also—since, with all my supposed *astuteness*, to foresee the consequences is not so easy that I can be sure there is no chance, once confidence in me is lost, of this proving far more disadvantageous than all the ills I now think to avoid—whether it may not be a *more prudent* action to proceed here on a general maxim and make it my habit not to give a promise except with the intention of keeping it. Yet it becomes clear to me at once that such a maxim is always founded solely on fear of consequences. To tell the truth for the sake of duty is something entirely different from doing so out of concern for inconvenient results; for in the first case the concept of the action already contains in itself a law for me, while in the second case I have first of all to look around elsewhere in order to see
19 what effects may be bound up with it for me. When I deviate from
403 the principle of duty, this is quite certainly bad; but if I desert my prudential maxim, this can often be greatly to my advantage, though it is admittedly safer to stick to it. Suppose I seek, however, to learn in the quickest way and yet unerringly how to solve the problem 'Does a lying promise accord with duty?' I have then

to ask myself 'Should I really be content that my maxim (the maxim of getting out of a difficulty by a false promise) should hold as a universal law (one valid both for myself and others)? And could I really say to myself that every one may make a false promise if he finds himself in a difficulty from which he can extricate himself in no other way?' I then become aware at once that I can indeed will to lie, but I can by no means will a universal law of lying; for by such a law there could properly be no promises at all, since it would be futile to profess a will for future action to others who would not believe my profession or who, if they did so over-hastily, would pay me back in like coin;[1] and consequently my maxim, as soon as it was made a universal law, would be bound to annul itself.

Thus I need no far-reaching ingenuity to find out what I have to do in order to possess a good will. Inexperienced in the course 20 of world affairs and incapable of being prepared for all the chances that happen in it, I ask myself only 'Can you also will that your maxim should become a universal law?' Where you cannot, it is to be rejected, and that not because of a prospective loss to you or even to others, but because it cannot fit as a principle into a possible enactment of universal law. For such an enactment reason compels my immediate reverence, into whose grounds (which the philosopher may investigate) I have as yet no *insight*,[1] although I do at least understand this much: reverence is the assessment of a worth which far outweighs all the worth of what is commended by inclination, and the necessity for me to act out of *pure* reverence for the practical law is what constitutes duty, to which every other motive must give way because it is the condition of a will good *in itself*, whose value is above all else.

### [*Ordinary practical reason.*]

In studying the moral knowledge of ordinary human reason we have now arrived at its first principle. This principle it admittedly does not conceive thus abstractly in its universal form; but it does always have it actually before its eyes and does use it as a norm of judgement. It would be easy to show here how human 404 reason, with this compass in hand, is well able to distinguish, in 21 all cases that present themselves, what is good or evil, right or

wrong—provided that, without the least attempt to teach it anything new, we merely make reason attend, as Socrates did, to
its own principle; and how in consequence there is no need of
science or philosophy for knowing what man has to do in order
to be honest and good, and indeed to be wise and virtuous. It
might even be surmised in advance that acquaintance with what
every man is obliged to do, and so also to know, will be the affair
of every man, even the most ordinary. Yet we cannot observe
without admiration the great advantage which the power of
practical judgement has over that of theoretical in the minds of
ordinary men. In theoretical judgements, when ordinary reason
ventures to depart from the laws of experience and the perceptions
of sense, it falls into sheer unintelligibility and self-contradiction,
or at least into a chaos of uncertainty, obscurity, and vacillation.
On the practical side, however, the power of judgement first begins
to show what advantages it has in itself when the ordinary mind
excludes all sensuous motives from its practical laws. Then
ordinary intelligence becomes even subtle—it may be in juggling
with conscience or with other claims as to what is to be called
22 right, or in trying to determine honestly for its own instruction
the value of various actions; and, what is most important, it can
in the latter case have as good hope of hitting the mark as any
that a philosopher can promise himself. Indeed it is almost surer
in this than even a philosopher, because he has no principle different
from that of ordinary intelligence, but can easily confuse his
judgement with a mass of alien and irrelevant considerations and
cause it to swerve from the straight path. Might it not then be
more advisable in moral questions to abide by the judgement of
ordinary reason and, at the most, to bring in philosophy only in
order to set forth the system of morals more fully and intelligibly
and to present its rules in a form more convenient for use (though
still more so for disputation)—but not in order to lead ordinary
human intelligence away from its happy simplicity in respect of
action and to set it by means of philosophy on a new path of
enquiry and instruction?

[*The need for philosophy.*]

Innocence is a splendid thing, only it has the misfortune not
405 to keep very well and to be easily misled. On this account wisdom

itself—which in any case consists more in doing and not doing than in knowing—does require science as well, not in order to learn from it, but in order to win acceptance and durability for its own 23 prescriptions. Man feels in himself a powerful counterweight to all the commands of duty presented to him by reason as so worthy of esteem—the counterweight of his needs and inclinations, whose total satisfaction he grasps under the name of 'happiness'. But reason, without promising anything to inclination, enjoins its commands relentlessly, and therefore, so to speak, with disregard and neglect of these turbulent and seemingly equitable claims (which refuse to be suppressed by any command). From this there arises a *natural dialectic*—that is, a disposition to quibble with these strict laws of duty, to throw doubt on their validity or at least on their purity and strictness, and to make them, where possible, more adapted to our wishes and inclinations; that is, to pervert their very foundations and destroy their whole dignity—a result which in the end even ordinary human reason is unable to approve.

In this way the *common reason of mankind* is impelled, not by any need for speculation (which never assails it so long as it is content to be mere sound reason), but on practical grounds themselves, to leave its own sphere and take a step into the field of *practical philosophy*. It there seeks to acquire information and precise instruc- 24 tion about the source of its own principle, and about the correct function of this principle in comparison with maxims based on need and inclination, in order that it may escape from the embarrassment of antagonistic claims and may avoid the risk of losing all genuine moral principles because of the ambiguity into which it easily falls. Thus ordinary reason, when cultivated in its practical use, gives rise insensibly to a *dialectic* which constrains it to seek help in philosophy, just as happens in its theoretical use; and consequently in the first case as little as in the second will it anywhere else than in a critique of our reason be able to find peace.

## PASSAGE FROM POPULAR MORAL PHILOSOPHY
## TO A METAPHYSIC OF MORALS

*[The use of examples.]*

If so far we have drawn our concept of duty from the ordinary use of our practical reason, it must by no means be inferred that we have treated it as a concept of experience. On the contrary, when we pay attention to our experience of human conduct, we meet frequent and—as we ourselves admit—justified complaints that we can adduce no certain examples of the spirit which acts out of pure duty, and that, although much may be done *in accordance with* the commands of *duty*, it remains doubtful whether it really is done *for the sake of duty* and so has a moral value. Hence at all times there have been philosophers who have absolutely denied the presence of this spirit in human actions and have ascribed everything to a more or less refined self-love. In so doing they have not cast doubt on the rightness of the moral concept. They have spoken rather with deep regret of the frailty and impurity of human nature, which is on their view noble enough

26 to take as its rule an Idea so worthy of reverence, but at the same time too weak to follow it: the reason which should serve it for making laws it uses only to look after the interest of inclinations, whether singly or—at the best—in their greatest mutual compatibility.

407    In actual fact it is absolutely impossible for experience to establish with complete certainty a single case in which the maxim of an action in other respects right has rested solely on moral grounds and on the thought of one's duty. It is indeed at times the case that after the keenest self-examination we find nothing that without the moral motive of duty could have been strong enough to move us to this or that good action and to so great a sacrifice; but we cannot infer from this with certainty that it is not some secret impulse of self-love which has actually, under

the mere show of the Idea of duty, been the cause genuinely determining our will. We are pleased to flatter ourselves with the
false claim to a nobler motive, but in fact we can never, even
by the most strenuous self-examination, get to the bottom of our
secret impulsions; for when moral value is in question, we are
concerned, not with the actions which we see, but with their
inner principles, which we cannot see.

Furthermore, to those who deride all morality as the mere 27
phantom of a human imagination which gets above itself out of
vanity we can do no service more pleasing than to admit that
the concepts of duty must be drawn solely from experience (just
as out of slackness we willingly persuade ourselves that this is
so in the case of all other concepts); for by so doing we prepare
for them an assured triumph. Out of love for humanity I am
willing to allow that most of our actions may accord with duty;
but if we look more closely at our scheming and striving, we
everywhere come across the dear self, which is always turning up;
and it is on this that the purpose of our actions is based—not on
the strict command of duty, which would often require self-denial.
One need not be exactly a foe to virtue, but merely a dispassionate
observer declining to take the liveliest wish for goodness straight
away as its realization, in order at certain moments (particularly
with advancing years and with a power of judgement at once made
shrewder by experience and also more keen in observation) to
become doubtful whether any genuine virtue is actually to be
encountered in the world. And then nothing can protect us against
a complete falling away from our Ideas of duty, or can preserve
in the soul a grounded reverence for its law, except the clear
conviction that even if there never have been actions springing
from such pure sources, the question at issue here is not whether 408] 28
this or that has happened; that, on the contrary, reason by itself
and independently of all appearances commands what ought to
happen; that consequently actions of which the world has perhaps
hitherto given no example—actions whose practicability might
well be doubted by those who rest everything on experience—
are nevertheless commanded unrelentingly by reason; and that,
for instance, although up to now there may have existed no loyal
friend, pure loyalty in friendship can be no less required from
every man, inasmuch as this duty, prior to all experience, is

contained as duty in general[1] in the Idea of a reason which determines the will by *a priori* grounds.

It may be added that unless we wish to deny to the concept of morality all truth and all relation to a possible object, we cannot dispute that its law is of such widespread significance as to hold, not merely for men, but for all *rational beings as such*—not merely subject to contingent conditions and exceptions, but *with absolute necessity*.[2] It is therefore clear that no experience can give us occasion to infer even the possibility of such apodeictic laws. For 29 by what right can we make what is perhaps valid only under the contingent conditions of humanity into an object of unlimited reverence as a universal precept for every rational nature? And how could laws for determining *our* will be taken as laws for determining the will of a rational being as such—and only because of this for determining ours—if these laws were merely empirical and did not have their source completely *a priori* in pure, but practical, reason?

What is more, we cannot do morality a worse service than by seeking to derive it from examples. Every example of it presented to me must first itself be judged by moral principles in order to decide if it is fit to serve as an original example—that is, as a model: it can in no way supply the prime source for the concept of morality. Even the Holy One of the gospel must first be compared with our ideal of moral perfection before we can recognize him to be such. He also says of himself: 'Why callest thou me (whom thou seest) good? There is none good (the archetype of the good) but one, that is, God (whom thou seest not)'. But where do we 409 get the concept of God as the highest good? Solely from the *Idea* of moral perfection,[1] which reason traces *a priori* and conjoins inseparably with the concept of a free will. Imitation has no place 30 in morality, and examples serve us only for encouragement—that is, they set beyond doubt the practicability of what the law commands; they make perceptible what the practical law expresses more generally; but they can never entitle us to set aside their true Original, which resides in reason, and to model ourselves upon examples.

### [*Popular philosophy.*]

If there can be no genuine supreme principle of morality which is not grounded on pure reason alone independently of all experience, it should be unnecessary, I think, even to raise the question whether it is a good thing to set forth in general (*in abstracto*) these concepts which hold *a priori*, together with their corresponding principles, so far as our knowledge is to be distinguished from ordinary knowledge and described as philosophical. Yet in our days it may well be necessary to do so. For if we took a vote on which is to be preferred, pure rational knowledge detached from everything empirical—that is to say, a metaphysic of morals—or popular practical philosophy, we can guess at once on which side the preponderance would fall.

It is certainly most praiseworthy to come down to the level of popular thought when we have previously risen to the principles of pure reason and have done so to our full satisfaction. This could be described as first *grounding* moral philosophy on meta- 31 physics[1] and subsequently winning *acceptance* for it by giving it a popular character after it has been established. But it is utterly senseless to aim at popularity in our first enquiry, upon which the whole correctness of our principles depends. It is not merely that such a procedure can never lay claim to the extremely rare merit of a truly *philosophical popularity*, since we require no skill to make ourselves intelligible to the multitude once we renounce all profundity of thought: what it turns out is a disgusting hotchpotch of second-hand observations and semi-rational principles on which the empty-headed regale themselves, because this is something that can be used in the chit-chat of daily life. Men of insight, on the other hand, feel confused by it and avert their eyes with a dissatisfaction which, however, they are unable to cure. Yet philosophers, who can perfectly well see through this deception, get little hearing when they summon us for a time from this 410 would-be popularity in order that they may win the right to be genuinely popular only after definite insight has been attained.

We need only look at the attempts to deal with morality in this favoured style. What we shall encounter in an amazing medley is at one time the particular character of human nature (but along with this also the Idea of a rational nature as such), at another perfection, at another happiness; here moral feeling and there the 32 fear of God; something of this and also something of that. But it never occurs to these writers to ask whether the principles of morality are to be sought at all in our acquaintance with human nature (which we can get only from experience); nor does it occur to them that if this is not so—if these principles are to be found completely *a priori* and free from empirical elements in the concepts of pure reason and absolutely nowhere else even to the slightest extent—they had better adopt the plan of separating off this enquiry altogether as pure practical philosophy or (if one may use a name so much decried) as a metaphysic* of morals; of bringing this to full completeness by itself alone; and of bidding the public which demands popularity to await in hope the outcome of this undertaking.

Nevertheless such a completely isolated metaphysic of morals, 33 mixed with no anthropology, no theology, no physics or hyperphysics, still less with occult qualities (which might be called hypophysical), is not only an indispensable substratum of all theoretical and precisely defined knowledge of duties, but is at the same time a desideratum of the utmost importance for the actual execution of moral precepts. Unmixed with the alien element of added empirical inducements, the pure thought of duty, and in general of the moral law, has by way of reason alone (which first learns from this that by itself it is able to be practical as well as theoretical) an influence on the human heart so much 411 more powerful than all the further impulsions** capable of being called up from the field of experience that in the consciousness of its own dignity[1] reason despises these impulsions and is able

32    *We can, if we like, distinguish pure moral philosophy (metaphysics) from applied (applied, that is, to human nature)—just as pure mathematics is distinguished from applied mathematics and pure logic from applied logic. By this terminology we are at once reminded that moral principles are not grounded on the peculiarities of human nature, but must be established *a priori* by themselves; and yet that from such principles it must be possible to derive practical rules for human nature as well, just as it is for every kind of rational nature.

33    **I have a letter from the late distinguished Professor *Sulzer*,[1] in which he asks me what it is that makes moral instruction so ineffective, however convincing it may be in the eyes of reason. Because of my efforts to make it complete, my answer came too late. Yet it is just this: the teachers themselves do not make their concepts pure, but—since they try to do too well by hunting everywhere for inducements to be moral—they spoil their medicine altogether by their very attempt to make it really powerful. For the most ordinary observation shows that when 34 a righteous act is represented as being done with a steadfast mind in complete disregard of any advantage in this or in another world, and even under the greatest temptations of affliction or allurement, it leaves far behind it any similar action affected even in the slightest degree by an alien impulsion and casts it into the shade:[1] it uplifts the soul and rouses a wish that we too could act in this way. Even children of moderate age feel this impression, and duties should never be presented to them in any other way.

gradually to become their master. In place of this, a mixed moral philosophy, compounded of impulsions from feeling and inclination and at the same time of rational concepts, must make the 34 mind waver between motives which can be brought under no single principle and which can guide us only by mere accident to the good, but very often also to the evil.

### [Review of conclusions.]

From these considerations the following conclusions emerge. All moral concepts have their seat and origin in reason completely *a priori*, and indeed in the most ordinary human reason just as much as in the most highly speculative: they cannot be abstracted from any empirical, and therefore merely contingent, knowledge. In this purity of their origin is to be found their very worthiness to serve as supreme practical principles, and everything empirical added to them is just so much taken away from their genuine influence and from the absolute value of the corresponding actions.[1] It is not only a requirement of the utmost necessity in respect of theory, where our concern is solely with speculation, but is also 35 of the utmost practical importance, to draw these concepts and laws from pure reason, to set them forth pure and unmixed, and indeed to determine the extent of this whole practical, but pure, rational knowledge—that is, to determine the whole power of pure practical reason. We ought never—as speculative philosophy[1] does allow and even at times finds necessary—to make principles depend on the special nature of human reason. Since moral laws have to 412 hold for every rational being as such, we ought rather to derive our principles from the general concept of a rational being as such,[2] and on this basis to expound the whole of ethics—which requires anthropology for its *application* to man—at first independently as pure philosophy, that is, entirely as metaphysics[3] (which we can very well do in this wholly abstract kind of knowledge). We know well that without possessing such a metaphysics it is a futile endeavour, I will not say to determine accurately for speculative judgement the moral element of duty in all that accords with duty—but that it is impossible, even in ordinary and practical usage, particularly in that of moral instruction, to base morals on their genuine principles and so to bring about pure moral dispositions and engraft them on men's minds for the highest good of the world.

36    In this task of ours we have to progress by natural stages, not merely from ordinary moral judgement (which is here worthy of great respect) to philosophical judgement, as we have already done,[1] but from popular philosophy, which goes no further than it can get by fumbling about with the aid of examples, to metaphysics. (This no longer lets itself be held back by anything empirical, and indeed—since it must survey the complete totality[2] of this kind of knowledge—goes right to Ideas, where examples themselves fail.) For this purpose we must follow—and must portray in detail —the power of practical reason from the general rules determining it right up to the point where there springs from it the concept of duty.[3]

### [Imperatives in general.]

Everything in nature works in accordance with laws. Only a rational being has the power to act *in accordance with his idea* of laws—that is, in accordance with principles—and only so has he a *will*. Since *reason* is required in order to derive actions from laws,[4] the will is nothing but practical reason. If reason infallibly determines the will, then in a being of this kind the actions which are recognized to be objectively necessary are also subjectively necessary—that is to say, the will is then a power to choose *only that* which reason independently of inclination recognizes to be

37 practically necessary, that is, to be good. But if reason solely by itself is not sufficient to determine the will; if the will is exposed also to subjective conditions (certain impulsions) which do not always harmonize with the objective ones; if, in a word, the will

413 is not *in itself* completely in accord with reason (as actually happens in the case of men); then actions which are recognized to be objectively necessary are subjectively contingent, and the determining of such a will in accordance with objective laws is *necessitation*. That is to say, the relation of objective laws to a will not good through and through is conceived as one in which the will of a rational being, although it is determined[1] by principles of reason, does not necessarily follow these principles in virtue of its own nature.

The conception of an objective principle so far as this principle is necessitating for a will is called a command (of reason), and the formula of this command is called an **Imperative**.

All imperatives are expressed by an 'ought' (*Sollen*). By this they mark the relation of an objective law of reason to a will which is not necessarily determined by this law in virtue of its subjective constitution (the relation of necessitation). They say that something would be good to do or to leave undone; only they say it to a will which does not always do a thing because 38 it has been informed that this is a good thing to do. The practically *good* is that which determines the will by concepts of reason, and therefore not by subjective causes, but objectively—that is, on grounds valid for every rational being as such. It is distinguished from the *pleasant* as that which influences the will, not as a principle of reason valid for every one, but solely through the medium of sensation by purely subjective causes valid only for the senses of this person or that.*

A perfectly good will would thus stand quite as much under 414] 39 objective laws (laws of the good), but it could not on this account be conceived as *necessitated* to act in conformity with law, since of itself, in accordance with its subjective constitution, it can be determined only by the concept of the good. Hence for the *divine* will, and in general for a *holy* will, there are no imperatives: '*I ought*' is here out of place, because '*I will*' is already of itself necessarily in harmony with the law. Imperatives are in consequence only formulae for expressing the relation of objective laws of willing to the subjective imperfection of the will of this or that rational being—for example, of the human will.

*The dependence of the power of appetition on sensations is called an inclination, 38 and thus an inclination always indicates a *need*. The dependence of a contingently determinable will on principles of reason is called an *interest*. Hence an interest is found only where there is a dependent will which in itself is not always in accord with reason: to a divine will we cannot ascribe any interest. But even the human will can *take an interest* in something without therefore *acting from interest*. The first expression signifies *practical* interest in the action; the second *pathological* interest in the object of the action. The first indicates only dependence of the will on principles of reason by itself; the second its dependence on principles of reason at the service of inclination—that is to say, where reason merely supplies a practical rule for meeting the need of inclination.[1] In the first case what interests me is the action; in the second case what interests me is the object of the action (so far as this object is pleasant to me). We have seen in Chapter I that in an action done for the sake of duty we must have regard, not to interest in the object, but to interest in the action itself and in its rational principle (namely, the law).

F

[*Classification of imperatives.*]

All *imperatives* command either *hypothetically* or *categorically*. Hypothetical imperatives declare a possible action to be practically necessary as a means to the attainment of something else that one wills (or that one may will). A categorical imperative would be one which represented an action as objectively necessary in itself apart from its relation to a further end.

Every practical law represents a possible action as good and therefore as necessary for a subject whose actions are determined 40 by reason. Hence all imperatives are formulae for determining an action which is necessary in accordance with the principle of a will in some sense good. If the action would be good solely as a means *to something else*, the imperative is *hypothetical*; if the action is represented as good *in itself* and therefore as necessary, in virtue of its[1] principle, for a will which of itself accords with reason, then the imperative is *categorical*.

An imperative therefore tells me which of my possible actions would be good; and it formulates a practical rule for a will that does not perform an action straight away because the action is good—whether because the subject does not always know that it is good or because, even if he did know this, he might still act on maxims contrary to the objective principles of practical reason.

A hypothetical imperative thus says only that an action is good for some purpose or other, either *possible* or *actual*. In the 415 first case it is a **problematic** practical principle; in the second case an **assertoric** practical principle. A categorical imperative, which declares an action to be objectively necessary in itself without reference to some purpose—that is, even without any further end—ranks as an **apodeictic** practical principle.

41    Everything that is possible only through the efforts of some rational being can be conceived as a possible purpose of some will; and consequently there are in fact innumerable principles of action so far as action is thought necessary in order to achieve some possible purpose which can be effected by it. All sciences have a practical part consisting of problems which suppose that some end is possible for us and of imperatives which tell us how it is to be attained. Hence the latter can in general be called imperatives of **skill.** Here there is absolutely no question about the rationality

or goodness of the end, but only about what must be done to attain it. A prescription required by a doctor in order to cure his man completely and one required by a poisoner in order to make sure of killing him are of equal value so far as each serves to effect its purpose perfectly. Since in early youth we do not know what ends may present themselves to us in the course of life, parents seek above all to make their children learn things *of many kinds*; they provide carefully for *skill* in the use of means to all sorts of *arbitrary* ends, of none of which can they be certain that it could not[1] in the future become an actual purpose of their ward, while it is always *possible* that he might adopt it. Their care in this matter is so great that they commonly neglect on this account to form and correct the judgement of their children about the worth of the things which they might possibly adopt as ends.    42

There is, however, *one* end that can be presupposed as actual in all rational beings (so far as they are dependent beings to whom imperatives apply); and thus there is one purpose which they not only *can* have, but which we can assume with certainty that they all *do* have by a natural necessity—the purpose, namely, of *happiness*. A hypothetical imperative which affirms the practical necessity of an action as a means to the furtherance of happiness is **assertoric.** We may represent it, not simply as necessary to an uncertain, merely possible purpose, but as necessary to a purpose which we can presuppose *a priori* and with certainty to be present in every man because it belongs to his very being. Now skill in the choice 416 of means to one's own greatest well-being can be called *prudence** in the narrowest sense.[1] Thus an imperative concerned with the choice of means to one's own happiness—that is, a precept of 43 prudence—still remains *hypothetical*: an action is commanded, not absolutely, but only as a means to a further purpose.

Finally, there is an imperative which, without being based on, and conditioned by, any further purpose to be attained by a certain line of conduct, enjoins this conduct immediately. This imperative

*The word 'prudence' (*Klugheit*) is used in a double sense: in one sense it can 42 have the name of 'worldly wisdom' (*Weltklugheit*); in a second sense that of 'personal wisdom' (*Privatklugheit*). The first is the skill of a man in influencing others in order to use them for his own ends. The second is sagacity in combining all these ends to his own lasting advantage.[1] The latter is properly that to which the value of the former can itself be traced; and of him who is prudent in the first sense, but not in the second, we might better say that he is clever and astute, but on the whole imprudent.

is **categorical.** It is concerned, not with the matter of the action and its presumed results, but with its form and with the principle from which it follows; and what is essentially good in the action consists in the mental disposition, let the consequences be what they may. This imperative may be called the imperative of **morality.**

Willing in accordance with these three kinds of principle is also sharply distinguished by a *dissimilarity* in the necessitation of the will. To make this dissimilarity obvious we should, I think, name these kinds of principle most appropriately in their order if we said they were either *rules* of skill or *counsels* of prudence or *commands (laws)* of morality. For only *law* carries with it the concept of an *unconditioned,* and yet objective and so universally

44 valid, *necessity*; and commands are laws which must be obeyed— that is, must be followed even against inclination. *Counsel* does indeed involve necessity, but necessity valid only under a subjective and contingent condition—namely, if this or that man counts this or that as belonging to his happiness. As against this, a categorical imperative is limited by no condition and can quite precisely be called a command, as being absolutely, although practically,[1] necessary. We could also call imperatives of the first kind *technical*

417 (concerned with art); of the second kind *pragmatic*★ (concerned with well-being); of the third kind *moral* (concerned with free conduct as such[2]—that is, with morals).

## [*How are imperatives possible?*]

The question now arises 'How are all these imperatives possible?' This question does not ask how we can conceive the execution of an action commanded by the imperative, but merely how we can conceive the necessitation of the will expressed by the imperative in setting us a task.[3] How an imperative of skill is possible requires no special discussion. Who wills the end, wills

45 (so far as reason has decisive influence on his actions) also the means

44 ★It seems to me that the proper meaning of the word '*pragmatic*' can be defined most accurately in this way. For those *Sanctions* are called Pragmatic which, properly speaking, do not spring as necessary laws from the Natural Right of States, but from *forethought* in regard to the general welfare.[1] A *history* is written pragmatically when it teaches *prudence*—that is, when it instructs the world of to-day how to provide for its own advantage better than, or at least as well as, the world of other times.

which are indispensably necessary and in his power. So far as willing is concerned, this proposition is analytic: for in my willing of an object as an effect there is already conceived[1] the causality of myself as an acting cause—that is, the use of means; and from the concept of willing an end the imperative merely extracts the concept of actions necessary to this end. (Synthetic propositions are required in order to determine the means to a proposed end, but these are concerned, not with the reason for performing the act of will, but with the cause which produces the object.) That in order to divide a line into two equal parts on a sure principle I must from its ends describe two intersecting arcs—this is admittedly taught by mathematics only in synthetic propositions; but when I know that the aforesaid effect can be produced only by such an action, the proposition 'If I fully will the effect, I also will the action required for it' is analytic; for it is one and the same thing to conceive something as an effect possible in a certain way through me and to conceive myself as acting in the same way with respect to it.

If it were only as easy to find a determinate concept of happiness, the imperatives of prudence would agree entirely with 46 those of skill and would be equally analytic. For here as there it could alike be said 'Who wills the end, wills also (necessarily, if he accords with reason) the sole means which are in his power'. 418 Unfortunately, however, the concept of happiness is so indeterminate a concept that although every man wants to attain happiness, he can never say definitely and in unison with himself what it really is that he wants and wills. The reason for this is that all the elements which belong to the concept of happiness are without exception empirical—that is, they must be borrowed from experience; but that none the less there is required for the Idea of happiness an absolute whole, a maximum of well-being in my present, and in every future, state. Now it is impossible for the most intelligent, and at the same time most powerful, but nevertheless finite, being to form here a determinate concept of what he really wills. Is it riches that he wants? How much anxiety, envy, and pestering might he not bring in this way on his own head! Is it knowledge and insight? This might perhaps merely give him an eye so sharp that it would make evils at present hidden from him and yet unavoidable seem all the more frightful, or

would add a load of still further needs to the desires which already
47 give him trouble enough. Is it long life? Who will guarantee that
it would not be a long misery? Is it at least health? How often
has infirmity of body kept a man from excesses into which perfect
health would have let him fall!—and so on. In short, he has no
principle by which he is able to decide with complete certainty
what will make him truly happy, since for this he would require
omniscience. Thus we cannot act on determinate principles in
order to be happy, but only on empirical counsels, for example,
of diet, frugality, politeness, reserve, and so on—things which
experience shows contribute most to well-being on the average.
From this it follows that imperatives of prudence, speaking strictly,
do not command at all—that is, cannot exhibit actions objectively
as practically *necessary*; that they are rather to be taken as recom-
mendations (*consilia*), than as commands (*praecepta*), of reason; that
the problem of determining certainly and universally what action
will promote the happiness of a rational being is completely
insoluble; and consequently that in regard to this there is no imperative possible which in the strictest sense could command us to do
what will make us happy, since happiness is an Ideal, not of reason,
but of imagination—an Ideal resting merely on empirical grounds,
419 of which it is vain to expect that they should determine an action
48 by which we could attain the totality of a series of consequences
which is in fact infinite. Nevertheless, if we assume that the means
to happiness could be discovered with certainty, this imperative
of prudence would be an analytic practical proposition; for it
differs from the imperative of skill only in this—that in the latter
the end is merely possible, while in the former the end is given.
In spite of this difference, since both command solely the means
to something assumed to be willed as an end, the imperative which
commands him who wills the end to will the means is in both
cases analytic. Thus there is likewise no difficulty in regard to the
possibility of an imperative of prudence.

   As against this, the question 'How is the imperative of *morality*
possible?' is the only one in need of a solution; for it is in no way
hypothetical, and consequently we cannot base the objective
necessity which it affirms on any presupposition, as we can with
hypothetical imperatives. Only we must never forget here that it
is impossible to settle *by an example*, and so empirically, whether

there is any imperative of this kind at all: we must rather suspect that all imperatives which seem to be categorical may none the less be covertly hypothetical. Take, for example, the saying 'Thou shalt make no false promises'. Let us assume that the necessity for this abstention is no mere advice for the avoidance of some further 49 evil—as it might be said 'You ought not to make a lying promise lest, when this comes to light, you destroy your credit'. Let us hold, on the contrary, that an action of this kind must be considered as bad in itself, and that the imperative of prohibition is therefore categorical. Even so, we cannot with any certainty show by an example that the will is determined here solely by the law without any further motive, although it may appear to be so; for it is always possible that fear of disgrace, perhaps also hidden dread of other risks, may unconsciously influence the will. Who can prove by experience that a cause is not present? Experience shows only that it is not perceived. In such a case, however, the so-called moral imperative, which as such appears to be categorical and unconditioned, would in fact be only a pragmatic prescription calling attention to our advantage and merely bidding us take this into account.

We shall thus have to investigate the possibility of a *categorical* imperative entirely *a priori*, since here we do not enjoy the advantage 420 of having its reality given in experience and so of being obliged merely to explain, and not to establish, its possibility.[1] So much, however, can be seen provisionally—that the categorical imperative alone purports to be a practical **law,** while all the rest may be 50 called *principles* of the will but not laws; for an action necessary merely in order to achieve an arbitrary purpose can be considered as in itself contingent, and we can always escape from the precept if we abandon the purpose; whereas an unconditioned command does not leave it open to the will to do the opposite at its discretion and therefore alone carries with it that necessity which we demand from a law.

In the second place, with this categorical imperative or law of morality the reason for our difficulty (in comprehending its possibility) is a very serious one. We have here a synthetic *a priori* practical proposition;* and since in theoretical knowledge there is

*Without presupposing a condition taken from some inclination I connect an 50 action with the will *a priori* and therefore necessarily (although only objectively so —that is, only subject to the Idea of a reason having full power over all subjective

so much difficulty in comprehending the possibility of propositions of this kind, it may readily be gathered that in practical knowledge the difficulty will be no less.

### [*The Formula of Universal Law.*]

51     In this task we wish first to enquire whether perhaps the mere concept of a categorical imperative may not also provide us with the formula containing the only proposition that can be a categorical imperative; for even when we know the purport of such an absolute command, the question of its possibility will still require a special and troublesome effort, which we postpone to the final chapter.

When I conceive a *hypothetical* imperative in general, I do not know beforehand what it will contain—until its condition is given. But if I conceive a *categorical* imperative, I know at once what it contains. For since besides the law this imperative contains only
421 the necessity that our maxim* should conform[1] to this law, while the law, as we have seen, contains no condition to limit it, there remains nothing over to which the maxim has to conform except
52 the universality of a law as such; and it is this conformity alone that the imperative properly asserts to be necessary.

There is therefore only a single categorical imperative and it is this: '*Act only on that maxim through*[1] *which you can at the same time will that it should become a universal law*'.

Now if all imperatives of duty can be derived from this one imperative as their principle, then even although we leave it unsettled whether what we call duty may not be an empty concept, we shall still be able to show at least what we understand by it and what the concept means.

impulses to action). Here we have a practical proposition in which the willing of an action is not derived analytically from some other willing already presupposed[1] (for we do not possess any such perfect will[2]), but is on the contrary connected immediately[3] with the concept of the will of a rational being as something which is not contained in this concept.

51     *A *maxim* is a subjective principle of action and must be distinguished from an *objective principle*—namely, a practical law. The former contains a practical rule determined by reason in accordance with the conditions of the subject (often his ignorance or again his inclinations): it is thus a principle on which the subject *acts*. A law, on the other hand, is an objective principle valid for every rational being; and it is a principle on which he *ought to act*—that is, an imperative.[1]

## [*The Formula of the Law of Nature.*]

Since the universality of the law governing the production of effects constitutes what is properly called *nature* in its most general sense (nature as regards its form)² —that is, the existence of things so far as determined by universal laws—the universal imperative of duty may also run as follows: '*Act as if the maxim of your action were to become through your will a* UNIVERSAL LAW OF NATURE.'

## [*Illustrations.*]

We will now enumerate a few duties, following their customary division into duties towards self and duties towards others and into 53 perfect and imperfect duties.*

1. A man feels sick of life as the result of a series of misfortunes that has mounted to the point of despair, but he is still so far in 422 possession of his reason as to ask himself whether taking his own life may not be contrary to his duty to himself. He now applies the test 'Can the maxim of my action really become a universal law of nature?' His maxim is 'From self-love I make it my principle to shorten my life if its continuance threatens more evil than it promises pleasure'. The only further question to ask is whether this principle of self-love can become a universal law of nature. It is then seen at once that a system of nature by whose law the very same feeling whose function (*Bestimmung*) is to stimulate the 54 furtherance of life should actually destroy life would contradict itself and consequently could not subsist as a system of nature.¹ Hence this maxim cannot possibly hold as a universal law of nature and is therefore entirely opposed to the supreme principle of all duty.

2. Another finds himself driven to borrowing money because of need. He well knows that he will not be able to pay it back; but he sees too that he will get no loan unless he gives a firm promise to pay it back within a fixed time. He is inclined to make such a promise; but he has still enough conscience to ask 'Is it not

*It should be noted that I reserve my division of duties entirely for a future 53 *Metaphysic of Morals* and that my present division is therefore put forward as arbitrary (merely for the purpose of arranging my examples). Further, I understand here by a perfect duty one which allows no exception in the interests of inclination,¹ and so I recognize among *perfect duties*, not only outer ones, but also inner.² This is contrary to the accepted usage of the schools, but I do not intend to justify it here, since for my purpose it is all one whether this point is conceded or not.

unlawful and contrary to duty to get out of difficulties in this way?' Supposing, however, he did resolve to do so, the maxim of his action would run thus: 'Whenever I believe myself short of money, I will borrow money and promise to pay it back, though I know that this will never be done'. Now this principle of self-love or personal advantage is perhaps quite compatible with my own entire future welfare; only there remains the question 'Is it right?' I therefore transform the demand of self-love into a universal law and frame my question thus: 'How would things stand if my maxim became a universal law?' I then see straight away that this maxim can never rank as a universal law and be
55 self-consistent, but must necessarily contradict itself. For the universality of a law that every one believing himself to be in need may make any promise he pleases with the intention not to keep it would make promising, and the very purpose of promising, itself impossible, since no one would believe he was being promised anything, but would laugh at utterances of this kind as empty shams.

3. A third finds in himself a talent whose cultivation would
423 make him a useful man for all sorts of purposes. But he sees himself in comfortable circumstances, and he prefers to give himself up to pleasure rather than to bother about increasing and improving his fortunate natural aptitudes. Yet he asks himself further 'Does my maxim of neglecting my natural gifts, besides agreeing in itself with my tendency to indulgence, agree also with what is called duty?' He then sees that a system of nature could indeed always subsist under such a universal law, although (like the South Sea Islanders) every man should let his talents rust and should be bent on devoting his life solely to idleness, indulgence, procreation, and, in a word, to enjoyment. Only he cannot possibly **will** that this should become a universal law of nature or should be
56 implanted in us as such a law by a natural instinct. For as a rational being he necessarily wills that all his powers should be developed, since they serve him, and are given him, for all sorts of possible ends.

4. Yet a *fourth* is himself flourishing, but he sees others who have to struggle with great hardships (and whom he could easily help); and he thinks 'What does it matter to me? Let every one be as happy as Heaven wills or as he can make himself; I won't deprive

him of anything; I won't even envy him; only I have no wish to contribute anything to his well-being or to his support in distress !' Now admittedly if such an attitude were a universal law of nature, mankind could get on perfectly well—better no doubt than if everybody prates about sympathy and good will, and even takes pains, on occasion, to practise them, but on the other hand cheats where he can, traffics in human rights, or violates them in other ways. But although it is possible that a universal law of nature could subsist in harmony with this maxim, yet it is impossible to **will** that such a principle should hold everywhere as a law of nature. For a will which decided in this way would be at variance with itself, since many a situation might arise in which the man needed love and sympathy from others,[1] and in which, by such a law of nature sprung from his own will, he would rob himself of all hope of the help he wants for himself.                        57

### [*The canon of moral judgement.*]

These are some of the many actual duties—or at least of what we take to be such—whose derivation from the single principle cited above leaps to the eye. We must *be able to will* that a maxim 424 of our action should become a universal law—this is the general canon for all moral judgement of action. Some actions are so constituted that their maxim cannot even be *conceived* as a universal law of nature without contradiction, let alone be *willed* as what *ought* to become one. In the case of others we do not find this inner impossibility, but it is still impossible to *will* that their maxim should be raised to the universality of a law of nature, because such a will would contradict itself. It is easily seen that the first kind of action is opposed to strict or narrow (rigorous) duty, the second only to wider (meritorious) duty;[1] and thus that by these examples all duties—so far as the type of obligation is concerned (not the object of dutiful action)[2]—are fully set out in their dependence on our single principle.

If we now attend to ourselves whenever we transgress a duty, we find that we in fact do not will that our maxim should become 58 a universal law—since this is impossible for us—but rather that its opposite should remain a law universally: we only take the liberty of making an *exception* to it for ourselves (or even just for this once) to the advantage of our inclination. Consequently if we weighed it all up from one and the same point of view—that of reason—we should find a contradiction in our own will, the contradiction that a certain principle should be objectively necessary as a universal law and yet subjectively should not hold universally but should admit of exceptions. Since, however, we first consider our action from the point of view of a will wholly in accord with reason, and then consider precisely the same action from the point of view of a will affected by inclination, there is here actually no contradiction, but rather an opposition of inclination to the precept of reason (*antagonismus*), whereby the universality of the principle (*universalitas*) is turned into a mere generality (*generalitas*) so that the practical principle of reason may meet our maxim half-way. This procedure, though in our own impartial judgement it cannot be justified, proves none the less that we in fact recognize the validity of the categorical imperative and (with all respect for it) merely

59 permit ourselves a few exceptions which are, as we pretend, inconsiderable and apparently forced upon us.

425    We have thus at least shown this much—that if duty is a concept which is to have meaning and real legislative authority for our actions, this can be expressed only in categorical imperatives and by no means in hypothetical ones. At the same time—and this is already a great deal—we have set forth distinctly, and determinately for every type of application, the content of the categorical imperative, which must contain the principle of all duty (if there is to be such a thing at all). But we are still not so far advanced as to prove *a priori* that there actually is an imperative of this kind—that there is a practical law which by itself commands absolutely and without any further motives, and that the following of this law is duty.

### [*The need for pure ethics.*]

For the purpose of achieving this proof it is of the utmost importance to take warning that we should not dream for a moment of trying to derive the reality of this principle from *the special characteristics of human nature*. For duty has to be a practical, unconditioned necessity of action; it must therefore hold for all rational beings (to whom alone an imperative can apply at all), and *only because of this* can it also be a law for all human wills. Whatever, on the other hand, is derived from the special predisposition of humanity, from certain feelings and propensities, 60 and even, if this were possible, from some special bent peculiar to human reason and not holding necessarily for the will of every rational being—all this can indeed supply a personal maxim, but not a law: it can give us a subjective principle—one on which we have a propensity and inclination to act—but not an objective one on which we should be *directed* to act although our every propensity, inclination, and natural bent were opposed to it; so much so that the sublimity and inner worth of the command is the more manifest[1] in a duty, the fewer are the subjective causes for obeying it and the more those against—without, however, on this account weakening in the slightest the necessitation exercised by the law or detracting anything from its validity.

It is here that philosophy is seen in actual fact to be placed in a precarious position, which is supposed to be firm although neither in heaven nor on earth is there anything from which it depends or on which it is based. It is here that she has to show her purity as the authoress of her own laws—not as the mouthpiece of laws whispered to her by some implanted sense or by who knows what tutelary nature, all of which laws together, though they may always be better than nothing, can never furnish 426 us with principles dictated by reason. These principles must have an origin entirely and completely *a priori* and must at the same time derive from this their sovereign authority—that they expect nothing from the inclinations of man, but everything from the 61 supremacy of the law and from the reverence due to it, or in default of this condemn man to self-contempt and inward abhorrence.

Hence everything that is empirical is, as a contribution to the principle of morality,[1] not only wholly unsuitable for the purpose, but is even highly injurious to the purity of morals; for in morals the proper worth of an absolutely good will, a worth elevated above all price, lies precisely in this—that the principle of action is free from all influence by contingent grounds, the only kind that experience can supply. Against the slack, or indeed ignoble, attitude which seeks for the moral principle among empirical motives and laws we cannot give a warning too strongly or too often; for human reason in its weariness is fain to rest upon this pillow and in a dream of sweet illusions (which lead it to embrace a cloud in mistake for Juno)[2] to foist into the place of morality some misbegotten mongrel patched up from limbs of very different ancestry and looking like anything you please, only not like virtue, to him who has once beheld her in her true shape.*

62    Our question therefore is this: 'Is it a necessary law *for all rational beings* always to judge their actions by reference to those maxims of which they can themselves will that they should serve as universal laws?' If there is such a law, it must already be connected (entirely *a priori*) with the concept of the will of a rational being as such.[1] But in order to discover this connexion we must, however much we may bristle, take a step beyond it—that is, into metaphysics, although into a region of it different from that of speculative philosophy, namely, the metaphysic of morals.[2] In

427 practical philosophy we are not concerned with accepting reasons for what *happens*, but with accepting laws of what *ought to happen*, even if it never does happen—that is, objective practical laws. And here we have no need to set up an enquiry as to the reasons why anything pleases or displeases; how the pleasure of mere sensation differs from taste, and whether the latter differs from a universal approval by reason;[3] whereon feelings of pleasure and displeasure are based; how from these feelings there arise desires and inclinations; and how from these in turn, with the co-operation of reason, there arise maxims. All this belongs to empirical

63 psychology, which would constitute the second part of the doctrine of nature, if we take this doctrine to be the *philosophy of nature* so far as grounded on *empirical laws*.[1] Here, however, we are discussing objective practical laws, and consequently the relation of a will to itself as determined solely by reason. Everything related to the empirical then falls away of itself; for if *reason by itself alone* determines conduct (and it is the possibility of this which we now wish to investigate), it must necessarily do so *a priori*.

61    *To behold virtue in her proper shape is nothing other than to show morality stripped of all admixture with the sensuous and of all the spurious adornments
62 of reward or self-love. How much she then casts into the shade all else that appears attractive to the inclinations can be readily perceived by every man if he will exert his reason in the slightest—provided he has not entirely ruined it for all abstractions.

## [*The Formula of the End in Itself.*]

The will is conceived as a power of determining oneself to action *in accordance with the idea of certain laws.* And such a power can be found only in rational beings. Now what serves the will as a subjective[2] ground of its self-determination is an *end*; and this, if it is given by reason alone, must be equally valid for all rational beings. What, on the other hand, contains merely the ground of the possibility of an action whose effect is an end is called a *means*.[3] The subjective ground of a desire is an *impulsion* (*Triebfeder*); the objective ground of a volition is a *motive* (*Bewegungsgrund*). Hence the difference between subjective ends, which are based on impulsions, and objective ends, which depend 64 on motives valid for every rational being. Practical principles are *formal* if they abstract from all subjective ends; they are *material*, on the other hand, if they are based on such ends and consequently on certain impulsions.[1] Ends that a rational being adopts arbitrarily as *effects* of his action (material ends) are in every case only relative; for it is solely their relation to special characteristics in the subject's power of appetition which gives them their value. Hence this value can provide no universal principles, no principles valid and necessary for all rational beings and also for every volition[2]—that is, no practical laws. Consequently all these relative ends can be the 428 ground only of hypothetical imperatives.

Suppose, however, there were something *whose existence* has *in itself* an absolute value, something which as *an end in itself* could be a ground of determinate laws; then in it, and in it alone, would there be the ground of a possible categorical imperative—that is, of a practical law.

Now I say that man, and in general every rational being, *exists* as an end in himself, *not merely as a means* for arbitrary use by this or that will: he must in all his actions, whether they are directed to himself or to other rational beings, always be viewed *at the same time as an end.* All the objects of inclination have only 65 a conditioned value; for if there were not these inclinations and the needs grounded on them,[1] their object would be valueless. Inclinations themselves, as sources of needs, are so far from having an absolute value to make them desirable for their own sake that it must rather be the universal wish of every rational being to be wholly free from them.[2] Thus the value of all objects that can *be produced* by our action is always conditioned. Beings whose existence depends, not on our will, but on nature, have none the less, if they are non-rational beings, only a relative value as means and are consequently called *things*. Rational beings, on the other hand, are called *persons* because their nature already marks them out as ends in themselves—that is, as something which ought not to be used merely as a means—and consequently imposes to that extent a limit on all arbitrary treatment of them (and is an object of reverence). Persons, therefore, are not merely subjective ends whose existence as an effect of our actions has a value *for us*: they are *objective ends*—that is, things whose existence is in itself an end, and indeed an end such that in its place we can put no other end to which they should serve *simply* as means; for unless this is so, nothing at all of *absolute* value would be found anywhere.

66 But if all value were conditioned—that is, contingent—then no supreme principle could be found for reason at all.

If then there is to be a supreme practical principle and—so far as the human will is concerned—a categorical imperative,[1] it must be such that from the idea of something which is necessarily an end for every one because it is an *end in itself* it forms an *objective*

429 principle of the will and consequently can serve as a practical law. The ground of this principle is: *Rational nature exists as an end in itself*. This is the way in which a man necessarily conceives his own existence: it is therefore so far a *subjective* principle of human actions. But it is also the way in which every other rational being conceives his existence on the same rational ground which is valid also for me;* hence it is at the same time an *objective* principle, from which, as a supreme practical ground, it must be possible to derive all laws for the will. The practical imperative will therefore be as follows: *Act in such a way that you always treat humanity*,[2] *whether in your own person or in the person of any other, never simply*[3]

67 *as a means, but always at the same time as an end*. We will now consider whether this can be carried out in practice.

### [*Illustrations.*]

Let us keep to our previous examples.

*First*, as regards the concept of necessary duty to oneself, the

66    *This proposition I put forward here as a postulate. The grounds for it will be found in the final chapter.[1]

man who contemplates suicide will ask 'Can my action be compatible with the Idea of humanity *as an end in itself*?' If he does away with himself in order to escape from a painful situation, he is making use of a person merely as *a means* to maintain a tolerable state of affairs till the end of his life. But man is not a thing—not something to be used *merely* as a means: he must always in all his actions be regarded as an end in himself. Hence I cannot dispose of man in my person by maiming, spoiling, or killing. (A more precise determination of this principle in order to avoid all misunderstanding—for example, about having limbs amputated to save myself or about exposing my life to danger in order to preserve it, and so on—I must here forego: this question belongs to morals proper.)

*Secondly*, so far as necessary or strict duty to others is concerned, the man who has a mind to make a false promise to others will see at once that he is intending to make use of another man *merely as a means* to an end he does not share. For the man whom 68 I seek to use for my own purposes by such a promise cannot possibly agree with my way of behaving to him, and so cannot himself share the end of the action. This incompatibility with the 430 principle of duty to others leaps to the eye more obviously when we bring in examples of attempts on the freedom and property of others. For then it is manifest that a violator of the rights of man intends to use the person of others merely as a means without taking into consideration that, as rational beings, they ought always at the same time to be rated as ends—that is, only as beings who must themselves be able to share in the end of the very same action.*

*Thirdly*, in regard to contingent (meritorious) duty to oneself, it is not enough that an action should refrain from conflicting 69 with humanity in our own person as an end in itself: it must also *harmonize with this end*. Now there are in humanity capacities for greater perfection which form part of nature's purpose for

---

*Let no one think that here the trivial '*quod tibi non vis fieri, etc.*'[1] can serve 68 as a standard or principle. For it is merely derivative from our principle, although subject to various qualifications: it cannot be a universal law[2] since it contains the ground neither of duties to oneself nor of duties of kindness to others (for many a man would readily agree that others should not help him if only he could be dispensed from affording help to them), nor finally of strict duties towards others; for on this basis the criminal would be able to dispute with the judges who punish him, and so on.

G

humanity in our person.[1] To neglect these can admittedly be compatible with the *maintenance* of humanity as an end in itself, but not with the *promotion* of this end.

*Fourthly*, as regards meritorious duties to others, the natural end which all men seek is their own happiness. Now humanity could no doubt subsist if everybody contributed nothing to the happiness of others but at the same time refrained from deliberately impairing their happiness. This is, however, merely to agree negatively and not positively with *humanity as an end in itself* unless every one endeavours also, so far as in him lies, to further the ends of others. For the ends of a subject who is an end in himself must, if this conception is to have its *full* effect in me, be also, as far as possible, *my* ends.

## [*The Formula of Autonomy.*]

This principle of humanity, and in general of every rational agent, *as an end in itself* (a principle which is the supreme limiting condition of every man's freedom of action) is not borrowed from experience; firstly, because it is universal, applying as it does to all rational beings as such, and no experience is adequate to determine universality; secondly, because in it humanity is conceived, not as an end of man (subjectively)—that is, as an object which, as a matter of fact, happens to be made an end—but as an objective end—one which, be our ends what they may, must, as a law, constitute the supreme limiting condition of all subjective ends and so must spring from pure reason. That is to say, the ground for every enactment of practical law lies *objectively in the rule* and in the form of universality which (according to our first principle) makes the rule capable of being a law (and indeed a law of nature); *subjectively*, however, it lies in the *end*; but (according to our second principle) the subject of all ends is to be found in every rational being as an end in himself. From this there now follows our third practical principle for the will—as the supreme condition of the will's conformity with universal practical reason—namely, the Idea *of the will of every rational being as a will which makes universal law.*

By this principle all maxims are repudiated which cannot accord with the will's own enactment of universal law. The will **71** is therefore not merely subject to the law, but is so subject that

431] **70**

it must be considered as also *making the law* for itself and precisely on this account as first of all subject to the law (of which it can regard itself as the author).

### [*The exclusion of interest.*]

Imperatives as formulated above—namely, the imperative enjoining conformity of actions to universal law on the analogy of a *natural order* and that enjoining the universal *supremacy* of rational beings in themselves *as ends*—did, by the mere fact that they were represented as categorical, exclude from their sovereign authority every admixture of interest as a motive. They were, however, merely *assumed* to be categorical because we were bound to make this assumption if we wished to explain the concept of duty. That there were practical propositions which commanded categorically could not itself be proved, any more than it can be proved in this chapter generally; but one thing could have been done—namely, to show that in willing for the sake of duty renunciation of all interest,[1] as the specific mark distinguishing a categorical from a hypothetical imperative, was expressed in the very imperative itself by means of some determination inherent in it. This is what 432 is done in the present third formulation of the principle—namely, in the Idea of the will of every rational being as *a will which makes universal law.*

Once we conceive a will of this kind, it becomes clear that 72 while a will *which is subject to law* may be bound to this law by some interest, nevertheless a will which is itself a supreme law-giver cannot possibly as such depend on any interest; for a will which is dependent in this way would itself require yet a further law in order to restrict the interest of self-love to the condition that this interest should itself be valid as a universal law.[1]

Thus the *principle* that every human will is *a will which by all its maxims enacts universal law**—provided only that it were right in other ways—would be *well suited* to be a categorical imperative in this respect: that precisely because of the Idea of making universal law it is *based on no interest* and consequently can alone among all possible imperatives be *unconditioned*. Or better still—to

*I may be excused from bringing forward examples to illustrate this principle, 72 since those which were first used as illustrations of the categorical imperative and its formula can all serve this purpose here.

convert the proposition—if there is a categorical imperative (that is, a law for the will of every rational being), it can command us only to act always on the maxim of such a will in us as can
73 at the same time look upon itself as making universal law; for only then is the practical principle and the imperative which we obey unconditioned, since it is wholly impossible for it to be based on any interest.

We need not now wonder, when we look back upon all the previous efforts that have been made to discover the principle of morality, why they have one and all been bound to fail. Their authors saw man as tied to laws by his duty, but it never occurred to them that he is subject only to *laws which are made by himself* and yet are *universal*, and that he is bound only to act in accordance with a will which is his own but has for its natural purpose[1] the function of making universal law. For when they thought of man merely as subject to a law (whatever it might be), the law had to
433 carry with it some interest in order to attract or compel, because it did not spring as a law from *his own* will: in order to conform with the law his will had to be necessitated by *something else* to act in a certain way. This absolutely inevitable conclusion meant that all the labour spent in trying to find a supreme principle of duty was lost beyond recall; for what they discovered was never duty, but only the necessity of acting from a certain interest. This interest might be one's own or another's; but on such a view the imperative was bound to be always a conditioned one and
74 could not possibly serve as a moral law. I will therefore call my principle the principle of the **Autonomy** of the will in contrast with all others, which I consequently class under **Heteronomy**.

### [*The Formula of the Kingdom of Ends.*]

The concept of every rational being as one who must regard himself as making universal law by all the maxims of his will, and must seek to judge himself and his actions from this point of view, leads to a closely connected and very fruitful concept— namely, that of *a kingdom of ends*.

I understand by a '*kingdom*' a systematic union of different rational beings under common laws. Now since laws determine ends as regards their universal validity, we shall be able—if we abstract from the personal differences between rational beings, and also from all the content of their private ends—to conceive a whole of all ends in systematic conjunction (a whole both of rational beings as ends in themselves and also of the personal ends[1] which each may set before himself); that is, we shall be able to conceive a kingdom of ends which is possible in accordance with the above principles.

For rational beings all stand under the *law* that each of them should treat himself and all others, *never merely as a means*, but 75 always *at the same time as an end in himself*. But by so doing there arises a systematic union of rational beings under common objective laws—that is, a kingdom. Since these laws are directed precisely to the relation of such beings to one another as ends and means, this kingdom can be called a kingdom of ends (which is admittedly only an Ideal).

A rational being belongs to the kingdom of ends as a *member*, when, although he makes its universal laws, he is also himself subject to these laws. He belongs to it as its *head*, when as the maker of laws he is himself subject to the will of no other.[1]

A rational being must always regard himself as making laws 434 in a kingdom of ends which is possible through freedom of the will—whether it be as member or as head. The position of the latter he can maintain, not in virtue of the maxim of his will alone, but only if he is a completely independent being, without needs and with an unlimited power adequate to his will.

Thus morality consists in the relation of all action to the making of laws whereby alone a kingdom of ends is possible. This making of laws must be found in every rational being himself and must 76 be able to spring from his will. The principle of his will is therefore never to perform an action except on a maxim such as can also be a universal law, and consequently such *that the will can regard itself as at the same time making universal law by means of its maxim*. Where maxims are not already by their very nature in harmony with this objective principle of rational beings as makers of universal law, the necessity of acting on this principle is practical necessitation—that is, *duty*. Duty does not apply to the head in a kingdom of ends, but it does apply to every member and to all members in equal measure.

The practical necessity of acting on this principle—that is, duty

—is in no way based on feelings, impulses, and inclinations, but
only on the relation of rational beings to one another, a relation
in which the will of a rational being must always be regarded as
*making universal law*, because otherwise he could not be conceived
as *an end in himself*. Reason thus relates every maxim of the will,
considered as making universal law, to every other will and also
to every action towards oneself: it does so, not because of any
further motive or future advantage, but from the Idea of the
77 *dignity* of a rational being who obeys no law other than that which
he at the same time enacts himself.

## [*The dignity of virtue.*]

In the kingdom of ends everything has either a *price* or a
*dignity*. If it has a price, something else can be put in its place as
an *equivalent*; if it is exalted above all price and so admits of no
equivalent, then it has a dignity.

What is relative to universal human inclinations and needs has
a *market price*; what, even without presupposing a need, accords
with a certain taste—that is, with satisfaction in the mere purpose-
435 less play of our mental powers[1]—has a *fancy price* (*Affektionspreis*);
but that which constitutes the sole condition under which anything
can be an end in itself has not merely a relative value—that is, a
price—but has an intrinsic value—that is, *dignity*.

Now morality is the only condition under which a rational
being can be an end in himself; for only through this is it possible
to be a law-making member in a kingdom of ends. Therefore
morality, and humanity so far as it is capable of morality, is the
only thing which has dignity. Skill and diligence in work have a
78 market price; wit, lively imagination, and humour have a fancy
price; but fidelity to promises and kindness based on principle
(not on instinct) have an intrinsic worth. In default of these, nature
and art alike contain nothing to put in their place;[1] for their worth
consists, not in the effects which result from them, not in the
advantage or profit they produce, but in the attitudes of mind—
that is, in the maxims of the will—which are ready in this way
to manifest themselves in action even if they are not favoured by
success. Such actions too need no recommendation from any
subjective disposition or taste in order to meet with immediate

favour and approval; they need no immediate propensity or feeling for themselves; they exhibit the will which performs them as an object of immediate reverence; nor is anything other than reason required to *impose* them upon the will, not to *coax* them from the will—which last would anyhow be a contradiction in the case of duties. This assessment reveals as dignity the value of such a mental attitude and puts it infinitely above all price, with which it cannot be brought into reckoning or comparison without, as it were, a profanation of its sanctity.

What is it then that entitles a morally good attitude of mind—or virtue—to make claims so high? It is nothing less than the *share* 79 which it affords to a rational being *in the making of universal law*, and which therefore fits him to be a member in a possible kingdom of ends. For this he was already marked out in virtue of his own proper nature as an end in himself and consequently as a maker of laws in the kingdom of ends—as free in respect of all laws of nature, obeying only those laws which he makes himself and in virtue of which his maxims can have their part in the making of universal law (to which he at the same time subjects himself). 436 For nothing can have a value other than that determined for it by the law. But the law-making which determines all value must for this reason have a dignity—that is, an unconditioned and incomparable worth—for the appreciation of which, as necessarily given by a rational being, the word 'reverence' is the only becoming expression. *Autonomy* is therefore the ground of the dignity of human nature and of every rational nature.

### [Review of the Formulae.]

The aforesaid three ways of representing the principle of morality are at bottom merely so many formulations of precisely the same law, one of them by itself containing a combination of the other two. There is nevertheless a difference between them, which, however, is subjectively rather than objectively practical: that is to say, its purpose is to bring an Idea of reason nearer to intuition (in accordance with a certain analogy) and so nearer to feeling. 80 All maxims have, in short,

1. a *form*, which consists in their universality; and in this respect the formula of the moral imperative is expressed thus:

'Maxims must be chosen as if they had to hold as universal laws of nature';

2. a *matter*—that is, an end; and in this respect the formula says: 'A rational being, as by his very nature an end and consequently an end in himself, must serve for every maxim as a condition limiting all merely relative and arbitrary ends';

3. a *complete determination*[1] of all maxims by the following formula, namely: 'All maxims as proceeding from our own making of law ought to harmonize with a possible kingdom of ends as a kingdom of nature'.* This progression may be said to take place through the categories of the *unity* of the form of will (its universality); of the *multiplicity* of its matter (its objects—that is, its ends); and of the *totality* or completeness of its system of ends.[2] It is, however, better if in moral *judgement* we proceed always in

81 accordance with the strictest method and take as our basis the universal formula of the categorical imperative: '*Act on the maxim*

437 *which can at the same time be made a universal law*'. If, however, we wish also to secure acceptance for the moral law, it is very useful to bring one and the same action under the above-mentioned three concepts and so, as far as we can, to bring the universal formula[1] nearer to intuition.

### [Review of the whole argument.]

We can now end at the point from which we started out at the beginning—namely, the concept of an unconditionally good will. The *will* is *absolutely good* if it cannot be evil—that is, if its maxim, when made into a universal law, can never be at variance with itself. This principle is therefore also its supreme law: 'Act always on that maxim whose universality as a law you can at the same time will'. This is the one principle on which a will can never be at variance with itself, and such an imperative is categorical. Because the validity of the will as a universal law for possible actions is analogous to the universal interconnexion of existent things in accordance with universal laws—which con-

80   *Teleology views nature as a kingdom of ends; ethics views a possible kingdom of ends as a kingdom of nature. In the first case the kingdom of ends is a theoretical Idea used to explain what exists. In the second case it is a practical Idea used to bring into existence what does not exist but can be made actual by our conduct—and indeed to bring it into existence in conformity with this Idea.

stitutes the formal aspect of nature as such²—we can also express the categorical imperative as follows: '*Act on that maxim which can at the same time have for its object³ itself as a universal law of nature*'. In this way we provide the formula for an absolutely good 82 will.

Rational nature separates itself out from all other things by the fact that it sets itself an end. An end would thus be the matter of every good will. But in the Idea of a will which is absolutely good—good without any qualifying condition (namely, that it should attain this or that end)—there must be complete abstraction from every end that has to be *produced* (as something which would make every will only relatively good). Hence the end must here be conceived, not as an end to be produced, *but as a self-existent end*. It must therefore be conceived only negatively¹—that is, as an end against which we should never act, and consequently as one which in all our willing we must never rate *merely* as a means, but always at the same time as an end. Now this end can be nothing other than the subject of all possible ends himself, because this subject is also the subject of a will that may be absolutely good; for such a will cannot without contradiction be subordinated to any other object. The principle 'So act in relation to every rational being (both to yourself and to others) that he may at the same time count in your maxim as an end in himself' is thus at bottom the same as the principle 'Act on a maxim which at the same time contains in itself its own universal validity for every rational being'. 438 For to say that in using means to every end I ought to restrict my maxim by the condition that it should also be universally 83 valid as a law for every subject is just the same as to say this— that a subject of ends, namely, a rational being himself, must be made the ground for all maxims of action, never *merely* as a means, but as a supreme condition restricting the use of every means— that is, always also as an end.

Now from this it unquestionably follows that every rational being, as an end in himself, must be able to regard himself as also the maker of universal law in respect of any law whatever to which he may be subjected; for it is precisely the fitness of his maxims to make universal law that marks him out as an end in himself. It follows equally that this dignity (or prerogative) of his above all the mere things of nature carries with it the necessity

of always choosing his maxims from the point of view of himself—and also of every other rational being—as a maker of law (and
this is why they are called persons). It is in this way that a world
of rational beings (*mundus intelligibilis*) is possible as a kingdom
of ends—possible, that is, through the making of their own laws
by all persons as its members. Accordingly every rational being
must so act as if he were through his maxims always a law-making
member in the universal kingdom of ends. The formal principle
84 of such maxims is 'So act as if your maxims had to serve at the
same time as a universal law (for all rational beings)'. Thus a
kingdom of ends is possible only on the analogy of a kingdom
of nature; yet the kingdom of ends is possible only through maxims
—that is, self-imposed rules—while nature is possible only through
laws concerned with causes whose action is necessitated from
without. In spite of this difference, we give to nature as a whole,
even although it is regarded as a machine, the name of a 'kingdom
of nature' so far as—and for the reason that—it stands in a relation
to rational beings as its ends.[1] Now a kingdom of ends would
actually come into existence through maxims which the categorical
imperative prescribes as a rule for all rational beings, *if these maxims
were universally followed*. Yet even if a rational being were himself
to follow such a maxim strictly, he cannot count on everybody
else being faithful to it on this ground, nor can he be confident
that the kingdom of nature and its purposive order will work
in harmony with him, as a fitting member, towards a kingdom of
ends made possible by himself—or, in other words, that it will
439 favour his expectation of happiness.[2] But in spite of this the law
'Act on the maxims of a member who makes universal laws for
a merely possible kingdom of ends' remains in full force, since its
command is categorical. And precisely here we encounter the
85 paradox that without any further end or advantage to be attained
the mere dignity of humanity, that is, of rational nature in man—
and consequently that reverence for a mere Idea—should function
as an inflexible precept for the will; and that it is just this freedom
from dependence on interested motives which constitutes the
sublimity of a maxim and the worthiness of every rational subject
to be a law-making member in the kingdom of ends; for otherwise he would have to be regarded as subject only to the law
of nature—the law of his own needs. Even if it were thought

that both the kingdom of nature and the kingdom of ends were united under one head and that thus the latter kingdom ceased to be a mere Idea and achieved genuine reality, the Idea would indeed gain by this the addition of a strong motive, but never any increase in its intrinsic worth; for, even if this were so, it would still be necessary to conceive the unique and absolute law-giver himself as judging the worth of rational beings solely by the disinterested behaviour they prescribed to themselves in virtue of this Idea alone. The essence of things does not vary with their external relations; and where there is something which, without regard to such relations, constitutes by itself the absolute worth of man, it is by this that man must also be judged by everyone what-soever—even by the Supreme Being. Thus *morality* lies in the relation of actions to the autonomy of the will—that is, to a possible making of universal law by means of its maxims. An 86 action which is compatible with the autonomy of the will is *permitted*; one which does not harmonize with it is *forbidden*. A will whose maxims necessarily accord with the laws of autonomy is a *holy*, or absolutely good, will. The dependence of a will not absolutely good on the principle of autonomy (that is, moral necessitation) is *obligation*. Obligation can thus have no reference to a holy being. The objective necessity to act from obligation is called *duty*.

From what was said a little time ago we can now easily explain how it comes about that, although in the concept of duty we think of subjection to the law, yet we also at the same time attribute to the person who fulfils all his duties a certain sublimity and 440 *dignity*. For it is not in so far as he is *subject* to the law that he has sublimity, but rather in so far as, in regard to this very same law, he is at the same time its *author* and is subordinated to it only on this ground. We have also shown above[1] how neither fear nor inclination, but solely reverence for the law, is the motive which can give an action moral worth. Our own will, provided it were to act only under the condition of being able to make universal 87 law by means of its maxims—this ideal will which can be ours is the proper object of reverence; and the dignity of man consists precisely in his capacity to make universal law, although only on condition of being himself also subject to the law he makes.

## Autonomy of the Will
### *as the supreme principle of morality.*

Autonomy of the will is the property the will has of being a law to itself (independently of every property belonging to the objects of volition). Hence the principle of autonomy is 'Never to choose except in such a way that in the same volition the maxims of your choice are also present as universal law'. That this practical rule is an imperative—that is, that the will of every rational being is necessarily bound to the rule as a condition—cannot be proved by mere analysis of the concepts contained in it, since it is a synthetic proposition. For proof we should have to go beyond knowledge of objects and pass to a critique of the subject—that is, of pure practical reason—since this synthetic proposition, as commanding apodeictically, must be capable of being known entirely *a priori*. 88 This task does not belong to the present chapter. None the less by mere analysis[1] of the concepts of morality we can quite well show that the above principle of autonomy is the sole principle of ethics. For analysis finds that the principle of morality must be a categorical imperative, and that this in turn commands nothing more nor less than precisely this autonomy.

441

## Heteronomy of the Will
### *as the source of all spurious principles of morality.*

If the will seeks the law that is to determine it *anywhere else* than in the fitness of its maxims for its own making of universal law—if therefore in going beyond itself it seeks this law in the character of any of its objects—the result is always *heteronomy*. In that case the will does not give itself the law, but the object does so in virtue of its relation to the will. This relation, whether based on inclination or on rational ideas, can give rise only to hypothetical imperatives: 'I ought to do something *because I will something else*'. As against this, the moral, and therefore categorical, imperative, says: 'I ought to will thus or thus, although I have 89 not willed something else'. For example, the first says: 'I ought not to lie if I want to maintain my reputation'; while the second says: 'I ought not to lie even if so doing were to bring me not the slightest disgrace'. The second imperative must therefore abstract from all objects to this extent—they should be without any *influence*[1] at all on the will so that practical reason (the will) may not merely administer an alien interest but may simply manifest its own sovereign authority as the supreme maker of law. Thus, for example, the reason[2] why I ought to promote the happiness of others is not because the realization of their happiness is of consequence to myself (whether on account of immediate inclination or on account of some satisfaction gained indirectly through reason), but solely because a maxim which excludes this cannot also be present in one and the same volition as a universal law.

## CLASSIFICATION

*of all possible principles of morality based on the assumption of heteronomy as their fundamental concept.*

Here, as everywhere else, human reason in its pure use—so long as it lacks a critique—pursues every possible wrong way before it succeeds in finding the only right one.

All the principles that can be adopted from this point of view are either *empirical* or *rational*. The **first** kind, drawn from the 90 principle of *happiness*, are based either on natural, or on moral, 442 feeling. The **second** kind, drawn from the principle of *perfection*, are based either on the rational concept of perfection as a possible effect of our will or else on the concept of a self-existent perfection (God's will) as a determining cause of our will.

## [*Empirical principles of heteronomy.*]

*Empirical principles* are always unfitted to serve as a ground for moral laws. The universality with which these laws should hold for all rational beings without exception—the unconditioned practical necessity which they thus impose—falls away if their basis is taken from the *special constitution of human nature* or from the accidental circumstances in which it is placed. The principle of *personal happiness* is, however, the most objectionable, not merely because it is false and because its pretence that well-being always adjusts itself to well-doing is contradicted by experience; nor merely because it contributes nothing whatever towards establishing morality, since making a man happy is quite different

from making him good and making him prudent or astute in seeking his advantage quite different from making him virtuous; but
because it bases morality on sensuous motives which rather undermine it and totally destroy its sublimity, inasmuch as the motives
91 of virtue are put in the same class as those of vice and we are
instructed only to become better at calculation, the specific difference between virtue and vice being completely wiped out. On
the other hand, moral feeling, this alleged special sense* (however
shallow be the appeal to it when men who are unable to *think*
hope to help themselves out by *feeling*, even when the question
is solely one of universal law, and however little feelings, differing
as they naturally do from one another by an infinity of degrees,
can supply a uniform measure of good and evil—let alone that
one man by his feeling can make no valid judgements at all for
others)—moral feeling still remains closer to morality and to its
dignity in this respect: it does virtue the honour of ascribing to
443 her *immediately* the approval and esteem in which she is held, and
does not, as it were, tell her to her face that we are attached to
her, not for her beauty, but only for our own advantage.

### [*Rational principles of heteronomy.*]

Among the *rational* bases of morality—those springing from
92 reason—the ontological concept of *perfection*[1] (however empty,
however indefinite it is, and consequently useless for discovering
in the boundless field of possible reality the maximum reality
appropriate to us; and however much, in trying to distinguish
specifically between the reality here in question and every other,
it shows an inevitable tendency to go round in a circle and is
unable to avoid covertly presupposing the morality it has to explain)
—this concept none the less is better than the theological concept
which derives morality from a divine and supremely perfect will[2];
not merely because we cannot intuit God's perfection and can only
derive it from our own concepts, among which that of morality
is the most eminent; but because, if we do not do this (and to

---

91    *I class the principle of moral feeling with that of happiness because every
empirical principle promises a contribution to our well-being merely from the
satisfaction afforded by something—whether this satisfaction is given immediately
and without any consideration of advantage or is given in respect of such advantage.
Similarly we must with *Hutcheson*[1] class the principle of sympathy for the happiness
of others along with the principle of moral sense as adopted by him.

do so would be to give a crudely circular explanation), the concept of God's will still remaining to us—one drawn from such characteristics as lust for glory and domination and bound up with frightful ideas of power and vengefulness—would inevitably form the basis for a moral system which would be in direct opposition to morality.

Yet if I had to choose between the concept of moral sense and that of perfection in general[3] (both of which at least do not undermine morality, though they are totally incompetent to support it as its foundation), I should decide for the latter; for this, since it 93 at least withdraws the settlement of this question from sensibility and brings it before the court of pure reason, even although it there gets no decision, does still preserve unfalsified for more precise determination the indeterminate Idea (of a will good in itself).

### [The failure of heteronomy.]

For the rest I believe I may be excused from a lengthy refutation of all these systems. This is so easy and is presumably so well understood even by those whose office requires them to declare themselves for one or other of these theories (since their audience will not lightly put up with a suspension of judgement) that to spend time on it would be merely superfluous labour. But what is of more interest to us here is to know that these principles never lay down anything but heteronomy as the first basis of morality and must in consequence necessarily fail in their object.

Wherever an object of the will has to be put down as the basis 444 for prescribing a rule to determine the will, there the rule is heteronomy; the imperative is conditioned, as follows: 'If, or because, you will this object, you ought to act thus or thus'; consequently it can never give a moral—that is, a categorical—command. However the object determines the will—whether by means of inclination, as in the principle of personal happiness, or by 94 means of reason directed to objects of our possible volitions generally, as in the principle of perfection—the will never determines itself immediately by the thought of an action, but only by the impulsion which the anticipated effect of the action exercises on the will: 'I ought to do something because I will something else'.

And the basis for this must be yet a further law in me as a subject, whereby I necessarily will this 'something else'—which law in turn requires an imperative to impose limits on this maxim.¹ The impulsion supposed to be exercised on the will of the subject, in accordance with his natural constitution, by the idea of a result to be attained by his own powers belongs to the nature of the subject—whether to his sensibility (his inclinations and taste) or to his understanding and reason, whose operation on an object is accompanied by satisfaction in virtue of the special equipment of their nature—and consequently, speaking strictly, it is nature which would make the law. This law, as a law of nature, not only must be known and proved by experience and therefore is in itself contingent and consequently unfitted to serve as an apodeictic rule of action such as a moral rule must be, but it is *always merely heteronomy of the will*: the will does not give itself the law, but an 95 alien impulsion does so through the medium of the subject's own nature as tuned for its reception.

[*The position of the argument.*]

An absolutely good will, whose principle must be a categorical imperative, will therefore, being undetermined in respect of all objects, contain only the *form* of *willing*, and that as autonomy. In other words, the fitness of the maxim of every good will to make itself a universal law is itself the sole law which the will of every rational being spontaneously imposes on itself without basing it on any impulsion or interest.

*How such a synthetic* a priori *proposition is possible* and why it is necessary—this is a problem whose solution lies no longer within 445 the bounds of a metaphysic of morals; nor have we here asserted the truth of this proposition, much less pretended to have a proof of it in our power. We have merely shown by developing the concept of morality generally in vogue that autonomy of the will is unavoidably bound up with it or rather is its very basis. Any one therefore who takes morality to be something, and not merely a chimerical Idea without truth, must at the same time admit the 96 principle we have put forward. This chapter, consequently, like the first, has been merely analytic. In order to prove that morality is no mere phantom of the brain—a conclusion which follows if the categorical imperative, and with it the autonomy of the will, is true and is absolutely necessary as an *a priori* principle—we require a *possible synthetic use of pure practical reason*.[1] On such a use we cannot venture without prefacing it by a *critique* of this power of reason itself—a critique whose main features, so far as is sufficient for our purpose, we must outline in our final chapter.

# PASSAGE FROM A METAPHYSIC
# OF MORALS TO A
# CRITIQUE OF PURE PRACTICAL REASON

### The Concept of Freedom
### is the Key to Explain Autonomy of the Will

WILL is a kind of causality belonging to living beings so far as they are rational. *Freedom* would then be the property this causality has of being able to work independently of *determination* by alien causes; just as *natural necessity* is a property characterizing the causality of all non-rational beings—the property of being determined to activity by the influence of alien causes.

The above definition of freedom is *negative* and consequently unfruitful as a way of grasping its essence; but there springs from it a *positive* concept, which, as positive, is richer and more fruitful. The concept of causality carries with it that of *laws* (*Gesetze*) in accordance with which, because of something we call a cause, 98 something else—namely, its effect—must be posited (*gesetzt*). Hence freedom of will, although it is not the property of conforming to laws of nature, is not for this reason lawless: it must rather be a causality conforming to immutable laws, though of a special kind; for otherwise a free will would be self-contradictory. Natural necessity, as we have seen, is a heteronomy of efficient causes; for every effect is possible only in conformity with the law that something else determines the efficient cause to causal 447 action. What else then can freedom of will be but autonomy— that is, the property which will has of being a law to itself? The proposition 'Will is in all its actions a law to itself' expresses, however, only the principle of acting on no maxim other than one which can have for its object[1] itself as at the same time a universal law. This is precisely the formula of the categorical imperative and the principle of morality. Thus a free will and a will under moral laws are one and the same.[2]

Consequently if freedom of the will is presupposed, morality, together with its principle, follows by mere analysis of the concept of freedom. Nevertheless the principle of morality is still a synthetic proposition, namely: 'An absolutely good will is one whose maxim can always have as its content itself considered as a universal law'; for we cannot discover this characteristic of its maxim by analysing 99 the concept of an absolutely good will. Such synthetic propositions are possible only because two cognitions[1] are bound to one another by their connexion with a third term in which both of them are to be found. The *positive* concept of freedom furnishes this third term, which cannot, as in the case of physical causes, be the nature of the sensible world (in the concept of which there come together the concepts of something as cause and of *something else* as effect in their relation to one another). What this third term is to which freedom directs us and of which we have an Idea *a priori*, we are not yet in a position to show here straight away,[2] nor can we as yet make intelligible the deduction of the concept of freedom from pure practical reason and so the possibility of a categorical imperative: we require some further preparation.

## FREEDOM MUST BE PRESUPPOSED AS A PROPERTY OF THE WILL OF ALL RATIONAL BEINGS

It is not enough to ascribe freedom to our will, on whatever ground, unless we have sufficient reason for attributing the same freedom to all rational beings as well. For since morality is a law 100 for us only as *rational beings*, it must be equally valid for all rational beings; and since it must be derived solely from the property of freedom, we have got to prove that freedom too is a property of the will of all rational beings. It is not enough to demonstrate freedom from certain alleged experiences of human nature (though to do this is in any case absolutely impossible and freedom can be 448 demonstrated only *a priori*)[1]: we must prove that it belongs universally to the activity of rational beings endowed with a will. Now I assert that every being who cannot act except *under the Idea of freedom* is by this alone—from a practical point of view—really free; that is to say, for him all the laws inseparably bound up with freedom are valid just as much as if his will could be pronounced free in itself on grounds valid for theoretical

philosophy.* And I maintain that to every rational being possessed
101 of a will we must also lend the Idea of freedom as the only one
under which he can act. For in such a being we conceive a reason
which is practical—that is, which exercises causality in regard to
its objects. But we cannot possibly conceive of a reason as being
consciously directed from outside in regard to its judgements[1];
for in that case the subject would attribute the determination of his
power of judgement, not to his reason, but to an impulsion.
Reason must look upon itself as the author of its own principles
independently of alien influences. Therefore as practical reason,[2]
or as the will of a rational being, it must be regarded by itself
as free; that is, the will of a rational being can be a will of his
own only under the Idea of freedom, and such a will must therefore—from a practical point of view—be attributed to all rational
beings.

### The Interest Attached to the Ideas of Morality
#### [Moral interest and the vicious circle.]

We have at last traced the determinate concept of morality
back to the Idea of freedom, but we have been quite unable to
demonstrate freedom as something actual in ourselves and in human
449 nature: we saw merely that we must presuppose it if we wish to
102 conceive a being as rational and as endowed with consciousness
of his causality in regard to actions—that is, as endowed with a
will. Thus we find that on precisely the same ground we must
attribute to every being endowed with reason and a will this
property of determining himself to action under the Idea of his
own freedom.[1]

From the presupposition of this Idea[2] there springs, as we
further saw, consciousness of a law of action, the law that subjective principles of action—that is, maxims—must always be
adopted in such a way that they can also hold as principles
objectively—that is, universally—and can therefore serve for our
own enactment of universal law. But why should I subject myself

100    *This method takes it as sufficient for our purpose if freedom is presupposed
merely *as an Idea* by all rational beings in their actions; and I adopt it in order to
avoid the obligation of having to prove freedom from a theoretical point of view
as well. For even if this latter problem is left unsettled, the same laws as would bind
a being who was really free are equally valid for a being who cannot act except
under the Idea of his own freedom. In this way we can relieve ourselves of the
burden which weighs upon theory.[1]

to this principle simply as a rational being and in so doing also subject to it every other being endowed with reason? I am willing to admit that no interest *impels* me to do so since this would not produce a categorical imperative; but all the same I must necessarily *take* an interest in it and understand how this happens; for this 'I ought' is properly an 'I will' which holds necessarily for every rational being—provided that reason in him is practical without any hindrance. For beings who, like us, are affected also by sensibility—that is, by motives of a different kind—and who do not always act as reason by itself would act, this necessity is expressed 103 as an 'I ought,' and the subjective necessity is distinct from the objective one.[1]

It looks as if, in our Idea of freedom, we have in fact merely taken the moral law for granted—that is, the very principle of the autonomy of the will—and have been unable to give an independent proof of its reality and objective necessity. In that case we should still have made a quite considerable gain inasmuch as we should at least have formulated the genuine principle more precisely than has been done before. As regards its validity, however, and the practical necessity of subjecting ourselves to it we should have got no further. Why must the validity of our maxim as a universal law be a condition limiting our action? On what do we base the worth we attach to this way of acting—a worth supposed to be so great that there cannot be any interest which is higher? And how does it come about that in this alone man believes himself to feel his own personal worth, in comparison with which that 450 of a pleasurable or painful state is to count as nothing? To these questions we should have been unable to give any sufficient answer.

We do indeed find ourselves able to take an interest in a personal characteristic which carries with it no interest in mere states,[1] but 104 only makes us fit to have a share in such states in the event of their being distributed by reason. That is to say, the mere fact of deserving happiness can by itself interest us even without the motive of getting a share in this happiness. Such a judgement, however, is in fact merely the result of the importance we have already assumed to belong to moral laws (when we detach ourselves from every empirical interest by our Idea of freedom). But on this basis we can as yet have no insight into the principle that we ought to detach ourselves from such interest—that is, that we ought to regard ourselves as free in our actions and yet to hold ourselves bound by certain laws in order to find solely in our own person a worth which can compensate us for the loss of everything that makes our state valuable. We do not see how this is possible nor consequently *how the moral law can be binding*.

In this, we must frankly admit, there is shown a kind of circle, from which, as it seems, there is no way of escape. In the order of efficient causes we take ourselves to be free so that we may conceive ourselves to be under moral laws in the order of ends; and we then proceed to think of ourselves as subject to moral laws on the ground that we have described our will as free. Freedom and the will's enactment of its own laws are indeed both autonomy
105 —and therefore are reciprocal concepts[1]—but precisely for this reason one of them cannot be used to explain the other or to furnish its ground. It can at most be used for logical purposes in order to bring seemingly different ideas of the same object under a single concept (just as different fractions of equal value can be reduced to their simplest expression).

### [*The two standpoints.*]

One shift, however, still remains open to us. We can enquire whether we do not take one standpoint when by means of freedom we conceive ourselves as causes acting *a priori*, and another standpoint when we contemplate ourselves with reference to our actions as effects which we see before our eyes.

One observation is possible without any need for subtle reflexion and, we may assume, can be made by the most ordinary intelligence—no doubt in its own fashion through some obscure
451 discrimination of the power of judgement known to it as 'feeling.' The observation is this—that all ideas coming to us apart from our own volition (as do those of the senses) enable us to know objects only as they affect ourselves: what they may be in themselves remains unknown. Consequently, ideas of this kind, even
106 with the greatest effort of attention and clarification brought to bear by understanding, serve only for knowledge of *appearances*, never of *things in themselves*. Once this distinction is made (it may be merely by noting the difference between ideas given to us from without, we ourselves being passive, and those which we produce entirely from ourselves, and so manifest our own activity), it follows

of itself that behind appearances we must admit and assume something else which is not appearance—namely, things in themselves —although, since we can never be acquainted with these, but only with the way in which they affect us, we must resign ourselves to the fact that we can never get any nearer to them and can never know what they are in themselves. This must yield us a distinction, however rough, between the *sensible world* and the *intelligible world*, the first of which can vary a great deal according to differences of sensibility in sundry observers, while the second, which is its ground, always remains the same. Even as regards himself—so far as man is acquainted with himself by inner sensation[1]—he cannot claim to know what he is in himself. For since he does not, so to say, make himself, and since he acquires his concept of self not *a priori* but empirically, it is natural that even about himself he should get information through sense—that is, through inner sense—and consequently only through the mere appearance of his own nature and through the way in which his 107 consciousness is affected. Yet beyond this character of himself as a subject[1] made up, as it is, of mere appearances he must suppose there to be something else which is its ground—namely, his Ego as this may be constituted in itself; and thus as regards mere perception and the capacity for receiving sensations[2] he must count himself as belonging to the *sensible world*, but as regards whatever there may be in him of pure activity (whatever comes into consciousness, not through affection of the senses, but immediately)[3] he must count himself as belonging to the *intellectual world*, of which, however, he knows nothing further.

A conclusion of this kind must be reached by a thinking man about everything that may be presented to him. It is presumably 452 to be found even in the most ordinary intelligence, which, as is well known, is always very much disposed to look behind the objects of the senses for something further that is invisible and is spontaneously active; but it goes on to spoil this by immediately sensifying this invisible something in its turn—that is to say, it wants to make it an object of intuition, and so by this procedure it does not become in any degree wiser.

Now man actually finds in himself a power which distinguishes him from all other things—and even from himself so far as he is 108 affected by objects. This power is *reason*.[1] As pure spontaneity reason is elevated even above *understanding* in the following respect. Understanding—although it too is spontaneous activity and is not, like sense, confined to ideas which arise only when we are affected by things (and therefore are passive)—understanding cannot produce by its own activity any concepts other than those whose sole service is *to bring sensuous ideas under rules* and so to unite them in one consciousness: without this employment of sensibility it would think nothing at all. Reason, on the other hand—in what are called 'Ideas'—shows a spontaneity so pure that it goes far beyond anything sensibility can offer: it manifests its highest function in distinguishing the sensible and intelligible worlds from one another and so in marking out limits for understanding itself.[2]

Because of this a rational being must regard himself *qua intelligence* (and accordingly not on the side of his lower faculties) as belonging to the intelligible world, not to the sensible one. He has therefore two points of view from which he can regard himself and from which he can know laws governing the employment of his powers and consequently governing all his actions. He can consider himself *first*—so far as he belongs to the sensible 109 world—to be under laws of nature (heteronomy); and *secondly*— so far as he belongs to the intelligible world—to be under laws which, being independent of nature, are not empirical but have their ground in reason alone.

As a rational being, and consequently as belonging to the intelligible world, man can never conceive the causality of his own will except under the Idea of freedom; for to be independent of determination by causes in the sensible world (and this is what reason must always attribute to itself) is to be free. To the Idea of freedom there is inseparably attached the concept of *autonomy*, and to this in turn the universal principle of morality—a principle 453 which in Idea[1] forms the ground for all the actions of *rational* beings, just as the law of nature does for all appearances.

The suspicion which we raised above is now removed—namely, that there might be a hidden circle in our inference from freedom to autonomy and from autonomy to the moral law; that in effect we had perhaps assumed the Idea of freedom only because of the moral law in order subsequently to infer the moral law in its turn from freedom; and that consequently we had been able to assign no ground at all for the moral law, but had merely assumed it by begging a principle which well-meaning souls will gladly concede us, but which we could never put forward as a demonstrable proposi- 110 tion. We see now that when we think of ourselves as free, we transfer ourselves into the intelligible world as members and recognize the autonomy of the will together with its consequence—morality; whereas when we think of ourselves as under obligation, we look upon ourselves as belonging to the sensible world and yet to the intelligible world at the same time.

## HOW IS A CATEGORICAL IMPERATIVE POSSIBLE?

A rational being counts himself, *qua* intelligence, as belonging to the intelligible world, and solely *qua* efficient cause belonging to the intelligible world does he give to his causality the name of '*will*'. On the other side, however, he is conscious of himself as also a part of the sensible world, where his actions are encountered as mere appearances of this causality. Yet the possibility of these actions cannot be made intelligible by means of such causality, since with this we have no direct acquaintance; and instead these actions, as belonging to the sensible world, have to be understood as determined by other appearances—namely, by desires and inclinations. Hence, if I were solely a member of the intelligible world, all my actions would be in perfect conformity with the principle of the autonomy of a pure will; if I were solely a part of the sensible world, they would have to be taken as in complete conformity with the law of nature governing desires and inclinations—that is, with the heteronomy of nature. (In the first case 111 they would be grounded on the supreme principle of morality; in the second case on that of happiness.) *But because the intelligible world contains the ground of the sensible world and consequently also of its laws,* and because it therefore legislates immediately[1] with respect to my will (which belongs entirely to the intelligible world)[2] and must also be conceived as so doing, it follows that—in spite of regarding myself from another point of view as a being belong- 454 ing to the sensible world—I shall have to recognize that, *qua* intelligence, I am subject to the law of the intelligible world— that is, to the reason which contains this law in the Idea of freedom, and so to the autonomy of the will. Consequently I must look on the laws of the intelligible world as imperatives for me, and on the actions which conform to these principles as duties.

And in this way categorical imperatives are possible because the Idea of freedom makes me a member of an intelligible world. This being so, if I were solely a member of the intelligible world, all my actions *would* invariably accord with the autonomy of the will; but because I intuit myself at the same time as a member of the sensible world, they *ought* so to accord. This *categorical* 'ought' presents us with a synthetic *a priori* proposition, since to my will as affected by sensuous desires there is added the Idea of the same will,[3] viewed, however, as a pure will belonging to the intelligible
112 world and active on its own account—a will which contains the supreme condition of the former will, so far as reason is concerned. This is roughly like the way in which concepts of the understanding, which by themselves signify nothing but the form of law in general, are added to intuitions of the sensible world and so make synthetic *a priori* propositions possible on which all our knowledge of nature is based.

The practical use of ordinary human reason confirms the rightness of this deduction. There is no one, not even the most hardened scoundrel—provided only he is accustomed to use reason in other ways—who, when presented with examples of honesty in purpose, of faithfulness to good maxims, of sympathy, and of kindness towards all (even when these are bound up with great sacrifices of advantage and comfort), does not wish that he too might be a man of like spirit. He is unable to realize such an aim in his own person—though only on account of his desires and impulses; but yet at the same time he wishes to be free from these inclinations, which are a burden to himself. By such a wish he shows that having a will free from sensuous impulses he transfers himself in thought into an order of things quite different from that of his desires in the field of sensibility; for from the fulfilment of this wish he can expect no gratification of his sensuous desires and consequently no state which would satisfy any of his actual or
113 even conceivable inclinations (since by such an expectation the very Idea which elicited the wish would be deprived of its superiority); all he can expect is a greater inner worth of his own
455 person. This better person he believes himself to be when he transfers himself to the standpoint of a member of the intelligible world. He is involuntarily constrained to do so by the Idea of freedom—that is, of not being dependent on *determination* by

causes in the sensible world; and from this standpoint he is conscious of possessing a good will which, on his own admission, constitutes the law for the bad will belonging to him as a member of the sensible world—a law of whose authority he is aware even in transgressing it. The moral 'I ought' is thus an 'I will' for man as a member of the intelligible world; and it is conceived by him as an 'I ought' only in so far as he considers himself at the same time to be a member of the sensible world.

## THE EXTREME LIMIT OF PRACTICAL PHILOSOPHY
### [The antinomy of freedom and necessity.]

All men think of themselves as having a free will. From this arise all judgements that actions are such as *ought to have been done*, although they *have not been done*. This freedom is no concept of experience, nor can it be such, since it continues to hold although experience shows the opposite of those requirements which are regarded as necessary[1] under the presupposition of freedom. On 114 the other hand, it is just as necessary that everything which takes place should be infallibly determined in accordance with the laws of nature; and this necessity of nature is likewise no concept of experience, precisely because it carries with it the concept of necessity and so of *a priori* knowledge. The concept of nature is, however, confirmed by experience and must inevitably be presupposed if experience—that is, coherent knowledge of sensible objects in accordance with universal laws—is to be possible. Hence, while freedom is only an *Idea* of reason whose objective reality is in itself questionable, nature is a *concept of the understanding*, which proves, and must necessarily prove, its reality in examples from experience.

From this there arises a dialectic[2] of reason, since the freedom attributed to the will seems incompatible with the necessity of nature; and although at this parting of the ways reason finds the road of natural necessity much more beaten and serviceable than that of freedom for *purposes of speculation*, yet for *purposes of action* the footpath of freedom is the only one on which we can make use of reason in our conduct. Hence to argue freedom away is 456 as impossible for the most abstruse philosophy as it is for the most 115 ordinary human reason. Reason must therefore suppose that no genuine contradiction is to be found between the freedom and the natural necessity ascribed to the very same human actions; for it can abandon the concept of nature as little as it can abandon that of freedom.

All the same we must at least get rid of this seeming contradiction in a convincing fashion—although we shall never be able to comprehend how freedom is possible. For if the thought of freedom is self-contradictory or incompatible with nature—a concept which is equally necessary—freedom would have to be completely abandoned in favour of natural necessity.

[*The two standpoints.*]

From this contradiction it would be impossible to escape if the subject who believes himself free were to conceive himself *in the same sense*, or *in precisely the same relationship*, when he calls himself free as when he holds himself subject to the law of nature in respect of the same action. Hence speculative philosophy has the unavoidable task of showing at least this—that its illusion about the contradiction rests on our conceiving man in one sense and relationship when we call him free and in another when we consider 116 him, as a part of nature, to be subject to nature's laws; and that both characteristics not merely *can* get on perfectly well together, but must be conceived as *necessarily combined* in the same subject; for otherwise we could not explain why we should trouble reason with an Idea which—even if it can *without contradiction* be combined with a different and adequately verified concept—does yet involve us in a business which puts reason to sore straits in its theoretical use. This duty is incumbent on speculative philosophy solely in order that it may clear a path for practical philosophy. Thus it is not left to the discretion of philosophers whether they will remove the seeming contradiction or leave it untouched; for in the latter case the theory on this topic becomes *bonum vacans*,[1] of which the fatalist can justifiably take possession and can chase all morality out of its supposed property, which it has no title to hold.

Nevertheless at this point we cannot yet say that the boundary of practical philosophy begins. For practical philosophy has no part in the settlement of this controversy: it merely requires specula-457 tive reason to bring to an end the dissension in which it is entangled on theoretical questions so that practical reason may have peace and security from external attacks capable of bringing into dispute the territory which it seeks to occupy.

The lawful title to freedom of will claimed even by ordinary 117 human reason is grounded on a consciousness—and an accepted presupposition—that reason is independent of purely subjective determination by causes which collectively make up all that belongs to sensation and comes under the general name of sensibility. In thus regarding himself as intelligence man puts himself into another order of things, and into relation with determining causes of quite another sort, when he conceives himself as intelligence endowed with a will and consequently with causality, than he does when he perceives himself as a phenomenon in the sensible world (which he actually is as well) and subjects his causality to external determination in accordance with laws of nature. He then becomes aware at once that both of these can, and indeed must, take place at the same time; for there is not the slightest contradiction in holding that a *thing as an appearance* (as belonging to the sensible world) is subject to certain laws of which it is independent *as a thing* or being *in itself*. That he must represent and conceive himself in this double way rests, as regards the first side, on consciousness of himself as an object affected through the senses; as concerns the second side, on consciousness of himself as intelligence—that is, as independent of sensuous impressions in his use of reason (and so as belonging to the intelligible world).

Hence it comes about that man claims for himself a will which 118 does not impute to itself anything appertaining merely to his desires and inclinations; and, on the other hand, that he conceives as possible through its agency, and indeed as necessary, actions which can be done only by disregarding all desires and incitements of sense. The causality of such actions lies in man as intelligence and in the laws of such effects and actions as accord with the principles of an intelligible world. Of that world he knows[1] no more than this—that in it reason alone, and indeed pure reason independent of sensibility, is the source of law; and also that since he is there his proper self only as intelligence (while as a human being he is merely an appearance of himself), these laws apply to him immediately[2] and categorically. It follows that incitements from desires and impulses (and therefore from the whole sensible world of nature) cannot impair the laws which govern his will 458 as intelligence. Indeed he does not answer for the former nor impute them to his proper self—that is, to his will; but he does impute to himself the indulgence which he would show them if he admitted their influence on his maxims to the detriment of the rational laws governing his will.

### [*There is no knowledge of the intelligible world.*]

By *thinking* itself into the intelligible world practical reason does not overstep its limits in the least: it would do so only if it sought to *intuit or feel itself* into that world. The thought in question 119 is a merely negative one with respect to the sensible world: it gives reason no laws for determining the will and is positive only in this one point, that it combines freedom as a negative characteristic with a (positive) power as well—and indeed with a causality of reason called by us 'a will'—a power so to act that the principle of our actions may accord with the essential character of a rational cause, that is, with the condition that the maxim of these actions should have the validity of a universal law. If practical reason were also to import an *object of the will*—that is, a motive of action—from the intelligible world, it would overstep its limits and pretend to an acquaintance with something of which it has no knowledge. The concept of the intelligible world is thus only *a point of view*[1] which reason finds itself constrained to adopt outside appearances *in order to conceive itself as practical*. To conceive itself thus would not be possible if the influences of sensibility were able to determine man; but it is none the less necessary so far as we are not to deny him consciousness of himself as intelligence and consequently as a rational cause which is active by means of reason—that is, which is free in its operation. This thought admittedly carries with it the Idea of an order and a legislation different from that of the mechanism of nature appropriate to the world of sense. It makes necessary the concept of an intelligible world (that is, of the totality of rational beings as ends in themselves); but it makes not the 120 slightest pretension to do more than conceive such a world with respect to its *formal* condition—to conceive it, that is, as conforming to the condition that the maxim of the will should have the universality of a law, and so as conforming to the autonomy of the will, which alone is compatible with freedom. In contrast with this all laws determined by reference to an object give us heteronomy, which can be found only in laws of nature and can apply only to the world of sense.

## [*There is no explanation of freedom.*]

Reason would overstep all its limits if it took upon itself to *explain how* pure reason can be practical. This would be identical with the task of explaining *how freedom is possible*.

459

We are unable to explain anything unless we can bring it under laws which can have an object given in some possible experience. Freedom, however, is a mere Idea: its objective validity can in no way be exhibited by reference to laws of nature and consequently cannot be exhibited in any possible experience. Thus the Idea of freedom can never admit of full comprehension, or indeed of insight,[1] since it can never by any analogy have an example falling under it. It holds only as a necessary presupposition of reason in a being who believes himself to be conscious of a will—that is, of a power distinct from mere appetition (a power, namely, of determining himself to act as intelligence and consequently to act in accordance with laws of reason independently of natural instincts). 121 But where determination by laws of nature comes to an end, all *explanation* comes to an end as well. Nothing is left but *defence*— that is, to repel the objections of those who profess to have seen more deeply into the essence of things and on this ground audaciously declare freedom to be impossible. We can only show them that their pretended discovery of a contradiction in it consists in nothing but this: in order to make the law of nature apply to human actions they have necessarily had to consider man as an appearance; and now that they are asked to conceive him, *qua* intelligence, as a thing in himself as well, they continue to look upon him as an appearance in this respect also. In that case, admittedly, to exempt man's causality (that is, his will) from all the natural laws of the sensible world would, in one and the same subject, give rise to a contradiction. The contradiction would fall away if they were willing to reflect and to admit, as is reasonable, that things in themselves (although hidden) must lie behind appearances as their ground, and that we cannot require the laws of their operations to be identical with those that govern their appearances.

## [*There is no explanation of moral interest.*]

The subjective impossibility of *explaining* freedom of will is
122 the same as the impossibility of finding out and making compre-
460 hensible what *interest*★ man can take in moral laws; and yet he
does in fact take such an interest. The basis of this in ourselves
we call 'moral feeling'. Some people have mistakenly given out
this feeling to be the gauge of our moral judgements: it should
be regarded rather as the *subjective* effect exercised on our will by
the law and having its objective ground in reason alone.

If we are to will actions for which reason by itself prescribes
an 'ought' to a rational, yet sensuously affected, being, it is
admittedly necessary that reason should have a power of *infusing*
a *feeling of pleasure* or satisfaction in the fulfilment of duty,[1] and
consequently that it should possess a kind of causality by which
123 it can determine sensibility in accordance with rational principles.
It is, however, wholly impossible to comprehend—that is, to make
intelligible *a priori*—how a mere thought containing nothing
sensible in itself can bring about a sensation of pleasure or displeasure; for there is here a special kind of causality, and—as with
all causality—we are totally unable to determine its character *a
priori*: on this we must consult experience alone. The latter cannot provide us with a relation of cause and effect except between
two objects of experience—whereas here pure reason by means of
mere Ideas (which furnish absolutely no objects for experience)
has to be the cause of an effect admittedly found in experience.
Hence for us men it is wholly impossible to explain how and why
the *universality of a maxim as a law*—and therefore morality—should
interest us. This much only is certain: the law is not valid for us
*because it interests us* (for this is heteronomy and makes practical

122 ★An interest is that in virtue of which reason becomes practical—that is,
becomes a cause determining the will. Hence only of a rational being do we say
that he takes an interest in something: non-rational creatures merely feel sensuous
impulses. Reason takes an immediate interest in an action only when the universal
validity of the maxim of the action is a ground sufficient to determine the will.
Such an interest alone is pure. When reason is able to determine the will only by
means of some further object of desire or under the presupposition of some special
feeling in the subject, then it takes only a mediate interest in the action; and since
reason entirely by itself without the aid of experience can discover neither objects
for the will nor a special feeling underlying the will, the latter interest would be
merely empirical, and not a pure rational interest. The logical interest of reason
(interest in promoting its own insight) is never immediate, but presupposes purposes
for which reason can be employed.

reason depend on sensibility—that is to say, on an underlying 461
feeling—in which case practical reason could never give us moral
law); the law interests us because it is valid for us as men in virtue
of having sprung from our will as intelligence and so from our
proper self; *but what belongs to mere appearance is necessarily subordinated by reason to the character of the thing in itself.*

### [*General review of the argument.*]

Thus the question 'How is a categorical imperative possible?' 124
can be answered so far as we can supply the sole presupposition
under which it is possible—namely, the Idea of freedom—and
also so far as we can have insight into the necessity of this presupposition. This is sufficient for the *practical use* of reason—that
is, for conviction of the *validity of this imperative*, and so too of the
moral law. But how this presupposition itself is possible is never
open to the insight of any human reason. Yet, on the presupposition
that the will of an intelligence is free, there follows necessarily its
*autonomy* as the formal condition under which alone it can be
determined. It is not only perfectly *possible* (as speculative philosophy
can show) to presuppose such freedom of the will (without contradicting the principle that natural necessity governs the connexion
of appearances in the sensible world); it is also *necessary*, without
any further condition, for a rational being conscious of exercising
causality by means of reason and so of having a will (which is
distinct from desires) to make such freedom in practice—that is,
in Idea—underlie all his voluntary actions as their condition.[1] But
*how* pure reason can be practical in itself without further motives
drawn from some other source; that is, how the bare *principle of
the universal validity of all its maxims as laws* (which would admittedly 125
be the form of a pure practical reason) can by itself—without any
matter (or object) of the will in which we could take some ante-
cedent interest—supply a motive and create an interest which could
be called purely *moral*; or, in other words, *how pure reason can be
practical*—all human reason is totally incapable of explaining this,
and all the effort and labour to seek such an explanation is wasted.

It is precisely the same as if I sought to fathom how freedom
itself is possible as the causality of a will. There I abandon a
philosophical basis[1] of explanation, and I have no other. I could, 462

I

no doubt, proceed to flutter about in the intelligible world, which still remains left to me—the world of intelligences; but although I have an *Idea* of it, which has its own good grounds, yet I have not the slightest *acquaintance* with such a world, nor can I ever attain such acquaintance by all the efforts of my natural power of reason. My Idea signifies only a 'something' that remains over when I have excluded from the grounds determining my will everything that belongs to the world of sense: its sole purpose is to restrict the principle that all motives come from the field of sensibility by setting bounds to this field and by showing that it does not comprise all in all within itself, but that there is still more
126 beyond it; yet with this 'more' I have no further acquaintance. Of the pure reason which conceives this Ideal, after I have set aside all matter—that is, all knowledge of objects—there remains nothing over for me except its form—namely, the practical law that maxims should be universally valid—and the corresponding conception of reason, in its relation to a purely intelligible world, as a possible efficient cause, that is, a cause determining the will. Here all sensuous motives must entirely fail; this Idea of an intelligible world would itself have to be the motive or to be that wherein reason originally took an interest. To make this comprehensible is, however, precisely the problem that we are unable to solve.

#### [*The extreme limit of moral enquiry.*]

Here then is the extreme limit of all moral enquiry. To determine this limit is, however, of great importance in this respect: by so doing reason may be kept, on the one hand, from searching around in the sensible world—greatly to the detriment of morality —for the supreme motive and for some interest, comprehensible indeed, but empirical; and it may be kept, on the other hand, from flapping its wings impotently, without leaving the spot, in a space that for it is empty—the space of transcendent concepts known as 'the intelligible world'—and so from getting lost among mere phantoms of the brain. For the rest, the Idea of a purely intelligible world, as a whole of all intelligences to which we ourselves belong as rational beings (although from another point of view we are members of the sensible world as well), remains always a serviceable and permitted Idea for the purposes of a rational belief, though all knowledge ends at its boundary: it serves to produce in us a lively 127 interest in the moral law by means of the splendid ideal of a universal kingdom of *ends in themselves* (rational beings), to which we can belong as members only if we are scrupulous to live in 463 accordance with maxims of freedom as if they were laws of nature.

## CONCLUDING NOTE

The speculative use of reason *in regard to nature* leads to the absolute necessity of some supreme cause of the *world*; the practical use of reason *with respect to freedom* leads also to absolute necessity— but only to the absolute necessity *of the laws of action* for a rational being as such. Now it is an essential *principle* for every use of reason to push its knowledge to the point where we are conscious of its *necessity* (for without necessity it would not be knowledge characteristic of reason). It is an equally essential *limitation* of the same reason that it cannot have insight into the *necessity* either of what is or what happens, or of what ought to happen, except on the basis of a *condition* under which it is or happens or ought to happen. In this way, however, the satisfaction of reason is merely postponed 128 again and again by continual enquiry after a condition. Hence reason unrestingly seeks the unconditionally necessary and sees itself compelled to assume this without any means of making it comprehensible—happy enough if only it can find a concept compatible with this presupposition. Thus it is no discredit to our deduction of the supreme principle of morality, but rather a reproach which must be brought against reason as such, that it cannot make comprehensible the absolute necessity of an unconditioned practical law (such as the categorical imperative must be). For its unwillingness to do this by means of a condition— namely, by basing this necessity on some underlying interest— reason cannot be blamed, since in that case there would be no moral law, that is, no supreme law of freedom. And thus, while we do not comprehend the practical unconditioned necessity of the moral imperative, we do comprehend its *incomprehensibility*. This is all that can fairly be asked of a philosophy which presses forward in its principles to the very limit of human reason.

# NOTES

*(The first figure given is the page of the second edition, and the cross-references also refer to these pages.)*

# PREFACE

ii, n. 1. There can, however, be an applied logic; *see* p. 32 footnote.

v, n. 1. That is, a metaphysic of morals.

vi, n. 1. Anthropology is roughly equivalent to what we should now call psychology, though the latter title is usually reserved by Kant for theories about the soul as an incorporeal substance.

vi, n. 2. 'Idea'—with a capital I—is a technical term for a concept of the unconditioned (especially of an unconditioned totality or whole), and on Kant's view duty is unconditioned (or absolute). On the other hand, 'idea'—with a small i—is used in the ordinary English sense: it is a translation of the German *Vorstellung*. For 'Idea' *see* also the analysis of pp. 127–28. We find 'Idea' used also more loosely, as on page x, for the concept of an organic whole—e.g., a science.

vi, n. 3. Kant seems to have in mind such a precept as 'Honesty is the best policy'. This commends the universal duty of honesty by an appeal to the empirical motive of self-interest.

vii, n. 1. But *see* also p. 35. It is only the ultimate principles that require no anthropology.

vii, n. 2. Inclinations are for Kant *habitual* desires.

viii, n. 1. That is, a metaphysic of morals—not of nature.

ix, n. 1. This work by Christian Wolff was published in 1738–39.

x, n. 1. Kant has in mind his own Transcendental Logic (as set forth in the *Critique of Pure Reason*)—the logic of pure *a priori* knowledge, not of all thinking as such.

xi, n. 1. Metaphysics is here the metaphysic of nature.

xii, n. 1. That is to say, it is liable to fall into contradictions (antinomies) and illusions.

2, n. 1. This sentence should be noted as it affirms what Kant is commonly supposed to deny.

2, n. 2. That is, these qualities are not good when they are incompatible with a good will.

2, n. 3. An affection (*Affekt*) is a sudden passion like anger and is compared by Kant to intoxication. A passion (*Leidenschaft*) is a lasting passion or obsession like hate and is compared by Kant to a disease.

6, n. 1. The use of the word 'misology' is one of the passages which show the influence of Plato's *Phaedo* on Kant's ethical theory. This was due to the publication in 1767 of Moses Mendelssohn's *Phädon*—a work which is in great part a translation of Plato.

7, n. 1. Kant never claims—as it is too commonly said—that a good will is the sole good.

7, n. 2. Observe Kant's recognition of the 'contentment' found in good action. The view that he regarded this—or even a more mundane satisfaction —as diminishing or destroying the goodness of an action is a pure fabrication.

8, n. 1. Kant's view is always that obstacles make a good will more *conspicuous*—not that a good will is shown only in overcoming obstacles.

9, n. 1. The example refers, not to the preceding sentence, but to the one before that. It is not so easy as Kant suggests to distinguish between actions done from duty and actions done from self-interest—even a grocer may have a conscience. Nevertheless he is right in saying that an action done solely out of self-interest is not commonly regarded as morally good.

9, n. 2. For 'maxim' *see* the footnotes to pp. 15 and 51.

10, n. 1. Strictly speaking, it stands on the same footing as an *action* done from other inclinations.

12, n. 1. Happiness, as is indicated immediately below, is the *satisfaction* of all inclinations as a sum.

13, n. 1. It should be noted that Kant has neglected—presumably by an oversight—to state his *first* proposition in a *general* form.

13, n. 2. That is, as Kant indicates below, the controlling maxim must be formal, not material, where an action is done for the sake of duty.

16, footnote, n. 1. Strictly speaking, it is reverence (and not the law) which is analogous to fear and inclination.

17, footnote, n. 1. *See* pp. 55–56.

19, n. 1. This looks like falling back on mere self-interest, but Kant's point is that there could be *no promises at all* if this maxim were universally followed. *See* p. 18 above, also pp. 55 and 49.

20, n. 1. The highest grades of knowledge are for Kant 'insight' and (above insight) 'comprehension.' *See* pp. 120 and 123, and also *K.M.E.*, I 334.

## CHAPTER II

28, n. 1. It should be noted that it is contained as *duty in general*—not as a specific duty.

28, n. 2. This need not mean that one rule cannot over-ride another.

29, n. 1. This whole passage again suggests the influence of Plato. For the special point about the concept of God *see* p. 92.

31, n. 1. Metaphysics is here a metaphysic of morals.

33, n. 1. Dignity is a technical term for intrinsic value. *See* p. 77.

33, footnote, n. 1. Professor J. G. Sulzer (1720–79) translated Hume's *Inquiry* into German in 1755.

34, n. 1. Here again Kant is warning us only against contaminating moral *principles* by the addition of non-moral motives. To do this is to diminish the value of corresponding actions, as when we advocate honesty on the ground that it is the best policy.

35, n. 1. Speculative or theoretical philosophy has to allow, not only that human reason is discursive (in the sense that its concepts give us no knowledge apart from sensuous intuition), but also that for knowledge it is dependent on pure intuitions of space and time, which may be *peculiar* to human beings.

35, n. 2. We cannot, however, derive moral principles by mere *analysis* of the concept 'rational being'; *see* p. 50, footnote. For such derivation we require a *synthetic* use of reason; *see* p. 96.

35, n. 3. Metaphysics is here a metaphysic of morals.

36, n. 1. In Chapter I.

36, n. 2. Ideas in a metaphysic of morals (as elsewhere) go to a 'complete totality' such as can never be given in experience.

36, n. 3. We must pass from subjective principles (or maxims) to conditioned objective principles (hypothetical imperatives), and from them to the unconditioned categorical imperative of duty (especially the imperative of autonomy—pp. 69 ff.—which prepares the way for the concept of freedom). This can be clear only on a second reading.

36, n. 4. If this 'derivation' were logical deduction, we could hardly infer from it that the will is practical reason. Kant seems to have in mind something more like what Aristotle called a *practical* syllogism—one whose conclusion is not a proposition, but an action.

37, n. 1. 'Determined' here means '*objectively* determined'—not '*subjectively* determined' as it means in a later sentence on this page.

38, footnote, n. 1. Such a rule is a hypothetical imperative.

40, n. 1. The word 'its' refers to the will.

41, n. 1. The edition of the Berlin Academy strikes out the German word equivalent to 'not'.

42, n. 1. Prudence might perhaps better be described as rational self-love.

42, footnote, n. 1. This is one of the places where Kant indicates that prudence is concerned, not merely with means, but with the harmonization of ends.

44, n. 1. To be practically necessary is to be objectively necessary; compare page 50 footnote. To be theoretically necessary would be to fall under the necessity of nature, which is something quite different. *See* p. 97.

44, n. 2. This will become clearer in Chapter III.

44, n. 3. That is to say, we are concerned, not with finding out the means necessary to an end, but with the obligation to use these means when they are known.

44, footnote, n. 1. A pragmatic sanction is an imperial or royal decree having the effect of a fundamental law. Examples are the edict of Charles VII of France in 1438—the basis of the liberties of the Gallican church; and that of the Emperor Charles VI in 1724 determining the Austrian succession. Kant considers such sanctions to be prudential—not as following from the system of natural law which applies to all States as such.

45, n. 1. We are dealing—as Kant indicates in the next clause—with the *concept* of willing an end. In analytic propositions we have to distinguish sharply between the *concept* of the subject and the subject itself (usually a thing and not a concept).

49, n. 1. We have to show, not only *how* a categorical imperative is possible, but also *that* it is possible.

50, footnote, n. 1. The willing of an action enjoined by a categorical imperative cannot be derived by analysing the concept of willing an end (as is done in the case of a hypothetical imperative).

50, footnote, n. 2. We shall, however, find in Chapter III—*see* especially pp. 111–12—that the *Idea* of such a perfect will is necessary in order to establish the synthetic *a priori* practical propositions of morality.

50, footnote, n. 3. To say that the categorical imperative connects an action *immediately* with the concept of a rational will is to say that the connexion is not derived from the presupposed willing of some further end. Yet in spite of this *immediate* connexion the proposition remains synthetic: the willing of the action is *not* contained in the concept of a rational will.

51, n. 1. The maxim in question is a *material* maxim.

51, footnote, n. 1. An objective principle is an imperative only for finite agents who are imperfectly rational.

52, n. 1. The use of a preposition here (and elsewhere) may seem an unnecessary complication. Perhaps Kant wishes to emphasize the *interpenetration* of the material and formal maxim. In willing in accordance with a material maxim I will *at the same time* that this maxim should be a universal law. As a material maxim is based on sensuous motives, this formula by itself disposes of the traditional doctrine that in a morally good action a sensuous motive can never, on Kant's view, be present at the same time as the moral motive.

52, n. 2. When we speak of 'nature', we may take it in a *material* sense as equivalent to the sum total of *phenomena*; or we may take it in a *formal* sense as equivalent to the sum total of the *laws* governing the existence of natural phenomena. This second usage is more akin to popular phrases like 'the nature of man' and 'the nature of the world'. Hence we might say, speaking popularly, that it is the nature of the world to be governed by the law of cause and effect. In spite of this, Kant treats the laws of nature as purposive when he asks if our maxims can be conceived or willed as laws of nature. *See* also pp. 81, 84, and 80, footnote.

53, footnote, n. 1. This is explained in my analysis of the argument. It has nothing to do with the over-riding of one duty by another, as I mistakenly suggested in *T.C.I.*, p. 147.

53, footnote, n. 2. Outer duties are duties to others; inner duties are duties to myself.

54, n. 1. Many commentators say that Kant condemns suicide on the ground that if everyone committed suicide there would be no one left to do so! There is clearly no trace of such an argument here (or indeed anywhere else, so far as I know), and the reader should be on his guard against such absurdities.

56, n. 1. This is put in a prudential way, but Kant's doctrine is not prudential, as can be seen from p. 11 and p. 68, footnote.

57, n. 1. This distinction is the same as that between perfect and imperfect duties.

57, n. 2. Kant is dealing only with the four main types of duty (perfect and imperfect, inner and outer). Every type has different kinds of obligation falling under it according as it is concerned with different kinds of object. For example, perfect duties to others include duties not to assail their freedom or steal their property, as well as not to borrow on false pretences. *See* p. 68.

60, n. 1. Kant is again dealing with degrees of conspicuousness, not with degrees of excellence. *See* n. 1. on p. 8.

61, n. 1. The point is that we must not introduce empirical considerations into the *principle of morality*. The moral principle must by itself be sufficient to determine action, but this does not mean that other motives may not be present *at the same time*.

61, n. 2. By embracing a cloud in mistake for Juno Ixion became the father of the 'mongrel' race of centaurs.

62, n. 1. The proposition establishing this *a priori* connexion is, however, not analytic but synthetic. *See* p. 50, footnote.

62, n. 2. Here a metaphysic of morals is taken to include a critique of practical reason. The latter is specially concerned with *justifying* the *a priori* connexion between the moral law and a rational will as such. *See* pp. 87 and 95–96.

62, n. 3. These differences—between the pleasant, the beautiful, and the good—are discussed in the *Critique of Judgement*, e.g. in §. 5.

63, n. 1. As we have seen (pp. i–iii), physics (or natural philosophy) must have an empirical, as well as an *a priori*, part. This empirical part is in turn divided into two parts, the first of which is concerned with the world of physical nature, while the second (which is here in question) is concerned with mind.

63, n. 2. I have here ventured to amend the text by substituting 'subjective' for 'objective'. 'An objective ground'—if it could mean anything here—would have to mean 'a ground in objects'. This sense is very rare in Kant and would be most confusing in a passage where everywhere else 'objective' means valid for every rational being as such. On the other hand Kant always emphasizes that ends (whether objective or subjective) must be subjectively chosen—we can never be compelled to make anything our end. *See*, for example, the use of the word 'subjectively' on p. 70, especially the second use of it. Every end is a subjective ground of the will's self-determination. If it is given solely by reason, it becomes an objective ground as well.

63, n. 3. A means considered as the ground (or cause) of the possibility of an action seems to be an instrument. Thus, for example, a hammer is (or contains) the ground of the possibility of knocking in a nail. In practice, however, Kant usually treats an action itself as a means (the means enjoined by a hypothetical imperative).

64, n. 1. Compare p. 14.

64, n. 2. If Kant means 'every volition' strictly, he must have in mind universal *principles* only—not particular moral laws.

65, n. 1. We might expect inclinations to be grounded on needs, but Kant appears usually to take the view that needs are grounded on inclinations.

65, n. 2. Kant is not usually so hostile to inclinations. Is his attitude here perhaps due to the influence of the *Phaedo*?

66, n. 1. Here Kant distinguishes clearly between a supreme practical *principle* valid for all rational beings as such and a corresponding categorical *imperative* valid for imperfectly rational agents such as men. This distinction should always be kept in mind where it is not made explicitly.

66, n. 2. Strictly speaking, 'humanity' should be 'rational nature as such', but the only rational nature with which we are acquainted is to be found in man. Kant himself makes this distinction at the beginning of the previous paragraph.

66, n. 3. The word 'simply' is essential to Kant's meaning since we all have to use other men as means.

66, footnote, n. 1. The reference is to pp. 99–100 and 101–02. A rational being can act only under the Idea of freedom, and so must conceive himself as autonomous and therefore as an end in himself.

68, footnote, n. 1. 'Don't do to others what you don't want done to yourself'.

68, footnote, n. 2. It should be observed that here Kant regards a law as universal only if it covers *all* duties and so is an ultimate principle. So far as he uses 'universal law' in this sense, his claim that it is independent of knowledge of human nature is at least not palpably absurd.

69, n. 1. The *purpose (or end) of nature* for humanity is to be sharply distinguished from the *natural purpose (or end)* which all men seek (as in the paragraph immediately following). The first conception supposes nature to have a final end or aim which is not to be found in nature itself. The second rests on observation of nature and can be confirmed by such observation. See *Critique of Judgement*, §. 67.

71, n. 1. Here Kant is not bidding us to renounce all interests: we have, for example, a right, and even an indirect duty, to seek our own happiness. What he is saying is that the categorical imperative cannot be based on any interest: it excludes from its *sovereign authority* 'every admixture of interest as a motive'. Our judgement of duty must in no way be influenced by our interests—this is the only sense in which all interests must be renounced.

72, n. 1. Kant is considering the hypothesis that we are bound to obey moral laws only because of self-interest. He argues that a will bound by self-interest would not always issue in right actions unless it was bound by a *further* law bidding it act on maxims of self-interest *only* when these maxims were capable of being willed as universal laws; *see* also p. 94. Hence a will bound by self-interest could not be a *supreme* law-giver nor would it make *universal* law.

73, n. 1. Kant seems to have in mind here a purpose of nature rather than a natural purpose. *See* n. 1 on p. 69 above.

74, n. 1. Here we are not considering the *content* of personal ends (which has just been excluded). What we are considering is only the *form* of a kingdom of ends composed of persons capable of willing personal ends (whatever be their content) *in conformity with universal law*.

75, n. 1. Kant may have in mind that *members* of the kingdom of ends are rightly subjected to the sanctions of State law and so to force exerted by the will of others.

77, n. 1. This is a reference to Kant's own aesthetic theory. I use the term 'fancy price' (in the absence of a better) to mean a value for fancy or imagination.

78, n. 1. It may seem a moralistic prejudice on Kant's part thus to put moral value so far above aesthetic value. Yet when we consider what we think of men who combine the finest aesthetic taste with fiendish cruelty (as happened in some cases during the war), we may begin to incline towards Kant's view.

80, n. 1. A complete determination combines both form and matter.

80, n. 2. Unity, multiplicity (or plurality), and totality are the three categories of *quantity*, the last of which combines the other two.

81, n. 1. It would be a more natural rendering to say 'bring the *action* nearer to intuition'. But an action is already near to intuition, and what we require to bring nearer to intuition is the universal formula (or the Idea of reason, as on pp. 79–80 above).

81, n. 2. *See* also n. 2. on p. 52.

81, n. 3. It is not clear whether 'object' means object of thought or object (purpose) of will. On p. 98 'object' is apparently equated with 'content', but this again is ambiguous.

82, n. 1. Kant forgets that in the case of imperfect (or wider) duties the end in itself is conceived positively.

84, n. 1. Rational beings are here regarded as the *ends (or purposes) of nature*. *See* n. 1 on p. 69. This teleological assumption is also made in Kant's use of the universal law of nature as an analogy for the universal law of morality (or freedom).

84, n. 2. The introduction of happiness as a reward for virtue is a trifle crude. It would be more satisfactory to say, as Kant does elsewhere, that without the co-operation of nature the good will could not be successful in realizing its ends.

86, n. 1. The reference is to pp. 14 ff., especially to the footnote on pp. 16–17.

88, n. 1. Analysis of concepts seems here to produce synthetic propositions. Does Kant refer to an analytic argument? *See* my analysis of p. xiv.

89, n. 1. This is not the inhuman doctrine that a good man should not be influenced by any desire for objects, but that he should not allow his desire for any object to interfere with his judgement of duty.

89, n. 2. Kant is referring to the reason which is the basis of the categorical imperative. This reason cannot be merely that I happen to be interested in the happiness of others.

91, footnote, n. 1. Francis Hutcheson (1694–1747), Professor of Moral Philosophy in the University of Glasgow, was the leading exponent of the doctrine of moral sense. Kant was himself for some time influenced by this doctrine.

92, n. 1. Kant has in mind the doctrines of Christian Wolff (1679–1754) and his followers. *See* n. 1. on p. ix.

92, n. 2. The reference is primarily to the doctrine of Crusius (1712–76).

92, n. 3. The reference is to the *ontological* concept of perfection mentioned above.

94, n. 1. If any object of will is made the basis for morality, we require (1) a law binding us to pursue this object, and (2)—if the law is to issue always in right actions—a *further* law bidding us act on the maxim of pursuing this object *only* when the maxim is capable of being willed as a universal law. *See* n. 1. on p. 72.

95, n. 1. This passage (together with p. xiv) suggests a connexion between a synthetic argument and synthetic propositions. I do not see how this can be so since the same propositions must appear in both analytic and synthetic arguments. *See* my analysis of the argument of p. xiv and also my note on p. 88.

# INDEX OF PROPER NAMES
# AND GENERAL INDEX

*The page numbers in both these indices refer to the smaller numbers given in the margin of the translation. These correspond to the numbers of the pages in the second edition of the original.*